W9-DES-624

Language Exploration and Awareness

A Resource Book for Teachers

Third Edition

E. Petch (signature)

Language Exploration and Awareness

A Resource Book for Teachers

Third Edition

Larry Andrews
University of Nebraska–Lincoln

2006
LAWRENCE ERLBAUM ASSOCIATES, PUBLISHERS
Mahwah, New Jersey   **London**

Copyright © 2006 by Lawrence Erlbaum Associates, Inc.
All rights reserved. No part of this book may be reproduced in any form, by photostat, microform, retrieval system, or any other means, without prior written permission of the publisher.

Lawrence Erlbaum Associates, Inc., Publishers
10 Industrial Avenue
Mahwah, New Jersey 07430

Cover design by Kathryn Houghtaling Lacey

Library of Congress Cataloging-in-Publication Data

Andrews, Larry.
Language exploration and awareness : a resource book for teachers /
Larry Andrews.— 3rd ed.
    p. cm.
    Includes bibliographical references (p.) and index.
ISBN 0-8058-4308-6 (paper : alk. paper)
1. Language arts. 2. Activity programs in education.
3. Teaching. I. Title.

LB1576.A625 2006
372.6—dc22

                                                2005043512

Books published by Lawrence Erlbaum Associates are printed on acid-free paper, and their bindings are chosen for strength and durability.

Printed in the United States of America
10 9 8 7 6 5 4 3 2 1

For
Forestine and Clarence Mabin

Contents

CHAPTER 5 WORDS AND LEXICOGRAPHY 97

CHAPTER 6 GRAMMAR, SPELLING, AND GOOD ENGLISH 130

CHAPTER 7 DISCOURSE ROUTINES AND SOCIAL CONVENTIONS 167

CHAPTER 8   REGIONAL, SOCIAL, AND HISTORICAL VARIATIONS   203

CHAPTER 9 **MEANINGS AND GENERAL
SEMANTICS   251**

CHAPTER 10 **THE LANGUAGES OF INTOLERANCE
AND DISCRIMINATION   287**

CHAPTER 11 **WHEN SOME OF THEM DON'T
SPEAK ENGLISH   316**

Preface

Language Exploration and Awareness: A Resource Book for Teachers (Longman, 1993; Lawrence Erlbaum Associates, 1998) has enjoyed a rewarding journey. The journey began when I was teaching a linguistics course for pre- and in-service teachers; it was a challenge for me early on because there were no appropriate textbooks available. I used texts about language, although none addressed the specific needs of classroom teachers, then we made accommodations for classroom applications in the classes. I thought my students would be better served, however, if there were a language text specifically for teachers.

When I spent a sabbatical semester as a visiting fellow at the University of London Institute of Education, I had the opportunity to work with individuals I had met previously, but only as footnotes. My associations with these world-class linguists, all of whom had genuine interests in language study in the schools, helped me to clarify and organize my ideas. The results of the seminars, the department meetings, the meetings of professional linguistics societies, the conversations, and my continued reading and study, each provoked and encouraged the creation of the approach to language study I've called language exploration.

Toward the end of my appointment in London I began to organize my thoughts in a more formal manner and started to write what you'll read in this text as chapter 3. As my reading and writing continued, my courses back home were becoming more clarified and organized in my thoughts, and a book emerged from those reflections. You are reading the third edition of that book.

From the beginning of this journey, I have tried to accomplish several goals: first, to share my enthusiasm for language and the numerous ways it enables us to define and understand ourselves and our world, to celebrate the bright intervals in life, and to offer solace and support when needed. My second goal was to provide an alternative approach to language study, one that didn't rely on the naming of parts, writing labels for parts of speech above every word in a sentence, memorizing 25 spelling words selected by someone somewhere who somehow divined that *these* are the 25 words the students need to learn to spell this week, and to write idealized sentences that represented Proper English but not real language real people use for real communicative purposes.

Third, I've tried to expand the view of language in the language arts curriculum. Too often the language curriculum has been limited to an illusive target: Standard English Grammar. As you'll read in this text and then, I hope, come to appreciate, the "standard" in that term is often difficult to define with any degree of precision. Even more, other aspects of language are frequently ignored. Students seldom have the opportunity to consider semantics, dialects, lexicography, social discourse, and the like. This is their loss because topics like these represent significant aspects of language and communication.

Apparently the first edition found several homes; it was adopted for many courses at colleges and universities in the United States. My editor, Naomi Silverman, encouraged me to prepare a second edition and it, too, was well-received. I've received numerous complimentary e-mail messages and telephone calls from students and professors at other universities, citations in other university-level texts, and invitations to speak. The reception for *Language Exploration and Awareness* over the years has been gratifying. Now I'm pleased to bring you the third edition.

WHAT'S NEW IN THE THIRD EDITION

The third edition of *Language Exploration and Awareness* discusses the importance of No Child Left Behind (NCLB) legislation and the state standards movement in chapter 1; chapters 2 and 3 describe imbalances in the English-language curriculum and how they can be corrected. Chapter 4 renews a discussion of some basic properties of human communication. Chapter 5 discusses how words are created, and how an event—like 9/11—can produce a need for new expressions. Chapter 6 frames the discussion about traditional grammar by distinguishing between English *use* and English *usage*, and by illustrating that Standard English and Standard American English (SAE) meet varying standards.

Chapter 7 reviews social-discourse conventions with expanded attention given to e-mail and how e-mail may affect written discourse. Dialects are discussed in chapter 8, with clarifications regarding mutual intelligibility, variations within the SAE umbrella, and some interesting distinctions between SAE and British English. Chapter 9 is devoted to general semantics and meaning, and illustrates how current events and newer experiences can drive our search for meaningful words (like *rebels, insurgents, terrorists*).

Chapter 10, a unique chapter, reviews intolerant language and includes newer discussions of how words and concepts fit into the mix of national and international politics. Chapter 11 presents some suggestions for successful strategies to use with learners for whom English is a new language.

Finally, every chapter in Section II, chapters 4 through 11, concludes with several *new* Student Explorations, classroom activities designed by pre- and in-service teachers that you can use in your classroom with your students.

SPECIAL FEATURES IN THIS BOOK

At the beginning of each chapter you'll find a special, introductory paragraph with the boldfaced heading, **Before you read this chapter**. We've learned from the field of cognitive science that if we activate and focus on what we already know about a topic before we read new information about that topic, our comprehension will be greater. Thinking about the questions in this section will help your comprehension of the chapter; discussing the questions with others will enhance your comprehension even more.

For your inquiry and practice activities in each chapter give you some recommendations about ways you can either apply or expand a topic or concept presented in the chapter.

Reviewing the Chapter sections, found at the end of every chapter are presented in two, varying formats. One format is what those engaged in the field of content literacy recognize as three-level reading guides. These postreading statements ask you to connect what you've understood with the chapter's literal language, to arrive at meaningful inferences about what is stated in the text, and to link the information in the text to knowledge you already have. The other format, the Question-Answer-Relationship postreading guide, provides an alternate way to make the same cognitive connections as the three-level guides.

You'll notice that this book does not have a glossary of technical terms and their definitions. To the contrary, when technical terminology is used, its is in **boldface** and defined by the surrounding context of use. This is the most common way people learn language, so I'm repeating the strategy here.

WHO THE THIRD EDITION IS FOR

As noted earlier, the first and second editions of *Language Exploration and Awareness* found many homes.

First, I wrote the texts specifically for pre- and in-service teachers of the English language arts. Most undergraduate methods courses no longer use a single, omnibus text but use one (or more) texts for examining the pedagogies of teaching literature, writing and language. *Language Exploration and Awareness* is the language-teaching book.

Many universities offer special courses in the teaching of English language for upper-level undergraduate students and beginning-level graduate students. This text is for that course. This book can also be used in an Introduction to Language or an Introduction to Linguistics course, especially if those courses emphasize language study from a sociocultural perspective.

The sociolinguistic perspective will also make this textbook very appealing to ELL teachers. Though several universities have used this text in their ELL teacher certification programs, I would like to mention another book I have written that may be even more suitable for them: *Linguistics for L2 Teachers* (Lawrence Erlbaum Associates, 2001).

The subtitle of this book, "A Resource Book for Teachers," indicates that it is also intended for current classroom teachers. I see this text occupying a special place on the desk of every English/language arts teacher in today's classrooms.

A desk or collegiate dictionary—still one of the best bargains in any bookstore—will be needed to accompany some of the learning activities in this book. There are several editions available at most bookstores. Small, paperback dictionaries sold at supermarkets and discount stores omit word histories, variant spellings, alternate pronunciations, and too much other information to make them useful, either to professional educators or to their students.

A WORD ABOUT WEB SITES

Another new feature in the third edition is found throughout several chapters in the text, references to Web sites you and your students might find useful. My students and I have used them and have found them very useful. I need to caution you, however, that Web sites tend to come and go, for a variety of reasons. Some aren't maintained, some are closed after a time, others just "drift away." Indeed, my friend and colleague, Professor David W. Brooks, has discovered that some sites simply deteriorate over time, regardless of whether they receive many or few hits.[1] I hope the sites I mention will be useful to you.

ACKNOWLEDGMENTS

I've been extremely fortunate to have enjoyed some gifted students in my classes. Through their questions, observations, and exemplary efforts in their own classrooms, they have helped me to understand much better aspects of language in use that I thought I really knew. I'm grateful to them for the help they've given me.

As with the first and second editions, a number of pre- and in-service classroom teachers also contributed to this book by lending classroom explorations they have prepared and that appear at the ends of chapters 4 through 11. I am grateful to the following for helping to make this a more useful book for teachers: Shelby Aaberg, Laurel Barrett, JoAnn Barry, Jennifer Becker, Debra Bundy, Sally Burt, Sonia Christiansen, Tim Coniglio, Anne Cowser, Lynne Danielsen, Michele Diedrichsen, Joan Doyle, Erin Egan, Linda Enck, Jim Fields, Amy Finlay, Carol Floth, Pamela Gannon, Elizabeth Gillis, Sheri Gross, Michelle Hayduska, Laurie Hokom, Joan Jorgensen, Marilee Kabes, Jodi Knoll, Shelly Kropp, Elizabeth Lickei, Jessica McAndrew, Frank McCahill, Cindy Meyer, Kelly Meyers, Amy Moylan, Judy Obert, Paul Orvis, Amy Poindexter, Beverly Redwine, Steve Reiter, Lorilyn Rennings, Verla Ringenberg, Sheri Rogers, Dana Schaefer, John Skretta, Rita Lyon Smith, Amy Steager, April Stocker, Jared Sutter, Emily Turek, Louis Whitmore, Beverly Wilhelm, Emily Wlaschin, Kelly Wood, and Sharon Yoder,

Naomi Silverman, my acquisitions editor at Lawrence Erlbaum Associates, has been my editor and coach for 13 years. She brings luster to the publishing profession; I'm grateful to her for her wisdom and guidance over

---

[1]John Markwell and David W. Brooks, "'Link Rot' Limits the Usefulness of Web-Based Educational Materials in Biochemistry and Molecular Biology," *Biochemistry and Molecular Biology Education,* 31 (2003): 69–72.

the years. Thanks, too, to Erica Kica, Associate Editor at Erlbaum. Erica is a skilled manager and proves that speed and efficiency *can* go together.

For their recommendations regarding this edition of *Language Exploration and Awareness*, I want to acknowledge and thank Professors Nancy L. Hadaway, University of Texas at Arlington; Mary Jeanot, Gonzaga University; and, Terry A. Osborn, University of Connecticut.

With more than the customary and predictable sentiments, for their continual support and encouragement, I am thankful to my daughters Wyn and Sally, and to my wife, Ruthie.

Introduction

Since the publication of the first edition of *Language Exploration and Awareness* (Longman, 1993), there have been profound changes in U.S. schools and in the nation.

The Whole Language movement was discredited, replaced by reading/language arts programs presenting what many saw as a more balanced view of literacy. State governing boards of K–12 education established content standards that students in schools were expected to meet, and if they did not, the schools would realize potential penalties. Nationally, No Child Left Behind (NCLB) legislation represented federal participation in K–12 curricula at historic levels. Political discourse in Washington, DC, became more partisan and parsimonious. The events of 9/11 revealed a vulnerability many thought we were immune to. The United States engaged in a war, an action praised by some and denounced by others, furthering national divisions and intensifying the political debate.

Sociologically, the African-American population in the United States was replaced as the second-largest ethnic identity group by Hispanics; immigrant and refugee families arrived in the United States in record-setting numbers. The social fabric changed.

Given these enormous changes at the local, state, and national levels, it is my belief that the need to understand language and how it works in society has seldom been more necessary or more important.

The historic obsession with traditional grammar instruction in schools in the United States has all but preempted attention to other aspects of language. Attention to grammar and usage is obviously a *part* of a K–12 language arts curriculum, but only one part. I recommended a more balanced approach to the study of the English language in our schools in the first edition of this text, and I'm repeating that suggestion with even more enthusiasm as I begin the third edition.

1

The English-language curriculum needs to go beyond its traditional focus on grammar and usage, balancing this concentration by including similar focus on general semantics, regional and social dialects, social language conventions and habits, the relationship between language and culture, and the like. These aspects of English are as important in the process of interpreting and ascribing meaning to language as are grammar and usage.

A more balanced English language curriculum is also important to each individual in our schools, students and teachers alike. Ludwig Wittgenstein reminded us that *the limits of my language are the limits of my universe.* Our students deserve the widest universe they are capable of conceptualizing. When we offer them a more balanced language curriculum, one that demonstrates that communicative language results from human choices, not mere obedience to a fixed code of rules, then our students are well on their way to a larger personal cosmos. The third edition of *Language Exploration and Awareness* is my contribution to that goal. I hope you'll enjoy reading it as much as I enjoyed writing it.

Language Exploration and Awareness: The Rationale

CHAPTER **1**

Language Exploration and Awareness: What It Is

The study of our language opens all kinds of doors.
—David Crystal, *Who Cares About English Usage?*

Before you read this chapter, try to recall from your long-term memory some of the English-language lessons—the drills, exercises, worksheets, and the like—you completed in your earlier schooling. Were you asked to identify the part of speech for every word in a sentence? Did you ever underline subjects once and predicates twice? Were you asked to unhinge dangling participles? Did you ever have an assignment that asked you to write sentences containing a particular feature, like a predicate nominative, a predicate adjective, a direct or indirect object? What do you think were the purposes of these activities?

Language is patently important to us. As Jim Cummins has observed, we try to make sense of the world through language. We express our ideas through language. Language can either bring us together or set us apart. Though it can be an inclusive activity, bridging barriers between cultures, religions, and worldviews, it can also be an exclusive activity, excluding others through xenophobic, racist, or sexist uses.[1]

Our lives are so intricately related to our language that it is difficult, if not impossible, to imagine human experience without language. Steven Pinker has pointed out that whenever two or more people are together

---

[1] Jim Cummins, "Language and the Human Spirit," *TESOL Matters,* 23, no. 1 (2003): 1.

anywhere in the world, they'll soon be *talking*. Even when there's no one to talk with, we often talk to ourselves, to our pets, or even to our house-plants! Consider all of your human relations and interactions: The race is not always won by the swift, but more often by the *verbal*.[2]

Language is important for a socio-educational reason, too: It's taught in schools, more often than any other subject. In classrooms in the United States, learners study English each year so that they will improve their language competencies and, as a result, either they will be better writers, readers, or speakers, or they will be better prepared for the next grade, for middle or high school, for college, or for a job. For a century, and with few exceptions, the all but exclusive focus of this study has been the *structure* of English, most usually traditional grammar and usage.

The results from a considerable body of research, however, which are confirmed by the experiences, observations, and conclusions of thousands of teachers and their students, make it abundantly clear that the traditional approach to teaching about the English language, and its focus on traditional grammar, has been generally ineffective, especially when you consider the amount of time and emphasis allocated to it.

At the end of this chapter you'll find a feature that recurs throughout the book, an activity called "For Your Inquiry and Practice"; this one invites you to interview five to six people (but no English/language arts pre- or in-service teachers), asking them what they remember about their study of English from their K–12 school days. Many of my students, who are both pre- and in-service English teachers, complete this activity and are routinely disappointed with the results. The respondents, former English learners, recall literature they read, often with fond memories. They frequently mention favorite writing opportunities. When they describe their language memories, however, they are hard-pressed to use complimentary terms. The vast majority mention worksheets, then some additional worksheets, then, you got it, more worksheets. Despite all this, you can observe many speakers and writers today who don't have the foggiest idea about the distinctions between "its" and "it's," or whether it's appropriate to say "between you and me" or "between you and I." (I hear and read the latter construction so often these days that I'm sometimes not sure anymore!).

George Hillocks has concluded that studying traditional grammar and the parts of speech—as they have been traditionally taught—has made little appreciable difference in students' reading, writing, or speaking proficiencies.[3]

---

[2]Steven Pinker, *The Language Instinct* (New York: Morrow and Company, 1994), 1.

[3]George Hillocks, *Research on Written Composition* (Urbana, IL: National Council of Teachers of English, 1986), 227, 248.

Ironically, no matter how convincing the evidence might be that teaching traditional grammar and parts of speech has little to no effect on the speaking and writing of learners in schools, nothing seems to diminish the urges and compulsions for too many teachers to continue teaching traditional grammar in an isolated, decontextualized manner.[4]

I hear some teachers rationalize this situation by saying "I know this [teaching traditional grammar] doesn't help much, but (Select one of the following.) my administrators . . . my department chair . . . the parents . . . the students . . . the community . . . my colleagues . . . the state standards . . . expect it from me. Some additional reasons for these dismal practices, largely historical and not pedagogical, are discussed in more detail in chapter 3.

For the moment, let's consider one more possible reason for the failure of traditional school language study to accomplish what its advocates claim it either will, might, or ought to accomplish. I can illustrate this reason with a true story, and it goes like this.

A certified teacher, seeking employment in a large metropolitan school district in the Midwest, thought her chances of being hired would be improved if she served the district as a substitute teacher. In this capacity she reported to duty one morning in a seventh-grade class. After the bell rang and the students settled into their seats, she picked up the regular teacher's gradebook and began to call the roll.

"Anderson?" (No answer.)

"Brown?" (No answer.)

"Cunningham?" (Again, no answer.)

This sub was experienced enough to know full well the games students sometime play with substitute teachers. "All right, class, let's have some cooperation here," she sternly ordered. Then, she returned to calling the roll.

"Davis?" (Still, no reply!)

At 8:23 a.m., she thought she'd already had a long day. She sat down, looked at the gradebook, then glared at the students, then returned her attention to the gradebook. About this time a sympathetic youngster from the

---

[4]Peter Elbow, *What Is English?* (New York: The Modern Language Association and the National Council of Teachers of English, 1990), 15; and Patrick Hartwell, "Grammar, Grammar, and the Teaching of Grammar," *College English,* 47 (1985): 105–27.

front row stood and approached the substitute. He quietly said to her, "Lady, you're on the wrong page."

There are those who have labored in the fields of language teaching by emphasizing traditional grammar and usage to the virtual exclusion of any other aspects of language. Like the substitute teacher, they have either been on the wrong page in the wrong book, or have remained on the same page for the wrong period of time.

Of course, grammar and usage are important elements in a language arts curriculum. For decades, the society that has supported our schools has told us that. But, there's more to the study of language than only traditional grammar.

If medical schools educated their students they way we often educate students about language, the medical school curriculum would consist of little more than Anatomy I, Anatomy II, and Anatomy III. Learning about the structure of the body is important for physicians, but there's much more they need to know. Learning about the structure of the language is important for teachers and their students, too, but there's much more they need to know.

METALINGUISTIC AWARENESS AND THE LANGUAGE ELEPHANT

Many of our students are following or have followed what is described in this book as a "traditional curriculum" in English language study, with its emphasis on grammar. They are reminiscent of the fable, the Six Wise Men of Hindustan. In this fable, the six wise men, each one blind, want to know what an elephant is like. The wise man holding the elephant's tusk believes the elephant is built like a spear. The one touching the elephant's side believes the elephant is built like a wall; the one holding the trunk believes the elephant is like a snake, and so on. When our students follow only a traditional language curriculum, they are, as Wilson describes them, like the blind men in the fable, each having a "limited personal experience of that elephant, language."[5]

The approach to language study I call language exploration and awareness (LEA) views the study of the English language from a larger, more expanded perspective. This more comprehensive view will, as Wilson puts

---

[5]Kenneth G. Wilson, *Van Winkle's Return: Change in American English 1966–1986* (Hanover, NH: University Press of New England, 1987), 37.

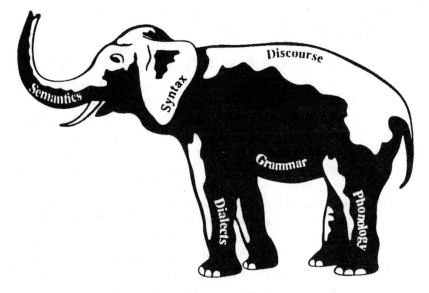

FIG. 1.1.   The Language Elephant.

it, "help those of us blinded by our personal provincialities to see the language elephant whole."[6]

Before learners are likely to gain insights into how they and other speakers and writers might manipulate specific grammatical features, they must see a *reason* to attend to these issues. These reasons will become increasingly apparent as the learners explore authentic language use in the real world, how language changes and varies from one geographic region to another, from one generation to another, from one social class to another; how a dictionary provides a history of these variations; how words are created; how people attach meanings to words.

Another major purpose of the LEA approach is go study *language as language*. In the traditional curriculum, the rationale for studying the English language is often a statement of how mastering grammar will help the students write better reports in science class or reports in social studies, and the like. Although this may be true to some extent, the fact remains that students seldom study language as language.

More pointedly, Peter Elbow points out that in the view of many people, English is viewed primarily as an "ancillary" school subject. English has

---

[6]Ibid.

tended to be, Elbow says, "a handmaiden to the other disciplines in the humble sense of that metaphor: a 'service discipline.'"[7]

The view of English as a service discipline, its primary purpose being to enable students to read, write, think, and speak better in *other* school subjects, presents a number of negative outcomes. Among them is the expectation that the English teacher is the faculty member who is responsible for teaching students how to spell all of the technical terms they need to know in all of their other subjects. The "handmaiden" view suggests that it is the English teacher alone, like an all-knowing knight-on-a-mission, who is responsible for teaching students how to master all of the expository writing structures required for successful writing in history, chemistry, psychology, and any other subjects the students might be studying.

How did we arrive at this "handmaiden," service-course predicament? I don't have *the* definitive answer to this question, but I suspect part of the reason is that many people believe that in English courses students are expected to learn how to write and talk *properly*. The idea that students might study language as language is a rather foreign notion to them.

James and Leslie Milroy offer another partial explanation when they say, "There is a depressing general ignorance of the nature of language and the complexity of linguistic issues in society."[8]

Exaggerations, you think? Recently my wife and I were having dinner at one of our favorite restaurants. The diners at a nearby table were especially friendly and talkative. We exchanged greetings and made the usual introductions. "And, what does your husband teach," I heard one ask? My wife replied, "Linguistics," and the other diner, trying gallantly to be attentive, commented, "Oh, linguistics. How interesting. What's that?"

LANGUAGE STUDY IN THE
TRADITIONAL CURRICULUM

The traditional language curriculum has assumed a narrow focus since the beginning of public schooling in the United States Citizens have expected that students will learn *proper* English in their English classes; "how to rite and talk gud," [*sic*] Alfred E. Newman might say. Generation after generation has studied grammar and usage, but little else from the field of English language.

---

[7]Elbow, *What Is English?*, 12.

[8]James Milroy and Leslie Milroy, *Authority in Language* (London: Routledge & Kegan Paul, 1985), 175.

In a national survey of U.S. high schools having reputations for excellence in teaching English, teachers and department heads estimated that they allocate approximately 50% of their time to the study of literature, 27% of their time to writing, and about 10% to the study of language. The remainder of time was allocated to a variety of activities like sustained silent reading, research papers, and the like.[9]

These percentages reveal an increase in the time allocated to writing, according to an older national survey.[10] The increase in writing reported in the more recent study came at the expense of language study, speech, and other activities.[11]

If we were to conduct today a similar survey of middle and high school English curricula, I suspect the amount of time allocated to the broader aspects of language study would be even less, largely because of No Child Left Behind (NCLB).[12] The focus for language study will be a few items listed in the school's state standards.

NCLB is the most recent revision of the Elementary and Secondary Education Act, which was enacted in 1965. The goals of NCLB are, essentially:

1. By the school year 2013–2014, all students will be proficient in mathematics and reading.
2. All students will be proficient in reading at the end of the third grade by 2013–2014.
3. All students for whom English is a new language (ESL, ELL) will be proficient in English.
4. All students will be taught by highly qualified teachers by 2005–2006.
5. All students will graduate from high school.[13]

---

[9] Arthur N. Applebee, *The Teaching of Literature in Programs With Reputations for Excellence in English* (Albany, NY: University of New York-Albany Center for the Learning and Teaching of Literature, Report 1.1, 1989).

[10] James R. Squire and Roger K. Applebee, *High School English Instruction Today* (New York: Appleton–Century–Crofts, 1968).

[11] Applebee, *The Teaching of Literature*, 10.

[12] See http://www.nochildleftbehind.gov, the government's official Web site, for a complete description of the requirements established by NCLB.

[13] John E. Readance, R. Scott Baldwin, and Thomas W. Bean, *Teaching Content Literacy: An Integrated Approach,* 8th ed. (Dubuque, IA: Kendall/Hunt Publishing Company, 2004), 4.

NCLB has imposed federal control over public education at historic levels, making it a piece of legislation praised by some and condemned by others. NCLB is not merely public, political posturing; to the contrary, NCLB is very serious business.

NCLB has a schedule all public schools in all of the states are to adhere to as they create their plans for meeting the goals enumerated earlier, as well as state reading standards. If schools do not make satisfactory annual yearly progress, severe penalties are assessed, the most severe being the termination of employment of a school's faculty and staff, then turning the school over to a private company.[14]

NCLB relies heavily on group standardized test scores. I know of some school districts in which building principals have been told that if they want to retain their administrative positions, the standardized test scores for the children in their building *must* improve.

These threats notwithstanding, making satisfactory annual progress has become the mantra for many schools in the United States. Allocating more classroom time to meeting state reading and writing standards and improving test-taking skills have assumed new levels of importance and have taken up a larger portion of the school day for teachers and their students. In fact, there are suggestions circulating that even more tests will become a feature of NCLB.

Though NCLB has been very controversial,[15] it remains the law of the land. The extent to which NCLB represents education reform of a lasting and positive nature is something only time will tell. In the meantime, teachers cannot ignore it.

I believe that the approach to language study described in this book will enable students to learn more about language because LEA is a more student-friendly and more inviting approach. Further more, because classroom time has become more compressed in today's "high stakes testing" climate, teachers aren't as likely to offer several 2- to 3-week units of instruction in which their students will examine aspects of language; the shorter, exploratory activities described in this text will be more fruitful. Of course, you're expected to help your students to meet the standards; how you get them there is a matter of your judgment and choice.

The traditional language curriculum has too often operated from the assumption that there is a fixed code of oral and written expressions that represent "Good English" that is to be used in all and every communication

---

[14]Ibid.

[15]See especially David Marshak, "No Child Left Behind: A Foolish Race Into the Past," *Phi Delta Kappan*, November 2003, 229–231.

events, and that it's the teacher's responsibility to transmit that fixed code to the learners. This view all but ignores some basic issues: What constitutes an act of communication? How do we communicate in ways other than through speech and writing? How does language vary, inevitably and legitimately, between and among groups of speaker/writers? Questions like these are seldom asked in a traditional language curriculum where there is just one standard or benchmark of what represents "Good English."

One of the primary outcomes of an LEA approach to the study of language is the development of the students' reflective or **metalinguistic awareness** (overt, extrinsic knowledge about one's language uses) of a wider, more complete range of language features and principles. As students become more aware of the totality of language (the whole elephant, that is, not just the trunk, tusk, or leg) and how its use varies, normally and legitimately, from setting to setting, they will become more sensitive to the communication demands in each context and will become more competent in using language confidently and deliberately.

GROWTH IN AND THROUGH LANGUAGE

There is widespread and general agreement among language scholars that thought and language are related. Linguists, psychologists, anthropologists, learning theorists, and cognitive scientists have discussed for many years and at great length the degree of this relationship.

For example, Lev Vygotsky argued that the verbal behavior of a child comes first, making later cognitive growth possible.[16] Similarly, but in stronger terms, Sapir and Whorf hypothesized that the vocabulary and structure of the language one learns will predetermine how an individual will name and classify events, concepts, and the like, thus shaping how the individual perceives the world.[17]

Jean Piaget, on the other hand, suggested that thinking comes first and that the early cognitive concepts of children establish a structure for their later understandings, learnings, and uses of language.[18]

---

[16]Lev Vygotsky, *Thought and Language* (Cambridge, MA: MIT Press, 1962).

[17]See Benjamin Whorf, "A Linguistic Consideration of Thinking in Primitive Communities," in *Language, Thought, and Reality*, ed. John Carroll (Cambridge, MA: MIT Press, 1956), 65–86; and David Mandelbaum, *The Selected Writings of Edward Sapir* (Berkeley: University of California Press, 1949).

[18]Jean Piaget, *The Language and Thought of the Child* (London: Routlege & Kegan Paul, 1965).

Similar to the age-old riddle of whether the chicken or the egg came first, you can see there is no agreement regarding whether language creates thought or thought creates language. This brief discussion of this matter should lead you to understand, nevertheless, that language and thought are inextricably related; and, in my view, they are interdependent.

It is beyond the scope of this introductory chapter to provide a more thorough discussion of these theories describing the relationships between thought and language. This relationship is, as the noted linguist Jean Aitchison describes it, "a vast and wooly subject."[19] Given this vastness and wooliness, you will come to understand and appreciate, I hope, the LEA approach is not based on any one of these theories to the exclusion of the others. The approach to language study that is advocated in this book recognizes the similarities among the several theories and that language and cognitive development are separable yet interdependent functions, one growing in a mutually supportive fashion with the other, at least in normal circumstances.

In a similar vein, language has traditionally been seen as a *vehicle of thought*, a means of shaping a person's thoughts and ideas so that they can be made both clearer and more communicable to others.[20] Language is also sometimes thought of as the *content* as well as the *vehicle* of thought. Can you and I negotiate a compromise, at least for the purposes of this book, and agree that language is, simultaneously, both the medium and the message?

At the risk of oversimplification, let me offer that as the school learner becomes more adept with language, and can use language more spontaneously, and with increasing levels of elaboration and precision, then thoughts and ideas—that is to say, meanings—of more complex natures can be formed, articulated, synthesized, and evaluated by the language user. Thus, as students grow *in* language, they continue to grow *through* language.

ACQUIRING AND LEARNING LANGUAGE

You will encounter a similar interposition in this book with regard to how people acquire and learn language. As we discuss in chapter 2, language learning is a continuous process and it isn't completed by the ages of 5 or 6, or 12 or 13. The language of children, adolescents, and young adults is still

---

[19]Jean Aitchison, *The Articulate Mammal* (London: Unwin Hyman, 1989), 5.

[20]Edward Finegan and Niko Besnier, *Language, Its Structure and Use* (New York: Harcourt Brace Javonovich, 1989), 2.

developing. Throughout grades K–12, the learners are serving *linguistic apprenticeships*.

Some scholars adhere to theoretical or psycholinguistic models of language learning whereas others believe that sociolinguistic models are more accurate. I suggest that we need to take *both* schools of thought into account as you and your students examine their personal and social uses of language.

Psycholinguistics is the study of language in relation to mental processes used as people understand, acquire, and produce language. A psycholinguistic approach to language study examines what is happening *inside* the individual—mentally, cognitively, psychologically—and usually does not consider the language learner's interactions between, with, and among people.[21] Rather, the focus of psycholinguistics is more likely to be on the roles of one's memory, perception, and concept development. The study of psycholinguistics has clarified what happens as a child acquires sound patterns (**phonology**), meaning patterns (**semantics**), and word and sentence structures (**morphology** and **grammar**), and has been a major school of language study in the United States for the past half-century.[22]

Sociolinguistics, on the other hand, is the study of how one's language is acquired and used in relation to any number of social factors, such as the language user's socioeconomic status, age, gender, ethnic identity, educational level, occupation, geographic location, and the like.[23] Sociolinguists study, for example, how the social networks composed of family, friends, neighbors, and coworkers might shape a person's language choices in grammar, vocabulary, and pronunciation. In summary, the study of how one's communicative competence and linguistic performances are shaped through socialization processes is the domain of what we call sociolinguistics.

James Paul Gee says that there are good reasons to claim that during the past several years the two fields of psycholinguistics and sociolinguistics have been merging.[24] For example, Giles and Robinson[25] point out that although the 1957 publication of Noam Chomsky's *Syntactic*

---

[21]Aitchison, *The Articulate Mammal*, 1.

[22]Jack Richards, John Platt, and Heidi Weber, *Longman Dictionary of Applied Linguistics* (London: Longman, 1989), 234.

[23]Ibid.

[24]James Paul Gee, "Literacy, Discourse, and Linguistics," *Boston University Journal of Education* 171, no. 1 (1989): 5–25.

[25]Howard Giles and Peter Robinson, *Handbook of Language and Social Psychology* (New York: John Wiley & Sons, 1990), 2.

Structures[26] invigorated both linguistics and psychology and came to dominate the field of linguistics, it quickly became apparent to a number of other scholars that there was more to acquiring language than Chomsky's psycholinguistic Language Acquisition Device (LAD). Language acquisition also required a sociolinguistic Language Acquisition Support System (LASS).[27]

For example, Chomsky's LAD attempts to explain how the brain enables language learning. The LAD makes it possible for the language learner to perceive, understand, and ultimately reproduce the phonetic distinctions between "pin" and "pit" or between "nip" and "tip" and to associate these oral or written characters with their respective referents. Furthermore, the LAD helps the language learner to acquire, first incidentally and indirectly without formal, direct instruction, the rules underlying the morphology and grammar of one's language and then to generate sentences that abide by these rules.

The LASS, on the other hand, recognizes that people do not acquire and learn language in isolation. As the language learner *interacts* with his or her adult caregivers, older siblings, relatives, and members of other speech networks, the language learner embodies what Wells is talking about when he says, "Learning to talk is more than acquiring a set of linguistic resources; it is also discovering how to use them in conversation with a variety of people and for a variety of purposes."[28] And with this single observation, Wells describes the merger of the psycholinguistic and sociolinguistic theories, and how LAD is supported by LASS.

As we noted earlier, examples of LASS include one's parent(s), older sibling(s), friends, relatives, and neighbors. The LASS both supports and shapes language as it establishes both general and specific cultural norms and cultural expectations. The LASS educates the language learner sometimes very directly and other times quite incidentally, about the social rules governing language as it is used: when to say "Please" and when to say "Thank you"; what to say in reply to, "Hi. How are you?"; when "Once upon a time . . ." is more appropriate in some circumstances

---

[26]Noam Chomsky, *Syntactic Structures* (The Hague: Mouton), 1957.

[27]Jerome S. Bruner, *Child's Talk* (New York: W. W. Norton), 1981.

[28]Gordon Wells, *The Meaning Makers: Children Learning Language and Using Language to Learn* (London: Heinemann, 1986), 15.

and "Say, have you heard the one about . . .?" is more appropriate in other circumstances. Or, how the word *neither* might be pronounced NIGH-ther or KNEE-ther (and, by the way, the same with EE-ther and EYE-ther).

The view presented in this book is a merged perspective. There are obvious psycholinguistic underpinnings that help to account for the language children have acquired. By the same token, as you'll see in chapters 2 and 3, this language is seldom learned or used in isolation from other people and is rarely used in a social vacuum. Language and the social surroundings in which it is used are virtually inseparable. Anyone who has observed young adults for any period of time will notice that they have already acquired the basic linguistic structures used in English; that is, they unconsciously and naturally use subject-verb-object sentence patterns (S-V-O, as in "I like pizza."), and the like. Furthermore, regardless of their uniquely individual traits and attributes, the language of children and adolescents has many common features. They use the same slang terms, the same words for expressing approval and disapproval, the same words to greet each other, and so on. The same is true for older language users, such as bankers, butchers, automobile mechanics, sports reporters, truck drivers, lawyers, etc and so on. It is a fact that people talk *like* the people they talk *with*. The LAD and the LASS seem to get along nicely with each other as coworkers.

FOR YOUR INQUIRY AND PRACTICE:

My niece Leah wrote these sentences when she was 5 years old:

1. Mi dog went to another fens. she plad and had fun she stad overnit. mi dog iz nis. she ez prete I lik her.
2. Santa clos ez cmin 2 ton. he nos ef u r slepn he nos ef u r awak he nos ef u bn good r bad.
3. Santa clos bregs us toes. he is fat. 1 ov hes renders es namd rudof.
4. Valentinz ez soon. It will be febuera 14. We will have a porte. we will have koekes and candi. we wil hav fun.

What understandings about language had Leah learned at the age of 5 years?

LANGUAGE EXPLORATION
AND AWARENESS: THE CRITERIA

LEA is an approach to the study of *several* aspects of language, not just traditional grammar, usage, and spelling, that will enhance students' sensitivity to and awareness of language as it is used in diverse contexts by real people for different purposes in day-to-day life.

LEA provides opportunities for students to learn about regional and social variations in pronunciations, vocabulary, and grammar; how words enter and leave the language, and how dictionaries record those comings and goings; how the sentences we exchange in the parking lot at church, mass, or synagogue are different from the sentences we exchange in the aisles at the grocery store, a party, and the like, and yet all follow predictable and rigorously enforced social conventions; how language can either reinforce or attempt to remove stereotypes about men, women, and members of religious or racial groups different from your own.

The idea of *explorations* isn't new to many educators. Many middle schools and high schools already have elective "taster" or "exploratory" courses in art, music, foreign languages, the world of work and technology, and the like, for either one semester or a shorter period of time. A taster course gives students an opportunity to explore and investigate a field of study in order to determine whether they might have any more serious interest in it.

Explorations in language not only provide this same introductory purpose, but they also give students essential experiences with the larger domain of the English language as they explore language features often omitted from the traditional curriculum. Through these explorations, students become more aware of and sensitive to the complexity and diversity of language.

Most of the explorations demonstrated at the ends of the chapters in Section II of this book can be accomplished in 15 to 20 minutes. Some may take longer, of course. In the creation of the explorations illustrated in this text, my students and I have used the following criteria:

The Activities Emphasize Meaning. One of the most basic reasons human beings bother to communicate with each other is to impart some kind of *meaning*. To the extent that this is an accurate statement regarding the general public, it is all but axiomatic for school-age learners! Consequently, the activities in the LEA approach focus on the meaning(s) emerging from a language observation or event. The importance of meaning is usually illustrated when you say to yourself "Hmmm. I wonder what she meant by that?" We seldom, if ever, ask ourselves "Hmmm. I wonder why he began that statement with a sentence-initial gerund?"

Although the grammar of a written or spoken sentence is obviously important, it should be discussed only when a student question or comment about grammatical structure enters the discussion, or when the student's oral or written language is being discussed with the teacher in an individual writing conference or small-group discussion.

It is a questionable investment of time to assign to an entire class of learners a worksheet asking the students to underline, circle, diagram, or identify in some other manner an isolated grammatical feature. The time spent on activities like "Underline the personal pronouns in the following sentences" will be much better spent if the students are engaged in a more productive activity, like reading a book of their choosing, finishing an LEA activity, writing in their personal or class journals, talking about a piece of writing with a partner, or even telling a good joke. These alternatives, all emphasizing *meaning*, help to create more positive dispositions toward language learning!

LEA Activities Use Authentic Language Found in Genuine Social Circumstances. "Real" language frequently looks and sounds different from other-world language used in textbook examples. Consequently, LEA stresses real language as it is used by real people for real purposes. This is, after all, the type of language people will actually use in social and civic contexts for the remainder of their lives. Real people seldom write, for example, "practice" letters applying for a nonexistent job with a fictitious firm, an activity I observed recently in a class of 14-year-old learners.

This spurious activity could have been replaced by a *real* letter to Reebok or Nike, complaining about a pair of shoes that wore out too soon. Or, the student who disagrees with a movie review might write a *real* letter taking exception with the newspaper's or television station's movie reviewer's judgments.

Similarly, throughout this book you'll encounter many examples from newspapers, magazines, junk mail, advertising supplements, restaurant menus, and so on. These examples further illustrate how real and authentic language can be at the center of language explorations.

The foregoing does not mean that the only legitimate real language is found in business letters. Students will also write expressively, writing journal/diary entries, free-writing, poems, song lyrics, dialogue, and numerous other forms of written expression. The distinction I'm trying to make is that their written uses of language should emerge from authentic, genuine contexts, not phony ones created by writers who work for a publisher thousands of miles away.

The alternative writing activities such as those described previously are much more real to the student. The authentic letters represent a statement the student *wants* to make, rather than a statement the student has been assigned to make. Students are more likely to "own" the letters they want to write, and this ownership leads to a greater investment of their time and attention. This is pretty much common sense.

The Activities Provide for a Developmental View. The activities should correspond with the level of language development attained by adolescents and must take into account that the young adults' language proficiencies are still developing.

Classroom teachers who hold this view are patient. They understand that language development is a long-term endeavor. They understand that the focus in their classrooms is on the students' continuing language development, not short-cuts or one-shot vaccinations for a level of "correct" language use observed in some adults.

Adopting a developmental view enables the teacher to respond to students with the knowledge and conviction that student language production will not match or duplicate adult proficiency, but it will look and sound like language in the process of *becoming* more mature, more adult. Adult language models may be used in some language activities, but more as illustrations, not standards to be met.

The Activities Develop Awareness of Several Aspects of Language. Rather than stressing one aspect of language, *grammar*, the activities enable the students to examine a variety of language elements: signs, symbols, language change, regional and social varieties, lexicography, semantics, spelling, and so on. Although the ultimate goal of a K–12 language arts curriculum is for the students to achieve control over language and to be able to produce spontaneous, clear, cohesive, and elaborated oral and written utterances, LEA operates from the notion that reflective awareness how all of language "works" is a prerequisite to a sense of a need to control language.

The Activities are Student Centered and Inquiry Oriented. Lecturing adolescents about any topic, especially language usage, is risky business and ineffective teaching. Just try it and watch their eyes glaze over! Nevertheless, the best estimates of classroom talk indicate that the bulk of oral discourse in classrooms is carried on by the teacher, sending an implicit message that the most appropriate pupil response is passivity.[29]

---

[29]Michael Stubbs, *Discourse Analysis* (Oxford: Basil Blackwell, 1983), 64. See also Richard Allington, "What I've Learned About Effective Reading Instruction," *Phi Delta Kappan*, June 2002, 744–745.

An example of classroom discourse that promotes student passivity is the traditional lecture, or a lecture thinly disguised as a discussion. Within the context of the lecture hall or the classroom, it is assumed by everyone that it is the teacher/lecturer's job to talk; the student/listener's job is to listen, perhaps writing down some notes about what they are hearing.

Another example of classroom discourse that is likely to induce student passivity is the following:

Teacher: Who can tell me the capital of Texas?
Pupil 1:   Austin?
Teacher: Right. What about Iowa?
Pupil 2:   Des Moines?
Teacher: Right.

When students are talked at for a substantial period of time during the school year, for several years, or when they "participate" in a classroom discussion by supplying one-word answers, learner passivity should be expected.

People do not normally acquire language through a passive process, but through an interactive, rule-making, hypothesis-testing process. This idea is, however, contrary to a popular language myth, a myth that suggests that there is, somewhere in the language teacher's files, a codified list of "the correct way" to write or speak phrases, clauses, and sentences. All that is required by the language learner, according to this myth, is memorization of the list. Raymond Harris calls this the "fixed code fallacy."[30] This view sees language learners as empty heads waiting to be filled with Good'n' Proper Language Facts by the teacher.

A more accurate account of how language learners actually acquire and learn language has them actively constructing possible ways of using language, based in part on what they've seen and heard and in part on their attempts to produce language and the responses these attempts evince. For example, early on the language learner observes that plurality is usually indicated with the –s marker and will learn, incidentally and indirectly, to use "cats," "boys," and "hats" appropriately, but may overgeneralize and form plurals like "foots," and "mans." In time, most children will learn the conventional uses of both the regular and irregular plurals, as you did.

The point of this illustration is that the child is learning how to mark plurality by implicitly and indirectly observing and by applying the results

---

[30]Raymond Harris, *The Language Myth* (London: Duckworth & Company, Ltd., 1981), 10.

of these observations of the language around them. Older learners, adolescents and young adults, will follow similar patterns as they encounter new linguistic content, new language demands, and widening circles of social contexts in which language will be used.

Through similar applications, language learners arrive at an astounding number of positive generalizations about how successful language works. Normal children grow up with the capacity to communicate with others in their language networks without (or, in spite of) any direct teaching.

With some obvious modifications, LEA activities should follow the model of the *active* language acquisition model insofar as possible. It may sound simplistic, but I'll say it anyway: People learn language by using it. Consequently, in order for LEA to be successful, the students must be actively doing the activities.

The Activities Require Reflection. Learners make language choices all the time in the real world outside of school. Asking them to be even more reflective about their language choices will cause them to be more aware and thoughtful about what they hear, read, write, and say. We do not want them to become constrained to a smaller universe of language proficiency, a realm Paulo Freire calls a *silent culture* in which control of language has been either withheld or wrested from the speaker/writer by way of prescriptive commands.[31]

Furthermore, if adolescent and young-adult learners are going to become reflective users of language, and if they are going to develop metalinguistically (having overt knowledge about their personal language use), exercising a wider range of choices from a growing array of options, they must practice being reflective about language and its uses.

FOR YOUR INQUIRY AND PRACTICE:

Interview five to six persons from career fields other than teaching, asking them about the activities and content of language study they can remember from their K–12 school days. What was emphasized? After you have completed your interviews, review your notes. To what extent do your respondents' experiences agree with the six LEA criteria described in this chapter?

---

[31]Paulo Freire, "The Adult Literacy Process as Cultural Action for Freedom," *Harvard Educational Review,* 40 (1970): 205–221.

At the end of each chapter in this book you will find a series of questions or statements. The questions or statements will help you to clarify and enlarge your understanding of the chapter. The directions will be simple.

REVIEWING THE CHAPTER

Part One: *Place a (✓) in the space beside each statement that is explicitly stated in this chapter.*

_____ 1. Learning to talk requires more than learning how to pronounce words.

_____ 2. The formation of a thought usually precedes the language required to express it.

_____ 3. Some view English as a "service" course to other school courses.

_____ 4. The traditional curriculum reserves language study for Grades 9–12.

_____ 5. Students are more apt to learn something if they see a purpose for learning it.

Part Two: *Place a (✓) in the space beside each statement you think the author would agree with.*

_____ 6. Students' writing errors are best alleviated through minilessons.

_____ 7. People learn grammar without direct instruction.

_____ 8. People first look for meaning in language, unless the structure is confusing.

_____ 9. *Contrived* language for one student might be *authentic* for another.

_____ 10. "Standards of usage" is such a relative term that almost anything the student says or writes will be acceptable.

Part Three: *Based on your understanding of this chapter, and taking into account what you've learned as an educator, place a (✓) in the space beside each statement you agree with.*

_____ 11. No pain, no gain.

_____ 12. Practice makes perfect.

_____ 13. You can accomplish anything if you try hard enough.

_____ 14. The whole is often greater than the sum of the parts.

_____ 15. Some groves of trees don't make a forest.

CHAPTER 2

Language Exploration and Awareness: Why It Is

They have been at a great feast of languages, and stolen the scraps.
—William Shakespeare, *Love's Labour's Lost*

Before you read this chapter, think about how the language you use changes as you encounter different people in different situations throughout a typical day. How would you describe the language you use when you are talking with a close friend? Your pastor, priest, or rabbi? A clerk at the mall? An elementary, middle-level, or high school student? Which of these uses is "good English" or "proper English," as these terms are customarily used?

Contrary to our pride in being human beings, we must recognize some indisputable facts: Despite what Olympic weight-lifters can accomplish, the lion is stronger. When it comes to speed, humans are no match for the ostrich. The dolphin can outswim any human. And, we humans see less acutely than a hawk. There is, however, one area where we humans are superior: in the use of symbols.[1]

As a teacher of the English language, you may be interested in any number of symbol systems we humans use, and the symbols we call *words* will feature prominently in your list. As one who has assumed the responsibility and challenge of helping others learn about the power of these symbols, you face a number of tasks.

---

[1] Ernest L. Boyer, "Literacy and Learning," in *The First R: Every Child's Right to Read,* eds. Michael F. Graves, Paul Van Den Broek, and Barbara M. Taylor (New York: Teachers College Press, and Newark, DE: The International Reading Association, 1996), 1.

Snow and Fillmore, for example, have described five teacher functions in which language is central:

1. Teachers are educators, responsible for content instruction, selecting materials, and strategies that promote language learning.
2. Teachers are evaluators, making decisions about students that have important consequences.
3. Teachers are educated people, possessing information about language.
4. Teachers are communicators, and have strategies for understanding the ways their students use language.
5. Teachers are agents of socialization, helping students learn the norms, expectations, and communication patterns that are used both in and outside of school.[2]

You have taken on some impressive responsibilities!

After having read only one chapter in this book, you have already discovered that I have strong feelings about the English language, especially how it might be, could be, or ought to be taught in schools. The exploration of language can and should be an instructive and enjoyable aspect of one's life, unless it is reduced to a blizzard of classroom worksheets asking students to engage in atomistic analyses of abstract bits and pieces of language for which they see no realistic application to their lives.

THE FOCUS AND CONTEXTS OF LANGUAGE STUDY

There are two important terms of interest we need to examine as they apply to language: the **prescriptive** and the **descriptive** approaches to the study of language.

Edward Finegan contrasts the two approaches this way: "Descriptive grammarians ask the question, 'What is English like—what are its forms and how do they function in various situations?' By contrast, prescriptive grammarians ask, 'What *should* English be like—what forms should people use and what functions should they serve?'"[3]

---

[2]Lily Wong-Fillmore and Catherine Snow, *What Teachers Need to Know About Language*) (Washington, DC: Clearinghouse on Language and Linguistics 2000), http://www.cal.org.ericcll/teachers.pdf.

[3]Edward Finegan, *What Is "Correct" Language?* (n.d.), available from the Linguistic Society of America, http://www.lsadc.org/fields/index.htm.

The prescriptive approach to language use involves the laying down of rules by those who claim to have special or expert knowledge of a language. Prescriptive advice "tends to be conservative, [language] changes being regarded with suspicion, if not disdain."[4]

There are both prescriptive and descriptive linguists active today, although I suspect the majority are descriptivists. Whether it's a statistically significant difference, I don't know. Descriptivists examine how people actually use the language, then they report the results of their research without making judgments about whether the results represent "proper English" or "bad English."

In the United States there is a long-standing tradition, nevertheless, of the general public wanting directions for the ways they *should* use English. I experience this often when people stop me in the corridor in my office building, in the parking lot at church, in the aisle at the supermarket, and even in some telephone calls to my home and office: "Larry, what's correct, for me to say *less than* or *fewer than*?", or some other aspect of usage. Be prepared, teacher; people will ask you, too, questions like this, if they haven't already started!

Here's a classic, similar to several of the questions I've received, a letter written to a newspaper advice column: "I am in my 90's and have been telling my friends that I am 'slowing down.' The other day I had a note from a retired Dean of a college. He wrote, 'I am 77 and have slowed up.' So, what's correct, 'slowing down' or 'slowing up?'"[5] Another letter to the same advice column asked a similar usage question: "When my granddaughter kept ordering her dog to 'lay down,' I told her she ought to say 'lie down.' 'No wonder they don't mind me,' my granddaughter said."[6]

I'm not including these letters because they represent the epitome of linguistic thought in the United States. These citations are here only because they illustrate notions ordinary people have about language and how it ought to be used correctly. These letters also illustrate that some people believe there is one—and only one—right way to say something; the other way is the wrong way.

In my view, any apparent distinctions between *slowing up* or *slowing down* are distinctions without a difference. Either expression is equally acceptable. Furthermore, the schoolroom grammar distinctions between

---

[4]Jesse Sheidlower, "Elegant Variation and All That," *The Atlantic Monthly*, December 1996, 112.

[5]Dear Abby, *The Lincoln* (NE) *Star*, August 12, 1992.

[6]Dear Abby, *The Lincoln* (NE) *Star*, August 4, 1993.

lie and *lay* have all but disappeared in American English. The merger of the *lie/lay* distinction from days of old represents an unwitting need or desire by speakers in the United States to regularize American English grammar. Moreover, I'm confident the granddaughter's dog is equally obedient to either command.

I cite these letters because they illustrate a continuing belief in "correct" or "proper English," beliefs illustrating a prescriptive attitude toward English usage.

Once introduced, a prescriptive rule is all but impossible to eradicate, no matter how awkward or ridiculous it might be. "Do not begin a sentence with an adverb" is a good example of a prescriptive rule, which we'll discuss in more detail later in this chapter. Prescriptive language rules survive by the same dynamic that perpetuates other school behavior; like reserving special or preferential seating for the high school seniors either during school assemblies or in the cafeteria at lunch time; I went through it and am none the worse, so why should you have it any different?

Birch wonders why grammar standards in the United States seem so firmly rooted in the *past* whereas, at the same time, people in the United States expect constant innovation in fashion, technology, and the media.[7] You tell me.

Perhaps more important, some prescriptive rules are so unnatural that only those people who have realized the benefits of privileged schooling can abide by them. In this case, prescriptive rules can become social markers, distinguishing the *elite* from the *riffraff*.[8]

You should be wondering at this point, where did these prescriptive rules come from? In his history of English teaching in the United States, Arthur Applebee notes that the subject called English did not appear in school curricula until the end of the 19th century. English grammar was the first formal study of English to become widespread in the schools.[9]

In the late 1800s, the purpose of the U.S. high school was divided between two philosophies. Traditional educators saw the high school as a college preparatory institution, dividing the student body into two groups: the college prep track and the terminal or "general" track. Students in these two tracks were typically selected according to economic, social, and ethnic backgrounds. In 1892 the National Education Association

---

[7]Cited in Jiang Yajun, "Metaphors the English Language Lives By," *English Today*, July 2002, 59.

[8]Steven Pinker, *The Language Instinct* (New York: Penguin, 1990), 374.

[9]Arthur N. Applebee, *Tradition and Reform in the Teaching of English: A History* (Urbana, IL, National Council of Teachers of English, 1974), 5–8.

addressed this issue by appointing the Committee of Ten to establish a standard high school curriculum. The Committee of Ten, chaired by Charles Eliot, president of Harvard University, issued several recommendations. Among them was the recommendation that in addition to the study of classical Latin and Greek, more courses in foreign languages, mathematics, science, English, and history should be made available to *all* students, not just the college prep.[10]

As one writer has observed, the ghosts of the 1892 Committee of Ten continue to haunt us today.[11] Because there was no existing tradition of English instruction already in place that might serve as a guide as to how one's *native* language might be taught, the schools looked to other forms of language study in the curriculum, the teaching of Latin and Greek for the college prep students, for instructional methods and models.[12]

The emphasis in teaching the classical languages was traditional grammar, and it emphasized two elements: the learning of grammar rules and the application of grammar rules. These elements were learned through "sentence parsing," which was and is analyzing sentences, diagramming sentences, and correcting usage errors. This approach to the study of Latin and Greek was adopted as the curriculum model to follow in the study of English. What evolved in the study of English in U.S. high schools, then, was an extraordinary switch from a method of *teaching* a classical/foreign language—Latin or Greek—to a method of *correcting* a native language, English.[13]

As we've discussed and illustrated earlier in this chapter, the prescriptive tradition is alive and well today. Just try to introduce any language topic into a conversation (using dictionaries, writing letters, speaking extemporaneously, speaking dialects, etc.), and within 15 minutes the conversation will devolve into issues of what's "correct English." Indeed, the ghosts of the 1892 Committee of Ten haunt us, even today.

Many of the prescriptive rules of language "experts" simply make no sense. As Steven Pinker, an MIT cognitive scientist with a particular concern for language learning and language use, has written, "There are bits of folklore that originated for screwball reasons several hundred years ago and have perpetuated themselves ever since." Furthermore, as long as these prescriptive rules have existed, people have "broken" them, bringing

---

[10]Allan Ornstein and Daniel U. Levine, *Foundations of Education* (Boston: Houghton Mifflin, 1993), 174–175.

[11]Carol Aulbach, "The Committee of Ten: Ghosts Who Still Haunt Us," *English Journal*, March 1994, 16.

[12]Applebee, *Tradition and Reform*, 7.

[13]Ibid.

forth anguished complaints from the "experts" about the decline and decay of language.[14]

As a pre- or in-service teacher of English, you either need to know, or you've already learned, that most people who speak English are language "experts."

This is just a bit ironic. Those who balance checkbooks use math, but don't consider themselves expert mathematicians. People who prepare hamburgers on the patio grill don't think they're expert chefs. Weekend golfers, tennis players, or poker players seldom consider themselves "experts." Nevertheless, almost anyone who speaks English is an "expert" about how English ought to be used. Go figure.

Often, Pinker suggests, this expertise goes unchallenged. For example, imagine that an expert makes an announcement concerning a grievous error. The correct name for the city in Ohio that people call Cleveland is really Cincinnati, and the correct name for the town people call Cincinnati is really Cleveland. The expert gives no reasons why this error is an error. The expert simply states that people who care about the language will adopt this usage, immediately. If this were to happen, you would surely think this person is either crazy or stupid. But when an "expert" makes similar pronouncements about language use in an editorial, a newspaper column, or a letter to the editor, he or she is not seen as crazy or stupid but is admired as a champion of high standards and as a defender of literacy![15]

Sometimes similar pronouncements are voiced in classrooms. (It's those ghosts again!) A student in one of my classes recently completed the "For Your Inquiry and Practice" activity that appears at the end of chapter 1. The adults she interviewed gave these comments about their English language studies in school:

- "Sometimes the teacher would dictate whole sentences and paragraphs and we wrote them down. It was difficult because the sentences were unrelated."
- "There were isolated words that the whole class had to memorize."
- "Eighty percent of the students spoke a different dialect. In school we were allowed to use only the classical style. As soon as I left school for home I went back to my own dialect. I didn't know it was 'slang.'"

---

[14]Pinker, *The Language Instinct*, 373.

[15]Pinker, *The Language Instinct*, 383.

- "We were encouraged to write letters and to send them to our grandparents. I learned that postcards were the easiest."
- "Letter-writing assignments were form centered. The teacher gave us the ideas to write, then we sent the letters to mythical, far-off places."
- "We never did personal journal writing. Language learning was never fun but was a chore."

WEAKNESSES OF TRADITIONAL LANGUAGE STUDY

Most of the respondents interviewed in this "For Your Inquiry and Practice" activity described their language studies as "traditional." The traditional approach typically fails to present a more comprehensive view of language uses and users, and has been relatively ineffective for a variety of reasons, which include but aren't limited to the following:

The Traditional Approach Emphasizes Structure Rather Than Meaning. In the traditional approach, 9-, 10-, or 11-year-old students begin a 6- to 8-year study of written language structures using Latinate grammatical analyses. Never mind, of course, that English grammar is Germanic in origin, not Latinate. In many cases, it's not actually an 8-year program, but is a 1-year course of study repeated eight times. Students memorize definitions of nouns, verbs, adverbs, and conjunctions; subjective and nominative case; and the categories of phrases, causes, and sentences. By labeling the parts of speech of each word in a sentence, and through related analyses of individual sentences, the students are expected to be able, as a consequence, to create sentences that will duplicate the adult sentences they have been studying.

In addition to confusing the application of rules appropriate for a Romance language grammar, Latin, to a grammar more Germanic in nature, English, there is little attention given to the distinctions between passive memorizing and active learning. The focus of this type of language study is on the "pure meaning" of illustrative and idealized sentences that are supposed to be representative of adult language mastery. The sentences are often presented in list form and are examined independent of any real context of use.

For example, an English handbook I have on my desk presents the following pairs of sentences, each pair representing a type of sentence:

A. A **declarative** sentence makes a statement.

1. Dexter grows broccoli in his garden.

2. Our boat has leaked since last fall.

B. An **interrogative** sentence asks a question.

1. Wouldn't you like a pillow for your head?

2. What will an extra night in the hotel cost?

C. An **imperative** sentence gives a command.

1. Wait for me, Mario.

2. Chauncey, stop that barking!

D. An **exclamatory** sentence expresses strong emotion or feeling.

1. Willie's sister said her first word!

2. Oh, what a surprise I have for Lon![16]

These categories and their examples need some commentary. First, the categories are not only *simplistic* but are *patently incorrect* when we consider how people actually use language. "Wait for me, Mario" offered in the preceding list as an example of an imperative sentence, a sentence giving a command, may be, in a real context of use, a *request*, even a *plea* if it's spoken by a younger brother or sister to an older brother or sister.

Recall with me a scene from Jean Shepherd's seasonal TV classic, *A Christmas Story*. Ralphie and Randy are trudging through the snow to school. Randy falls down and can't get up; Ralphie helps Randy to his feet and quickly returns to Flick and the group of friends. Randy cries out, "Ralphie, wait up!" Like "Wait for me Mario," Randy's "Ralphie, wait up" is *not* a command; it's an *appeal*, a *plea*, a *supplication*!

Until you know the context in which a sentence is used, classifying the sentence by any typology is, at best, an iffy proposition. You must look at the *function* of the sentence, not just its *form*.

Similarly, another sentence that from a textbook point of view might be labeled as an **interrogative** sentence, might actually be something else. For example, when a teacher asks a student, "Will you please close the door?" or when my wife calls me on the telephone and asks me, "Can you pick up a loaf of French bread on your way home from campus?" the

---

[16]Mary Ellen Snodgrass, *The Great American English Handbook* (Jacksonville, IL: Perma-Bound, 1987), 27.

sentences are more likely to be imperative sentences, commands. The range of acceptable replies to these two sentences is rather limited; no student is likely to say to the teacher, "No thank you." I'm not likely to say that to my wife, either! The *imperatives* spoken by the teacher and by my wife are disguised as *interrogatives* because they sound nicer and are more polite; this is routine behavior in a culture that values politeness.

Continuing our form-versus-function discussion, consider also so-called *interrogative* sentences, sentences ending with a question mark. Sentences or statements that sometimes look like interrogative can actually be exclamatory sentences. "Are you kidding?", for example, is frequently spoken when the speaker means "Wow!" Just because a sentence looks like an interrogative in *form*, you need to examine its *function* in a real context.

These traditional textbook categories emphasize structure, form, rather than meaning, function, as it emerges through authentic use in a real context.

These traditional definitions emphasizing structure rather than meaning have one more dubious achievement worth noting, and that is historical precedent. One of the examples quoted earlier tells the reader that "An **imperative** sentence gives a command." This is like an older definition, "A sentence which gives an order is a command." This latter example comes from one of the texts in my personal collection of *antique* books, an text published in the United States in 1889![17]

Imagine the public outcry if science or geography teachers used facts, definitions, or concepts from the 19th-century knowledge base. When English-language curricula continue to use 19th-century ideas, then our profession is no better off than the physics teacher who denies Newtonian or quantum physics or the geography teacher who continues to use maps that show that the Earth is flat.

Though structure in language is clearly important, it is one of the last linguistic features the typical language learner pays attention to. *Meaning* is the first, and for most language users, the most enduring interest and perceived need. From the onset of language acquisition until young adulthood, and well into adulthood, language users are most concerned with what they talk *about*, not what they talk *with*. The paramount and over-riding linguistic interest of normal speakers and writers is *meaning*. When was the last time you paid more attention to form, instead of meaning, and asked yourself, "Why did she use a sentence-initial gerund in that sentence?"

---

[17]C. C. Long, *New Language Exercises for Elementary Schools* (Cincinnati, OH, and New York: Van Antwerp Bragg and Company, 1889), 31.

This does not mean that structure should never be included in the language arts curriculum. To omit grammar study from the classroom would be as professionally irresponsible as teaching *only* grammar and no other aspects of language. I am suggesting, however, that the history of English language instruction in the United States is largely one of grammar instruction. The other aspects of language, like those topics included in the table of contents in this textbook, have received fleeting or no attention.

Part of the reason for this can be found in our earlier discussion of how the subject of English was first introduced into the school curriculum. (Those ghosts keep reappearing.) Additionally, most of the scholarship in linguistics in the United States has emphasized structure. As Widdowson has noted, "Linguists, at least since Chomsky (1959, 1965), if they have been concerned with language acquisition, have been concerned principally with grammatical competence."[18] Oller is even more outspoken when he puts the matter bluntly: "The focus of American linguistics, I found, with few exceptions was almost exclusively on some aspect of phonetics, phonology, or syntax, with almost active indifference toward meaning and a near defiant oblivousness to the world of experience."[19] Clarke tempers the discussion to a degree and acknowledges that although recent research "has moved beyond the acquisition of grammatical competence, performance—the messy business of actual language use—is not accorded much attention."[20]

The fact is most people use language because of what it can accomplish for them. Toddlers do not learn words like *milk, cookie, doll*, or *ball* because they feel some heightened sense of visceral pleasure by manipulating their lips, tongue, and teeth to form those words. Nor are they learning these words because they are "correct." They learn these and other words because saying the words brings results. They are expressing needs, wants, wishes, and demands. Crying is rather vague; saying a word is more precise. So, words are learned and used to express a variety of meanings.

Similarly, adolescents have learned, usually incidentally and indirectly, what language can accomplish. They have learned, for example, that the adoption of the code words of their respective social networks simultaneously establishes and symbolizes their identity, their group affiliation, their *belonging*. These are meaning-making language choices of the most

---

[18]Cited in Mark A. Clarke, "The Dysfunctions of the Theory/Practice Discourse," *TESOL Quarterly*, Spring 1994, 15.

[19]Ibid.

[20]Ibid.

personal type, and are virtually universal among all language learners, especially adolescents and young adults.

Remember, the unstated but nevertheless nearly unanimous motto for most students in our schools is "Death before uncool." The sense of the motto is clear: Death is preferred over committing an act others might interpret as uncool. Of course, the surest way to avoid being uncool is to gain the affirmation and identity that results from belonging to a social group of one's choice. How is this accomplished? Dress like they dress and *talk* like they *talk*!

School-age learners use language for several reasons: to share ideas, dreams, secrets, fantasies, and thoughts with their friends, or with those they want or yearn to be friends; to negotiate and construct questions, answers, and interpretations of information about their social and academic worlds in ways their peers consider acceptable and "with it." Using language that will satisfy all these outcomes is a tall order.

Furthermore, it is a generally accepted sociolinguistic fact that people will adopt the language of the group or network they either belong to or aspire to belong to. This is true for adults as well as for adolescents. The use of group-codified slang terms, like *bling-bling, metrosexual, minizzle, tanorexic,* and *sweet* are terms used because others in the group or network use them. If you use these terms, you're part of the group.

I might add that trying to be knowledgeable about current slang is a bit like putting salt on the tail of a squirrel; it changes quickly. Indeed, by the time you read this book the five italicized examples listed here may have already be passed out of fashion.

You have no doubt observed that some adults, perhaps even some English teachers, identify themselves through their behavior as **language cops**. Language cops, agents from the Department of [Linguistic] Corrections, patrol classrooms and corridors, poised to pounce on and apprehend linguistic miscreants who live outside the Pilazzo of Paragraph Purity.

In one of my classes, one teacher proudly described how he "dealt with" the word *humongous*, a word he said he "detested." He explained that he told his students that they could use the words in his room (How gallant and heroic!), but because *humongous* is not in the dictionary, they must not use it anywhere else. *Humongous,* as a matter of fact, most certainly is in "the dictionary." It is included in two dictionaries I have in my office. Here is an example of a language cop who only thinks he's arresting what he considers poor language use, but he's also spreading false information about the dictionary to his students. That's inexcusable.

Yeah, I'm from the Department of
Corrections, and what you've been doing
with your passive sentences is known by us.

FIG. 2.1.   Department of (linguistics) corrections cop.

Sometimes attempts by language cops to command and control language use are downright funny. In a four-page section headed "Frequently Misused Words and Phrases," for example, a language handbook cited earlier admonishes its adolescent audience to "avoid using **amongst**, which is an outdated form."[21]

A recently published dictionary, *Merriam-Webster's Collegiate Dictionary (11th edition)*, published in 2003, includes the preposition *amongst* as a recognized variant of *among*, but does not use a **label of time** beside the entry word to indicate that *amongst* is "obsolete," "archaic," or "older." Why, one must wonder, did the author of the language handbook select *amongst* as a frequently misused word and by what authority can the writer claim that *amongst* is an "outdated form?" The writer doesn't mention closely related words like *whilst*, *amidst*, or *against*, by the way. Shouldn't we at least expect consistency from language cops?

The word *amongst* is routinely used by the Queen of England and members of her family and court, the Archbishop of Canterbury, my British friends Tony Tickner who lives in Newcastle-upon-Tyne and Graham and Kathleen Shaw who live in Barnes (a London suburb), as well as millions of speakers who live in the United Kingdom, Canada, Australia, and other countries heavily influenced by British English.

---

[21]Snodgrass, *The Great American English Handbook*, 36.

Are these speakers and other language users—seen and heard frequently on news programs broadcast by ABC, NBC, MSNBC, CBS, Fox, NPR, CNN, and C-SPAN, just to name a few—guilty, at least according to one language cop, of using "outdated" language? Of course not.

Granted, *amongst* will be used either more or less frequently depending on the speech habits and conventions of different language groups and networks. How different groups and networks use variant forms of a word, illustrating regional or social dialects, are more honest and more productive issues to bring to a class. (see chaps. 5, 7 and 8.)

No amount of adult, teacher, or parent ridicule, discouragement, attempted control, or fun making will likely cause Lisa or Brad to stop saying *humongous*, or *like*, as in "Can we, *like*, stop at that 7-Eleven?" The adult who casts him or herself in the language cop role will most likely be received by the adolescent language user with stony silence, cold stares, or temporary and reluctant compliance accompanied by under-the-breath mutterings like, "Man, this is dumb."

The Traditional Approach Assumes Language Homogeneity Instead of Recognizing Language Variability. Several years ago I asked my university to release me from my then current administrative appointment so that I could return to my first academic loves: to teach, to read, to conduct research, and to write. Shortly after my decision became public knowledge, the dean of one of our colleges met me on the street. As our curbside conversation came to an end, the dean said to me, "By the way, do me a favor: Make sure your students know *not* to begin sentences with 'Hopefully.' Teach them that adverbs can't begin sentences. That just drives me up the wall!"

Students and faculty on my campus know this dean to be a kind, intelligent, and tolerant individual. His comments about adverbs in general and *hopefully* in particular, however, demonstrate another of the myths about "proper English" or "good English."

Hopefully has, for some reason, been identified by some as a major misuse of an adverb. Why *hopefully* in the sentence-initial position should create so much controversy is a linguistic mystery. Nevertheless, resistance to the use of *hopefully* has been voiced by several writers, Lipton among them, who compares the relatively widespread use of *hopefully* to a relentless advance by a bunch of linguistic Vandals and Huns. He observes that "*Hopefully* is marching roughshod through sentences, modifying every word on the eleven o'clock news but the right one."[22]

---

[22]James Lipton, *An Exaltation of Larks* (New York: Viking Penguin, 1991), 13.

The traditional argument against *hopefully* goes like this: The adverb *hopefully* comes from the adjective *hopeful,* meaning "in a manner full of hope." Therefore, some experts say, *hopefully* can be used only when the sentence refers to a person who is doing something in a manner full of hope. It simply isn't true, however, that an English adverb must indicate only the manner in which the actor or agent performs the action because there are two forms of adverbs, **verb phrase adverbs** and **sentence adverbs**.

A verb phrase adverb refers to the agent or actor identified in the sentence. A sentence adverb, on the other hand, indicates the doer's attitude toward the content of the sentence. Examples of commonly used sentence adverbs include *accordingly, basically, candidly, generally, incidentally,* and *seriously,* to name but a few. Understandably, the use of *hopefully* has been around since the 1930s.[23]

Few experts given to criticizing the public's use of language vent their spleens in a similar fashion regarding other sentence adverbs like "*Naturally,* I think so, too," "*Surprisingly,* we went first," or "*Fortunately,* she was there on time."

Amazingly, despite all the fuss surrounding the use of *hopefully,* other sentence-initial adverbs seem to be more acceptable.

Whether the issue is the proper placement of adverbs, the use of split infinitives ("To boldly go . . ."), the preferred pronunciation of *nuclear,* the dropping of /r/ in "Pahk the cah heah," or dropping the /g/ as in "Stop that runnin'," or a multitude of other possibilities, there has been a persistent tendency among some language critics, classroom teachers, and textbook publishers to prescribe one language use over another, and to label the preferred use as "correct" and the other as "incorrect." Those items that are "correct" are often referred to as **Standard American English** (SAE). This is an illusive term and we discuss it several times throughout this text.

The traditional language curriculum has tended to follow the prescriptive approach to language study for more than a century in the United States, identifying "correct" and, therefore, SAE usage despite the indisputable evidence that language is neither "fixed" nor homogenous. Language varies. It varies in real time and it varies over time.

For example, you may be surprised to learn that there are some questions regarding what SAE actually is. Consider the following sentences:

1. Father was exceedingly fatigued subsequent to his extensive peregrination.
2. Dad was very tired after his lengthy journey.

---

[23]Pinker, *The Language Instinct,* 381.

3. Pop had a long, difficult trip.
4. Do you have any money?
5. Have you got any money?

Which of these sentences would you accept as SAE? I suspect most linguists in the United States would consider all five sentences to be representative of SAE. Sentence 1 is, of course, formal to the point of being stilted, what with the ridiculously prim *peregrination*, a word we seldom encounter. Sentences 2 and 3 say, essentially, the same thing as sentence 1; all three sentences have, generally, the same referential meaning. The same can be said about Sentences 4 and 5; they communicate, basically, the same message. In the United Kingdom, on the other hand, I imagine Sentence 5 might be more questionable as an example of Standard British English owing to the fact that *got* in a sentence like this one is more acceptable in the United States than in the UK.[24]

What these examples should help you understand is something I've suggested earlier: SAE isn't a fixed code. Speakers can express sentences in what is called SAE in a variety of ways. The traditional approach and language cops seldom accept this view in practice or in theory.

Turning to another aspect of SAE, pronunciation, my former pastor, the Rev. Dr. Ra Drake, always referred to the *membuhs* of her congregation. She dropped the /r/. I always pronounce the /r/ in *members*. The difference in our pronunciations of this word is not the result of her ordination as a pastor, or the lack of my ordination as a clergy person. The fact is, she was born and raised in Memphis, Tennessee, the U.S. Southern Dialect region. The majority of the speakers in this region drop the /r/ in the word *member*. I was born and raised in the U.S. Midwest Dialect region; the majority of the speakers in this region pronounce the /r/.

Similarly, born in the Midwest Dialect region, I grew up describing some foods as *greazy* (Note the /z/.) Both of my daughters, however, from an identical gene pool but born and raised in the Upper North Midland Dialect area, render that word as *greasy* (Note the /s/.) My former pastor, my daughters, and I are all speaking SAE, I contend. It's important to note that SAE is not a fixed code; it varies. What these variations illustrate is a seemingly simple but very profound axiom: People talk *like* the people they talk *with*.

Let's visit one more aspect of variability within SAE. At the university where I attended graduate school studying for my PhD, the word *data* was

[24]Peter Trudgill, "Standard English: What it Isn't," in *Standard English:The Widening Debate*, eds. Tony Bex and Richard J. Watts (London: Routledge, 1999), 117–28.

always a plural noun, as in *The data are conclusive.* Those students who treated *data* as a singular noun were corrected! Today, however, *data* is being used with great frequency as a singular noun. One of my collegiate dictionaries reflects this trend with the usage note "sing or pl." Clearly, the uses of *data* are changing, but I contend that at present both the singular and the plural fall within the range of SAE. Language is not homogenous. It varies.

There are additional examples of language variability, and they are typically ignored or discredited in the traditional program, which advocates a *single standard* for proper language use. One possible explanation for the imposition of a single standard has been suggested by James and Leslie Milroy: The written language has been studied, analyzed, and codified to a far greater extent than oral language and, consequently, that teachers and textbooks have imposed the standards for *written* language on *oral* language.[25]

Oral language is quite different from written language, as you already know. Oral language represents that "messy" business of actual language use we described earlier. In oral language we exhibit stuttering starts and stops, throwing in several "uhs" and "ers" to hold our place while we think about our next comment, overlapping the speech of our conversational partner, finishing a sentence for the person we're talking to. If we misspeak, we try to repair the error right away by saying, "What I mean is. . . ."

Written language seldom allows for any of this "messy" business. We can *edit* written language so that the fitful starts, stops, "ers," and repairs don't appear in print. Attempting to hold speakers accountable for the same conventions writers adhere to flies in the face of reality.

Furthermore, we must also remember that despite its codification and greater degree of standardization, written language varies, too. We've already illustrated this idea with the five SAE sentences we examined earlier. Consider additionally how a letter applying for a job, a note to the mail carrier, a shopping list, a letter to a friend, and a manuscript prepared for publication in a scholarly journal will each use a different style of written language. It is misleading to tell our students that the formal language in a scholarly manuscript is the one and only standard we will use in the assessment of all uses of written language. To extend this standard to oral language, too, seems far-fetched to me.

---

[25]James Milroy and Leslie Milroy, *Authority in Language* (London: Routledge & Kegan Paul, 1985), 71–72.

Some prescriptive statements about language use are downright foolish. To tell a student, for example, that using a double negative makes a statement positive is a misapplication of a principle from mathematics. If a speaker says "We don't have no money," only a fool or a knave would insist that the speaker has *some* money. We might discourage the use of double negation in sentences, but we'd better seek a reason for doing so that makes sense.

At the human level, prescriptive statements can be horrific, especially when a student is made to feel ashamed of the way she or he speaks. Michael Halliday and his colleagues said it best several years ago: "A speaker who is made ashamed of his own language habits suffers a basic injury as a human being. To make anyone, especially a child, feel so ashamed is as indefensible as to make him feel ashamed of the color of his skin."[26]

A modern English language arts curriculum ought to provide opportunities for students to observe and analyze aspects of language as these features *vary* as the speakers, writers, contexts and the communicative needs and intentions vary. Determining whether the language used under these circumstances is appropriate, convincing, or apropos requires more awareness of human language than does the application of a single standard of correctness.

The Traditional Approach Emphasizes Artificial Instead of Authentic Language.   As we saw earlier in our discussion of structure versus meaning, the traditional approach uses contrived examples of "proper English." Many of the sentences in these textbooks and workbooks are isolated and have no context of authentic use. These illustrative sentences do not represent the ways real people speak or write. Inasmuch as these sentences appear out of nowhere, other then the figment of someone's imagination, I don't understand how can any self-respecting educator can hold them up to students as examples of good models, of "proper English."

If we accept these ostensibly illustrative sentences literally and devoid of real contexts, we are ignoring one inescapable fact: **Real sentences always occur in real contexts**. Furthermore, in a given context, a sentence will likely carry more meaning that its literal content conveys.

For example, "Are you kidding?" can be either an interrogative sentence or an exclamatory utterance, depending on the context of use. Here

---

[26]M. A. K. Halliday, Angus McIntosh, and Peter Stevens, *The Linguistic Sciences and Language Teaching* (Bloomington: Indiana University Press, 1964), 105.

are two examples of that sentence, conversations between my wife and me, illustrating both the interrogative and the exclamatory functions of "Are you kidding?"

Example 1: During the recent World Series, I telephoned my wife while my night class was enjoying its regularly scheduled "comfort break." Being a life-long baseball fan, I was eager to know the score. "The other team is ahead," she said. Suspecting that she might be teasing me, not an unusual gambit on her part, I said "Are you kidding?" It was a genuine question, an interrogative sentence.

Example 2: I arrive at home after a day on campus, walk into the kitchen and see my wife talking on the telephone, not an unusual practice on her part. "That was Dad," she said. "When we go to Kansas City next Friday night, he wants to take us out to dinner at The Cheesecake Factory for your birthday, if you'd like." I replied with, "Are you kidding?" This reply was *not* a question, despite the use of the question mark. It was an exclamation, synonymous with "Of course," or "And how," or "I surely would like!"

We can more accurately describe, analyze, and assess sentences only when they are seen in a real context of use. Contrived, isolated sentences have no communicative contexts. The traditional program that emphasizes artificial instead of authentic language ignores a basic fact of communication: Normal people simply do not go around making unconnected, unprompted, or unsolicited comments about the world![27]

You'll find numerous activities following each chapter in Section II of this book that use authentic language used in real contexts.

The Traditional Program Emphasizes Adult Rather Than Developmental Models of Language.   In his autobiography, the British writer Laurie Lee recalls the disillusionment he experienced his first day at the village school. After arriving at school, he was taken to a chair and was told by the teacher, "Why don't you just sit here for the present." "I sat there all day," he writes, "but I never got it [the present]."[28] The adult's use of *present* was certainly different from the child's understanding of *present*! Roger Bruning, one of my colleagues, tells a related story about the young piano student who was particularly fond of the music of the French composer, "W.C." (Debussy).

---

[27]Michael Stubbs, *Discourse Analysis* (Oxford: Basil Blackwell, 1983), 150.

[28]Laurie Lee, *The Edge of Day: A Boyhood in the West of England* (New York: William Morrow and Company, 1960), 45.

Here you see two young people in relatively new territory. The young speakers in these two illustrations are not, through no fault of their making, communicating with the language of the adult world; the young people have imposed their own sense of reality on the reality of adult language. Similar misunderstandings can happen in classrooms when adult language models are used.

The traditional approach to language study glosses over the fact that the language of adolescents is still developing. The language of adolescents is neither fixed nor established. Young adults are still learning how to interpret the sociolinguistic features of speaker, intention, and situation in their daily conversations. How these understandings might transfer to writing activities isn't clear. Indeed, the use of socially stigmatized forms of language, like using double negatives or using *ain't*, is at its maximum in a speaker's adolescent years.[29]

Adolescents are still developing their fluency with language and will use false starts, voiced hesitations, and meaningless repetitions. (So do adults, by the way.) Complex noun phrases, some modal auxiliaries (*shall, may, ought to*), relative clauses introduced by *whom* or *whose* are just some of the grammatical features not that frequent in the language of adolescents.[30]

These are just a few examples of *normal* language development among adolescent learners. These illustrations do not exemplify students who are stupid, substandard, or lazy. What the examples illustrate is that young adults are, simply, still learning the language. They are still serving their *linguistic apprenticeships*, understandably unaware that anyone might care about the use of adverbs in the sentence-initial position.

Despite what we've learned about continuing language development among learners in their early teens, English-language handbooks and textbooks presuppose an ideal "speaker/writer," already equipped with an adult mastery of language. As most teachers know, however, this is a false assumption; many middle and high school students haven't reached this level of language proficiency. When students are given models of narrative or expository writing created by adult, professional writers, and are told, "Now, it's your turn. Can you write a similar piece?" they experience needless frustrations.

Some schools are using different approaches. Two approaches that allow for young writers to write more naturally, without being held up

---

[29]Suzanne Romaine, *The Language of Children and Adolescents* (Oxford: Basil Blackwell, 1984), 108.

[30]Katherine Perera, "The Language Demands of Schooling," in *Linguistics and the Teacher*, ed. Ronald Carter (London: Routledge & Kegan Paul, 1982), 115.

against an adult rubric, are the Six-traits, or 6+1 Traits writing model developed by the Northwest Regional Education Laboratory[31] and the approaches advocated trough the National Writing Project sites throughout most of the United States. Both of these approaches give teachers and students a vocabulary and vehicles for talking about writing, and neither approach assumes the young writers will be adult professionals!

The Traditional Approach Emphasizes Control Before Awareness. One of the greatest weaknesses of the traditional program of English-language study is that it attempts to teach students how to *control* isolated features of language before many of the students are *aware* of their own language, or the languages around them. Moreover, the traditional program too often emphasizes isolated features through *negative* examples, which is completely opposite to the normal way we acquire and learn language.

Several years ago a group of us organized a coed softball team for one of the city leagues, the league created for older "athletes" who refuse to admit that their playing days were over some time ago! You need to know that women my age came trough the school system long before either Title IX or the newer physical education curricula. Consequently, the coed softball team was their first opportunity to play an organized team sport. At a team practice session one Saturday afternoon while I was pitching batting practice, I told one female batter, "Don't swing if the ball isn't in the strike zone." The batter turned to the catcher and asked, "What's a strike zone?"

I was guilty of assuming the batter had *control* over something she wasn't even *aware* of

The traditional English language arts curriculum typically makes a similarly false assumption, namely, that students can control individual aspects of language before they are aware that they exist. This book is dedicated to the proposition that learners can and will learn more about exercising greater control over language, but their attainment of this outcome will be realized when they have opportunities to explore language, becoming more aware of the complexities of language, and how real people use language for authentic and very varied purposes.

Language handbooks and textbooks frequently present examples of sentences that the students are to "avoid" because they are "confusing," "weak," or "unacceptable." The inclusion of either ungrammatical or negative

---

[31]For information about this model, go to http://www.nwrel.org/assessment/department.asp?d=1.

examples under the heading of "Don't Say" is not the way language is normally acquired and learned.

Pinker provides a thorough analysis of whether negative, ungrammatical evidence (models, examples) is *ever* presented to the language learner. "Obviously," he says, "no one gives children ungrammatical sentences tagged with asterisks."[32] (In language texts, an asterisk is conventionally attached to ungrammatical or improbable sentences, as in *boy home the ran.*) Adult caregivers just don't talk like that to infants and toddlers!

Exactly how children acquire language with all its complex entanglements isn't totally understood. Most linguists tend to believe that language is acquired as children observe how language is used around them, and then they experiment, using words and sentences in newer contexts to see if they "work." Most of the feedback children receive from these efforts will focus on the success, or lack thereof, of the functional, meaning-centered uses of language in the home or social contexts, not grammaticality.[33] In whatever form the feedback is given, negative evidence or examples are seldom if ever used.

Briefly, this is one reason why the negative examples in textbooks and handbooks aren't likely to be useful to the learner's language growth. People simply do not learn language by imitating negative examples.

FOR YOUR INQUIRY AND PRACTICE:

Prepare a brief statement entitled "My Language Story." Explain how the language you use today is different from the language you used 5 years ago. Ten years ago. What and who have been the major influences on your evolving language?

REVIEWING THE CHAPTER

Part One: *Place a (✓) in the blank beside each statement found in this chapter.*

_____ 1. Prescriptivists study language as it is used.
_____ 2. Following descriptive rules can lead to social-class marking.

---

[32]Steven Pinker, *Learnability and Cognition: The Acquisition of Argument Structure* (Cambridge, MA: MIT Press, 1991), 6.

[33]Ibid., 11.

___ 3. Language curricula suffer because of the lack of linguistic authorities.

___ 4. Students and adults believe the prescriptive approach is beneficial.

___ 5. The study of grammar is unnecessary.

Part Two: *Place a (✓) in the blank beside each statement you believe the author would agree with.*

___ 6. Adult models are always instructionally effective.

___ 7. Both language form and language function are equally important.

___ 8. Language conformity is more important to adolescents than to adults.

___ 9. Older definitions are more accurate definitions.

___ 10. Oral and written language must meet the same standards of proper English.

Part Three: *Based on your understanding of this chapter, and taking into account what you've learned as an educator, place a (✓) beside each statement you can agree with.*

___ 11. If the shoe fits, wear it.

___ 12. All problems have solutions.

___ 13. You have to be true to yourself.

___ 14. Sometimes the best solution for a problem is to ignore it.

___ 15. It's easier to talk the talk than it is to walk the walk.

CHAPTER 3

Language Exploration and Awareness: Three Prerequisites

Language is not an abstract construction of the learned,
or of dictionary makers, but is something arising out of the work,
needs, ties, joys, affections, tastes, of long generations
of humanity, and has its bases broad and low, close to the ground.
—Walt Whitman, *Slang in America*

Before you read this chapter, recall from chapter 2 how the study of the English language was introduced into the school curriculum: It was a means of correcting the students' uses of English, their *native* language. In your view, what *ought to be* the purposes of studying the English language in schools? Name four to five major student outcomes for a K–12 English-language curriculum.

In chapters 1 and 2 you read what LEA is about, and you've read why I think becoming more aware of language through explorations is a more fruitful endeavor for language learners than is the memorizing of an assortment of rules. As language learners become more aware of the many nuances, complexities, purposes, and effects of how people use language, they are much more likely, in my view, to give their time and attention to the ways *they* use language. If this is going to happen in schools, we need to expunge simplistic rules of what either right or wrong language use is, and begin to define notions of correctness more complexly.[1]

---

[1]Gregory Shafer, "Reforming Writing and Rethinking Correctness," *English Journal*, September 2004, 66.

Many students who enter our classrooms are not aware of the questions and controversies surrounding language and ideas about what's "correct." Too often they see uses of language as objective, dispassionate endeavors that require them to simply follow a set of standard and fixed rules.[2]

A joke making the rounds several years ago goes like this:

Question: How many psychologists does it take to change a lightbulb?

Answer: Only one, but the lightbulb has to *want* to change.

There is more than just a germ of truth in this joke. Any psychologist or counselor knows that he or she can help clients modify their behavior— lose weight, stop smoking, stop drinking, control anger, and so on— successfully only when the client really wants to change his or her behavior. The same holds true for changing one's linguistic behavior, too.

The motivation for changing how one writes or talks is not likely to result from reading a collection of "Do say" and "Don't say" proclamations in a language textbook. Motivation for change is an individual and an internal matter. As Baron puts it, "Despite our best, and often our worst, efforts to change other people's language, it seems that language change can't be readily imposed by the language police, the word hucksters, or the usage mongers. It has to come from within."[3]

The approach to language study offered in this book will help to spur the school learner's language interests, wants, and needs. There are some prerequisites, however, for the success of the LEA approach to the study of language. Those three prerequisites are the major topics in this chapter:

1. Language success (correctness) is determined by the use of multiple criteria.
2. Language study should focus on authentic and germane uses of language.
3. There should be more opportunities for student talk in classrooms.

To introduce and illustrate the first topic, here's an autobiographical vignette. The incident reflects what I call a one-way view of the world ("My way, or the wrong way!") and it has a direct, albeit opposite, relationship to the expanded view of the English language curriculum suggested in this book.

---

[2]Ibid.

[3]Dennis Baron, *Guide to Home English Repair* (Champaign-Urbana, IL: National Council of Teachers of English, 1994), 60.

The setting: We are sitting in a circle in the main lodge at summer camp, finishing our final day of orientation for the new counselors on the summer's staff. Most of the young campers who will be joining us tomorrow have some kind of physical disability. Many come from homes of lower socioeconomic status. This final orientation session is designed to help us to understand better the needs of each camper and, therefore, how to provide for the physical and other needs of each camper.

At the conclusion of the meeting, one of the camp's codirectors is finishing the description of how the family-style meal service works and she ends her remarks by telling us, "Before I forget, make sure the campers break their bread. They never do and it looks just awful to see them chewing on a whole slice. Someday I'm going to have 'Break Your Bread' chiseled above the fireplace." We counselors dutifully nod, implicitly agreeing to teach the campers the importance of breaking a slice of bread in half at mealtime.

USING REAL DISCOURSE AND MULTIPLE CRITERIA TO DETERMINE CORRECTNESS

I'm sharing this summer camp experience because I believe it illustrates a stubborn and intolerant insistence on *one way* to define socially acceptable and correct behavior. It also illustrates cultures in conflict. The fact is, most of the children who attend this summer camp and their families survive during the school year by eating food provided by government commodities and surpluses. Breaking a piece of bread in half, putting their napkins in their laps, and the like, aren't items of etiquette high on their personal agendas!

Returning to the main points of this chapter, when it's applied to language behavior, the "my way or the wrong way" (Sometimes known as "my way is the *only* way") attitude should have been eradicated years ago, but like teenage acne, it's persistent. This view of language and language correctness—that it's an abstract construction possessed by the learned that must be imposed on other, needier and more linguistically challenged ne'er-do-wells—remains throughout U.S. culture and some classrooms much more than one might suppose or desire.

The children and young adults in our classrooms, however, know better. They have been observing real language at work for years and they have gained numerous *implicit* understandings about how authentic language actually works. If you've overheard youngsters playing "School," for example, you'll recognize the following passage:

(1) **Mary:**   Let's get quiet boys and girls . . .

(2) **Gary:**   [Teacher, Teacher . . .

(3) **Mary:**   Gary, I'm not ready for your questions. You need to pay . . .

(4) **Gary:**   [But, Teacher . . .

(5) **Mark:**   Gary, siddown!

(6) **Mary:**   (clapping hands) Boys! Boys! Do you want to be separated?

In Statement (1), Mary demonstrates her implicit knowledge of Teacher's routine way of talking to a class, directing its attention or activity and then redirecting focus when necessary. Mary learned this "script" and its related rules through observation. She, like Gary, Mark, and thousands of other school-age children, have learned how to play "School" in accordance to the rules without any direct instruction.

The game would break down if Mary would have started with either "Brothers and sisters of the household of faith . . ." or with "Gentlemen, start your engines!" Although the "class" would recognize these statements as grammatical, they would also, most likely, rule them as invalid in this context because the sentences don't represent things teachers say. Teachers don't typically use these scripts.

Similarly, had Mary said in Statement (6), "Ladies and gentlemen of the jury . . ." Gary and Mark would reject this alternative, too, because it isn't right, it just doesn't fit the setting. They understand, no matter how implicitly, that this statement, this particular script, doesn't fit the contextual or situational rules of classroom discourse.

In the various pretend or "play like" games of young language learners, rule violators are dealt with. If one of the players doesn't play by the rules of the game, they suffer immediate consequences. They either are assigned to another role, or are ignored, or they're excluded from the game altogether. You can validate this by observing children at play on any playground at school or in a public park.

I should add at this point that you and I as members of the adult culture treat rule violators in a similar fashion. How often, for example, have you decided *not* to ask someone a simple question for fear that you'd get a lecture instead of an uncomplicated answer?

GOOD ENGLISH IN THE CONTEXTS OF SOCIAL AVENUES

For a variety of reasons, these are important observations for teachers of English and the language arts. These illustrations remind us that kids learn easily and quickly how to shift their language to fit a particular circumstance. Based on their life experiences, they have learned how teachers talk. In other games, they assume the language scripts appropriate to a physician, a priest, pastor, or rabbi; they can mimic the school bus driver, a school nurse, and many others whom they have observed over time. Children learn early on that "correct" language use in their world is determined by its context and that as the contexts change, so do the criteria and standards for judging correctness. They have learned that there is no *single* standard for what is considered correct language use, but there are options within the sociolinguistic system. The correctness of the option selected is ultimately determined by the use of multiple criteria, or multiple "rules."

I have a major concern, though. As children learn these language lessons incidentally, indirectly, and implicitly, learnings I believe to be valid and amazingly sophisticated and complicated, what happens when they encounter a "this way or the wrong way" advocate or prescriptivist, either a teacher or some other adult prominent in their lives? Well, some children might think their language, their family, their friends, and so on, are somehow inferior. Or, some may believe there's a major *disconnect* between what they observe in their real world and in their school world; they may believe one of these worlds is out of step. This type of disconnect is serious.

Yet again, some may feel they've been duped. I vividly recall a lesson in my sophomore high school English class. We were learning to say and to write, "It is I." My classmates and I thought this sounded weird. Our teacher was a great human being whom we all loved. I later dedicated one of my published books to his memory because of the profound influence he had on my personal and professional lives. When we sophomores asked him, "What do you say when you answer the telephone and the caller asks for you?" our teacher admitted he said, "Yeah, it's me." instead of "It is I." What? Why would the Greatest Teacher on Earth tell us to do one thing, and then admit he doesn't do it? What are we supposed to do? Fake it? Give him the answer he wants on the unit exam, but carry on as usual in our real world? How can we reconcile this disconnect? Things like this really bother 15-year olds. The credibility of the school and of schooling is a serious matter!

Our teacher was demonstrating, on the other hand, the reality of multiple criteria for determining language correctness, although we didn't recognize it at the time. "Notions of language correctness *depend*—and always have. A political speech for a group of construction workers includes a different language than a commentary [written] for a political magazine.

Our notions of appropriateness are different for a journal than for a business letter to a potential client."[4]

Even among academic journals there is no unanimity about what constitutes language correctness. The same is true for publishers of academic books. For example, some require total elimination of the first-person writer whereas others embrace a more informal style, the text you're reading right now being an example of the latter.[5]

Adolescents are learning and are beginning to implicitly understand that language use is a contextually driven, socially determined behavior. They know what "good English" is when they're talking with friends on the school bus. It's language that includes nicknames (flattering or rude), insider jokes, and a lot of *ya know, sweet, like, dork, doofus*, and similar words that maintain the bridges of social relationships. On the other hand, they are also learning that when they greet the building principal, ask a question in science class, or talk with the drama teacher at after-school rehearsal, another type of language, more formal, will be needed. Later on in the same day, they'll switch back to a more informal register when they talk with a friend on the telephone about what happened at school that day.

They're learning that in each of these several circumstances they'll make different language choices, talking in different yet pointedly suitable and appropriate ways. Although they may not yet be fully aware of all of the overt changes they're making, they unconsciously shift linguistic gears because the social avenues demand it. They are, on the other hand, fully aware of how their society comes to terms with rule violators and they do not want to be reassigned, ignored, or left out. They desperately crave, far above anything else, to remain a member in good standing with their friends, their *group*.

SCHOOL AS A SOCIAL EVENT

As almost any parent or experienced teacher can attest, most students do not regard school as *school*, an institution dedicated to learning and teaching. Instead of thinking of their school, whether middle level or high school, as an academic institution, most of the learners regard their school as a *social organization*, the center of their social lives. Ask 10 students "What happened at school today?" and 9 of them will tell you what Tammy

---

[4]Shafer, "Reforming Writing," 67.

[5]Ibid.

FIG. 3.1. Young adults see school as a social organization

said to Ashley about Mark, what Sean said to Jason about Tracy, or who's "going with" whom (at this moment, that is), or some similar report on the social goings-on. This is a fact of adolescent development.

On a broader and more empirical scale, when 1,000 midwestern middle school and high school students were asked, "What's the best thing about school?", the most common replies were "being with my friends," "meeting new people," "spending time with my boy friend," and the like. In this study, references to peers overshadowed references to academics and extracurricular activities at every grade level from Grade 7 through Grade 12.[6]

Because social relationships, peer associations, groups, and networks are of central importance to school-age learners, there is logic behind the decision to focus more language study on its uses in society. Throughout their school years, students are coming into greater contact with an increasing number of peers from wider ranges of social classes as several elementary schools "feed" a middle-level school, and three middle schools "feed" a high school. They are also having more contacts with adults.

---

[6] B. Bradford Brown and Wendy Theobald, "Learning Contexts Beyond the Classroom: Extracurricular Activities, Community Organizations, and Peer Groups," in *The Adolescent Years: Social Influences and Educational Challenges*, Ninety-seventh Yearbook of the National Society for the Study of Education, eds. Kathryn Borman and Barbara Schneider (Chicago: University of Chicago Press, 1998), 112.

Their language networks are growing and they are increasingly becoming more socially aware and perceptive. A social perspective toward language and language users speaks to your students' natural and developmental interests.

LANGUAGE AS A SOCIAL EVENT

Approaching language study as a social activity, a view recognizing the importance of authentic discourse in real, social circumstances would seem to be a natural choice for schools. Much of our language behavior, even beyond school, is a social phenomenon, based on and emerging from *social facts* found in one's culture.

Some social facts shape our personal attire. For example, as I prepare to leave home for my campus office I will gather my pens, pencils, car and office keys, an insurance form, football ticket order form, checkbook, appointment book, and any other paraphernalia I'll need. I may discover that I have too much "stuff" to put in my pockets. What will I do?

I probably will not borrow a purse from my wife's collection. One of her larger purses would certainly have more than enough room for my things, but there is a social fact in my culture that men don't carry purses. A few men in my culture might carry a small clutch bag, it is true, but this item is constructed in such a way that it is not likely to be mistaken for a woman's purse or handbag.[7]

Some social facts determine how we stand in line. In the United States a social fact suggests that we form a line while waiting our turn at a ticket window, at the counter of a fast-food establishment, or any other occasion where we honor the "first come, first served" tradition. In the United States a social fact says that we will stand in line and won't flit about like a bunch of nervous tadpoles, and, furthermore, when we enter the waiting line, we go to the rear, working our way forward in a democratic, egalitarian fashion. Exceptions to this social fact are common at airports, when the elderly or those with young children are boarded first.

Similarly, there is a social fact determining how we stand in elevators: We face the doors. The existence of this social fact can be validated the next time you enter an elevator; instead of facing the doors like everyone else, face the back wall of the elevator and notice the reactions of the other passengers you'll be facing.

---

[7]The discussion of *social facts* is based on Geoffrey Sampson, *Schools of Linguistics: Competition and Evolution* (London: Century House, 1987), 43–44.

Social facts like these are not written down anywhere, are seldom taught directly, but are learned and known by everyone. The *social fact* is in the collective mind of society and exists over and above the individual members of society.[8]

FOR YOUR INQUIRY AND PRACTICE:

Why is it that the person *initiating* a telephone call doesn't speak first? No, it's the one who *answers* the telephone, the person being called, who is expected to speak first, either by saying "Hello" or, if it's a business telephone, by identifying the organization or firm. What happens when a social fact like this is violated? The next time you answer your residential telephone, pick up the handset and say *nothing*. What happens?

There are also social facts successful language users must observe: how to ask questions politely, how to ask for directions, how and when to use appropriate terms of address, like Sir, Madam, Dr., Pastor, Aunt, Rabbi, a nickname, Professor, and the like.

Moreover, another reason to study language in authentic social circumstances is found in the observation that most of the "errors" that native speakers of English make in their language use violate social facts and are, consequently, *social errors*, not language or grammatical errors. As Shafer points out, "Language is not simply a matter of right and wrong—of correct and incorrect—and when we reduce such cultural issues to monolithic simplicities, we invariably exclude the richness of language as it reflects the energy of our culturally diverse society."[9]

Native English speakers already know, for the most part, how to pronounce words like the other members of their language networks, and they also know how to put words together into meaningful sentences and other utterances. Under normal circumstances, the native English speaker will never say or write *live United the States in I*. Instead of learning primarily or only about the basic syntactical patterns of English, the school student will profit more by examining the social facts that affect language options.

Parents of younger language learners know, for example, that *please* and *thank you* are relatively easy words to teach someone to learn how to

---

[8]Ibid., 44.

[9]Shafer, "Reforming Writing," 67.

pronounce. The challenge is helping children learn the social facts that tell us *when* they are appropriate words to say and then to remember to say them.[10] How many times have you heard a parent or adult caregiver prompt and remind a child with, "What do you say?" The adult isn't teaching *please* or *thank you*; the adult is teaching the social context in which those words are supposed to be used.

Adults sometimes try to teach linguistic social facts and etiquette so directly that young children can become either confused or just downright bored with the process. For example, several years ago my niece, Courtney, 4 years old at the time, spent the night with her great-grandmother, whom we called Mother Ruth. Mother Ruth was a real stickler for doing things right, like saying "Thank you" and "Please."

The following conversation took place at the breakfast table:

Mother Ruth: Courtney, would you like some eggs for breakfast?
Courtney: No, thank you.
Mother Ruth: Would you like some pancakes?
Courtney: No, thank you.
Mother Ruth: Would you like some oatmeal?
Courtney: No, thank you.
Mother Ruth: Would you like some cold cereal?
Courtney: No, thank you.
Mother Ruth: Would you like some toast?
Courtney: (becoming weary) No.
Mother Ruth: "No" what?
Courtney: No toast.
Mother Ruth: (flustered, to Courtney's mother) Is she being smart?

Courtney wasn't confused, but she certainly was bored with this "Miss Manners" interrogation.

TEACHING THE ENGLISH LANGUAGE AS A SOCIAL ACTIVITY

Teaching the English language as a social activity governed by social rules and social facts can be illustrated by the following examples, all of which have been used successfully in classrooms.

---

[10]Gordon Wells, *The Meaning Makers: Children Learning Language and Using Language* (London: Hoder & Stoughton, 1986), 41.

For our first example, let's consider these recurring questions: Where did language come from and how did people learn to use it? These are significant issues in an individual's becoming more aware of and sensitive to the wonder and the power of language. Sue Spilker, a teacherfriend of mine, tried to help some of her students understand these questions better by helping them create a word. All of the members of the class were sworn to secrecy abut the creation of the word, then they were told to use it around the school when its use would be normal and appropriate. Within 5 school days, Sue tells me, members of her class told her that "their word" had been in gym class, in the cafeteria, and in the corridor one morning before classes began.

"What does this tell us," Mrs. Spilker asked, "about where language comes from, or about how people learn language?" The resulting discussion was both perceptive and lively, based on the students' real observations and experiences, and it helped them understand better these two essential issues about language.

Another teacher, Paula Cvitek, uses role playing with one of her classes. Based on her observations of her students' recent language behavior, she will select a social-usage item like complaint/apology. Then she frames for the class a social setting in which a conversation will take place:

> You are at an awards dinner-ceremony in the school cafeteria and there's something massively wrong with the entrée. Four of you are sitting with the new building principal, who asks how you're enjoying the meal. What will you say, and how will you say it?

After this role play has run its course, another scene is set, substituting a popular teacher for the principal. In this role-play, the students are much more forthcoming in their remarks. A third option substitutes another student known to everyone, rather than the principal or the teacher. The conversation undergoes significant revisions again!

Following these brief role plays, Mrs. Cvitek helps the class make observations about the influences setting and participants exert on a conversation, about how the age, gender, and social or professional standing will help to shape the language used. The students see the issues of "good English" and "bad English" in a different and more genuine perspective, one that differs from a traditional textbook definition.

Students studying language as a social activity can correspond through e-mail with students of the same age in a school in another state, noting the language similarities and differences they and their correspondents evince. This activity can also help to illustrate the "good English" versus "bad English" discussion and it can serve as an introduction to regional dialects or regional language variations. If you want to try this activity, go to your favorite search engine and enter "pen pals," "e-pals," or a related key word; you'll discover many opportunities for exchanges.

Students studying language as a social activity can also compare and contrast the language (i.e., uses of adjectives, pronouns, simple vs. complex sentences, active vs. passive sentences, etc.) used in the daily announcements at their school with the language used by the speakers on the school's public address system. For example, why do some accusatory sentences in the daily announcements lack an agent, as in "It has been reported that some students are parking their cars in the No Parking area in the parking lot."

Two or three English/language arts teachers could expand this list 10 fold with one pot of coffee and 50 uninterrupted minutes in the staff lounge. Their efforts will be received enthusiastically by their students. In time, the students will have gained numerous insights into the nature of *their* language, the languages used around them, and the rigorous demands imposed by multiple criteria of "correctness" or "good English."

THE INSEPARABILITY OF LANGUAGE AND SITUATION

LEA recognizes that the language people use varies from situation to situation throughout any given day. Language and situation, or context, are virtually inseparable. This is true whether we're talking about language used by children, by adolescents and young adults, or by adults.

Neil Postman expanded this idea several years with his description of **semantic environment**. A semantic environment has at least four components: (a) people, their formal and informal social and political relationships; (b) their purposes, to convince, describe, apologize, flatter, obscure, and so on; (c) the general discourse rules through which the conversation operates; and (d) the talk being used, whether it's formal, informal, intimate, hortatory, and so on.[11]

For example, the settings (or contexts) of a *witness box*, a *batter's box*, or a *confessional box* represent three distinctly different semantic environments, but each has definite purposes and rules that are implicitly understood by those stepping into one of the boxes.

---

[11]Neil Postman, *Crazy Talk, Stupid Talk* (New York: Delacorte Press, 1976), 9–11.

As you read in chapter 1, participants who disrupt a semantic environment by making inappropriate language choices will suffer serious consequences. For example, if a member of a baseball team steps into the batter's box, turns to the umpire behind home plate and says, "Father, forgive me for I have sinned . . . ," either he is making a really stupid joke, or is flirting with ejection from the game and a subsequent referral for professional care. Similarly, one who steps into a witness box is not likely to remain in the courtroom long if he or she swears to tell the truth, the whole truth, and nothing but the truth, at least *mostly,* if it's convenient.[12]

Postman calls these violations of semantic environments examples of either "crazy talk" or "stupid talk." If you abhor unnecessarily complicated technical vocabulary, you will find this description refreshing!

For another example, Postman asks us to imagine an attractive young thing who is beginning to have romantic feelings on a beach in Waikiki. Attractive young thing turns to his or her partner and sighs, with heavy breathing, "Isn't this a gorgeous sunset?" Similarly attractive partner, soon to be a former significant other, earnestly and seriously replies, "Well, strictly speaking, the sun is not setting. Nor does it ever do so. The sun, you see, is in a relatively fixed position in relation to the earth. So, to speak precisely, one ought to say that the earth is rising."[13]

As you can appreciate, the comments from the soon to be *former* significant other are accurate, from a scientific point of view, but in this context, in this semantic environment, they are unquestionably dumb and moronic, clearly violating the semantic environment. The significant other in this illustration has completely misunderstood the relationship between language and situation and has revealed him- or herself as either crazy or just plain stupid![14]

LEA emphasizes the relationships between language and situation (context), given the learners' present stage of development and their heightened awareness of and sensitivity to the processes of socialization. Quite unlike studying the traditional list(s) of isolated, decontextualized, and anonymous sentences just waiting to get parsed, this approach is built on the commonsense view that when language is used, it's used by real people who not only talk, but they talk to each other![15] The traditional

---

[12]Ibid.

[13]Ibid.

[14]Ibid.

[15]M. A. K. Halliday, "Linguistics in Teacher Education," in *Linguistics and the Teacher,* ed. Ronald Carter (London: Routledge & Kegan Paul, 1982), 11.

language program has seldom reflected this view of either language or people.

The traditional approach seems to operate from the fixed-code, cart-before-the-horse belief that language doesn't exist for people, but that people were made for language, and if people would only roll up their sleeves, pull up their socks, and try harder, then their language would be "good English." Language does, however, exist for people and their many uses of it. Regarding language as a real activity used in real society by real people for authentic and real purposes is a necessary foundation for LEA. Language study in the classroom should not, in my view, be reduced to rudimentary analyses of the structure of isolated, decontextualized, phony, and contrived sentences. Rather, language study should approach language as a multidimensional activity in all its human complexities.

REMEMBERING PAIN, BOREDOM, OR NOTHING

In some cases, though, language study has devolved to the study of "Do say" and "Don't say" directives. The results of this approach have not been satisfactory. In his cogent and witty text, *Who Cares About English Usage?*, David Crystal observes that "Something has gone seriously wrong when so many people find themselves looking back at the English grammar lessons at school remembering only the pain, the boredom—or nothing."[16] This is, indeed, a frustrating irony. The learners' developing stages of social, psychological, and linguistic sensitivities ought to make language study one of their favorite school activities. It is not.

According to the most recent nation wide study of schools, Goodlad and his associates found that English is the subject in school the *fewest* middle school and high school students in the United States rate as "Interesting."[17] Ouch!

To illustrate Crystal's observation and Goodlad's research, any teacher of English can recall numerous instances when a seatmate in an airplane or a new acquaintance at a social gatherings has asked, "And what do you do for a living?" When the reply to this question is, "I'm an English teacher," the next line in the conversation is fairly predictable: "An English teacher, huh? I'd better watch out how I talk around *you*!" Though math and

---

[16]David Crystal, *Who Cares About English Usage?* (London: Penguin Books, 1984), 10.

[17]John Goodlad, *A Place Called School* (New York: McGraw-Hill, 1984).

science teachers may suffer similar social and psychic indignities, I've never heard comments like, "Oh, you're a family sciences teacher? I guess I'd better be careful what I eat in front of you!" Nor have I heard, "So, you teach history? I'd best watch my dates, huh?"

Peter Elbow says that "For an explanation [of this public perception] we need only look at our tradition. English has tended to stand for two things: the teaching of grammar and the teaching of literature." Elbow continues by suggesting that grammar and literature lessons bore students with details they consider insignificant, models of civility they believe are unattainable, leaving them with feelings of incompetence, of being "unwashed" and "not right."[18]

The professional pride you and I share might tempt us to discredit and deny the negative (and we hope isolated) results reported by Goodlad and described by Elbow. Well, I'm sorry to say, you can dismiss that temptation. Elbow holds our feet to the fire when he also points out that that the public's pessimistic assessments do not come from an angry few. To the contrary, the public has taken more English language arts courses than *any other* subject![19] At almost any time during the regular school day, in most K–12 school buildings and on any college or university campus, more students are in English classes than in any other class.

Remember that the school subject we call "English" came into the curriculum using a model and a method of *correcting* the learners' native language. Unfortunately, despite some notable exceptions, over the years since many have continued to believe that the students' language is imperfect, often requiring austere remediation. Thus the public's perception of who English teachers are and what they do: They repair other people's language faults.

LANGUAGE LEARNING GOES ON, AND ON

It is important for us professional English language teachers to remember that one of the most important "givens" for the language arts curriculum is the fact that language learning and development *continue* well into adolescence and adulthood. Mike Stubbs, an eminent, world-class linguist with whom I have studied emphasized this point several years ago with a

---

[18]Peter Elbow, *What Is English?* (New York: The Modern Language Association, and Champaign-Urbana, IL: The National Council of Teachers of English, 1990), 111.

[19]Ibid., 112.

characteristically wise subtitle to one of his articles. It bears repeating here: "Why Children Aren't Adults."[20] Students in our classrooms aren't fully-matured adults, but some teachers and the curricula they follow tend to forget or ignore this fact.

Acquiring proficiency in language performance is not completed by some arbitrarily selected age, whether it's age 11, 14, or 17. Adolescent learners, therefore, still have much to learn about how to use the language with precision, for differing purposes, and in numerous and always changing contexts.

Indeed, even adults continue to learn about language. When an adult is in a new context—joins a new professional or civic organization, takes a new job, visits a new church, travels to another city, or watches the evening news on television and learns about events in another part of the world— new words, expressions, terms, and other ways of behaving linguistically are often needed. In these examples, as the adult's universe expands and grows, the adult's language will expand and grow, too, in order to accommodate or assimilate the new information. If this is true for adults, who have had more practice with language and who are more experienced language users, then it would seem obvious that it's true for the young people in school.

Nevertheless, there is a persistent tendency among some adults to expect young people to possess a completed language that reflects adult mastery. As an example, consider how adults respond in confounding ways to young people who are learning language. On the one hand, we hear a 2-year old exclaim, "Daddy goed to work," and we smile, nodding approval and encouragement to the speaker of this overgeneralized verb form. It's cute. On the other hand, the 13- or 16-year-old who injects "like", "I mean", or "ya know" into his or her statements is scolded for being either lazy, imprecise, slangy, or all three!

Actually, the 13-year-old who uses "I mean" is including it in sentences for a variety of reasons: The other speakers in his or her network probably use it, and one way to be identified with a group, a prepotent need for all school learners (any many adults), is to talk the way the members of the group talk.

"Ya know", "I mean", "like", and other verbal tics may also be serving either as linguistic fillers, used at one level to maintain social bridges between the speakers and listeners, or as conversational turn holders.

---

[20]Michael Stubbs, "The Sociolinguistics of Writing: Or, Why Children Aren't Adults," in *Readings on Language, Schools, and Classrooms*, eds. Michael Stubbs and Hillary Hiller (London and New York: Methuen & Company, 1983), 279.

Grammatically, "I mean" and "ya know" are used in fairly predictable positions in sentences in order to introduce a justification for a previous claim or to connect two propositions included in the sentence.[21] These can be illustrated by a couple of sentences I heard recently. "That's a neat song, ya know; don't you just love it?" And the other, "I'm not riding in his car; I mean, he's crazy."

We also hear young speakers consistently use *one* as a vague, generic adjective, as in, "Do you know that *one* guy?" Or, "Where is that *one* book?" Teachers frequently condemn usage like these examples, but they result from two interrelated causes: The young speaker hasn't yet learned more precise alternatives or options, and hasn't had sufficient practice talking in contexts where those options might be used.

These examples are used here to help demonstrate a few features of normal usage by adolescents whose language is still developing and growing. It is within the context of this development that language curricula become operational. The classroom is an ideal setting both for the *exploration* of those options, as well as for *practicing* their use.

By way of analogy, think of it this way: If you go to your favorite department store and select a pair of slacks you think you want to purchase, the department store will have a fitting room where you can put on the slacks to see if they fit. The classroom ought to be a language fitting room.

SOME ESSENTIAL LANGUAGE OBJECTIVES

Any curriculum follows some kind of design. Today, curricular designs and plans fit within a broad matrix of requirements established by the federal government, additional requirements established in state standards, requirements established by regional accrediting agencies, as well as requirements developed over the years by the local board of education in response to the views and needs expressed by the patrons, businesses, and other groups in the community. Curriculum development is a daunting responsibility.

At the risk of adding more building blocks to an already heavy load, I propose three long-term goals that have major applications in the realm of language proficiency. The three goals are: **spontaneity**, **precision**, and **elaboration**.

---

[21]Brit Erman, *Pragmatic Expressions in English: A Study of "You know," "You See," and "I Mean" in Face-to-Face Conversation* (Stockholm: University of Stockholm, Stockholm Studies in English, 1987), 206–07.

Spontaneity refers to one's ability to speak freely and with confidence, so that the speaker allocates her or his attention to *what* is being said, the message, or the communication to be shared. The spontaneous user of language engages comfortably in social conversations, classroom discussions, and classroom presentations, and can speak in front of an audience in a reasonably poised and confident manner. For the purposes of this book, the opposite of spontaneous might be *reluctant*. Reluctant language users do not use language freely, are often embarrassed and self-conscious, and demonstrate—both verbally and nonverbally—uncertainties about themselves and their abilities to express their ideas.

Precision describes the quality of exactness. The precise language user demonstrates the ability to utilize a more expanded repertoire of words in order to say more directly and more cogently what the speaker is trying to accomplish. The precise language user might be described as facile, or even loquacious. The opposite of precision in this particular discussion might be *vagueness*. The vague language user will overuse words devoid of real meaning, like *thing*, *that one*, *doohickey*, and the familiar *whatchamacallit*. The speaker who has not attained the goal of precision—the vague language user—will frequently stop in the middle of a deeply-felt utterance and say, as if in complete linguistic surrender, "Oh, you know what I mean." These are among the saddest words in the English language.

Elaboration refers to the ability to use more complex language structures, weaving phrases that provide support, subordination, clarification, and greater specificity into the natural fabric of a sentence or series of sentences. An elaborative language user demonstrates the ability to combine and coordinate several ideas and propositions in a coherent and cohesive manner, and will use, rather automatically, what the speaker has learned and already knows about story or expository structures, the larger frames of discourse.

As used in this book, the opposite of elaboration might be *fragmentation*. A speaker whose language is fragmented will utilize chains of simple subject–verb sentences that are presented in a dull, tedious, inarticulate, and very brief manner. Instead of presenting an elaborated idea, these simple sentences are characterized by "mentioning," where one idea is mentioned, then perhaps another, and perhaps one more, as if to say, "There's this, and there's this, and there's this . . . etc." The larger frames of language structure are missing.

These objectives are related to each other in a broader way, too. Before language users attend to the control over language that spontaneity, precision, and elaboration describe, they must first be *aware* of, be *reflective* about, and be *sensitive* to the roles language plays in their lives.

LANGUAGE LEARNING REQUIRES PRACTICE

Spontaneity, precision, and elaboration are, you'll recall, long-term objectives. Like most language objectives, they require time for their development and fulfillment. These three proficiencies will not become permanent abilities because one or two 45- or 50-minute class sessions have been devoted to one of them. Time alone, however, is not enough. The time involved in language learning needs to include numerous opportunities for language learners to experience and to practice using language, and to do so in ways they believe to be meaningful. One of the simplest ways to surround learners with meaningful language is to provide more opportunities for student talk in classrooms.

There is a fairly common assumption among some adults that if a speaker is articulate in one dimension of language use, the social, for example, then that ability automatically transfers to other language domains, a more formal context, perhaps. Classroom teachers know this assumption is false.

It is not at all unusual for students to carry on spirited, lively social conversations with their friends on the school bus, in the parking lot, or in the school corridor. When they come into the classroom, however, they can be reduced to discombobulated inarticulacy when they are expected to talk in front of the class, or when they are asked to explain or justify an answer. The cause of this linguistic imbalance is relatively simple: Students have had more practice with social talk than with school, or academic talk.

Sometimes students even have difficulty with oral expression when they are reading aloud from a text or a script. In a sophomore English class studying Shakespeare's *Julius Caesar*, I recently heard a 15-year-old "Brutus" anxiously and nervously read aloud, "A soothsayer bids you beware the *ideas* of March."

Recommending more student talk in any classroom may sound muddle-headed to teachers who believe they already spend more time than they'd like trying to redirect and refocus the attention of a "busy" group of chatty adolescents. "Surely," I can hear one of those teachers say, "if my students know anything, it's how to talk." Moreover, classroom talkers are frequently seen as troublemakers.

The classroom talk I'm recommending, let me hasten to clarify, is not a verbal free-for-all in which students are allowed or directed to talk or visit while the teacher attends to other business. Quite to the contrary, regularly scheduled group talking activities ought to have some important distinctions:

1. They have a definite purpose or direction.
2. The effectiveness of the discussion will be assessed.

First, the direction or purpose should be established through the selection of an issue *the students* see as meaningful, if not urgent, like the surprise cancellation of a school dance or party, new building regulations, or whatever a local "hot" topic might be at the moment. Lana and Dennie Smith suggest the following topics a possibilities:

- Censorship of movies or music.
- Gun control.
- School dress codes, grooming.
- Smoking in public areas.
- Individual rights of free speech in newspapers, radio, TV.
- Required schooling for parents.
- Sexism, lack of opportunities for women to advance in the corporate world.
- Equal health benefits or legal counsel for everyone.
- Current issues in the newspaper.[22]

Initially, the teacher can select the topic. The responsibility for topic selection can be shifted gradually to the class as soon as feasible in order to ensure its authenticity in their eyes.

Second, following the discussion the class should be helped to become amateur linguists, carefully observing such matters as:

1. What topic was discussed?
2. By whom?
3. To whom?
4. For what purposes?
5. With what effectiveness?

Interpreting their observations of their group discussions using these or similar criteria might cause the students, for example, to recommend to Maria that she should stick to the point; or Mark should contribute more, because he has good ideas; or Ashley should try to include more speakers

---

[22]Lana J. Smith and Dennie L. Smith, "The Discussion Process: A Simulation," *Journal of Reading*, April 1994, 583.

in the discussion; or Mohammed's positions would be stronger if he gave some examples. Smagorinsky describes another strategy, using dramatic scenes created by the students, and how to meet and deal with the unexpected! A group of boys in one of his classes prepared and delivered a parody of Andrew Dice Clay, a scene that included many of Clay's trademark targets, particularly women. The material was sufficiently abusive and offensive to make most of the girls in class uncomfortable, despite their giggling. "I did not cut it off," he writes, "but at the end I made it clear that we had seen the last of Clay in my classroom and that any future performances needed to be respectful toward the feelings of their classmates."[23] You might think ahead and determine what ground rules you'll want to establish for your classroom.

If the talk groups portrayed earlier seem too regimented for your tastes, you might consider an alternative Roller calls Group Talk. In Roller's classroom, each day class begins with 10 minutes of unstructured talking, which might include a conversation about a currently popular or controversial movie, a recently televised athletic event, a favorite hobby, or a report on a pet. Group Talk provides opportunities to build a sense of community in a classroom as students share more and learn more about each other. The students become more comfortable and more facile speakers. "Group talk is a time when [the students'] competence is spotlighted."[24]

Finally, Finders and Hynds have identified several types of oral language activities, and how the following might be adapted for use in your classroom will be limited only as far as your imagination extends: interviews, debates, memorized speeches, dramatic improvisations, recitations, extemporaneous speeches, panel discussions, dramatic monologues, choral reading, oral demonstrations, jokes, skits, storytelling, oral reports, scripted dialogues, and poster sessions.[25]

ENHANCING LINGUISTIC AWARENESS

Student talk is an important element in the student's growth toward greater language awareness and linguistic maturity, owing to the experience and

---

[23]Peter Smagorinsky, "'Growth Through English' Revisited," *English Journal*, July 2002, 27.

[24]Cathy M. Roller, *Variability, Not Disability* (Newark, DE: International Reading Association, 1996), 15–16.

[25]Margaret Finders and Susan Hynds, *Literacy Lessons* (Columbus, OH: Merrill Prentice-Hall, 2003), 240.

practice with language that talk provides. All too often the language arts curriculum is prepared with the implicit view that the students already know, somehow, the central role of language in their lives. The official curriculum then leads the students and their teachers through exercises and activities designed to shape the learners' language competence and control. I contend that unless and until the learners are more *linguistically aware*, even the best-written and well-intentioned language curricula are *premature*, literally and figuratively.

Be giving students opportunities to be active participants in language lessons as they explore the uses of language in real-life settings—how language varies from region to region; how the languages of the media are similar and dissimilar; the implicit languages of uniforms, hairstyles, and wardrobe, and so on—the teacher is helping the students to gain *awareness* of the complexity of language options, uses, and patterns, which is both a legitimate learning outcome in and of itself, as well as a prequisite to the students' continued language learning. Subsequently, instead of remembering school language learning with either pain or boredom or, worse yet, remembering nothing at all, school learners who engage in exploration and awareness activities will remember when they learned more about the power and joy of language.

REVIEWING THE CHAPTER

Based on what you've read in this chapter and what you've learned elsewhere, please answer the following:

1. Why can't language modification be imposed from above?
2. Why should there be more opportunities for student talk in classrooms?
3. What does "Death before uncool" have to do with language use?
4. How are social facts related to language?
5. How are *perception* and *reality* related? Different?
6. What is a "semantic environment"?
7. When might adults learn a new language?
8. Why might a student use vague language?
9. How are *becoming* and *arriving* different?
10. Name three objectives for language proficiency.

SECTION II

Language Exploration
and Awareness:
The Elements

Each chapter in Section II is divided into two parts. Part 1 is for you, the classroom teacher, and it describes a basic aspect of language study. Part 2, on the other hand, is for your students. Part 2 contains illustrative language explorations for your students' classroom inquiries.

CHAPTER **4**

Properties of Communication and Language

Language study is not a subject, but a process.
—Peter Trudgill, *Accent, Dialect, and the School*

Before you read this chapter, please answer these questions: Where do you think language came from? How is human language different from animal signaling systems? Why do we teach the English language in schools?

We don't think about essential activities all of the time. We think the most about breathing, for example, when we have a cold and our lungs or nasal passages are congested. We think about swallowing only when we have a sore throat. We don't think twice about walking across the room to turn off a lamp until we have a sprained ankle. So it is with language. We use it every day, but scarcely give it a moment's notice until something goes awry.

We might become more attentive to language when we hear someone violate one of our pet linguistic peeves, like pronouncing NUKE-lear as NUKE-YA-lure, or REAL-tor as REAL-A-tor. We might pay closer attention to language if we hear some someone offer as a truthful statement something we know to be false. If someone fails to return a greeting we offer to them, we wonder what's wrong with them. Pet peeves aside, I tend to agree with Geoffrey Nunberg when he says that the worst offense people can commit against language is to fail to listen to it closely.[1]

---

[1]Geoffrey Nunberg, *Going Nucular: Language, Politics, and Culture in Confrontational Times* (New York: Perseus Books Group, 2004), xv.

Whatever the characteristics are that separate us humans from all of the other creatures on earth, complex language is certainly one of the most obvious and most important. The advantages bestowed by the ability to string together meaningful words in an infinite number of combinations and permutations are obvious to anyone who has ever struggled to communicate across a language barrier. Words are bridges to other minds, allowing us to cooperate in complex ways and knitting our communities together.[2]

This chapter is about communication, about language, what it is, where it might have come from, and how it is uniquely human. This chapter, and those that follow, will also help you and your students to listen to language more closely.

Having read, either in part or in whole, *Beowulf, The Canterbury Tales*, some plays and poems by Shakespeare, and perhaps the King James translation of the Holy Bible, you know that the English we use today is far different from the English found in those older selections. You already have an intuitive sense of linguistic change from an historical perspective. But, before these older examples, what did English look like? Moreover, where did language come from?

Answers to these questions have been offered over the years by parents, archeologists, theologians, and linguists, and the answers have been a curious mixture of opinion, fact, theory, speculation, and ideology. Whenever our available information falters, speculation becomes a ready reference, as numerous conversations at a family reunion or in the teachers' lounge will attest.

With regard to the question about the origin of language, where it came from, the simplest answer is easy: We don't know. There are no audio- or videotapes in the archives at the Smithsonian Institute recording the first utterances. The *National Enquirer* has not yet published an article, "Here! For the First Time! Language Begins!" Not even the ever-resourceful Oprah Winfrey has managed to schedule an interview with "Urg and Yhlms," we can almost hear her say, "those wonderfully creative folks who created language."

The popular arts have made some speculative contributions to the question about the origin of language. In the Bantam novels of Jean Auel, for example, (see *Clan of the Cave Bear, The Valley of Horses, The Plains of Passage*), Ayla and the other characters speak—in remarkably Modern English—with what can only be described as truly prodigious linguistic

---

[2]Elizabeth Culotta and Brooks Hanson, "First Words," *Science*, February 2004, 1315.

repertoires, given the fact that the novels are set in the Pleistocene Epoch when humans first appeared.

In *The Valley of Horses* there is this exchange, initiated when Ayla asks, "What are counting words?" Jondalar replies, "They are . . . names for the marks on your sticks, for one thing, for other things, too. They are used to say the number of . . . anything." Seeing that Ayla is close to grasping the notion of numeracy, Jondalar elaborates, " 'Let me show you,' he said. He lined [some stones] up in a row, and, pointing to each in turn, began to count. 'One, two, three, four, five, six, seven.' "[3]

Please. Give us a break.

Some popular movies, on the other hand, have reflected quite an opposite view in terms of the linguistic development of its characters. Raquel Welch (*1,000,000 B.C.*), Shelly Long, Ringo Starr and John Matuszak (*Prehistoric Women*) stumble and bumble around bushes and piles of rocks, wearing scanty clothes fashioned from the hides of their most recent kills, muttering either gritty and guttural "Argghhs" or suggestive and sensuous "Ummms."

Granted, neither the novels nor the movies cited here intended to be serious attempts at linguistic scholarship, but they do help to illustrate some of the diverse myths and notions about the beginnings of language. With both the novels and the movies set in approximately the same time periods, we see on the one hand linguistic development generally equivalent to what you and I are accustomed to in the 21st century, whereas on the other hand we hear only animal-like grunts and groans.

One of my favorite films, *Quest for Fire*, stands out as a remarkable exception. This film is a celebration of human persistence, courage, inquisitiveness, creativity, and communication. Aired with some regularity on the cable channels, *Quest for Fire* depicts three men (led by Ron Perlman) who embark upon a dangerous journey, seeking fire for their tribe. While their dialogue is prelinguistic, they demonstrate language-in-the-making. Their prelinguistic behavior is highlighted when they are befriended by a female member (Rae Dawn Chong) of another tribe, whose language is much more fully developed. The attempts at communication among the characters are both instructive and poignant.

THE ORIGIN OF LANGUAGE: SOME SPECULATIONS

There have been other attempts to account for the beginning of language and we examine just a few of them here. I'm not offering these theories

---

[3]Jean Auel, *The Valley of Horses* (New York: Bantam Books, 1982), 466–467.

because they represent scientific thought; they're here because some of them are amusing.

The **divine origin theory** is one attempt to explain how language began. According to the Judeo-Christian view, God created Adam (in Hebrew, one translation of *Adam* is "man") and language at the same time. In Genesis 2:19 (RSV), we read:

> God formed every beast of the field and every bird of the air, and brought them to the man to see what he would call them, and whatever the man called every living creature, that was its name.

The actual language spoken by Adam and Eve has received its share of attention, too. Andreas Kemke, a Swedish philologist who can only be described as a staunchly loyal Swedish patriot, claimed that in the Garden of Eden God spoke Swedish (of course!), Adam and Eve spoke Danish, and the evil serpent spoke French.[4] Clearly, Kemke the Swede had much higher regard for his neighbors from Denmark than he had for those from France!

In the Hindu tradition, language comes from Sarasvasti, wife of Brahma, the creator of the universe.[5] The Holy Qur'an gives the Islamic account:

> And among His Signs is the creation of the heavens
> And the earth, and the variations in your languages.[6]

Similar accounts of the divine origin theory of language appear in American Indian beliefs. It is probably safe to say that every religious denomination in the world asserts that language came from a divine source, inasmuch as the Divine Creator created everything else.[7]

Another view of the origin of language is the **natural sounds theory**, sometimes called the **bow-wow theory** or the **echoic theory**. This belief holds that the first words were actually human imitations or pantomimes of the sounds cave dwellers heard in the natural world. For example, when Pleistocene Peter observed a creature flying overhead making a *caw-caw* sound, he would imitate that naturally occurring sound in naming the bird. Similarly, when Pleistocene Paula walked by a stream and heard what she

---

[4]Fred West, *The Way of Language* (New York: Harcourt Brace Javonovich, Inc., 1975), 4.

[5]George Yule, *The Study of Language* (Cambridge: Cambridge University Press, 1985), 1.

[6]The Holy Qur'an, S.xxx.22.

[7]West, *The Way of Language*, 5.

interpreted as a *ripple* or a *babble*, then she used those words to describe to Peter what she had seen. Little by little, as a *bow-wow*, a *hiss*, a *boom*, and other sounds were encountered, these natural sounds became words, and thus, the vocabulary list grew.[8]

Of course, every language has a fairly full range of onomatopoetic words like these. For example, the English *boom* is *bum* in Spanish, and is *krawomms* in German. Nevertheless, how **abstract words** like *peace, love, justice, loyalty,* and *fidelity* might have come into the language according to this theory isn't explained.

Similar to the natural sounds theory is the **yo-heave-ho theory** of language origin. This theory goes something like this: When Pleistocene Peter was attempting to move a large boulder or tree from the path, he strained hard, expelling a burst of air through his lips. Unable to budge the heavy object he went for help and tried to explain his request for assistance. The result was another expulsion of air through his lips, like before, thus creating the word *push*. As more boulders were moved away from more paths, as heavy trees were felled and moved, as boats were launched and beached, the sounds made by the workers became prototype expressions for words.[9]

FOR YOUR INQUIRY AND PRACTICE:

Try to express the following by using natural sounds and gestures:

1. Help me move this refrigerator.
2. I see a dog.
3. I think the hypotenuse is wrong.
4. Is it raining?
5. My cat thinks she's the Queen of England.

Why are some of these statements easier—or more difficult—to express through gestures and natural sounds? What do your answers tell you about these theories?

Despite the fact that each of us has grunted and groaned during periods of physical exertion, like mowing the lawn, playing tennis, or lifting a heavy

---

[8]Ibid., 9.

[9]Yule, *The Study of Language*, 3.

suitcase, this theory has more than just a few limitations. An obvious one is a limitation cited earlier for the natural sounds theory: Try to explain "Life, liberty, and the pursuit of happiness" using yo-heave-ho talk.

Believe it or not, although these theories may seem outlandish today, at one time they had any number of followers and believers. The origin of language has provoked discussions and "experiments" dating back 3,000 years or more. The attempts to learn about the origin have been largely fruitless and, consequently, disappointing. In fact, so dissatisfied was one group of scholars back in the 19th century that they took drastic action: In 1866 the Linguistic Society of Paris published a proclamation banning discussion of the topic at their meetings![10]

Most researchers today tend to believe that language gradually emerged over a couple of hundred thousand years. All we know for certain, according to Steven Pinker, is that fully developed language was in place 50,000 years ago, when humans in Europe were creating art and burying their dead, symbolic behaviors that point to fluent language.[11]

PROPERTIES OF COMMUNICATION

Much of the human talk represented in these theories exhibit the **interactional** function of language in which the primary purpose is to establish and maintain social relations. Interactional language is contrasted with **transactional** language, whose primary focus is on the exchange of information.[12]

Interactional language is the language we use when we interact with others socially, showing friendliness, hostility, cooperation, pain, or pleasure. Interactional language is frequently listener oriented and intends to maintain effective relationships and social bridges.

Transactional language, on the other hand, is used to transmit knowledge, skills, and information. Transactional language is message oriented and its intention is to bring about a change in the listener's state of knowledge.[13]

There is good reason to believe that our earliest ancestors, in whatever language they used, employed both of these functions. The survival of

---

[10]David Crystal, ed., *The Cambridge Encyclopedia of Language*, 2nd ed. (Cambridge: Cambridge University Press, 1997), 290.

[11]Cited in Constance Holden, "The Origin of Speech," *Science*, February 2004, 1316.

[12]Jack C. Richards, *The Language Teaching Matrix* (Cambridge: Cambridge University Press, 1997), 68.

[13]Ibid.

humanity from its Pleistocene beginnings to today is evidence that there was both transactional language (as in "Beware of hairy elephants with long tusks." or "Don't eat the purple berries from that bush.") as well as inter-actional language (as in "Say, Fleet Foot, want a drink of this cold water?" or "Here, Soft Shoulders, cuddle with me under this bearskin blanket."). (Obviously, the English language wasn't in use during the Pleistocene Era. I'm exercising my author's license for the sake of illustration and lame humor.)

Human communication can also be described as either direct, inten-tional communication or as indirect, inferential communication. **Direct communication** results when the meaning potential of an expression offers a smaller range of alternative messages or understandings.[14] Direct communication is illustrated with statements like such as: "I want the red sweater." "Don't run in the halls." "Tell me the answer the problem to #2." There aren't many alternative meanings in these messages; the meaning potential is narrow because the statements are so direct.

When the meaning potential offers more alternatives, on the other hand, the communication is more indirect; it's **inferential communica-tion**. For example, if you observe a friend in the aisle following worship services or a colleague in the parking lot after school, and you note that your friend or colleague's characteristic smile is missing and he or she is walking with a weary plod, you begin to make an inference. You don't need to ask "Is something wrong?" Instead, you skip that part of the con-versation, infer that something is the matter, and you ask, "Do we need to talk?" Your friend or colleague replies with "My boss has done it again." Done what, you wonder? The meaning potential is wide open.

We make inferences all the time but they remain, nevertheless, chal-lenges to accurate communication. A U.S. tourist (one I know *very* well!), for example, may drive a rental car along the M4, a major motor-way in Great Britain, and observe a road sign bearing the words "Lay By." Having observed other vehicles pull off the M4 at earlier Lay By exits, and further observing that this type of exit does not appear to lead to a village, city, or a petrol station, the tourist makes the inference that a Lay By must be like a rest area one finds at intervals beside a U.S. inter-state highway and infers, moreover, that the Lay By will provide toilets, picnic areas, a public telephone, and a pet exercise area. This inference worked.

---

[14]M. A. K. Halliday, *Learning How to Mean: Explorations in the Development of Language* (London: Edward Arnold, 1975), 37.

On the other hand, this same tourist from the United States can enter a pub in Wales and notice a door displaying the sign "Rest Room." With a sigh and an enormous measure of relief, the tourist, having enjoyed four cups of tea at breakfast, hurries to the door, opens it, and discovers a small room containing a sofa and two overstuffed chairs. The room is not what the tourist anticipated. This rest room is just that: a room where people sit and they rest, just like the sign on the door advertised. Darn! Wrong inference!

SOME PROPERTIES OF LANGUAGE

Human beings aren't the only creatures on the planet capable of communicating. Animals communicate with others of their species and there is extensive testimony regarding pets communicating with their owners. Animal communication is largely direct, offering fewer alternatives in the meaning potential of one of their signals. If a dog goes to the door leading to the patio and barks, signaling an urgent need to go to the backyard, there's absolutely no mistaking what the dog wants or needs. The meaning potential is narrow.

If you've had a pet, you know that a hungry animal will bark, whine, or meow in order to signal that it wants food. If you ask your pet "Do you want the same thing you ate last night?," you'll most likely get the same bark, whine, or meow you received in the first instance. (Well, maybe not the same meow; the second meow will, no doubt, be accompanied by either a disinterested or an arrogant, imperious yawn!)

The pet's response to your question will be identical to the first signal because animals communicate in the here and now. They do not understand "last Monday," "next Monday," and certainly not "when you were just a puppy." A dog's bark cannot communicate "I really enjoyed barking at the squirrels when we walked in the new park last Saturday."

Human language, on the hand, is capable of transcending time and space. Humans can refer to past or future time, or places other than where they are presently situated. This transcendent property of language is called **displacement**. It appears that only humans have the capacity to talk about things other than the present, thus transcending *this* place at *this* time.[15] Bees apparently have some ability to return to the hive and

---

[15]Charles F. Hockett, "Logical Considerations in the Study of Animal Communication," in *The View From Language*, ed. Charkles F. Hockett (Athens: University of Georgia Press, 1977), 147.

communicate—through a "dance"—the location of nectar, indicating some *degree* of displacement, but the modification of degree must be emphasized. Scientists believe bees refer only to the most recent source of nectar, not a source located 3 weeks ago at First Avenue and Maple Street.[16]

Displacement enables humans to talk about not only things, places, people, and events removed from the here and now, but also those things, places, people, and events we're not even sure of. Displacement enables humans to communicate about the past and the future, to articulate hopes and wishes and other ideas that may be contrary to present fact, to create fiction and science fiction, and to write interpretations of history or predictions about the future. Animal communication does not have this property.

One reason human language is characterized by displacement, transcending space and time, is that human language is more symbolic than animal signals. Given this symbolic quality, human language is, therefore, characterized by yet another property: It is **arbitrary**. The property of arbitrariness means that there is no direct relationship between a referent, an object (a tree, for example), and the word (*'tree'*) used to symbolize the object. The relationship between a thing and its name is arbitrary.[17] Both *tree* and either *arbol* or *arbre* can signify the same physical object.

Similarly, the word *dog* has no direct relationship to the particular dog I mentioned earlier, the one barking at the door to the patio. If there were a direct relationship, then all the languages in the world would use the same word to name four-legged canine animals, *dog*. They do not, though, as everyone knows. Because of the arbitrary property of language, either a *dog*, a *perro*, a *chien*, or a *hund* can be a family pet.

Because symbols and meanings (or, senses) are arbitrary in human language, we know that words do not "fit" the objects, ideas, or the referents they denote or suggest. Animals, on the other hand, have a set and fixed sound for signaling conditions, such as pain, pleasure, hunger, fright, and the like.

This arbitrary property is important inasmuch as it enables another property of language used by humans, the property of **productivity**. Humans can manipulate their linguistic resources in order to create *new* statements, *new* expressions, *new* words, and *new* figures of speech.[18] The

---

[16]Yule, *The Study of Language*, 18.

[17]Hockett, "Logical Considerations," 142–43.

[18]Yule, *The Study of Language*, 19–20.

degree to which the property of productivity is evident in human language is clear when you consider the numbers of new words included in newly published dictionaries or when you access wordspy.com and note the new words and new expressions listed at this Web site. We say much more about word creation in chapter 5.

Animal signals lack the property of productivity. A cicada, for example, has four fixed signals available to use, not three, not five. A vervet monkey has 36 vocal signals, not 33, not 37. Given the permanency of their fixed signaling sounds, animals cannot alter their communicative output.[19]

Neither the cicada, the vervet monkey, nor any other animal has the capacity to create either a new sound or new strings of new sound combinations. Humans, however, can and do. Human language is anything but permanent; it is astonishingly productive. To validate this generalization you can talk with a grandparent and inquire about two areas of activity. First, what computer terms you know and use that they don't; most of those terms or definitions are relatively recent from a grandparent's perspective. Second, and with the same grandparent, discuss the names of some newer over-the-counter (OTC) drugs. There are new OTC drugs coming on to the market regularly; many of them (and their *names*) didn't exist when the grandparent was your age.

There are those who decry the process of change in language. As Aitchison observes, significant numbers of intelligent people resent and condemn changes in the language, regarding the changes as examples of human sloppiness, laziness, or ignorance.[20] Attitudes toward language change are examined in more detail in chapter 8. For our purposes here, however, it needs to be stressed that human language is unique precisely because it is so productive. When humans have a need for a new word, phrase, or sentence, they will create one.

Not only are most animal signals permanently fixed, they are also universal within each species. This is not the case with human language because of another property, **cultural transmission**. To illustrate the property of cultural transmission, consider the biological fact that humans inherit the color of their hair, the color of their eyes, and their skin pigmentation from a gene pool created by their parents, grandparents, great-grandparents, and so on. Regardless of where you happen to spend

---

[19]Ibid., 20.

[20]Jean Aitchison, *Language Change: Progress or Decay?* (New York: Universe Books, 1985), 16.

your adult life, your *physical characteristics* will have been shaped by the genes you inherited from your immediate ancestors. This is a biological fact, but not a linguistic fact. Language is not inherited; it is transmitted and learned through one's culture.[21]

Animals of the same species, on the other hand, not only inherit their physical characteristics, but they all make the same sounds worldwide. A German Shepherd dog born in Bonn, Germany, will make the same sounds as a German Shepherd dog born in London, England. A Manx cat born in Moscow, Russia, will make the same sounds as a Manx cat born in Moscow, Idaho. On the other hand, a newborn Nigerian infant adopted immediately after its birth by a couple in New York will grow up speaking either Manhattan, Long Island, or Brooklyn English rather than Ibo. Language is transmitted and acquired through one's culture, not through one's genes.[22]

FOR YOUR INQUIRY AND PRACTICE:

Charles Berlitz has collected the representations different languages use to describe the sounds made by some animals. Among them are:[23]

ANIMAL	*ENGLISH*	*JAPANESE*	*RUSSIAN*
Dog	bow-wow	wau-wau	gaf-gaf
Cat	meow	n'yao	myaou-myaou
Pig	oink-oink	bu-bu	kroo-kroo
Bird	chirp-chirp	pi-pi	tyu-tyu

Do these examples support or refute the claim that animal sounds are species specific?

Some speakers of U.S. English *wash* the dishes whereas other *warsh* them. Similarly, some speakers will place pieces of chicken in a *fry pan*, others in a *frying pan*, and still others in a *skillet*. Furthermore, some speakers in the United States will ask, "We're going to the movies; would

---

[21]Hockett, "Logical Considerations," 155.

[22]Yule, *The Study of Language*, 21.

[23]Charles Berlitz, *Native Tongues* (New York: Grosset & Dunlap, 1982), 146.

you like to go with us?" Other speakers might say, "We're going to the movies; do you want to go with?"

In the preceding paragraph, you've seen different pronunciations for the same word, different words for the same object, and different syntactical arrangements for what is, essentially, the same sentence. One pronunciation, word, or syntactical arrangement isn't better than the other. People learn their pronunciations, words, and syntax from their culture. Remember, we talk *like* the people we talk *with*. That's cultural transmission in the nutshell.

It is possible to distinguish between the pronunciations of *wash* and *warsh* because the sounds in human language are distinct, exemplifying another property of language, **discreteness**. The sounds used in creating human language are distinct and they are separable.[24]

For example, the differences we hear between the spoken /p/ and the spoken /b/ are not great, but they are extremely meaningful differences when we hear them at the beginning of words like *pack* and *back* or *pit* and *bit*. The differences in these four words are due to the difference between /p/ and /b/. Animal sounds are not separable like this.

The property of discreteness is helpful in examining the final property of language we consider in this chapter, the property of **duality**. Human language not only is organized at the discrete sound level, but it is also simultaneously organized at the word level. By manipulating the discrete sounds symbolized by the letters /r/, /d/, /a/, and /e/, for example, a speaker of English can generate *read*, *dear*, and *dare*. Then sound–symbol duality is unique to human language.

When a dog hears a noise—the doorbell, the arrival of the mail, or the screech of automobile tires—the dog might instinctively let out a *yip* or a *bow-wow* (or whatever sound your dog makes when it's startled). On some other occasion, however, the same dog cannot rearrange those sounds to form "piy", "wow-bow", or any other construction. Similarly, contented cows always *mooo*. They never "omoo".

A TENTATIVE SUMMARY

Communication and language are patently important. Through language we are able to shape and express ideas, plans, dreams, and emotions for ourselves and for others. Through language we become who we are; one's

---

[24]Hockett, "Logical Considerations," 145.

FIG. 4.1.   Duality is not a characteristic of animal sounds.

language is an inseparable part—a very large part—of one's personal and social identity.

Some attempts at communication are relatively clear and easy to understand. Others may be more obscure, depending on the nature of the message to be imparted, the ability of the sender to present the idea clearly and effectively, and the ability of the receiver to understand the message within its range of potential meanings.

I hope this chapter partially demonstrates that language is a complex system. But at the same time, I believe that the study of language in a classroom that reduces the range of linguistic inquiry to a series of isolated and decontextualized choices between *who* or *whom* or *lie* or *lay* either is assuming that the learners already understand and appreciate the complexities, or the complexities are being ignored, if not denied.

LEA provides opportunities for both the teacher and his or her students to explore various aspects of language and communication. Language may be complex, but is is complex because it is a human activity and humans are complex.

In studying a wider range of aspects of language, the students will become more familiar with the intricacies of language. The remaining chapters discuss additional features of language and provide several learning Explorations that will help your students understand and use language with greater clarity and sensitivity.

REVIEWING THE CHAPTER

Part One: *Place a (✓) in the blank beside any statement that says what the author says. Be prepared to defend your responses.*

___ 1.   Speculation and knowledge are sometimes interchangeable.
___ 2.   The natural sounds theory of language origination suggests that human language evolved in accord with human nature.
___ 3.   Social conversations are transactional.
___ 4.   Animal sounds are species specific within a culture.
___ 5.   Human language employs detached sound units.

Part Two: *Place a (✓) beside those statements you believe the author* would *agree with. Be prepared to defend your responses.*

___ 6.   Some theories of language origination are sociolinguistic.
___ 7.   Concrete language is more useful than abstract language.
___ 8.   Making inferences is a behavior we should avoid.
___ 9.   Cultural transmission requires a community.
___ 10. Human language is organized at the phomeme, word, and sentence levels simultaneously.

Part Three: *Based on your understanding of this chapter, and based on what you have learned as a teacher, place a (✓) beside each statement you can support. Be prepared to defend your responses.*

___ 11. Practice helps build theory.
___ 12. Avoid the obvious solution whenever possible.
___ 13. Telling isn't teaching; assigning isn't showing.
___ 14. Communication is seldom complete.
___ 15. Necessity forces creation and invention to happen.

STUDENT EXPLORATIONS FOR PROPERTIES OF COMMUNICATION AND LANGUAGE

EXPLORATION: Suite and Sour
DIRECTIONS: The teacher needs to bring to class display advertisements employing homonyms, like "suite" for "sweet," or ironic language like "Cool beans" advertising hot soup. The class will study the advertisements, then respond to the questions that follow:

1. What makes these ads clever?
2. Why do you understand the use of homonyms, or ironic language? How did you learn thse uses of language?
3. Suppose you weren't a native English language speaker/reader. How would you learn these uses of English?
4. How does this activity help you appreciate the challenge of learning a new language?

***** ***** *****

EXPLORATION: Scrabble
DIRECTIONS: Play a game of Scrabble with altered rules: The horizontal words must be read from right to left, and the vertical words must be read from the bottom upward.

1. Were you able to create as many words as you do when you play Scrabble the normal way?
2. What made this game more difficult for you?
3. How does this activity help you appreciate the challenge of learning a new language?

***** ***** *****

EXPLORATION: Uniforms
DIRECTIONS: Prepare a collage of photographs taken from magazines, newspapers, or your own collection of photos that shows people dressed in a variety of formal and informal "uniforms."

Then, be prepared to discuss answers to the following questions when you bring your collage to class:

1. Why do people wear uniforms?
2. What happens when someone is "out of uniform" when they are expected to be wearing it?
3. How many uniforms do you wear, and for what purposes or activities?
4. Why are the uniforms designed as they are? What "statement" is the uniform attempting to make?
5. Based on your study of uniforms, how would you describe the language(s) of uniforms? How is this language similar to or different from the language we typically speak?

[To the teacher: Vary this activity by asking some groups to focus on hairstyles, shoes, others on hats, shirts, blouses, sweaters, etc.]

***** ***** *****

EXPLORATION: Signs
DIRECTIONS: Collect from newspapers, magazines, and other publications illustrations of at least 10 interstate, road, or street signs. Explain what each sign means.

1. How do you know what each sign means? How did you learn this?
2. Who decided what these signs would "mean"?, How were the signs' designs and meanings agreed upon?
3. Prepare an alternate sign for each one in your collection and explain why you think yours is better.
4. Why do you think different states in the United States use the same interstate and other road signs?

***** ***** *****

EXPLORATION: Keep Off the Grass
DIRECTIONS: Regulatory signs like "Keep off the grass," "Stop," or "No running" were created by *someone* who thought that the actions of other people needed to be changed or directed. Pick out one change you'd like to see in other people's behavior, then create a sign with a shape, color scheme, and language telling them what to do.

1. Hang all of the signs on the walls in the classroom. Which signs do you especially like, and why?
2. Which signs will attract attention? Which ones are more likely to be ignored? What's the difference?
3. How do signs fit into the discussion of "good" or "bad" English? Which signs are good or bad?
4. What are the chances of one of the better signs being adopted by your school?

***** ***** *****

EXPLORATION: __ - __ - | __ __ __| | __ - - | __ | __ __ __
DIRECTIONS: Using the Morse Code, found on the next page, encode these sentences:

Meet me after school.
Are you busy Friday night?

1. Perhaps you are familiar with semaphore code. The Braille system is a code, too. What are some of the differences between an alphabet and a code?
2. Why are code systems used?
3. Can you think of any special languages that resemble codes?

Morse Code

A . —	N — .
B — . . .	O — — —
C — . — .	P . — — .
D — . .	Q — — . —
E .	R . — .
F . . — .	S . . .
G — — .	T —
H	U . . —
I . .	V . . . —
J . — — —	W . — —
K — . —	X — . . —
L . — . .	Y — . — —
M — —	Z — — . .

***** ***** *****

EXPLORATION: Wordless "Talk"
DIRECTIONS: Prepare a short skit in which you and the members ot your group conduct a conversation *without words, using* gestures, body language, hand clapping, finger snapping and pointing, and so on. The topics of the conversations should be agreed upon by the entire class beforehand (titles of songs, famous people, a significant event in U.S. history, and the like). The success of your skit will be determined by asking those in the class whether they understood your skit.

1. How do these "wordless" statements communicate?
2. How do we *know* what the gestures mean?
3. Are some people better at "wordless" talk?
4. Based on the skits you've seen, do you think "wordless" communication is as effective as speaking or writing?

***** ***** *****

EXPLORATION: Faces

DIRECTIONS: From newspapers, magazines, or your own collection of photos, bring to class at least seven photographs of people's faces, each one demonstrating a different mood or emotion.

1. How do we know which mood or emotion is being communicated?
2. How might these faces be related to common phrases like "two-faced," "evil eye," and the like?
3. How is your face part of your general language system?

***** ***** *****

EXPLORATION: Einbahnstrasse

DIRECTIONS: An American traveler in Germany once commented that "Einbahnstrasse" must be a popular street name in Germany because *every* town had one, and sometimes *two*, streets with that name! Later he was embarrassed to learn that "Einbahnstrasse" means "one-way street."

How many regulatory signs do you see every day? You know, signs telling you things like: "No exit," "No running," "Keep off the grass," "Entrance," "Drive Thru." Pick out one regulatory sign, then translate it into another language. Your school or public library/media center, a teacher of a foreign language, or a speaker of another language who lives in your community can help you. Prepare a copy of the sign, with the conventional shape and color scheme, using the alternate language. Post the signs in your classroom, in the corridors, or any other place where they'll be seen. Then, observe how others respond to these "new" versions of "old" signs.

1. Why do some regulatory signs tell people, in very direct and clear language, what *not* to do, then add "please" as an add-on?
2. What do the translations mean in the other language? Do they mean *exactly* the same thing as the English words?
3. As you observe other people reading your signs, how do they respond to a familiar shape bearing *new* language?

***** ***** *****

EXPLORATION: Do Clothes Make the Person?

DIRECTIONS: At one time or another, we have all made snap decisions about other persons based on inferences we make regarding their clothing, shoes, hairstyle, and the like. Some people decide what they will wear with the deliberate intention of making a statement through their attire; using clothes to make an intentional statement can be called a *specifically communicative signal*. On the other hand, some people don't. We might still make inferences about them, however, by interpreting the *unintentionally informative signals* their clothing sends.

Using the People-Watching Log, record information you gain—whether you think it's specifically or unintentionally informative—as you observe people you encounter during 1 day. (A sample entry is included as an example.) After you've completed your people-watching log, answer the following questions:

1. Share your interpretations of signals with members in your small group. Remember, these are *interpretations* and do not represent necessarily absolute or accurate statements.
2. If someone were observing you today, what interpretations might they make about you based on your clothing?
3. Invite members of your group to help you arrive at alternate interpretations of the signals you've recorded in your log.
4. What can you conclude about the distinctions between intentional and unintentional signals? How accurate are they? How permanent are they? How much of the observer is included in the interpretations?

PEOPLE-WATCHING LOG

Person Observed	Social Role	Signal	Interpretation
1. Mr. Sims	teacher	tie askew	preoccupied
2. Etc.			
3. Etc.			

*Specify whether a signal is *specifically communicative* or *unintentionally informative*, in your judgment.

***** ***** *****

EXPLORATION: Creating Dialogue
DIRECTIONS: The teacher will have a supply of wordless picture books available for you to use. Select one of the books, then read the wordless story. After you have decided on a narrative to fit the pictures, write appropriate dialogue for each page.

1. Reread your completed story, satisfying yourself that your dialogue is faithful to what you believe the author/illustrator is trying to convey.

2. Find another person in the class who has used the same wordless picture book and trade your dialogues. Discuss how your versions are similar. In what respects are they different?

3. Based on your conclusions in Item 2, what generalizations can you make about the information the illustrations convey in children's books? What is the purpose of dialogue in children's books?

[Some examples of wordless picture books appropriate for this activity are given in the following section.]

A SAMPLING OF WORDLESS PICTURE BOOKS

Martha Alexander (1970). *Bobo's Dream*. Dial.
Mitsumasa Anno (1982). *Anno's Britain*. Philomel.
_____ (1984). *Anno's Flea Market*. The Bodley Head.
_____ (1980). *Anno's Italy*. Collins.
Edward Ardizzone (1970). *The Wrong Side of the Bed*. Doubleday.
Raymond Briggs (1978). *The Snowman*. Random House.
Eric Carle (1971). *Do You Want to Be My Friend?* T. Crowell.
Tomie de Paola (1981). *The Hunter and the Animals*. Holiday House.
_____ (1978). *Pancakes for Breakfast*. Harcourt.
John Goodall (1977). *The Surprise Picnic*. Atheneum.
John Hamburger (1971). *The Lazy Dog*. Four Winds.
Iela Mari (1969). *The Magic Balloon*. Phillips.
Mercer and Marianna Meyer (1971). *A Boy, a Dog, a Frog, and a Friend*. Dial.
Mercer Meyer (1976). *Ah-choo*. Dial.
_____ (1974). *The Great Cat Chase*. Four Winds.
_____ (1976). *Hiccup*. Dial.
Ellie Simmons (1970). *Family*. McKay.
Chris Van Allsburg (1984). *The Mysteries of Harris Burdick*. Houghton Mifflin.
Lynd Ward (1973). *The Silver Pony*. Houghton Mifflin.
David Wiesner (1988). *Free Fall*. Lothrop, Lee & Shepard.

***** ***** *****

EXPLORATION: These Boots Were Made for . . .

DIRECTIONS: It is not unusual for people to be evaluated on first sight, typically as the result of how others assess their looks, clothes, hairstyle, and the like. A single feature, like shoes, can say something about the wearer to others. These images are often stereotypical and can be either fair or unfair.

1. What type of person do you think is most likely to wear the following?

Hushpuppies	Spiked high heels
Converse (canvas) sneakers	Saddle shoes
Air Jordans	Birkenstock sandals
Asics	Platform shoes
Western boots	Biker boots
Work boots	Oxfords
Wingtips	Penny loafers

Can you think of additions to this list?

2. What kind of shoes do you wear? Do your shoes "say" anything about you?

3. Can we always depend on judgments we make about others based on their shoes, their clothes? When is it helpful to use nonverbal clues? When might it be harmful?

***** ***** *****

EXPLORATION: Give Me a Sign

DIRECTIONS: At every sporting event, the officials—umpires, referees—use hand signals so that they can communicate to the timer, starter, score keeper, and the viewers. The baseball umpire jerks a thumb over his shoulder to communicate "You're out!" Or, the umpire will cross his hands horizontally to communicate "Safe!" Not only are signals like these used at sports events, they're also used by members of the ground crew at airports, and by drivers of large, tractor-trailer rigs as they pass each other on the interstate highway.

1. Consider the various signals mentioned in the directions. Where did these signals come from, do you think?

2. Interview a number of people who are employed and ask them about signals they use on the job. You can record the results of your interviews on the form found in the next section. Discuss your findings with others in your class.

3. How universal are the signals you learned about in your interviews? Would people from other jobs and in other parts of the country understand these signals? Why or why not?

4. Are these signals *language*?

SIGNALS: INTERVIEW LOG

1.0 Description of signal: _____

1.1 Signal given by: _____

1.2 Signal given to: _____

1.3 Intended meaning of signal: _____

2.0 Description of signal: _____

2.1 Signal given by: _____

2.2 Signal given to: _____

2.3 Intended meaning of signal: _____

3.0 Description of signal: _____

3.1 Signal given by: _____

3.2 Signal given to: _____

3.3 Intended meaning of signal: _____

4.0 Description of signal: _____

4.1 Signal given by: _____

4.2 Signal given to: _____

4.3 Intended meaning of signal: _____

***** ***** *****

EXPLORATION: Here's Looking at You, Kid

DIRECTIONS: We frequently communicate through body language, smiling when we're happy and frowning when we're not. Think about your body language and what your gestures or expressions "say" about you. Also, let's experiment: Pick a day when you'll adopt some unusual body language. Make an effort *not* to smile; use your hands in different ways—like holding them out at your side; look up in the air when you talk instead of looking at people, and so on.

1. What do you know about a smiling person? What about people who are frowning, yelling?

2. Is it possible to know how a friend is feeling if you can't see his or her body language?

3. Does body language change, depending on who you're with and where you are? To what extent is body language a form of communication?

***** ***** *****

EXPLORATION: Do You See What I See?
DIRECTIONS: Do this with a partner. First, select a picture of an ordinary object found in a house, apartment, or school. Describe the object to your partner without naming any of the object's parts or pieces; have your partner draw a picture, based on your description. Compare your partner's drawing with the original.

1. Did your partner get it right? Does the drawing look like the original?
2. How difficult was it to describe the object without naming the object or any of its parts?
3. After completing this activity, do you think effective communication is difficult or easy? Why?

***** ***** *****

EXPLORATION: Talking Between the Lines
DIRECTIONS: A teacher walks into a noisy classroom and asks, "Do I hear noise in here?" Examining a child's dirty hands, a parent asks, "You call this clean?" The answers to these "questions" are obvious; in fact, the questions really aren't *questions*, are they? The teacher and the parent are saying things *indirectly*.

1. Write some examples of indirect speech you've heard. What were the "real" messages?
2. Would someone from another country or from another social group or age group have difficulty interpreting the examples you've recorded?
3. Why do we talk "between the lines"? What do you need to know in order to interpret this type of communication?

***** ***** *****

EXPLORATION: Gestures on the Job
DIRECTIONS: Thinking about your activities throughout a week, consider the gestures you see people using: your pastor, school administrators, teachers, coaches, peers, family members, people driving cars, and so on.

1. How do you know how to interpret gestures?

2. Are some gestures "direct," having a small range of interpretation, whereas others are more "indirect," having more alternative interpretations?

3. How are gestures like/unlike spoken language? How might gestures vary from culture to culture? Are any gestures universal to all people around the world?

***** ***** *****

[Note to teacher: you'll need the game "Anagrams" for this Exploration.]
EXPLORATION: Let's Play Anagrams
DIRECTIONS: Play "Anagrams" until everyone in your group has five words. Remember, you may take a word from any player as long as you change the word by adding one or more letters.

1. How does the addition of *one* letter change either the pronunciation or meaning (or both) of a word?

2. How important are single letters in the ways we spell words?

***** ***** *****

EXPLORATION: Is This Intelligence Real, or What?
DIRECTIONS: The meanings of words are derived from both how they are spelled and how they are used in context; we can often understand a word even when it is misspelled. Computers with spell checkers can't do this; they rely on *form* alone. Humans and computers read language differently!

Using your computer or word processor, write a paragraph with at least four sentences in it on any topic of your choice. Misspell several words, being careful that the misspelling "sounds like" the true spelling. For example, don't misspell "dog" as "log." An example of a misspelled sentence might be: *The women wred the buk undre a trea.*

1. Spell-check the paragraph. When the spell checker suggests an alternative, accept the first one. Print the document, using the spell checker's first suggestions.

2. Read the document. Given your original intent in your paragraph, how close did the spell checker come in getting it right?

3. How do we obtain meaning from words—from form or from both form and context? What's more important, the form or the context?

***** ***** *****

EXPLORATION: Your Junk May Be My Treasure
DIRECTIONS: Bring to class several pieces of junk mail delivered to your home. Share the letters in a small group and examine them.

1. Who is the intended audience for this mail, and how do you know?
2. Does the junk mail appeal to emotions or to logic? Be specific, please.
3. Is some of the language more appealing or less appealing to some members of your group?
4. Why do words mean one thing to one person, and something else to another?

***** ***** *****

EXPLORATION: What's for Sale?
DIRECTIONS: Read the classified ad section of your local newspaper, using the following questions as your guide:

1. What kinds of things do people want to sell or buy?
2. What kinds of jobs are wanted or available?
3. What types of housing are available for rent or purchase?
4. What are people looking for in the "Personals"? Who reads this section, do you think?
5. Do these several ads create, in your judgment, a positive or negative picture of your community? What would they communicate to a visitor from another culture?
6. How is the language used in classified ads different from the language you use in conversations? In written assignments at school?

***** ***** *****

EXPLORATION: Picture This
DIRECTIONS: One of our earliest forms of communication was through the writing or drawing of pictures; these are called pictograms. A modern example is the sign seen on interstate highways featuring a knife and a fork, signifying that food is available at the next exit. As you go through your normal activities for the next day or two, make a list of pictograms you see.

1. Where do you see the pictograms and what were they trying to convey?
2. Why pictograms used instead of words?

3. Do you think pictograms are becoming more or less common? Why do you think this?

***** ***** *****

EXPLORATION: Quick on the Draw

DIRECTIONS: For the next day or two, look for examples of graffiti, writing and drawing on fences, buildings, walls, trains, and so on. Record what you've found and bring your list to class.

1. Do your graffiti contain few or many words?
2. Did you encounter graffiti using drawings instead of words?
3. Why do people draw graffiti?
4. What are graffiti: underground expression, secret code, pranks, vandalism?
5. How are graffiti similar to pictograms? What does this tell you about language and expression of ideas?

CHAPTER **5**

Words and Lexicography

> *Dictionopolis is the place where all*
> *the words in the world come from. They're*
> *grown right here in our orchards.*
> —Norton Juster, *The Phantom Tollbooth*

Before you read this chapter, think about all the words you've used today. Where did they come from? Who created them? Consider a related topic: dictionaries. People consult dictionaries every day. Why? What do they think they'll find in them?

We've already suggested that people use language every day, often with little thought or planning about which phonemes will be used in the formation of words or how the words might be connected to constitute longer utterances. We often take our abilities with language for granted. "The occasional frustration of having a word stuck on the tip of the tongue, the slow ordeal of composing a passage in a foreign language, and the agony of stroke victim struggling to answer a question remind us that our ordinary fluency is a precious gift."[1]

There have been, however, as you read in chapter 4, speculations about where language came from. You know that theories attempting to explain language origination have been around for hundreds of years. If you think that this kind of theorizing has come to a full stop, let me disabuse you of that notion. Stanley I. Greenspan and Stuart G. Shanker have recently published a book in which they claim that the previous theories about

---

[1]Steven Pinker, *Words and Rules: The Ingredients of Language* (New York: HarperCollins Publishers, 2000), 121.

language origination have been in error because theorists have assumed at the outset that a group of cave dwellers were sitting in a circle with a problem to solve—like killing a bison for food—and the cave dwellers' attempts to communicate with each other led to language. Not so, say Greenspan and Shanker. We need to approach this issue in a completely different manner, they say. Instead of thinking about cave-dwelling adults' attempts to communicate with each other, attention should focus instead on caregiver–infant interactions if we want to know how language began.[2] How this issue might be resolved, given the lack of prelinguistic or early linguistic evidence described in chapter 4, is anybody's guess.

The question of where words came from can be answered unequivocally and with a generally uncomplicated answer: The words used in a particular language came from the people who use that language. This is the best answer I can provide.

Word creation is relatively simple; when people need a new term or word, they'll either create one or borrow one from another language group. Sometimes an existing word will be used in a new context with a newer meaning. In an earlier day, for example, *crash* was something cars and stock markets did; today, computers *crash*, too. A car *crash* and a stock market *crash* aren't exactly the same kind of *crash*, you understand, but the words have been available to English language users for some time. The computer-age use of *crash* is more recent.

More recently, when the Twin Towers of the World Trade Center in New York were attacked by terrorists in hijacked airplanes, everyone had to dig deeply into their existing linguistic repertoires to describe new facts and new feelings. The event itself was initially described as "the World Trade Center disaster," or the "terrorist attacks on America," or "the hijacked planes in New York, Washington, and Pennsylvania." Eventually, these longer expressions were shortened and made less cumbersome by using *9/11* (pronounced either "nine-eleven" or "nine-one-one"). Early attempts using either "the missing" or "the dead" finally settled on *the lost*. The rather bland term "first responders" turned rather quickly to *heroes*. Finally, "ground zero," an established term signifying the exact location of a nuclear blast, or a slang term referring to Square One, became *the pit*, then *the site*.[3]

---

[2]Stanley I. Greenspan and Stuart G. Shanker, *The First Idea: How Symbols, Language, and Intelligence Evolved From Our Primate Ancestors to Modern Humans* (New York: De Capo Press, 2004).

[3]Jack Rosenthal, "9/11," *New York Times,* September 1, 2002, http://www.nytimes.com/2002/01/magazine/01ONLANGUAGE.html.

Sometimes a prefix (like *un-*) or a suffix (like *–ness*) will be added to an existing word, thereby altering the first and older meaning. This is how the words *unhappy* and *happiness* came into the language. Sometimes English-speaking people will borrow terms from other languages. For example, there are no English equivalent words for either *taco* or *pizza*, so English speakers borrowed these words from Spanish and Italian and converted them into English words.

Not only do we borrow names of foods from other languages, we can reach into other available languages in order to name other important elements in our lives. For example, have you considered where the names of the days of the week originated? Almost any collegiate dictionary will show that Sunday, the first day of the week, derives its name from the Anglo-Saxon *sunnan daeg*, "sun day," or "the sun's day." Monday is Sunday's Anglo-Saxon opposite, *monan daeg*, "moon day," or "the moon's day." An easy trip to your desk dictionary will reveal the sources for the names of the remaining days of the week. It would be relatively easy for you to create an Exploration activity for the names of the days of the week.

The names of the months show similar influences. The name *January* comes from the fact that the Romans dedicated the fist month of the year to Janus (the two-faced god, looking back on the previous year and looking ahead to the new year). March is the month named for the god of war, Mars. The month of May commemorates Maia, the mother of the god Mercury. Again, I invite you to use a quality collegiate dictionary, a dictionary containing word histories, to discover the sources for the remaining names of the months. As an alternative, you might create an Exploration activity for your students to accomplish the same thing.

Naming months after gods is one way the language of myth is used in language. There are other ways, too, and not all of them are constructive. For example, among the myths surrounding language in general and **lexicography** (the creation of dictionaries) in particular is the mistaken notion that words, their definitions, and their pronunciations come from *The Dictionary* in immutable, almost sacred form. Indeed, to hear some people talk, you'd think that when Moses descended Mt. Sinai, it wasn't The Law (Torah) he was bringing to the people, but it was *The Dictionary*!

You hear this attitude voiced when some speakers enter into a conversation a comment like, "Well, *the Dictionary* says . . . . " Similarly, some writers of letters to the editor of newspapers and magazines believe that they have decided a debate when they write, "According to *the Dictionary* . . . ." In either case, the speakers and writers seem to be suggesting that there

FIG. 5.1. Moses and *the Dictionary.*

is only *one* dictionary of the English language and it is the final arbiter regarding all questions about the proper meaning(s) of a word. This is not the case.

Another book is referred to in a similar manner: "Well, *the Bible* says . . . " or "According to *the Bible*. . . . " Many people refer to *the Bible* as if there were just *one* text with that title. Actually, there are dozens of Bible translations available. Whether one reads the *New International Bible, Today's New International Bible*, the *Revised Standard Version*, the *New American Standard* translation, the *King James Bible*, the *Oxford Annotated Bible*, or *The Message*, what is found in the different versions will vary.

In the best interests of fairness and intellectual honesty, people should give accurate citations for their quotes, whether their quotes come from a journal article, a textbook, a dictionary, or a Bible. You already know that textbooks and journal articles are not monoliths publishing just one view that is totally accepted by everyone. You can expect similar variation among Bibles, and dictionaries.

THE MULTIPLICITY OF DICTIONARIES

Those who refer to *The Dictionary* either ignore or are ignorant of the fact that there are numerous dictionaries and numerous *kinds* of dictionaries in print. There are law dictionaries, explaining the nuances of legal terminology; there are medical dictionaries, providing those who want or need to know the intricacies of the terms used by doctors and nurses. There are dictionaries of slang and there are translation dictionaries, providing Spanish-to-English, French-to-English, German-to-English, and almost any other language-to-English translation useful to the immigrant, the tourist, or the language student.

For example, Edward S. LeComte's *Dictionary of Last Words* lists the final words uttered by famous people on their death beds:

- "I do not understand what I have to do."—Leo Tolstoy
- "God bless you all. I feel myself again."—Sir Walter Scott
- "I believe we must adjourn this meeting to another place."—Adam Smith[4]

Josefa Heifitz Byrne, daughter of the famous violinist Jascha Heifitz, read hundreds of books, selected the more obscure words she encountered, and created *Mrs. Byrne's Dictionary of Unusual, Obscure, and Preposterous Words*. In this dictionary, you'll find definitions for words like *lalochezia* ("talking dirty to relieve tension"), *eroteme* ("a question mark"), *mytacism* ("excessive or incorrect use of the letter *m*"), and *adoxography* ("good writing on a trivial subject").[5]

Have you ever wondered about the distinctions between *dents* and *dense*? What about the differences among *air, heir, ere, err*, and *eyre*? If these terms are a challenge for you, see James B. Hobbs' *Homophones and Homographs: An American Dictionary*.

Did you know that the teeth on a comb are technically called *orlings*? Or, that paper clips have seven (7!) identifiable parts, each part having its

---

[4]Frances Flaherty, "Lexicography Odds and Ends," *The Atlantic Monthly,* 271, no. 1 (1993): 40.

[5]Ibid.

own name? Finally, what do you call a rainbow formed in the fog? *Ulloa's Ring*, of course. These and many others like them can be found in Dorothy Rose Blumberg's *Whose What? Aaron's Beard to Zorn's Dilemma*, yet another dictionary.[6]

There are scores of novelty dictionaries, dictionaries for almost every profession, and dictionaries for many special-interest and hobby groups. By now, I'm sure you get the idea—*the dictionary* is, at best, a vague term.

I understand and appreciate the fact, however, that when most people refer to *the dictionary*, they're referring to a dictionary of the English language. And there are scores of them available, too.

You'll remember our earlier use of the terms **prescriptive** and **descriptive** as they are used to describe approaches to the study of language. . . . These same terms can be applied to dictionaries as well. "Descriptivists believe that dictionaries should include all words that people use, even those most high school English teachers would deem 'ungrammatical.' Prescriptivists, on the other hand, want dictionaries to contain only words and definitions that they believe are 'proper English.'"[7]

The prescriptivist/descriptivist dictionary debate began in 1961 with the publication of Merriam Webster's *Third Unabridged International Dictionary*, known as the *W3*. Instead of consulting with a number of academics, asking them about words they use, the editors of *W3* turned instead to popular and academic publications in order to determine what words people were actually using in writing and speech.[8] The result of this historic methodilogical change was twofold. First, the first truly descriptive dictionary of current usage was published and, second, revolt. Because *W3* included all those words not only English teachers but Sunday school teachers as well couldn't endorse, magazines and newspapers called the *W3* "monstrous," "deplorable," and "a scandal and a disaster."[9]

Not only were four-letter taboo words, most notably *fuck*, included, but the inclusion of these words in a dictionary published by a respected lexicography house made a statement, according to the critics, of implicit approval of these words. Not since the days of Samuel Johnson's first dictionary of the English language has the publication of a dictionary created such a public fulminations.

---

[6]Ibid.

[7]Emily Shetier, "Dictionary Man," *VIP* (2004), http://www.jourmalism.nyu/pubzone/vip, 1.

[8]Ibid., 1.

[9]Ibid.

Should a dictionary attempt to describe all of the words in current use, or should a dictionary include those words authorities deem "proper English"? That's the basic issue.

Similar issues have led to the multiplicity of Bibles available in today's bookstores. Should Bibles maintain their traditional language, some of which is nearly undecipherable to today's reader? Should Bibles maintain language with an emphasis on masculine pronouns; should the Omnipotent always be referred to as "Father," never as "Mother"? You can find a heated argument on either side.

The American Heritage Dictionary, created as a response to the descriptive *W3*, is the most prescriptive U.S. English dictionary published today. The majority of the dictionaries published in the United States are largely descriptive. Which dictionary is better or superior depends on who's asking, as far as I'm concerned. I own a dozen dictionaries and consult several when I'm curious about any facet of knowledge about a word; as a student of language, you shouldn't limit your resources to just one reference, either, I should think.

WORD FORMATION PROCESSES

Whether the entries in a dictionary are selected from a descriptive or a prescriptive vantage point, the words have come from the people who use the language. As you'll read later in this chapter, the sources of new words vary, and we can identify several processes by which words have become a part of our **lexicon**, the pool of words available to us to use.

Coinage. Coinages are among the least common words, but they are the only ones representing entirely new, previously nonexistent words.[10] *Aspirin* is an example of a coinage. *Aspirin* was initially the brand name, or trade name, of a single pain-reducing product. Over the years the word *aspirin* has become more general.[11] Anytime a person undergoes a physical or emotional shock or trauma and develops a headache ("What? Grades are due tomorrow? Gimme an aspirin."), any brand of aspirin will do, whether its Anacin, Bayer, or St. Joseph's. You can even hear people call a *nonaspirin* like Tylenol an aspirin.

---

[10]Jeffrey Kaplan, *English Grammar: Principles and Facts* (Englewood Cliffs, NJ: Prentice-Hall, 1989), 21.

[11]George Yule, *The Study of Language* (Cambridge: Cambridge University Press, 1985), 51–52.

Another example of a coinage is the word *Kleenex*, created by a specific company for a specific product, a tissue. Like *aspirin, kleenex* has become generalized, too. You can see people who want a kleenex reach for a box of Puff's. Other examples of coinages are *Victrola, Frigidaire, Xerox, Zantac,* and *Pepscid.*

Derivation. The process of derivation may be the most common method for forming new words inasmuch as it builds on and expands existing words. The derivation process uses a large number of smaller bits and pieces of the language that carry lexical rather than inflectional meanings.[12] Derivational word parts include **affixes**, the prefixes and suffixes we add to words, like *un-, mis-, pre-, -ful, -less, -ish,* and *-ism.* Some examples of words created in this manner are *unhook, misapply, pretest, joyful, careless, boyish,* and *sadness.*

One of the more ubiquitous and older affixes is found in words like *attendee, examinee, employee,* and *refugee.* The **sense**, the general meaning or definition, of the *-ee* suffix is mainly passive, indicating a receiver or a sufferer of an action. Although the use of *-ee* can be traced back to 15th-century legal language (*assignee* is recorded in 1467, *grantee* in 1491, and *lessee* in 1495), *-ee* is an affix that is sometimes scorned by language cops.[13]

Language prescriptivists often flinch when some derivations enter the language. It is not unusual to hear complaints not only about the use of *-ee*, but also about the *-ize* suffix as used in *prioritize* or *hospitalize.* Why some language mavens complain about the *-ize* form, which creates a verb from an existing noun, is difficult to figure out. Here's an example of how *-ize* is used, albeit in the past tense, by Pat Truly, an established writer, a columnist and editorial writer for the Fort Worth (TX) *Star-Telegram*: "Very early in the debate about Haiti, one of my colleagues columnized on the subject."[14] If newspaper writers and editors are among those who help to standardize (See?) the language, how can Pat Truly be untrue?

Another relatively common derivation that has received complaining comments is the *-ish* suffix, as in "Let's do lunch, say, around noon-ish."

Comments about the other derivational parts of words (*-less* and *-ful*, for example) seldom receive as much negative attention. Regardless of our personal feelings about any of these affixes, derivation remains a common

---

[12]Kaplan, *English Grammar*, 87.

[13]Raymond Chapman, "A Versatile Suffix," *English Today* 7, no. 4 (1991): 39.

[14]Pat Truly, "Self-Censorship Growing Tedious," *Lincoln (NE) Star*, October 27, 1994.

route for new words to enter the language. To paraphrase Raymond Chapman, purism usually gives way to utility in language matters.[15]

Borrowing. Another common word-forming activity is the borrowing of a complete word from another language.[16] Sometimes borrowings are called "loan words," but I think "adopt" might be more accurate. It is doubtful, surely, that anyone in the United States asked the Italian government if English speakers could "borrow" the words *piano* or *pizza*. Similarly, no one asked the Japanese if we could borrow the word *karaoke*. We simply appropriated these (and many other) words, the same way rustlers in the Old West "acquired" new cattle, and the borrowed words are as much a part of our English vocabulary as are those words from our Anglo-Saxon stock.

Borrowings are common in English, as a glance at almost any page in a dictionary containing **etymologies** (word histories) will demonstrate. American English has borrowed thousands of words from other language families. A few additional examples of borrowings are *alcohol* (Arabic), *boss* (Dutch), *croissant* (French), *numero uno* (Spanish), *pretzel* (German), *yogurt* (Turkish), *kwanzaa* (Swahili), and *zebra* (Bantu). No one, I suggest, would call these words "foreign."

An extensive list of borrowings, for your information and reading pleasure, is available in Robert Hendrickson's delightfully readable *American Talk*.[17] When it comes to borrowing, as Hendrickson shows, English speakers are proven experts.

Compounding. English is not the only language that can create new words by joining together already existing words, but English users create new words this way with considerable skill. The new word, the compound, will be used as the same part of speech as the rightmost member of the newly compounded word. Consequently, the word *highchair* becomes a new noun (*high*, an adjective, is joined with *chair*, a noun).[18] Some common examples of compounds are *stir-fry, high school, teapot, globetrot, swearword, outhouse, sunburn, baseball, textbook, classroom,* and *waterbed*.

---

[15]Chapman, "A Versatile Suffix," 41.

[16]Yule, *The Study of Language,* 52.

[17]Robert Hendrickson, *American Talk: The Words and Ways of American Dialects* (New York: Penguin Books, 1986), 25–23.

[18]Adrian Akmajian, et al., *Linguistics: An Introduction to Language and Communication,* 3rd ed. (Cambridge, MA: MIT Press, 1990), 24.

There is some controversy over the use of hyphens in compound words because the conventions governing the use of hyphens are not consistent. Generally, however, when the new compounds are first created, they are hyphenated; when they become sustained entries in the vocabulary pool, they lose their hyphen. This is what happened with the word *baseball*. Originally, it was two words, *base ball*; later it was written *base-ball*. Not until the 1930s was it written *baseball*, a one-word, fully-conjoined compound.[19]

Blending. Blending is a word formation process similar to compounding, but with one major difference. A compound word will retain all parts of the original words; blends, on the other hand, use only parts of the original words.[20] For example, a relatively recent word, *infomercial* (*info*rmation + com*mercial*), has emerged to denote those 30- to 60-minute programs aired on television that pose as regularly scheduled programs. Infomercials have an overly jovial host, "guests" who have a product to sell, and enthusiastic audiences. These "programs" are, however, extended *commercials* advertising the benefits of woks, abs and buns of steel, bread machines, sets of kitchen knives, exercise machines, and financial success strategies, to cite but a few.

The word for the underwater *tunnel* under the English *ch*annel connecting Great Britain and France is *chunnel*. Older examples of blends are *brunch* (breakfast + lunch), *motel* (motor + hotel), and *smog* (smoke + fog).

Clipping. People will sometimes reduce the length of words of two or more syllables, especially in casual speech or in newspaper headlines, by "clipping" off one or more of the syllables in a word.[21] This is how *gas* was clipped from *gasoline*. Some additional examples are *fridge* from *refrigerator*, *ad* from *advertisement*, *fan* from *fanatic*, *frat* from *fraternity*, and *bus* from *omnibus*.

Acronym. Creating new words that are acronyms is another reduction process, however acronyms usually take the first letter in a sequence of words, like *l*ight *a*mplification by *s*timulated *e*mission of *r*adiation, producing the new word *laser*. We often refer to organizations not by their whole name, but

---

[19]Gerald Astor, *The Baseball Hall of Fame 50th Anniversary Book* (New York: Prentice-Hall, 1988), 7.

[20]Yule, *The Study of Language*, 53.

[21]Ibid.

by their initials, also acronyms: CIA, FBI, NCAA, NAACP, UNESCO, NATO, and NASA.[22]

Conversion. This word formation activity doesn't actually create a new form of a word, but rather, changes the *function* of an existing word; that is to say, it takes a word that is one part of speech and changes it to another part of speech. The word itself retains its spelling, but it is used in a new grammatical function. Conversion is sometimes called **functional shift**, which seems appropriate, or **zero derivation**.[23]

For example, numerous words in the English vocabulary were first used as verbs in sentences but have also come to be used as nouns. From *to walk*, we get *a walk;* from *to laugh* we get *a laugh;* and from *to guess* we get *a guess.* I'm sure you can add to this verb-to-noun list. Going the other way, some nouns have been converted into verbs, as in:

> We *papered* the bedroom.
> Please *butter* the toast.
> We *vacation* in August.

Sometime adjectives will be converted to verbs, as in:

> This is a *dirty* shirt. versus Who *dirtied* this shirt?
> This is an *empty* cup. versus Who *emptied* this cup?

Backformation. A specialized form of reduction, backformation will typically alter a noun like *television* and change it to a verb, like *televise.*[24] Some additional examples of backformation are *edit* from *editor, opt* from *option,* and *emote* from *emotion.*

For ages, it seems, language cops and usage mavens have expressed excruciating distress about the ways English speakers and writers convert nouns into verbs. Although this issue may seem inconsequential to you, it is a matter that has created considerable controversy.

Much to the chagrin of the language cops, however, is the fact nouns have been converted to verbs over the years. Consider these verbs, all of which were nouns initially: *to dialogue, to parent, to input, to interface, to host, to chair* (a meeting), *to contact,* and *to journal.*[25]

---

[22]Ibid.

[23]Kaplan, *English Grammar,* 86.

[24]Akmajian, et al., *Linguistics: An Introduction,* 14.

[25]Steven Pinker, *The Language Instinct* (New York: Morrow and Company, 1994), 8.

Converting nouns into verbs has been going on for centuries. This word formation activity is a distinctive characteristic of the English language. In fact, Pinker estimates that one fifth of all English verbs were nouns originally. Considering only those nouns related to the human body, for instance, when they are converted (or "verbed," as the case may be) we can *head* a committee, *scalp* football tickets, *nose* around, *jaw* at the umpire, *back* a candidate, *knuckle* under, *shoulder* a burden, *foot* the bill, *toe* the line, *belly* up to the bar, *stomach* someone's personality, and many other examples.[26]

Established writers have routinely converted nouns into verbs. In chapter 1 of *The Great Gatsby*, for example, F. Scott Fitzgerald has Nick say, "I had no intention of being *rumored* into marriage" (my emphasis).[27]

Just for the fun of it, let me introduce you to a recurring column in the *Atlantic Monthly*. In the monthly column "Word Fugitives," readers send in nominations for new words currently not available to describe certain experiences. Here are some recent examples:

1. What's a word to describe the feeling one experiences when stepping off a curb and not knowing the curb was there? *Curbigo* (from vertigo)? *Discurbed? Inadvertigo? Vertigone? Curbulance?*[28]
2. What do you call people who seem to have cell phones glued to their ears? *Audiots? Cellfish? Earheads? Earitants? Imbecells? Phonies?*[29]

I suspect you, you and your colleagues, and you and your students would enjoy trying to come up with acceptable words for these everyday experiences for which our vocabulary is currently lacking!

FOR YOUR INQUIRY AND PRACTICE:

Here are some words illustrating different word formation processes. Can you identify the process for each word? If not, consult your dictionary.

robot	Rolaids	password	gasohol	flu
opt	age (v.)	jeep	terrorism	MRI

---

[26]Ibid.

[27]F. Scott Fitzgerald, *The Great Gatsby* (New York: Collier Books, 1980), 20.

[28]Barbara Wallraf, ed., "Word Fugitives," *The Atlantic Monthly,* December 2004, 196.

[29]Ibid., May 2003, 144.

ATTITUDES TOWARD NEW WORDS

Ask anyone who might represent an "older" generation what they think of the "younger" generation and you'll likely hear a number of disparaging remarks about any number of traits, but certain to be among them will be music, hairstyles, and language. Previous generations commonly think more recent generations have no ear for "good music," like weird hairstyles, and use language that is sloppy and employs objectionable words. Change is not something many people embrace; in fact, there are days when I think the only people who look forward to change are babies with soiled diapers!

New words and new uses for existing words are as common as sunrise and sunset. You saw a glimpse of this in chapter 4 when we discussed the property of **productivity**. As the processes described in this chapter demonstrate, the relative ease with which new words can be created certainly makes English a productive language. The fact that it is relatively easy to create new words, and given the additional linguistic principle that says that whenever there's a need for a new word or a new form, a speech community will create one, we find one of the recurring paradoxes in language: New words are frequently controversial. General or widespread acceptance of a new word is often slower than its creation.

In fact, as you've already seen, some new words generate active opposition. John Simon, William Safire, Edwin Newman, and Charles, Prince of Wales, are just four examples of those who have written and spoken in opposition to words and other usages they consider bloated, obscure, imprecise, sloppy, or inaccurate. Language critics make statements about current language use because they understand and appreciate the intricacies of language and its relationships to the thoughts that language is attempting to convey. They speak from firmly held convictions that language, like any other creative tool, ought to be used properly.

Just last night my wife and I were having dinner with two of our closest friends and our table talk turned to language. The husband is a brilliant professional, quite successful in his chosen field. He's an avid reader and a keen observer of language. "I know people can use nouns as verbs," he said, "but I still don't like it." Life is a matter of taste. Differences in taste, nevertheless, will not change an immutable fact: Language is destined to change because the people who use it change. As Stuart Berg Flexner, editor of the *Dictionary of American Slang*, has observed, "It is impossible for any living vocabulary to be static."[30]

---

[30]Stuart Berg Flexner, "Preface' to the *Dictionary of American Slang*," in *Language Awareness*, 4th ed., eds. Paul Escholz, Alfred Rosa, and Virginia Clark (New York: St. Martin's Press, 1986), 182.

WORDS AS A REFLECTION OF CULTURE

It is a widely accepted sociolinguistic fact that language and culture are related. In fact, a colleague and a former PhD student of mine, Dr. Hamzah Al-Omari of the University of Jordan, commented several times during his doctoral studies that *language* and *culture* are almost synonyms. When he would say this, he was speaking in English, not his native Arabic. "Before I can speak or write using appropriate English usage conventions," he would say, "I must also translate the cultural conventions, and they're always changing in the U.S."

One of the reasons language changes is that the culture, the ways of life, the habits, customs, needs, and values of people are constantly changing. The language people use reflects these changing aspects of culture.

George Will, syndicated newspaper columnist, television political commentator, and avid baseball fan, has pointed out that, expressions such as "That'll make the Top Ten Highlights," and "That's a Web gem" are being used today to describe achievements in the social and political worlds. These expressions were first used by reporters on the all-sports channel, ESPN, and have edged their way into daily conversations.[31] The sports culture is reflected in general conversations.

This is not an isolated example. How often do you hear other sports-related figures of speech in nonsports contexts? A court case might be described as a "slam dunk" situation. Any hopeless circumstance might be described as "fourth and long." A person who has made a mistake has "dropped the ball." When someone "drops the ball," does he or she owe "a major-league apology" to the others in the office? Finally, what do you do when you're in absolute doubt? Punt?

These sports-related terms are meaningless in cultures unfamiliar basketball or football. Only in a culture familiar with these sports does their use in general language contexts mean anything. These terms reflect U.S. culture. By the same token, cricket metaphors would be lost on the general U.S. reader/listener. Cricket metaphors reflect United Kingdom, the culture of the or India, or any other country where cricket is a popular sport.

The popular media contribute to everyday language, and they have done so for years, although some of these linguistic cultural markers may have had short shelf-lives.

---

[31]George Will, "ESPN Pervades the Cultural World," *Lincoln (NE) Journal-Star*, November 7, 2004.

Fifty years ago *Fibber McGee and Molly* was a popular radio program. When the lead character, Fibber McGee, made a comment he thought was extremely clever and funny, his wife, Molly, would add to the conversation, "Taint funny, McGee." When people of the radio-listening era heard colleagues in offices, schools, and in other contexts offer lame attempts at humor, they reached into their cultural language resources and said, "Taint funny, McGee."[32]

As television become more widespread and popular, words from TV programs became more prevalent in social conversations. When *Get Smart*, starring Don Adams as a bungling spy (a spoof of the then popular James Bond 007 movies), was on prime-time television, Special Agent Smart (Adams) would make outlandish claims about his abilities, achievements, or the superhuman traits of his foes. When it became apparent to him that his claims were being doubted by those around him, he would quickly modify his claim downward by saying, "Would you believe . . . ?" During the life of *Get Smart*, this phrase became a part of society's general discourse. When *Get Smart* died the inevitable network death, so did society's use of the phrase.[33]

The point is, language and culture are related. A culture's mass media, its sports, its movies, its values, will contribute words and phrases to the language resources of that culture.

Some words are very culture specific. Recently, another professor on my campus and I were invited to meet with approximately 20 clergy from Russia and the Ukraine. They were touring the United States in order to understand better the relationships in the United States between religion and politics, religion and business, religion and culture, and the like. They were on our campus trying to learn more about the relationship between religion and higher education.

We were seated in a circle, joined by two translators who gave instantaneous translations from English to Russian and Russian to English. My colleague and I used a number of words and expressions that caused the translators to stop us, explaining that the word(s) we had just used had no translatable Russian equivalents. Some of the words were: *peer ministry, female clergy, endowed chair, hard-ball tactics, major* (academic), and *minor* (academic).

The Russian Orthodox church doesn't provide for either peer ministering or female clergy; many denominations in our culture do. The words we

---

[32]Larry Andrews, *Linguistics for L2 Teachers* (Mahwah, NJ: Lawrence Erlbaum Associates, 2001), 27.

[33]Ibid., p. 28.

used reflected our U.S. Protestant culture and reality, but not the Russian Orthodox culture and reality. Furthermore, Russian universities do not receive monetary gifts from private donors; consequently, an endowed chair reflects the university culture in the United States but not the university culture in Russia. *Hard-ball tactics* is a metaphor from baseball, generalized to any number of applications in U.S. culture; Russia is much more familiar with soccer and its metaphors. Our language was difficult for our guests because we used words we were familiar with, words derived from our culture. We weren't trying to be rude or evasive; we were simply using our normal language, even with all of its culture marking, somewhat automatically.

It's common in our culture, a culture valuing sports, to hear expressions like:

1. It's your turn to go to bat; see if you can get support for our proposal.
2. That law firm is really big-league.
3. That professor and his ideas are out in left field.
4. Linda works hard. She knows how to carry the ball.
5. Phil scored a touchdown on that exam![34]

These expressions, reflecting our culture, are so imbedded in our language that we use them without thinking about them. As I said earlier, we seldom give much thought to our casual and informal conversations. "Our conceptual system is not something we are normally aware of. In most of the little things we do every day, we simply think and act more or less automatically, along certain lines."[35]

THE ROAD TO THE DICTIONARY

As long as there are people using a language, that language will change. This evolutionary process is as natural, normal, and inevitable as the growth of an acorn into an oak or the development of a tadpole into a frog.

We know, on the other hand, that not all acorns or tadpoles will achieve maturity. The same is true of language changes generally, and for new

---

[34]Dilin Liu and Bryan Farha, "Three Strikes and You're Out," *English Today* 12, no. 1 (1996): 36–40.

[35]George Lakoff and Mark Johnson, *Metaphors We Live By* (Chicago: University of Chicago Press, 1980), 3.

words in particular. As people use language to describe new concepts, new social or technological phenomena, new words will often enter the language at the level of **slang**. Flexner defines slang as "words and expressions frequently used by a portion of the general American public, but not accepted as good, formal usage by the majority."[36] The field of slang is our linguistic laboratory where new ways of expressing ideas are tested. As slang words and expressions are used with either more or less frequency by either a growing or diminishing number of people, then the word will either become a sustained entry into the lexicon or die from disuse. When a word is in sustained use for a sufficient time, it will find its way into a dictionary.

Several words appearing first as slang terms have found popularity and sustainability among the general public. Some examples of words that were first used as slang terms but are now accepted entries in our lexicon are: *redcoat(s), greenhorn, fink, split-level* (house), *Yankee, Veep,* and *pony tail*.[37] Some examples of more recent slang that I've heard are *slammin'* (popular, "hot"), *dope* (quite good), *lame* (weak, not with it), *slacker* (lazy person), *dis* (to disrespect), *get outa here* (You must be kidding!), *hang, hang out* (to be at or with), and *phat* (cool, huge, very good, someone well-respected). By the time you read this book, some or all of these expressions may have been replaced by newer ones. How long these expressions remain fashionable will depend on the people using them. When it comes to settling questions about linguistic nuances, changes, new words, and the like, there is only one Supreme Court, the people who use the language.

"THE DICTIONARY" AND DICTIONARIES

It's as common as the air we breathe to hear people say, "Let's look it up in the dictionary." The use of the definite article *the* in this sentence is significant because it implies that there is, after all is said and done, only *one* dictionary (Remember our earlier discussion about *The Dictionary*?), published in varying shapes, colors, and bindings by different publishers. Alternatively, you might hear people say, "Let's look it up in Webster's." Noah Webster was the first major lexicographer in the United States. Using *Webster* and *dictionary* as synonyms is a classic example of an *eponym*, a word created from someone's name.

---

[36]Flexner, "'preface'", 180.

[37]Ibid., 183.

FOR YOUR INQUIRY AND PRACTICE:

The word *sandwich* is another example of an eponym. *Sandwich* is derived from the name of John Montagu, the Fourth Earl of Sandwich (1718–1792), a nonstop gambler who once spent 24 hours at a gaming table without taking a break for meals. All he had to eat was two slices of bread with a piece of cold meat in the middle so that his gambling wouldn't be interrupted. Here are some additional eponyms. Your desk dictionary will help you determine where they came from.

leotard	dunce	bloomer	maverick
derrick	hooligan	galvanize	diesel
zeppelin	shrapnel	amp	grog

As you read earlier in this chapter, referring to *the* dictionary is uninformed and misleading. There are *several* versions of American English dictionaries, each with its own set of editorial policies guiding the selection of entry words as well as what kind of information will be included for each word. Because book publishing is a highly competitive business, it should be obvious that the policies and the information contained in the published texts will differ.

The contents of dictionaries have evolved over the years and, as I've indicated previously, not all dictionaries contain identical information. There are, nevertheless, some features many dictionaries share. Many dictionaries, except for pictionaries and other dictionaries prepared for use in the primary grades, will include:

1. Head words or main entries, called **lemmata** by professional lexicographers, printed in boldface and arranged in strictly alphabetical order. The main entry will provide the word's conventional spelling and will also include a **variant spelling**, an acceptable option, when it's appropriate. Both *meager* and *meagre*, for example, are shown as acceptable spellings in three dictionaries in my office (see also *aluminum* and *aluminium*).

   Listing words in dictionaries in alphabetical order is an accident of history. It makes good organizational sense but it makes no semantic sense. For example, in the dictionary on your desk, regardless of who published it, you'll find *aunt* and *uncle*, clearly closely related words, at opposite ends of the dictionary. There is no pedagogical or semantic reason for this fact. The same can be said for words like *aardvark, bear, cat, dog,* and so on, all the way to *zoo.* Consider as well the placements of the words *hate* and *love, peace* and *war, constellation* and *star.* Only in special dictionaries, those advertised as **lexicons**, will you find the words listed in related, semantic fields. In a lexicon, the words *aunt, uncle, nephew,* and *niece* will be listed in close proximity. Consequently, a lexicon can be an invaluable tool for those learners for whom English is a new language.

2. A guide to the entry's pronunciation(s), usually using some form of phonetic respelling typically based on or derived from the International Phonetic Alphabet. The pronunciation guide will usually contain a more frequently heard pronunciation, but will also include **variant pronunciations** that are either optionally acceptable or regionally acceptable. The first pronunciation listed is **NOT** the "preferred" or the more accurate pronunciation. It may be the more frequent pronunciation in the judgment of the publisher, but it is not "preferred." Speakers from different regions of the United States are very likely to pronounce some words differently. The vowels in the word *oil*, for example, to select a very short word, can be rendered as the vowels heard in the word *all* or *coil.* To lift up one pronunciation as preferred rather than another acceptable pronunciation is an example of bigotry, classism, or linguicism, if not all three. There is a special room in Hell—with no windows, books, music, or sounds of children laughing—for the person who first suggested the idea that the first definition listed is "preferred."

3. The **etymology**, or history, of the entry word. The etymology will appear either at the end or at the beginning of the entry word's descriptive information. Where the etymology is situated within the entry ought to be of less concern to language teachers than whether the dictionary has etymologies. The etymology explains the family history of a word, how it came into the language. The word *dictionary*, for example, comes from the Medieval Latin *dictionarium* ("word book") in the early 16th century. *Redcoat*, on the other hand, a word mentioned earlier in this chapter, grew out of a description of British soldiers during the Revolutionary War. Every word has a story. Try *poinsettia*, for example, and *quiz.*

4. Each head word will also include several **senses**, or definitions. Sometimes the senses are listed in the chronological order they entered the language; sometimes frequency of use determines the order of presentation. It should be clear that the first sense listed, like the first pronunciation listed, is **NOT** the "preferred" definition. For example, one of the unabridged dictionaries in my office includes the head word *pitch*, and there are 48 senses listed for *pitch*, depending on whether it's used a transitive verb, an intransitive verb, or a noun. Until you've seen the word *pitch* as it's used in a sentence, how can anyone possibly claim one of the senses or definitions is "preferred?"

Learning individual words is a major task for all language learners and the dictionary can be one important tool in the vocabulary learning process. This is especially true when the language is English. I say this because so many words in the English language are **polysemous**; that is to say, they have multiple meanings and uses. Only when we examine the context of the sentence in which a word is used can we arrive at a sensible or appropriate definition. To validate this claim, look up the definitions for *school, class, run*, or almost any other common noun.[38]

Only by reading the front matter in a dictionary will the rationale of the order of presentation of the senses be known. By the way, there's an adjacent room in Hell for the person who first suggested that the first definition is "preferred."

5. Finally, many dictionaries will also include **labels of convenience** or **usage notes** indicating, when they might be appropriate, whether the editors consider the entry, its pronunciation, usage, or definition to be "archaic," "obsolete," "slang," or representative of a particular geographic region.[39]

FOR YOUR INQUIRY AND PRACTICE:

What labels of convenience, or usage notes, does your dictionary provide for the following italicized words?

---

[38] Andrews, *Linguistics for L2,* 18.

[39] The description of dictionary contents comes from Robert Burchfield, "The Oxford English Dictionary," in *Lexicography: An Emerging International Profession*, ed. Robert Ilson (Manchester, England: Manchester University Press, 1986), p. 19–20.

1. I'm *agin* it!
2. Are you *alright?*
3. Don't be so *judgemental.*
4. For supper we had beans and *light bread.*
5. *Irregardless,* we won't go.
6. Don't *argufy* with me.
7. *Ain't* he a piece of work?

Not all dictionaries will have all of these features. Only the *Oxford English Dictionary* (usually referred to as the *OED*) has consistently aimed to present all of them. Furthermore, only the OED has claimed to include every word in the English language; all other dictionaries are selective in choosing the entry words they will present.[40]

Let me introduce you to two books about the OED. The first, *The Meaning of Everything*, by Simon Winchester, gives an astounding history of the English language and the OED. That this vast enterprise was ever undertaken at all, let alone came to fruition, is a linguistic miracle. The second book, also by Winchester, is *The Professor and the Madman.* Winchester combines a murder mystery and a fascinating aspect of the OED's history: One of its most brilliant and prolific contributors of definitions and illustrative sentences was an inmate in Broadmoor, England's severest asylum for the criminally insane. You'll be delighted when you read these books.[41]

Some dictionaries will have precious little information. The inexpensive paperback dictionaries found near the other compulsive-purchase items at supermarket and discount store checkout counters have only the most Spartan entries and senses. They amount to little more than alphabetized words lists and are not suitable for your use or your students'. Save them for your next game of Scrabble, if then.

Perhaps the greatest activity in American lexicography in the past 50 years has been the development of the collegiate or desk dictionary. These one-volume dictionaries are peculiarly American, and they possess a number of attractive characteristics: They are relatively inexpensive, they are portable, they contain a great deal of information about each head word, and they are up-to-date.[42]

---

[40]Ibid.

[41]See Simon Winchester, *The Meaning of Everything* (Oxford: Oxford University Press, 2003), and *The Professor and the Madman* (New York: HarperCollins Publishers, 1998).

[42]Kenneth G. Wilson, *Van Winkle's Return* (Hanover, NH: University Press of New England, 1987), 18.

The typical unabridged dictionary is revised and republished every 25 to 30 years, whereas the publishing cycle for collegiate desk dictionaries is approximately every 10 years. Obviously, the desk dictionary will be able to reflect language change more rapidly.

Dictionaries serve a variety of purposes. In the middle school where I began my teaching career, I had a science-teaching colleague who punished rambunctious 14-year-olds by having them copy a page from a dictionary. I have an aunt who uses a dictionary as a doorstop. A dictionary, given its heft and size, can also serve as a bookend. I have a major problem with the teachers who use dictionaries as part of their discipline programs!

Dictionaries give information about meanings, pronunciations, and parts of speech. By examining the pronunciations, we can learn more about dialects. By studying the etymologies, the histories of the words, we can learn more about the history of the English language. All of these activities help us to understand better the concept of language change. I hope the activities in this chapter have renewed your interest in dictionaries.

FOR YOUR INQUIRY AND PRACTICE:

You'll need a collegiate dictionary to answer these questions:

1. What do the words *saxophone, silhouette,* and *cardigan* have in common?
2. What information does your dictionary provide for these spellings: *theater/theatre, center/centre, pajamas/pyjamas,* and *tire/tyre?*
3. What usage note does your dictionary give for *bye-bye?*
4. One of the words in the following list of word pairs is usually considered more prestigious that the other. Their etymologies may help you to explain why.

    hut vs. *cottage*
    aubergine vs. *eggplant*
    zucchini vs. *corgette*
    fat vs. *corpulent*

5. What pronunciations does your dictionary provide for the following words?

    creek
    garage
    orange
    white

REVIEWING THE CHAPTER

Part One: *Place a (✓) beside each statement found in this chapter.*

___ 1. Descriptive dictionaries will prefer one definition rather than others.
___ 2. Lexicographers include the culturally approved pronunciations of a word.
___ 3. Bibles and dictionaries are subject to translation.
___ 4. The word *baseball* is an example of blending.
___ 5. Converting nouns into verbs is a relatively recent practice.

Part Two: *Place a (✓) beside each statement you believe the text would support.*

___ 6. People, not dictionaries, will determine how a word should be used.
___ 7. Language change is part of a natural "drift" in human behavior.
___ 8. Dictionaries are history books, not law books.
___ 9. Reporters and teachers are among those who help to standardize the language.
___ 10. Some derivational changes result in slang.

Part Three: *Based on your experiences as an educator, and using your understanding of this chapter, place a (✓) beside each statement found in this chapter.*

___ 11. Be a lender, but not a borrower.
___ 12. What goes around usually comes around.
___ 13. Use it or lose it.
___ 14. I like what I know, and I know what I like.
___ 15. Keep up with the Joneses.

STUDENT EXPLORATIONS FOR WORDS AND LEXICOGRAPHY

EXPLORATION: New Words
DIRECTIONS: Dr. Seuss books have been popular for many years. Select one book by Dr. Seuss and identify as many new words as you can.

1. Are any of these words in a dictionary?
2. If a word isn't in a dictionary, is it still a *word*?

3. If a word is in a dictionary, what information is provided about the word formation process that was used in the creation of the word?

4. How does this activity help you understand how meanings become associated with words?

***** ***** *****

EXPLORATION: Houston, We Have a Problem
DIRECTIONS: Here are some well-known lines from some popular movies:

"Groovy, *baby*, yeah!"
"You can't handle the truth!"
"Duh!"
"That's your home. Are you too good for your home?"
"How *you* doin'."

1. Can you think of other lines from other movies that have found their way into recent conversations?

2. How often do you and your friends use language from movies or TV programs in you normal conversations?

3. Why do we use language from movies or TV programs in our conversations?

4. How important are the media as contributors to language? Will these contributions be long-lasting, do you think?

***** ***** *****

EXPLORATION: Animals Among Us
DIRECTIONS: Examine the italicized words in the following sentences, examples of figurative language, then write a *literal* definition for them.

a. It's a *dog eat dog* world.
b. The plan *seemed fishy* to me.
c. He acted like a *scaredy cat*.
d. *A little bird told me* it's your birthday.
e. When Mom saw my report card, she *had a cow*.
f. It's *raining cats and dogs* today.

1. Why do you suppose we use so many animal references in our idioms?
2. Can you actually write literal definitions for idiomatic expressions?
3. How important is the situational context in our understanding of the language we use on a daily basis?

***** ***** *****

EXPLORATION: Dictionary Acceptance
DIRECTIONS: Here is a list of *italicized*, informal "words" commonly used by the general public. Following each word is a longer sentence saying essentially the same thing.

a. *Umm.*   I don't know.
b. *Huh?*   What did you say?
c. *Peeyou!*   The smell is terrible!
d. *Yo.*   I'd like to talk with you.
e. *Humm.*   Let me think.
f. *Waz-up?*   How are you?

1. These expressions are commonly used in daily conversations, but seldom appear in dictionaries. Why do you think this is so?
2. Should these informal expressions be taught directly to the ELL students in your school? Why or why not?
3. Why are expressions like these seldom included in dictionaries?

***** ***** *****

EXPLORATION: Make-a-Word
DIRECTIONS: With the cooperation of everyone in your class, create a new word for something all of you know or have experienced (perhaps a new adjective meaning "good," or a new noun meaning "textbook"). Do not tell anyone outside your class about the new word, but use it freely around school whenever you have a chance.

1. How long does it take for people *outside* your class to begin using your word?
2. What does this tell you about where words come from? About how people learn language? About how people react to new and different words?

***** ***** *****

EXPLORATION: Launching New Words

DIRECTIONS: After you've created a word and have observed its degree of use and acceptance by those outside your English class, try creating *several* words. You might, for example, create another adjective for "good," and another new adjective to describe something "boring" or "bad." Similarly, create another noun to denote "textbook," or "teacher," or "student." Ultimately, select three or four new words, swearing everyone to secrecy, of course, then use this set of new words around school whenever you have an opportunity.

1. Again, observe how long it takes for people *outside* your class to begin using one or more of your set of new words.

2. From the complete set of new words, which one(s) catches on? Which words do not get used?

3. Are there any similarities between the accepted words? Do the unused/unaccepted words have similar characteristics?

4. After you have analyzed the "successful" and "unsuccessful" words, consider again what your analyses lead you to generalize about *where* words come from, *how* people learn language, and *why* people react to new and different words the way(s) they do.

***** ***** *****

EXPLORATION: Interview

DIRECTIONS: Schedule a visit with an older relative or a person in a retirement or rest home. Talk with this person about language use. You should prepare a list of questions before the interview, including the following:

1. What words did the person use at your age but that are no longer in use today?

2. What happened to these words?

3. What words are being used today on radio or television or in the newspapers that the person considers "new" words? Where did these words come from?

4. How does this person feel about these particular language changes, or any other language changes they've observed?

5. What do the results of your interview make you think about language change: Why does language change, how does language change, how do people feel about the change(s), and who changes language?

***** ***** *****

EXPLORATION: Variant stress

DIRECTIONS: You have heard a number of words pronounced in different ways. However, these words have alternate pronunciations for completely different reasons. Using your dictionary again, find out the reasons for the differences between the pronunciations for these pairs of words:

**CONduct/conDUCT conTENT/CONtent
conTRACT/CONtract EXploit/exPLOIT subJECT/SUBject
PERfume/perFUME conVICT/CONvict PREsent/preSENT**

Write a generalization or a "rule" describing what is happening with the pairs of words when you pronounce them differently.

***** ***** *****

EXPLORATION: Holiday Meals

DIRECTIONS: What favorite foods do you eat at particular holiday meals ? Roast turkey and stuffing (or dressing, as it is sometimes called) at Thanksgiving? Cranberry sauce? Fourth of July hot dogs? News Year's Day black-eyed peas? Make a list of four or five of your favorites. After you have your list, look up each name in a dictionary; where did these foods originate? Share your findings in a small group.

1. How many of the foods originated in another country?
2. How can you account for the inclusion of "foreign" foods on the menus of "American" holidays?
3. How do holiday meal traditions start? How and why are these traditions maintained from year to year?
4. Are the names of these foods "American" words?

***** ***** *****

EXPLORATION: Chocolate Moose

DIRECTIONS: **Homonyms** are words with different spellings but identical pronunciations, like *boar* and *bore* or *hall* and *haul*. Fred Gwynne uses homonyms in his book, *A Chocolate Moose for Dinner*. Before enjoying a dessert of chocolate moose, what meat would you want to eat: stake?

1. Can you plan a complete menu using homonyms?
2. When you hear a homonyms used in a conversation how do you know which word the speaker is using? What does this tell you about language?

***** ***** *****

EXPLORATION: Television Talk

DIRECTIONS: New words come into the general vocabulary almost every day, frequently without our being aware of their entry. Some of these new words originate as names for household products. Frequently television will give us new words and expressions. Brainstorm with your class, listing on the chalkboard as many phrases you can that are related to television ("boob tube," "tune in," "tune out," "wrong channel") but are used in other contexts as well.

1. Look up in at least two dictionaries—one older dictionary and one newer—some of the words on the list. Some of the words are likely to be in the newer dictionary but not in the older one. Why?

2. Ask your school librarian or media specialist to help you with some word research. When did the words or phrases from television first enter the language? Are there television expressions you're hearing today that you think might enter the general vocabulary?

3. Given your findings in this activity, be prepared to hypothesize why some words and expressions used on television enter our general vocabulary but others do not.

***** ***** *****

EXPLORATION: Lexicography Legwork

DIRECTIONS: Lexicographers, the special group of linguists who create dictionaries, are constantly "tracking" words, collecting evidence of new words and how they are used as well as observing newer uses and meanings for existing words. They use this evidence of how people use words when the information for a dictionary entry word is prepared. Here are six commonly used words:

run walk sleep car ball type

1. Based on examples of each word's use in speech or print, have your group write as many different definitions as you can think of for these six words. Remember to include both the *noun* and the *verb* functions, where appropriate.

2. How did your group decide which meanings or definitions to use? Which meanings were used first? Second? Third? Is one meaning "more correct" or "preferred"?

3. Explain how lexicographers arrive at the definitions and meanings they include in dictionaries. Where do the meanings and definitions come from?

***** ***** *****

EXPLORATION: Whoville
DIRECTIONS: Columbus, Ohio, was named after Christopher Columbus. Cambridge, England, got its name because it was the site of the *bridge* crossing the *Cam* river. Some places are named after nearby landforms, like Council Bluffs, Iowa. Knowing how places got their names can help us understand better the history of the region and the people who first settled there.

1. What do these suffixes mean when they are added on to the name of a place?

-ville	-mont
-ton	-burg (or bury)
-cester (or chester)	

2. Using a map or atlas, find an example of each of the suffixes shown in Item.

3. Can you think of places whose names end with the following?

-ford	-land
-field	-haven
-port	-hill

   What do these suffixes mean?

4. Can you think of five cities named for people? For other countries? With descriptive names?

5. For whom or what were the 13 original colonies in the United States named? (*The World Almanac* can help you answer this question.)

6. What conclusion can you draw about how people name the places where they live?[43]

***** ***** *****

EXPLORATION: Give Me Some Good Old American Pizza
DIRECTIONS: Write the name of the country or the national group from whom we get the following **boldface** foods:

---

[43]For additional resources on the study of place names, see the following: Kelsie B. Harder, *Illustrated Dictionary of Placenames, United States and Canada* (New York: Van Nostrand Reinhold Company, 1976); George R. Stewart, *American Place Names* (New York: Oxford University Press, 1970); Allan Wolk, *The Naming of America* (Nashville, TN: Nelson Publishing, 1977); and *The United States Dictionary of Places* (New York: Somerset Publishers, 1988).

1. An **eclair** is a _____ pastry.
2. The word **tortilla** is _____ for "pancake."
3. **Zwieback** (bread "baked twice") got its name from _____.
4. Cookies known to us as **macaroons** were first baked by _____.
5. Beaten egg whites baked on top of a pie are called **meringue**, which is a _____ word.
6. The word **chowder** means "thick soup." We got this word from the _____ people.

***** ***** *****

EXPLORATION: Tracking New Terms
DIRECTIONS: Look up the following items in your dictionary, then answer the questions that follow:

mini van	**word processor**
microwave	**VCR**
fax	**camcorder**
green mail	**MRI**

1. Are all of these terms listed in your dictionary? If not, why not? If they are, do the meanings in the dictionary agree with the way(s) you use the terms?
2. Do the spellings in your dictionary agree with the spellings used here?
3. From what other words do *fax*, *VCR*, and *camcorder* come from? How were these three words created?
4. Do you agree or disagree with the statement, "Words come from people, not from dictionaries?"

***** ***** *****

EXPLORATION: Logging On
DIRECTIONS: Innovations in technology often bring about new vocabularies to describe them. This has happened with the telegraph, telephone, radio, television, and the computer. Log on to the Internet—or read some articles about the Internet—and note especially any new words you encounter.

1. What kinds of new words did you find: coinages, borrowings, acronyms, blends, compounds?

2. Are any of these words and their intended definitions in your dictionary?

3. How do these words illustrate the principle that when people need a new word or definition for an existing one, they'll create one?

***** ***** *****

EXPLORATION: You're From Where?
DIRECTIONS: With another partner or two, look up the following words in your dictionary. Divide the words among your group and determine how they came into our vocabulary.

a. catch-22
b. golf
c. love (as used in tennis)
d. OK
e. posh
f. tip
g. nimrod
h. scot-free
i. quiz
j. widget

1. From where did these words originate, and when did they come into use?
2. How does language develop and change?

***** ***** *****

EXPLORATION: The Son-of-a-Gun Petered Out
DIRECTIONS: Here's a list of commonly used expressions. Visit your friendly dictionary and learn where they come from.

a. nail-biter
b. knee-slapper
c. hand-me-down
d. back-breaker
e. rule-of-thumb

    f. peter out

    g. son-of-a-gun

1. What do these terms mean, as you understand them?
2. Where did these phrases come from? What does this tell you about how language is created?

***** ***** *****

EXPLORATION: A Gift From God
DIRECTIONS: Many of the words we use have Greek and Roman roots. Here is a list with a number of surprises. Use your dictionary in order to learn from where the words on the left came:

MODERN WORD	DIETY	DEFINITION
lunar		
flora		
volcano		
insomnia		
psyche		
mercurial		
cereal		
vulcanize		
tantalize		
fortune		
terrain		

***** ***** *****

EXPLORATION: Just for the Halibut
DIRECTIONS: We get the words we use from many sources. If you like using your dictionary, and who doesn't, try looking up the sources of these common terms.

    a. caravan

    b. exit

    c. boulevard

    d. fettucine

    e. petite

    f. diploma

    g. gelatin

h. hors d'oeuvre

i. salon

j. orchestra

k. violin

l. typhoon

m. mustache

n. knapsack

o. robot

p. beret

CHAPTER 6

Grammar, Spelling, and Good English

When you're lying awake with a dismal
headache, and repose is tabooed by anxiety,
I conceive you may use any language
you choose to indulge in, without impropriety.
—W. S. Gilbert, *Iolanthe*

Before you read this chapter, come with me for a short, virtual visit to the teachers' lounge for a 15-minute break and a quick cup of coffee or tea. As you are sitting down, a faculty member from another subject matter area says to you, "What are you English types teaching these days? I have lots of your students who don't have the foggiest idea about the difference between *lie* and *lay*, or when to use *between* or *among*. Lots of them can't spell *sic'em*. All of that stuff I learned in middle school! Isn't anybody teaching proper English anymore?" What will you say? Be professional.

The next time you go to a meeting and you're milling around with the other attendees before the meeting is called to order, you'll likely engage in social small-talk. If you need some surefire conversation starters, here are a few suggestions:

- Are you people pro-life or pro-choice?
- Should schools teach evolution or creationism?
- Do schools teach enough grammar?

These topics will provide the discussion you're looking for.[1] Some people elevate the topic of grammar to the same heights as their deeply felt religious and political beliefs. As I've indicated earlier, whenever people are discussing any aspect of the English language, like dialects heard on TV commercials or writing proficiency in the workplace, within 15 to 20 minutes that conversation will have centered on "proper English" or "good grammar."

Many people have strong feelings about what constitutes "proper English." Here's a recent example sent to the widely syndicated newspaper feature, "Annie's Mailbox":

Dear Annie: You printed someone's pet peeve about the improper uses of "less" and "fewer." Please print mine. I have two. The first is the misuse of the apostrophe, either by omitting it in possessives ("the dogs tail") or inserting it in nonpossessive plurals ("table's for sale"). My second peeve is the comma splice, in which two complete sentences are joined by a comma, but lack a coordinating conjunction such as "or," "and," or "but" ("The water was cold, Jill went swimming anyway."). I had an English professor who automatically gave an "F" to any paper, no matter how good, that contained a comma splice.

—Author in Vermont

Dear Author: At the risk of having the grammar police on our tails, we are printing your letter and hope people will pay more attention to their punctuation. We agree that the misuse of the apostrophe is one of the most galling.[2]

It isn't just Annie's Mailbox that serves as a national sounding board for language issues. In the "Word Court" column in *The Atlantic Monthly*, we hear from a reader who objects to the wording, "She graduated high school." The editor of the column replies, "*Graduate* may be transitive ('The school graduated her with honors') but the graduating institution isn't allowed to be the object of the verb."[3]

I'm sharing these comments from the print media for one reason only: to demonstrate the fact that there are those in the general public who care

---

[1]Larry Andrews, *Linguistics for L2 Teachers* (Mahwah, NJ: Lawrence Erlbaum Associates, 2001), 38.

[2]Annie's Mailbox, *Lincoln (NE) Journal Star*, November 21, 2004.

[3]Word Court, *The Atlantic Monthly*, July 1996, 112.

enough about language usage to write public letters about their pet linguistic peeves in hopes that any readers who are guilty of the named infractions (And, they know who they are, don't they?) will change their behavior and shape up.

On the other hand, we are reminded by the W. S. Gilbert headnote to this chapter that there are times in our lives when we use language freely and expressively, without regard as to whether our usage is "proper." If you have a toothache, you don't particularly care how "properly" you describe it to your dentist or to anyone else. We want toothache relief, not grammatical approval.

When we visit with friends over a cup of coffee or a coke, or pizza and beer after a movie, when we're playing golf or tennis, or when we're joking with family members at a holiday dinner table, it's the *content* of what we say that matters most to us, not the *form* of our sentences. This is not a profound observation; you know this already because you've experienced it numerous times. Nevertheless, the belief in a *single standard of correctness* in language use is almost an obsession among people in the English-speaking world, even among those people who enjoy the informal and unguarded conversations described earlier.

There are two expressions that cause me to go cross-eyed and stiff-legged: The first is, "Is it hot (or cold) enough for you?" The second is, "Oh, you teach English? I guess I'd better watch how I talk in front of you!" My unspoken reply to the first question is, "Well, no it isn't, actually. I'm fond of physical discomfort." My similarly unspoken reply to the second question is, "You betcha! I don't want no language slobs' 'round me!" But, I don't say these things. I smile and change the subject to something that really matters, like baseball or bass fishing.

When I was a Visiting Professor at the University of London I was having Sunday afternoon tea at a friend's house. I was approached by the recently retired Head (In the United States, read "Principal.") of a local comprehensive school (In the United States, read "high school.") who asked me, "Professor Andrews, don't you think it's just terrible the way the Yanks have emasculated the language?" She continued by describing an encounter with a tourist from Chicago who had committed a split infinitive during their conversation at Sainsbury's, a well-known grocery chain in the UK.

Of all the topics in the conversational universe we might have talked about, she selected a split infinitive she met by the produce stand in a grocery store, generalized it to all Yanks, and then sought my agreement that this was, indeed, a very sorry state of affairs.

The notion of a *single standard of correctness* in language use is often perpetuated in the media. You've already read the items from Annie's Mailbox and The *Atlantic Monthly*. Here's another, in the same vein:

Dear Abby: When my granddaughter kept telling her dog to "lay down," I told her she should say "lie down." "No wonder [the dog] doesn't mind me," my granddaughter said.[4]

Author in Vermont was exercised enough about misused apostrophes and comma splices to write to Annie's Mailbox in order to vent his or her spleen; the reply is, "Yes, this really is the most galling." The reply given in the *Atlantic Monthly* column tells us that the "graduating institution isn't allowed to be the object of the verb." Finally, do you really believe the dog in the third letter can make a *lie/lay* distinction? Most humans don't have a clue.

What these three comments have in common is their belief in a *single standard* of correct language use.

Here's a short quiz for you. It covers the sorts of things some students, parents, other teachers, and friends have asked me about. Without a doubt, you'll be asked similar questions by similar people.

A SHORT ENGLISH USAGE TEST[5]

Part I Directions: Punctuate, spell, and capitalize correctly the following sentences, and for each correction you make, give the rule:

1. new york is the Largest of all american Cities.
2. a man named john right appeared in vue and was scene by sevral nabors he bore in his rite hand a peace of pottrey and a pain of glass to which he had no rite.

Part II Directions: Correct the following sentences, and for each correction give your reason:

3. Which do you like best, white meat or dark meat?
4. Yes, Your Honor, it was him who I saw.

---

[4]Dear Abby, *The Lincoln (NE) Journal Star*, August 4, 1992.

[5]The test is after Dennis Baron, *Guide to Home English Repair* (Champaign-Urbana, IL: National Council of Teachers of English, 1994), 15–20, with additions by the author.

5. Turn your hand this way, like I do.
6. Share the remainder between Tom, Dick, and Harry.
7. The wisdom and justness of his decision is now apparent.
8. None of the newer books were on the bargain table.
9. The whole team lost both it's cool and it's resolve.

If you discussed this test with others, I'll wager that there wasn't unanimous agreement about what was or was not an error. Indeed, when I've used this test in my classes I hear comments like the following:

- These sentences are really nit-picky.
- I'll never remember the difference between *who* and *whom*.
- I can't stand it when people misuse *it's*. It drives me crazy.
- Who really cares? I never learned these rules and don't intend to now.
- When I see this on a student paper, it's an automatic "F."

These comments come from people who have graduated from high school and have either been studying to become teachers of English for 4 years, or have been teaching English/language arts for several years. Why, do you suspect, is there so much disparity among their reactions?

Can you imagine, by the way, a preservice or in-service math teacher saying something like, "I never learned the multiplication table and don't intend to now." Or, can you envision a geography or social studies teacher saying, "These maps are really nit-picky."

Students in my classes have seen the items on the short usage test hundreds of times, beginning in the fourth or fifth grade through high school, yet they respond to them with an astonishing lack of consistency. Some view the "errors" as pesky, but generally insignificant linguistic gnats. Others see the "errors" as intolerable abominations. How can we account for the range of their responses, given the fact that they've had either the same or similar language study experiences?

Here's a digression. Or, maybe it's a critical point. In either event, consider the plight of the student. In one teacher's classroom, the student wanders in a carefree manner through *lie/lay*, *its/it's*, *between/among*, and the like, without ever being asked to make any distinctions. The following year our hypothetical student encounters another teacher, one who considers the ability to use *lie/lay*, *its/it's*, and *between/among* correctly as the only acceptable evidence of English language proficiency, always and without fail. Which teacher is right? The student, whose language use hasn't been questioned before, is confused. What's the student supposed to believe and do?

Owing to a variety of reasons, many of which we covered in chapters 1, 2, and 3, the English program in most schools in the United States has emphasized, to the virtual exclusion of all of the other areas of language study, the most difficult and most abstract, as well as the least productive aspect of school language study: *grammar*. This is, at best, odd, because the evidence demonstrating the ineffectiveness of traditional grammar instruction is generally conclusive.[6]

Traditional grammar instruction, with its goal of increased lexical and syntactical terminology creating improvements in students' oral and written language performance, has not been effective in the improvement of either students' writing or speaking competencies. Teaching students the names of the traditional parts of speech and the rules of prescriptive usage ("Do not end sentences with preparations." "The graduating institution isn't allowed to be the object of the verb.") may help them learn the names, or may help them learn some prescriptive rules that do not pertain to the English language (avoiding the split infinitive serving as a classic example), or it may help them learn something about social etiquette or social classism (linguicism), but it's not likely to help them to become better writers or speakers.

Some English teachers will take issue with what I've just said and will counter with, "But I just loved diagramming sentences." I have no right to deny their experience, and have no desire to do so. The fact remains, however, that most students did not enjoy diagramming sentences; ask 10 adults selected at random in any field of endeavor except teaching English and you'll see.

We can distill the several shortcomings of the traditional approach to language study, already cited here as well as in chapter 1, and group them

---

[6]See Richard C. Braddock, Richard Lloyd-Jones, and L. Schoer, *Research in Written Composition* (Champaign-Urbana, IL: National Council of Teachers of English, 1963); Stephen Sherwin, *Four Problems in Teaching English: A Critique of Research* (Scranton, PA, International Textbook Company for the National Council of Teachers of English, 1966); Arthur N. Applebee, *Contexts for Learning to Write: Studies in Secondary School Instruction* (Norwood, NJ: Ablex Publishing Corporation, 1984); George Hillocks, *Research on Written Composition: New Directions for Teaching* (New York: National Conference on Research in English, and Champaign-Urbana, IL: ERIC Clearinghouse on Reading and Communication Skills, 1986); Rei R. Noguchi, *Grammar and the Teaching of Writing: Limits and Possibilities* (Champaign-Urbana, IL: National Council of Teachers of English, 1991).

into one broad category: the erroneous belief that there is a *single standard* of what constitutes what some people believe represents "good English," "proper English," or "Standard English."

SOME IGNOTIONS ABOUT STANDARD ENGLISH

"Standard English" is one of those terms some people use with smug satisfaction, assuming everyone understands what it means. We've already seen earlier in this text that this is not the case. Among the several dialects of American English, a single variety called **Standard American English** (SAE) is used by many as the model for correct usage. This model is derived from the ways language is used by the most influential, social, cultural, economic, and political leaders.[7]

SAE is the language of people in positions of authority and power. How these people use the language is the model for SAE. Consequently, SAE is *socially correct,* and those who desire to be accepted socially will adopt these uses. Somewhere along the line SAE became more than just socially correct. It also came to be seen as *linguistically correct.* Today, SAE is not only considered socially superior, but it has been generally recognized and accepted as linguistically, logically, expressively, and aesthetically superior to other varieties.[8] SAE, however, is not as "fixed" in place as some seem to believe it is. SAE is a convenient abstraction whose precise features are all but impossible to pinpoint.[9]

Like all of the other living languages of the world, American English is constantly changing. Almost as soon as a schoolroom grammar text or a language handbook is published, part of it will be obsolete because of recent changes. The continuing evolution of language and the inevitable changes in membership among the people in positions of authority and power, the upper class, makes it fundamentally impossible to capture and codify the entirety of upper-class speech.[10]

For example, consider the word *nuclear.* I pronounce the word NUKE-lee-er. It's not a hard word to pronounce and I suspect most people, though not all, pronounce it as I do. President George W. Bush, however, pronounces

---

[7]Larry Andrews, *Language Exploration and Awareness: A Resource Book for Teachers* 2nd ed. (Mahwah, NJ: Lawrence Erlbaum Associates, 1998), 128.

[8]Ibid., 129.

[9]Ibid.

[10]Ibid.

it NUKE-ya-ler. *Nuclear* is similar to *likelier*, and you never hear anyone say LIKE-ya-ler. The elder President Bush and I pronounce the word the same way. So, where did Dubya pick up his NUKE-ya-ler?[11] Not from his family. If the President of the United States, clearly a person of authority and power, renders the word NUKE-ya-ler, will that make his alternative pronunciation more acceptable, more "standard"?

Similarly, students learning SAE were once taught that the three words *Mary*, *merry*, and *marry* were pronounced three different ways. Today, those distinctions are seldom evident in the United States, except as regional pronunciations. Likewise, the noun *loan* and the verb *lend* are used as synonyms today; they were not when my parents attended school. Today, "Loan me a pencil" and "Lend me a pencil" are equally acceptable.

The traditional insistence that people should adhere to all of the rules for "proper English" is simply a false issue. Native speakers of any language do, in fact, speak and write in accord with the grammar of their native language, similar to the unthinking and automatic ways they follow the other customs learned from their social communities and networks. Though native language users in the United States might not be able to articulate why they drive on the right-hand side of the road, other than to say "that's the way we do it," or be able to explain why they hold a knife in their right hand and their fork in the left, shifting the fork to the right hand after the bite of meat has been cut, or be able to name the parts of speech for words as they appear in a sentence, the native speaker will generate sentences that conform to the grammatical patterns those in their language network also use.

The fact is, no one *directly* teaches infants how the structure of their language of nurture actually works. Infants and toddlers learn language structure through immersion, observation, testing, trying, and through active participation and practice with the language surrounding them. It's through this constant interaction with older language users that the learner discovers how language is structured.

My nephew Cameron Kilgore visited us recently. At the age of 1;11 he's already learned many things: He knows where to get a glass when he wants milk or juice, where his clean socks are kept, where the clean plates are, where the forks and spoons are, and where his books are. He learned all of these things by watching his mother, father, sister, and brother put away these items, or fetch them when needed. After observing their actions and

---

[11]Geoffrey Nunberg, *Going Nucular: Language, Politics, and Culture in Confrontational Times* (New York: Public Affairs Perseus Books Group, 2004), 59–60.

participating in the drinking, eating, dressing, and reading episodes that ensued, Cameron learned, through repetition, what's been described here. This is also how he's learning their language.

Cameron doesn't speak French, Spanish, or Urdu for a simple reason. His immediate family, neighbors, and relatives don't speak French, Spanish, or Urdu. We speak English. Cameron doesn't say *book a have I* because no one models that kind of sentence structure when they talk to him. He will continue to learn and to use the sentence patterns used with him, and he will learn them incidentally and indirectly.

By way of contrast, a native SAE speaker might say, "My mother is a housewife." On the other hand, a Latino/a native Spanish speaker who has learned English as a new language might say, "My mother is the wife of the house." In terms of general meaning, the two sentences are clearly related, but the *structure* of the second sentence is patterned after Spanish grammar. The native English speaker, on the other hand, forms the first sentence according to the grammatical structure she learned: English.

Granted, it isn't likely, but if a native English speaker Cameron's age utters a construction like "I live in a house white," the older care givers aren't likely to say to him, "Now Cameron, remember that in English the adjective comes *before* the noun it modifies. In Romance languages, the adjective comes *after* the noun." To the contrary, the older caregiver is more likely to say, "Yes, that's right. We live in a white house," thereby presenting the conventional grammatical pattern through adult modeling.

Though my wife and I would prefer to think that nephew Cameron is an absolute linguistic genius, our earlier experiences with our children and my professional knowledge tell us that he's following the same route to language proficiency most native English language learners travel (Nevertheless, he is extremely smart!).

When children like Cameron start their formal schooling, too often there is an other-world, if not outlandish, assumption that either they have no understanding of language structure, or the language they think they understand is somehow incomplete, damaged, or downright incorrect.

This is where state standards enter the picture. Consider these two:

12.2.1 By the end of the twelfth grade, students will identify, describe, and apply knowledge of the structure of the English language and standard English conventions for sentence structure, usage, punctuation, capitalization, and spelling.

12.2.3 By the end of the twelfth grade students will demonstrate improvement in organization, content, word choice, voice, sentence fluency and standard English conventions after reviewing and editing their compositions.[12]

These standards are like hundreds of similar standards adopted by state education boards, agencies, and the like throughout the United States.

Standard 12.2.1 mandates knowledge of the structure of the English language. That's a bit of an overreach inasmuch as published reference grammar texts, pedagogical grammar texts, and prescriptive grammar texts don't always agree about structural matters. But, the standard sounds good and reeks of good, old-fashioned academic rigor that all politicians can champion and defend. The second half of standard 12.2.1 gives a litany of standard English conventions in sentence structure, usage, and so on. Once again, the available reference books don't agree on these issues, leaving school districts to their own devices as they determine which Linguistic Truths will be *their* and their students' Linguistic Truths.

Standard 12.2.3 mandates demonstrated improvement in these same areas as students review and edit their compositions. I know professional scholars who are still trying to clarify through their own scholarly activities and researches just what "all" of these conventions are. It's not unusual for the professionals to disagree. But, the standard sounds *so* good and reeks of good, old-fashioned academic rigor that all politicians can champion and defend. But, I repeat myself, violating a convention good writers should observe.

I don't intend for this chapter to take a right-angle turn and become a diatribe against state standards. That's a different issue.

Your school district has strategies in place for teachers to follow in order to prepare the students for their demonstrations that the standards have been satisfied. You will likely follow that plan because the political and economic stakes are too high not to follow it. Your challenge is to construe ways to provide for a more effective language curriculum, alongside the high-stakes mandates.

What bothers me the most about state standards like these are:

1. They are often a return to older views of language usage that weren't effective 100 years ago.
2. Continuing, and more critically, they muddle the distinctions between **English use** and **English usage.**

---

[12]*Nebraska Reading/Writing Standards, Grades K–12* (Lincoln: Nebraska State Board of Education, 1998).

ENGLISH USE AND USAGE

A student might learn how to label or create a basic S-V-O English sentence, such as "I like ice cream". This is an idealized sentence; it's grammatical. The student who can generate a sentence like this has demonstrated grammatical competence (**usage**). Even examined out of any real context of use, anyone familiar with English grammar will recognize "I like ice cream" as a well-formed sentence.

If you ask one of your students, "What part of town do you live in", it makes no difference whether the student replies with either "I like ice cream" or "Ice cream like I" because neither reply demonstrates correct **use** of the language.

The typical weakness of many grammar drills and worksheets, like those used in preparing students for high-stakes tests, is that although they may help the learner gain competence in English **usage**, they too often do little to help the student gain competence in learning how to **use** the language for authentic and meaningful purposes.[13] This is similar to an issue we visited earlier; emphasizing language *form* over *function* is dubious pedagogy!

Emphasizing language usage and form rather than language use and function is not new. Traditional English language arts curricula have done this for years as they have attempted to remedy the presumed faulty language behaviors of students. These attempts at remediation assume that in order to discover how American English works, one must look to a textbook, to logic, or to some other language—like Latin—rather than look at how people really use the language for different purposes in differing contexts. This misguided thinking further assumes that language is *pure* but people are impure.

These faulty assumptions and misguided thinking led early curriculum builders to look to Latin for solutions. Latin had been a school subject for years, and as you read in an earlier chapter, the methodology for learning Latin became the methodology for teaching English. Adopting this approach enabled, as well, the adoption of several rules of Latin grammar to be imposed on English, which makes as much sense as playing golf with a bowling ball.

WHERE YOU CAN PUT YOUR PREPOSITIONS

Many of the traditional rules of classroom grammar, having been borrowed from Latin, are simply not valid descriptions of the grammar of English.

---

[13]Andrews, *Linguistics for L2*, 41.

"Do not end a sentence with a preposition" is a prescriptive caution that mature and "proper" English users are expected to observe. Where did this prescriptive rule come from? Latin.

In the Latin language, it is physically impossible for words that indicate relations or locations in time or place (words we call prepositions, like *in, on, between, after*) to appear at the end of a sentence. This is why they're called **pre**positions and not **post**positions. As everyone knows, however, it is physically possible to put words suggesting relations or locations in time and place at the end of a sentence. In English, a preposition is a word you can end a sentence with.

Telling students to avoid placing prepositions at the ends of sentences is a *prescriptive* decision, not an accurate description of how English actually works. This prescription may be a rule of social class or of elitism, but that is no justification for its being taught in classrooms. So, why does it persist? Hill suggests that "Americans have been slow to give up their traditional Puritanism in matters linguistic."[14] Birch, furthermore, has wondered why grammar standards in the United States seem firmly rooted in the past while Americans expect constant innovation in fashion, technology, and media.[15]

Students in more prescriptive classrooms have also been told for generations, "Do not split infinitives." Most contemporary linguists don't even talk about this silly admonition anymore, but the prescription lives on in many classrooms. In Latin, Spanish, French, or any other dialect of any Romance language it is, indeed, impossible, physically impossible, to split an infinitive because it's *one word*. Infinitives in English, however, appear as two words (*to run, to read, to eat*). They are separable.

As we have said, in Latin it is not possible to split an infinitive. So, in English, the earliest authorities decided, it should not be possible to split an infinitive either. Why? There is no reason why we shouldn't split an infinitive any more than we should avoid automobiles and air travel because they weren't available to the Romans.[16]

HOW TO SPLIT AN INFINITIVE

The two-word English infinitive *to read* appears as the one-word infinitive *leer* in Spanish. In order to achieve special emphasis, I might tell one of

---

[14]Cited in Jiang Yajun, "Metaphors the English Language Lives By," *English Today*, July 2002, 59.

[15]Ibid.

[16]Bill Bryson, *Mother Tongue* (London: Penguin Books, 1991), 128.

my classes, "I want you **to** *carefully* **read** pages 105 to 108 in chapter 12." A teacher in a Spanish-speaking class will never be able to say that. Attempting to replicate this sentence in Spanish would yield a verb like **le** *con cuidado* **er**. Anyone familiar with Spanish would recognize this construction as noise, nothing else.

Like the preposition-final prescription, the "Don't split infinitives" statement is not an accurate description of how English sentences can be constructed. Grammatically, these old bromides are phony "rules." "Where are you *from?*" [Note the final preposition.] is a common question I hear almost daily. "Is it going **to** *really* **snow**?" [Note the split infinitive.] is a common wintertime question where I live. A teacher who insists that these "rules" must be observed is making *social* statements, not accurate *linguistic* statements about English.

LANGUAGE ERRORS REAL PEOPLE MAKE

Geoffrey Nunberg says there are two kinds of linguistic missteps: *typos* and *thinkos*. Typos are those word-processing glitches that sneak in between a thought and how we type it. Typos might make us look foolish, but they aren't signs of intellectual or ethical deficiencies the way thinkos are. It's the difference between a sentence that expresses an idea badly and a sentence that expresses a bad idea.[17]

Here are some examples of mistakes, errors, and thinkos:

- I recently reached for a book on the bookshelf beside my desk. I grabbed the wrong book. This was a *mistake*. No big deal.
- I was entertaining a widely known scholar with drinks on my patio some time ago, and I unthinkingly made a satirical comment (one I thought was extremely clever and funny, of course!) about a questionable statement I had recently read, forgetting that the statement was from one of *his* books. That was a *social* blunder, a real *thinko*!
- If they do no damage to people or property, many mistakes aren't all that serious. Social blunders, thinkos, sometimes are arrogant, frequently are stupid, and are almost always ignorant. They are also embarrassing!
- In one of my last softball games, a fly ball came floating out to me in center field. Instead of catching the ball in my glove, I misjudged

---

[17]Nunberg, *Going Nucular,* 59.

it. The ball hit my wrist and fell to the ground. What should have been an easy out was properly recorded in the scorebook as an *error* (E-8).

Errors are sometimes stupid, arrogant, or embarrassing, but they also imply a *standard* of correct behavior. The standard and correct behavior expected of a centerfielder is to catch a reachable fly ball. If the fly ball is within the player's reach but is booted, the player is guilty of incorrect behavior, a variation from the standard, an *error*.

We can apply the notions of *mistake*, *blunder*, and *error* to language use, too. For example, some language mistakes are what we call slips-of-the-tongue, as in the case of hearing someone say, "I wonder who invented crossword puzzles?" but actually referring to jigsaw puzzles. Another common example of a slip-of-the-tongue is a type of reversal, as in, "Look at the fuzzy patter-killer," but pointing to a caterpillar.[18]

Other examples of linguistic missteps might be illustrated by the following:

1. Houston is the Capitol of Texas.
2. Hopefully, it won't rain on our parade.
3. Pass the damn salt! [at a church potluck dinner]
4. Cleaning ladies can be fun.
5. The missionary was ready to eat.[19]

As you review these five sentences, which would you classify as a *mistake*, a *blunder*, or an *error*?

LINGUISTIC LEECHING

Why some school curricula have obsessively emphasized instruction in the overt knowledge of traditional grammar terminology and sentence parsing is somewhat mystifying. We have already observed that Americans tend to maintain a conservative Puritanism when it comes to language issues, but embrace changes in automobiles, kitchen appliances, automatic

---

[18]Jean Aitchison, *Words in the Mind* (Oxford: Basil Blackwell, 1987), 18–19.

[19]I heard Henry Widdowson use Sentences 4 and 5 as examples at an intercollegiate linguistics seminar at the University of London in April 1990. They were appreciated very much!

teller machines, 1-hour photograph developing, and hand held technologies. I have some additional conjectures that were described in chapters 1, 2, and 3 of this book. All of these reasons are, I hope, informed and reasoned possible explanations. They are not, however, in the detached meaning of the word, provable facts or certainties.

On the other hand, I do know and am certain of this: If I suffered from chronic pain in my knees and went to a physician for relief, I would scramble out of the physician's office as fast as possible if she tried to apply a leech to my arm, telling me that a good leeching would cure the pain in my knees. Leeching was believed to be a curative at the same time Robert Lowth published *A Short Introduction to Grammar* in 1762.[20] Medical practice, at least, has made significant progress since 1762. It is time for our profession to advance beyond the equivalent practice of linguistic leeching. Parsing sentences, identifying the part of speech for each word in a series of contrived sentences, and related classroom practices are not cures for any identifiable linguistic or other social disease.

A MORE MODERN ATTITUDE

In the LEA approach, we substitute the terms **conventional** or **appropriate** for the false notions of "correct" or "incorrect," which are built on the assumption of a *single criterion* for language usage. In keeping with more modern attitudes toward language performance, the determination of *conventional* or *appropriate* language use (and their counterparts, *unconventional* or *inappropriate*) can be made only by *observing* language as it is used in ever-changing contexts. LEA substitutes *information* derived from observations for misinformation or statements of someone's personal preferences. Further more, this approach enables another substitution: replacing a *single standard* for determining "correct" language use with *multiple standards*, which requires much more linguistic sensitivity and awareness by the user.

Lowth's *A Short Introduction to English Grammar* (1762) is one of the most significant English grammar texts ever published. In his Preface, Lowth wrote:

> The principal design of a Grammar of any Language is to teach us to
> express ourselves with propriety in that Language, and to be able to judge

---

[20]Robert Lowth, *A Short Introduction to English Grammar* (1762; rept. Menston, England: Scolar Press Facsimile, 1967).

of every phrase and form of construction, whether it be right or not. The plain way to do this is to lay down rules.[21]

Bill Bryson has pointed out that Lowth's *Grammar* enjoyed a "long and distressingly influential life" both in his native England and abroad. We can trace a number of prescriptive statements to the needed rules Lowth mentions in his Preface: the rule that you must say *different from* rather than *different to* or *different than*; the idea that two negatives make a positive; the rule that you must not say the superlative *heaviest* of two objects, but rather the comparative *heavier*; the distinction between *shall* and *will*; and the belief that *between* can apply only to two things and *among* to three or more (Share the money *between* Mike and Larry. vs. Share the money *among* Ruthie, Linda, and Marti.).[22]

Lowth theorized about how people *ought* to use the language, he wrote his grammar text, and in so doing he demonstrated how people were not meeting his standards of grammar. This approach can be described as a **theory-to-practice model** of language; that is, create a theory, then see if it's being met in actual practice.

To validate this approach, let's theorize that all 13-year-old eighth graders should possess the same vocabulary, their vocabularies should be the same size, and they should have identical words in their vocabulary pools. Now, think about *real* 13-year-old eighth graders from New York City, Boston, Dallas, Atlanta, Miami, San Francisco, Las Angeles, Minneapolis, Chicago, Denver, and East Thermopolis, Wyoming. How long will you support the 13-year-old vocabulary theory?

Most contemporary linguists follow the **practice-to-theory model**. The basic questions they ask are more in line with "How does the language actually work?" For example, a contemporary linguist will observe a variety of speakers in a variety of contexts in order to clarify whether speakers normally make a distinction between *will* and *shall*; normally say *different from*, *different to*, or *different than*, and the like, then they'll publish the results of their observations, free from judgments about the speakers or the results. Over time, theories are created using these analyses of practice.

This approach to language study does not suggest that one form of linguistic behavior is inherently superior to another. There is a long-standing adage that says a linguist doesn't explain what *ought* to be, but explains what *is*. When judgments about "right," "wrong," "superior," or "inferior"

---

[21]Quoted in Tony Fairman, "Mainstream English," *English Today*, January 2002, 58.

[22]Bryson, *Mother Tongue*, 132.

are made about language use, they don't come from linguists. They come from people.

DEFINING GOOD ENGLISH

"What is 'Good English?'"—that is to say, which usages of English are correct or incorrect, superior or inferior—is a recurring question. On earlier pages in this text, you've read about how some people advocate or practice a single standard of language use when they attempt to answer this question.

Sampson claims that this question is of particular concern in this country because many speakers and writers in the United States lack linguistic self-confidence. This lack of self-confidence stems from the fact that English language proficiency for a large proportion of the U.S. population is only one or two generations old.[23] In *The Americanization Syndrome: A Quest for Conformity*, Robert G. Carlson, on the other hand, paints a darker picture when he describes a long-lived fear of any form of human differences in the United States, and a resulting campaign for sameness, for homogeneity, for doctrinal conformity and orthodoxy in highly visible areas like personal habits, personal appearance, and language.[24] According to Carlson, we do not trust those who look or sound different from us.

"What is 'good English?'" is also a question appropriate for inquiry in your classroom. Using *multiple criteria*, which are suggested later on this section, your students will learn more about language as a *human* activity as they discuss this question. They should have a keen interest in the fact that many people—and not just in the United States—use language performance as a marker of social status; is this fair? At a more applied level, "What is 'good English?'" is often asked by parents, teachers, prospective and employers. They often answer this question by relying on prescriptions they learned in school.

The answer to this question that is closest to the approach to language study advocated in this book is the one suggested by Pooley:

"Good English" is marked by success in making language choices so that the fewest number of persons will be distracted by the choices.[25]

---

[23]Geoffrey Sampson, *Schools of Linguistics* (London: Century Hutchinson, 1987), 50.

[24]Robert G. Carlson, *The Americanization Syndrome: A Quest for Conformity* (New York, St. Martin's Press, 1987), 2.

[25]Robert C. Pooley, *The Teaching of English Usage* (Champaign-Urbana, IL, National Council of Teachers of English, 1974), 5.

This definition means that "good English" is as follows.

Appropriate to the Speaker/Writer's Purpose.   Our purposes for using language range from the highly formal to the extremely informal. According to this definition, users of "good English" are aware of the differences between a lecture and a casual conversation. They will use a language style of intimate informality when asking a close friend about the status of her father's health, but will choose a more formal style when speaking to a local civic club about the importance of the school bond issue on next month's election ballot. Confusing the purposes of language choices in these two examples could result in a friend's hurt feelings, astonished surprise, or disappointment among the members of the audience, or lost voter support.

Similarly, to return to the lecture–conversation dichotomy, people who continually conduct their language affairs in either a consistent formal manner or a constant chatty style will be judged by society as boors or as clowns who aren't to be listened to seriously. Either case is distracting and is an example of "bad English."

Appropriate to the Context.   If you're chairing a committee meeting of teachers in your building but continue to talk to your colleagues the way you talk to your students, you're clearly making language choices inappropriate to the context. I played bridge one evening with a second-grade teacher who kept referring to herself in the third person ("Mrs. Carter's going to bid two diamonds."). She wasn't joking. It was a tedious bridge party.

On the other hand, if you are supposed to give a report to the board of education and you use the same language style you use with your friends on the golf course, to show the board that you're just a "regular guy," then another context has been violated. The language choices you've made are distracting, you've used "bad English," and the board will think you're either crazy, or stupid, or both.

Comfortable to Both Speaker and Listener.   Perhaps the best way to describe this criterion is by way of an analogy. If you're having guests for dinner and you know that burning incense will cause one of them to sneeze, or that one of your guests is allergic to shrimp, you'll be courteous to your guests and you won't burn incense or serve shrimp. Similarly, you may regularly use four-letter taboo words with some of your friends, but probably not with your pastor, priest, or rabbi.

Users of "good English" are sensitive not only to their purposes for communicating and the context they find themselves in, but also to how their conversational partners are responding to *what* is being said and *how* it is being said. When people are comfortable with the language choices you make, communication is more likely to take place. Conversely, if your language choices make people uncomfortable, for whatever reason, distraction and miscommunication will surely follow. This is "bad English."

Some audiences or conversational partners will be distracted, for example, by the continual use of male nouns and pronouns, as in "All *men* are created equal" or "Each student should bring *his* book." Regardless of one's personal feelings about language that some regard as sexist, and knowing that some will be distracted by it but stubbornly insisting on using it, is "bad English."

If the participants in a language event are distracted by the speaker/writer's language choices, communication suffers. If the participants are distracted by *how* an idea is being offered, they will pay less attention to *what* is being said. When participants are distracted by the speaker/writer's language choices, they will discredit the speaker/writer as being either rude, unreliable, pretentious, intellectually deficient, or just plain dumb. Although these judgments may not be accurate, they will be made, correct or not. These judgments represent a **social tax**.

A social tax is levied by a society against those who violate either the society's norms or its expectations. If a person is eating dinner at a nice restaurant and noisily slurps his or her soup, those seated at the table will likely assess a social tax against the slurper, judging that either he has no table manners or he's as smart as a pile of dirt. "But, that's how I enjoy my soup," the person might say. Fine. Slurp away. Just be prepared for the social tax; it's your choice.

When speaker/writers violate the ways society expects language to be used, society will levy a social tax against the violators. The social tax is most often observed in the form of disdain, scorn, derisive laughter, or avoidance. Any of these is a high price to pay.

You should understand better by now how multiple criteria can replace a single standard of correct language use. These distinctions between "good English" and "bad English" are different from traditional classroom definitions. Contemporary thought about language study does not view language as an *object*, but as a human *event* that takes place in a particular *context* for a particular *purpose*. A more modern attitude toward language study sees *participants, intention, purpose*, and *context* as inseparable elements in the use, analysis, and examination of the effectiveness of language use.

What this means, in the final analysis, is that every question about the appropriateness of language use must be considered on a case-by-case basis.

Newer emphases in language study are clearly moving away from studying either words or sentences in isolation, with no context of use for a good reason: Normal people simply don't use language this way. Those who speak or write isolated words or sentences are usually diagnosed as bipolar or schizophrenic. When, for example, did you last pass someone in a corridor or on a sidewalk and hear them say, "All right. I'm ready for a Scrabble match. Put that trunk anywhere that it will fit. Aren't you interested in this drawing, Stan?"[26] These sentences are listed in isolation, devoid of any context, in a section in a recent English language handbook in order to illustrate what the handbook advocates as "good English." No, thanks just the same; sane people don't use language this way.

This text advocates a broader view when the effectiveness, the appropriateness, the legitimacy, or the accuracy of language use is in question. Multiple criteria must be used—*intention, purpose, participants*, and *context*—instead of a single standard. The use of a single standard conveniently ignores the fact that language *varies* according to intention, purpose, participants, and context.

When some people read the definition and ensuing discussion of "good English" presented in this text, I'll hear them say, in so many words, "Now I get it. It's okay for my students to break the rules from time to time." No, thank you. Now they don't get it. People who say this are still hobbled by the belief in a single standard of correctness.

What I'm saying is that instead of using a *single set* of rules, we should use *multiple sets* of rules. The rules governing "good English" must be observed or a social tax will be assessed, and the rules *change*, from one context to another context, and so on.

The definition of "good English" presented in this textbook does not mean that anything goes! It means that the simplistic view expressed in the single standard doesn't work because human beings will use language in an *infinite* number of contexts, or situations, and that each context or situation will be different by some degree from the last one and from the next one, and so on. That's why we use the multiple criteria described in this chapter. Granted, applying a single standard would be easier language teaching. It would also be a fraud. You want a better legacy than that.

---

[26]Mary Ellen Snodgrass, *The Great American English Handbook* (Jacksonville, IL: Perma-Bound, 1987), 38.

Another way to illustrate the ways language varies is to think about the paradigm that has been used in planning English language arts curricula and consider a newer one. The older paradigm used to plan language arts curricula consisted of a rather simple listing of the four traditional language arts. Experienced teachers will easily recognize the four-cell matrix in Fig. 6.1.

	SPOKEN	**WRITTEN**
PRODUCTIVE	Speaking	Writing
RECEPTIVE	Listening	Reading

FIG. 6.1.   The four traditional language arts.

DIALECT AND DIATYPE

As helpful as Fig. 6.1 might have been at one time, it leaves unexplained as much if not more than it illustrates. It cannot, for example, account for the essential principle of language variation, which has already been shown to be evident in the changing contexts, purposes, and intentions affecting our language choices. At a broad level, language variation can be described as:

1. **Dialect variation**. This is the term used to describe variations in language according to the individual user, as well as regional, social, and generational variations in pronunciation, word choice, and grammar.
2. **Diatype variation**. This is the term used to describe variations in language according to the use, and is sometimes used synonymously with *register* or *style*. Diatypic variations are also related to **field, tenor**, and **mode**.

Halliday describes *field, tenor*, and *mode* as the environmental determinants of a text. Field, for example, refers to the setting and the subject matter or topic, the field of action. Scientific discourse in a scholarly journal describing the behavior of ions and quarks will require different language choices from those choices needed in a discussion about knitting or gardening. Tenor refers to the socio political relationships between the discussants, that is, mother to daughter, principal to teacher, police officer to pedestrian, judge to defendant, and the like. These relationships require different language choices. Finally, mode refers to the channel of transmission, that is, written or oral, newspaper or television, e-mail or traditional mail. Each mode will require predictably different language choices.[27]

Using these features of diatypes, along with features of dialects, which are discussed in greater detail in chapter 8, Stubbs presents a paradigm quite different from the traditional four language arts (see Fig. 6.2).[28]

	DIALECT		DIATYPE		
	Regional	**Social**	**Field**	**Tenor**	**Mode**
phonology					
morphology					
lexis					
grammar					
semantics					
discourse					
graphology					

FIG. 6.2.   Dimensions of language variation

What Fig. 6.2 demonstrates is that we can examine language use as it varies and changes across two major dimensions, dialect and diatype. Dialect variations are those we observe in the *user* of language; diatype variations are those we observe in the *use* of language.

The Stubbs graphic demonstrates that comments about "good English" or "bad English" can be much more precise. Field, tenor, and mode clearly affect the types of language choices we make. For example, a simple question like "What have you been doing?" will require different responses in different contexts with different participants.

FOR YOUR INQUIRY AND PRACTICE:

What would you accept as "good English" answers to this question in the following contexts?

Question: *What have you been doing?*

---

[27]M. A. K. Halliday, *Learning How to Mean: Explorations in the Development of Language* (London: Edward Arnold, 1975), 130–32.

[28]Michael Stubbs, *Educational Linguistics* (Oxford: Basil Blackwell, 1986), 20–25.

1.   Professor to student at the library.
2.   Mother to daughter, coming home at 2:00 a.m.
3.   Manager to employee at office picnic.
4.   Rabbi to congregant who hasn't been to synagogue for 6 months.
5.   Social worker to parolee.
6.   Father to son, coming home at semester break.
7.   Coach to basketball player who just picked up her fifth foul.
8.   Aunt to nephew, whom she hasn't seen in 2 years.
9.   Building tenant to door man.
10. Brother to sister, who is hiding something in a bureau drawer.

When language is viewed as a social process and when learners have repeated opportunities to talk in classrooms exploring language events they have observed, they will become more adept at describing "good English." They will be able to do so, however, from a larger, more challenging, more interesting, and more accurate perspective. Furthermore, as they gain experience with analyses such as these, they will rely less on external and arbitrary prescriptions about language use and will become more sensitive and alert observers and users of language.

There are several learner activities at the end of this chapter. They can be used as starters for you and your students as they begin their language explorations. These activities are, however, only illustrations. Better language explorations will be discovered by you and your students as you go through your daily routines of listening to the radio, watching television, and reading newspapers, magazines, billboards, menus, as well as through your participation in hundreds of conversations each day. The analyses of these events will help your students become more aware of the power of language surrounding them.

What should we do, you might ask, when students' usages are at extreme variance with expectations? Well, there are several suggestions.

First, try to avoid the professional temptation English teachers sometimes find so alluring. Don't try to repair or rebuild the language of other people. If a student continues to mangle a usage item, take him or her off to one side and discuss the matter in private or in a teacher–writer conference. Explain to the student that society places a heavy stigma (the social tax we've described) against the usage in question and that if the students wants to be one who will be listened to, his or her usage needs to change. In the final analysis, the student will decide whether and when to heed your advice.

Students are more likely to pay attention to misusages when they detract from the meaning of something they have written. We have a good idea already concerning the most common errors found in student writings. Instead of trying to attend to all of the questionable usages you may read in your students' papers, I'd recommend that you aim for mastery of a more limited number. So, instead of bleeding red ink all over a piece of student writing, focus your attention on these items:

1. No comma after an introductory element.
2. Vague pronoun reference.
3. No comma in a compound sentence.
4. Wrong word.
5. A wrong or missing inflected element.
6. No comma in a nonrestrictive element.
7. Wrong or missing preposition.
8. Comma splice.
9. Possessive apostrophe error.
10. Shift in tense.
11. Unnecessary shift in person.
12. Sentence fragment.
13. Wrong tense or verb form.
14. Subject–verb agreement.
15. Lack of comma in a series.
16. Pronoun agreement.
17. Unnecessary commas.
18. Run-on or confused sentence.
19. Dangling or misplaced modifier.
20. Its/it's confusion.

These 20 elements represent the most frequently occurring errors in written language. Use them as a more targeted number of written language conventions you'll stress when you have individual writing conferences with your students. If your students master these 20 patterns, they're well on their way to being successful writers.[29]

---

[29]Robert J. Connors and Andrea A. Lunsford, "Frequency of Formal Error Patterns," *College Composition and Communication,* 39 (1988): 395–409.

WHAT ABOUT THE SPELLING PROBLEM?

What's wrong with spelling instruction? is a familiar cry among critics of schools. Clearly, they believe, no one cares enough to teach spelling the way they were taught (successfully, of course) 25 or 30 years ago. "The spelling problem" is also, like "the grammar problem," a favorite topic of the back-to-the-basics people. Nobody cares about correct language anymore; spelling isn't taught anymore; the progressives (liberals, educationists, etc., ad. lib.) have decided that "anything goes."

Correct spelling, like correct grammar, is sometimes viewed as a window to the student's moral code. Bad spellers, as viewed by the critics, are indolent, truculent, rebellious, marginal citizens who could do better if they would just try, or if they had teachers strong enough to *make* them try. The simple solution most frequently offered by the critics is a written test of selected spelling words, with both state and national standards for everyone to meet. Here's that good, old-fashioned academic rigor again that was fashionable years ago but is now, the critics say, passe.

The newspapers I read routinely report the results of spelling bees, demonstrating in human-interest writing the pride in the 13-year-old who won because she could accurately spell *sarcophagus*, winning over another young woman who couldn't spell *colluvies*.[30] If you miss these stories in the print media, you can watch *live* spelling bees on ESPN-TV. Even one of the downtown bars in the city where I live sponsors an annual spelling bee! Spelling is hot.

Why spelling success receives so much public attention is more than ironic inasmuch as *punctuation*, not spelling, obviously affects clear communication to a much greater degree. I've not yet heard or read about punctuation bees, or any other kind of punctuation competition. Punctuation is not hot.

Conventional English spelling is not regular, like Spanish spelling, but, by the same token, it isn't random, either. The fact is, English spelling does not have *a* system, but is the result of *many* systems.

Modern English spelling is the result of a number of historical influences. The Viking raids on what is now Great Britain replaced words that were leftovers from the earlier Norse raids. The Angles, Saxons, and Jutes waged similar forays, leaving behind the basic grammar foundation for what we would eventually call English. In 1066 William the Conqueror,

---

[30]Associated Press, "Wrong Turn on Foul Word Spells Loss," *The Lincoln (NE) Star*, September 24, 1991.

Duke of Normandy, was victorious at the Battle of Hastings, and enthroned French and Latin as the official languages of the church, government, the schools, and "society." The resulting co- mingling of French and Anglo-Saxon created a number of spelling changes that are still evident today. For example, the Germanic, or Anglo-Saxon, form of plurals (*house, housen; shoe, shoen*) was replaced with the French convention for plural marking, adding-*s* (*house, houses; shoe, shoes*). Only a few Anglo-Saxon plurals remain in use today (*ox, oxen; foot, feet; tooth, teeth; child, children*).

The "victory" of the French language over the Anglo-Saxon language also affected other spellings so that the Anglo-Saxon *cween* became the French-influenced *queen, cwellen* became *quell* and *cwencan* became *quench*, just to cite a few examples.

In order to fully appreciate the marvelous admixture of spelling systems at work in English, consider the following words, each one containing a different representation of what we call the long-*a* sound heard in the word *bay: ate, rain, gauge, ray, steak, veil*, and *obey*. Here we see many ways to symbolize (spell) the same sound! The etymologies of these words will reflect spelling influences from several languages; it's worth the time to read the etymologies in a dictionary.

Not only are the symbols for vowel sounds the results of numerous influences, so are the spellings of consonant sounds. Consider how we symbolize (spell) the consonant sound heard at the beginning of the word *shut*, and you wind up with *shoe, sugar, issue, mission, notion, suspicion, ocean, conscious, chaperon, schist, fuchsia*, and *pshaw*! Once again, use your dictionary to read the etymologies of these words and you'll appreciate that English spelling is the product of many influences.

What all of this illustrates, of course, is that there is no single system of English spelling. To the contrary, there are several systems in simultaneous use. These examples also illustrate another important fact: American English spelling is not the simple matter school critics would have us believe.

SPELLING COUNTS

How many times have you heard a student ask, "Does spelling count?" This question is most often asked by a student who is writing a paper or report in a science class, a social studies class, or some other content area. There are many possible answers to the question, but we focus on only two.

First, looking at the question from a sociological perspective, spelling certainly does count! American culture places a higher value on written language than any other form. Many English language teachers believe this emphasis is our of proportion to any long-range communicative value, but it's there, nonetheless. American culture assesses a heavy social tax against those who don't use conventional spellings (even those members of the culture who are, *themselves*, "spelling challenged").

Second, from the perspective of the writing students complete in school, spelling will or won't count as much, depending on the use, context, and purpose for writing. For example, accurate spelling isn't as important in a quick free write as it is in a polished piece of research.

The Monday pretest followed by the Friday spelling test has been resurrected in many schools as a result of the need to meet state standards. A spelling program like this is usually built on a scripted, prepackaged source of words selected by the editorial staff of the spelling text. The staff is typically situated in Boston, Dallas, Chicago, Los Angeles, or some other publishing home. The staff develops a list of 20 words to be assigned on a weekly basis during the school year. Any relationship between the weekly list of 20 words and the actual spelling needs of the students is, at best, haphazard. I invite you to prepare a list of 20 words *all* sixth, eighth, or 11th-grade learners in the United States need to know how to spell during the third week in September or the second week in April. Go ahead. Try it. But remember, you must include *all* sixth-, eighth-, or 11th-graders from New York City, from Boston, from Goshen, Vermont, from Osage Beach, Missouri, from Seattle, Washington, from San Antonio, Texas, and *all* points between. This is the challenge commercial spelling programs ignore.

An alternative approach is for a school building to create a spelling list of its own, which can be a workable plan if the list is based on the content area words students will need and if the list is revised annually. If the building list becomes fossilized, it's no better than a scripted or commercially prepared list.

Like other aspects of language study, spelling must be *contextualized*. For example, content area teachers should be responsible for teaching the vocabulary and the spelling of the vocabulary words they are using. The trigonometry teacher, not the English teacher, is responsible for helping students to use and spell accurately the word *exponential*. Other content area teachers have similar words and it's their job to teach them.

The third Student Exploration at the end of this chapter describes the use of *spelling logs* and represents a strategy I highly recommend. Please look at it now. Using spelling logs is an excellent way for your students to establish and maintain their own spelling program. Spelling logs place control, responsibility, and accountability where they belong: with the language user!

REVIEWING THE CHAPTER

Based on what you've read in this chapter and what you know, please answer the following questions:

1. How effective is the traditional approach to language study in the maturation of language use?
2. Which dialect of American English has the greatest prestige? Why?
3. Is using Standard American English a linguistic, social, economic, or political goal?
4. What parts of language do children learn indirectly? Directly?
5. What does the Linguistic Golden Rule (Those who have the gold rule.) mean to you as a teacher?
6. What's the difference between a linguistic error and a social error?
7. Who was Robert Lowth and why is he important?
8. Which theory of language usage do modern linguists follow?
9. Why should "good English" be determined on a case-by-case basis?
10. Does complexity increase or decrease with diversity?

STUDENT EXPLORATIONS FOR GRAMMAR, SPELLING AND GOOD ENGLISH

EXPLORATION: Radio Talk
DIRECTIONS: Listen to your favorite radio station for 15 minutes; then, listen to a radio station you don't want your friends to know you've ever listened to. Pay particular attention to the language in the lyrics of the songs, the language in the advertisements, the language used by the DJs.

1. What are some obvious differences between the languages used on these two radio stations?
2. How is the language used appropriate to the station's listening audience?

3. How does this analysis help you understand better the relationships between language and situation, or context? Language and people?

***** ***** *****

EXPLORATION: Casserole, Again?
DIRECTIONS: Although your significant other brags about his or her mother's tuna casserole, you hate tuna casserole. But when you're invited there for dinner, guess what: tuna casserole! It takes a lot of willpower, but you eat it. Describe how will you explain this experience to the following:

a. your best friend
b. your parent
c. your grandmother
d. your significant other

1. How do your descriptions change?
2. How are your language choices shaped by your relationship to the person you're talking to?

***** ***** *****

EXPLORATION: Keeping a Spelling Log
DIRECTIONS: One of the ways you can take charge of your own spelling growth is to keep a spelling log. Richard VanDeWeghe suggests the use of a log like the one you see here.[31] You can create your own log, or perhaps your teacher will prepare copies for everyone in the class. Keep the log with your writing drafts and make entries in it when you need to. The first entry is an example.

CONVENTIONAL SPELLING	MY SPELLING	WHY THE WORD IS CONFUSING	HELPS FOR REMEMBERING
1. meant	ment	I spell it like it sounds.	It's the past tense of *mean* not *men*.
2. Etc.			
3. Etc.			

***** ***** *****

---

[31]Richard VanDeWeghe, "Spelling and Grammar Logs," in *Non-Native and Nonstandard Dialect Students*, ed. Candy Carter (Champaign-Urbana, IL: National Council of Teachers of English, 1982) 101–05.

EXPLORATION: Language Diary
DIRECTIONS: Keep a language diary for 1 day, recording your language use. You can use the language diary form shown here. When you write your entries in your diary, be as complete as you can be. Bring your completed diary to class and either exchange it with a friend or analyze your own using the following questions as starters:

1. What observations can you make about who your primary language partners are during a typical day?
2. Is there a relationship between topic and language partner; topic and time of day; language partner and purpose; purpose and time of day?
3. Contrast your getting-out-of-bed, eating-breakfast, going-to-school, attending-school, after-school, and at-home languages. In how many ways do they differ?

LANGUAGE DIARY
Date _____

Time of day	Language partner(s)	Purpose of language	What was said
1.			
2.			
3.			
Etc.			

***** ***** *****

EXPLORATION: Slang
DIRECTIONS. Make a list of your most frequently used slang expressions.

1. Who else uses these expressions? Be specific by listing (a) the names of other people who use these expressions and (b) their relationship to you (best friend, neighbor next door, cousin).
2. Are there similar slang expressions you hear every day but would *never* use? Why? Who uses them?
3. Are there times during the day or week when you would not use any or some of the words on your list?
4. How do people decide when, where, and with whom slang expressions can or should not be used? How do people define "slang"?

***** ***** *****

EXPLORATION: "Oldies but Goodies" Slang
DIRECTIONS: Share the list of your slang with one or both parents, or with someone the same age as your parents.

1. How many words on your list do they recognize? How many do they know and use?

2. What terms or phrases did they use to express the same or similar ideas when they were your age?

3. Share your list with a grandparent, asking the same questions.

4. Why do different age groups use different slang expressions? Which terms, do you think, are more accurate or more expressive, the newer or the older slang?

5. How do people decide when, where, and with whom slang expressions can or should not be used?

***** ***** *****

EXPLORATION: Shifting gears
DIRECTIONS: You have an article of clothing—a shirt or a blouse, a pair of jeans—you don't like and hardly ever wear. In fact, it looks like new, although it isn't. Nevertheless, you're wearing it on a day when you meet several people. Each of the following persons will say "Is this a new shirt, blouse, etc.?" What answer are you most likely to give to their question (play fair; be honest), and *why* are your answers different?

a. your best friend

b. your pastor, priest, or rabbi

c. your favorite teacher

d. your father's best friend

e. your favorite aunt or uncle

f. your neighbor

g. the school principal

h. someone "hot" you want to impress

i. someone you don't particularly like

***** ***** *****

EXPLORATION: Good and Bad English

DIRECTIONS: Here are several conversational exchanges. Which ones demonstrate, in your view, "good" English? Which ones demonstrate "bad" English? How did you arrive at your answers? Might a "bad" reply sometimes be a "good" reply? Be prepared to defend your position.

1. A: Do you know what time it is?
   B: Yes, it's 10:30.
2. A: Do you know what time it is?
   B: Most assuredly; I own a timepiece.
3. A. Do you know what time it is?
   B. Yes. Do you?
4. A: Do you know what time it is?
   B: Yeah, babe. It's time we got it on!
5. A: Do you know what time it is?
   B: Time . . . It's an abstract and arbitrary notion, of which we are overmuch concerned, if not obsessed.

Based on your answers and other answers you've heard, what is your definition of "good" or "bad" English?

***** ***** *****

EXPLORATION: What Is a "Bad Sentence"?

DIRECTIONS: You have probably heard other people complain about the language use of others. Sometimes sentences are described by language critics as "using bad grammar." Sometimes sentences are described as "rude." What, if anything, is "wrong" in the following sentences?

a. The farmer drove the barn into the cows.
b. Females dominate conversations.
c. We was happy to be able to watch the movie.
d. St. Louis is east of New York.
e. The chicken was too hot to eat.
f. Males are more decisive.
g. Thanksgiving Day always falls on November 24.
h. Everyone should bring his money tomorrow.

    i.   The cow jumped over the moon.

    j.   One cannot always believe everything one hears.

    k.   She gave the dog it's food.

1. Analyze the "errors" you've identified in the sentences and see if they can be grouped into categories or families. How many different "types" of errors did you identify?

2. Rank the "errors" you've identified according to their seriousness. Are some errors more important than others?

3. There are probably differences of opinion among the members of your class concerning what is or is not an error, and how important or unimportant an error might be. Why?

***** ***** *****

EXPLORATION: How Many Ways Can You Say "I'm Sorry, But . . . "
DIRECTIONS: There are several ways we can apologize for something we've done, depending on the circumstances. Here are some examples. Read the examples, then answer the questions that follow.

> You arrive at school 30 minutes late (because the bus was late) and you must report to the principal's office before you can go to class.
> You are 30 minutes late meeting a friend.
> You are 30 minutes late for a study session with classmates.
> You are 30 minutes late for work for the second time this week.
> You are 30 minutes late picking up your mom at the grocery store.

1. Create an apology for each situation.

2. In how many ways are your apologies different? In how many ways are they similar?

3. Can you think of other circumstances that would require apologies in even more different forms?

4. Why did you use different forms of apologies in these situations? How do situations affect the language choices we make?

***** ***** *****

EXPLORATION: Intonations Are Meaningful
DIRECTIONS: Here are five simple sentences:

Jeff loves Kate.

We beat them.

Rambo likes school.

Bald is beautiful.

Lassie eats chickens.

1. Read each sentence three different ways: stressing the first word, the second word, and then the last word. How do the stress patterns affect the meaning?

2. Although intonation is not part of written language, it clearly affects a sentence's meaning. Explain how.

***** ***** *****

EXPLORATION: "Well, er, Like, You Know?"
DIRECTIONS: Keep a day record of all of the "fillers" you hear people using in their conversations. Fillers are expressions like "um," "er," "well," "like," and so on. Bring your list of observations to class.

1. What are the most common fillers used by speakers your age? Which fillers are more common among older or younger speakers?

2. Based on your observations, why do you think people use fillers? Do speakers use fillers all the time, or are they used in some circumstances but not in others?

3. What functions do fillers provide in oral language, in your judgment, based on your-day research?

***** ***** *****

EXPLORATION: Talking "Right" and Proper
DIRECTIONS: Can you recall the last time someone corrected your use of language? Perhaps a teacher, parent, or friend told you that you had misused a word or that something you had written was inaccurate or awkward. Write a paragraph about such an event in which you explain both (a) what language usage was "corrected," and (b) how you felt as a result of the correction.

1. Share your paragraphs in a small group and discuss *why* others have attempted to correct your language.

2. Was the attempt to correct your language successful? What do the others in your group report? Did they change their language?

3. Do corrections from others change your use of language, do you think? When are corrections successful? Unsuccessful? How do we learn different ways of using language?

***** ***** *****

EXPLORATION: Plain or Special: Both Work

DIRECTIONS: Some words are learned and used in everyday, ordinary conversations. Other words are learned and are used for special occasions. Here are several word pairs some people consider representative of ordinary/special terms.

fat/overweight	fire/conflagration
skinny/thin	talk/speech
stupid/ignorant	kids/children

1. Would it make any difference to you when you would use one of these instead of the other? Does it make a difference to others in your small group?

2. Does your dictionary make any distinctions between the meanings and possible uses of these words?

3. Why, in your judgment, do some people prefer one word in each pair instead of the other?

***** ***** *****

EXPLORATION: What a Trip!

DIRECTIONS: You have just returned from a week end trip. You spent time with friends and saw all the sights and did some crazy things, too. Now that you are home, several people want to hear about your adventures: your friends, your teachers, your parents, and so on.

1. Whom will you tell about a great party you went to?

2. Whom will you tell about the historical sites you visited?

3. When asked, "Did you have a good time?," how will your answer vary according to who's asking the question?

***** ***** *****

EXPLORATION: How Do I Agree With Thee? Let Me Count the Ways
DIRECTIONS: All of the following suggest agreement:

a. Yes

b. Yeah

c. Yep

d. Uh-huh

e. Affirmative

f. Correct

g. Sure

h. OK

i. Fine

j. All right

k. Okey-dokey

l. Right on

m. I agree

1. Which of these do you use? Which ones would you never use, and why?
2. With whom would you use each expression?
3. How do you decide which expressions are appropriate and which ones aren't?

***** ***** *****

EXPLORATION: You Say Tomato and I Say Tomahto . . .
DIRECTIONS: Circle the choice you believe is most correct:

shall	will
different from	different than
less	fewer
anyway	anyways
like	such as
that	which
you saying	your saying
It's me	It is I
yours and Sam's	your's and Sam's

1. Share your answers with a partner. Do you agree?
2. On what basis have you selected the "correct" form?
3. Can what is "correct"" in one situation *not* be "correct" in another?

***** ***** *****

EXPLORATION: Thank you. Thank you. Thank you.
DIRECTIONS: We can say almost anything in many different ways. What's "proper" in one situation may or may not be "proper" in another. In this case, we're looking at "Thank you." How would you *best* say "Thank you" in the following situations?

- To a police officer who has just given you a warning ticket.
- To an elderly relative who has just given you $5 for your birthday.
- To a 3-year-old, who has just offered you the gum she is chewing.
- To a classmate who has just given you a headache.
- To a school or church Santa Claus who has just given you a gag gift.
- To a friend, who has returned your favorite CD, after 2 months.
- To a stranger who has returned your lost wallet, with the money still in it.

1. What factors do you consider in determining whats the *best* way is to say "Thank you"?
2. How do *situation* and *participants* affect the language choices we make?
3. What price do we pay when we ignore *appropriateness*?

CHAPTER **7**

Discourse Routines
and Social Conventions

*Whether it's "Call me Harry" or "That's Ms. White," or
an unvoiced understanding that black men are not "boys"
and women are not "girls," we do what we can, often
unconsciously, to address people in ways they prefer.*
— Dennis Baron, *Declining Grammar*

Before you read this chapter, what will you say to the server at a
restaurant who comes to your table and asks, wearily, "What do you
people want?" What would you think if the public address announcer
at a concert or sporting event opens with, "Dearly beloved, we are
gathered have today . . . "? There's nothing grammatically wrong
with either statement. What *is* wrong?

Harvey is one of my favorite movies. Jimmy Stewart plays the role of
Elwood P. Dowd, a likeable and amiable drunk, who is accompanied
everywhere by his invisible companion, Harvey, a 6-foot, 3-inch white
rabbit. It isn't politically correct, I know, to refer to "a likeable and amiable
drunk," and I'm not advocating that condition for anyone. We're talking
about a movie.

Dowd has a very literal way with language, as these two passages
illustrate:

Bartender:	What can I do for you, Mr. Dowd?
Dowd:	What did you have in mind?

Man in conversation:	We should have lunch sometime.
Dowd:	Yes. When?

167

Elwood doesn't understand the bartender's question in the first passage. Instead of asking "What would you like to drink?" the bartender has opted for a more social and indirect question. In the second passage, Elwood doesn't understand a common leave-taking device. Instead of saying, "I need to leave now," which could sound curt or rude, the man in the conversation selects a throwaway line used hundreds of times every day in the city where you live. Elwood misses the point, believing the man is actually offering an invitation.

Both the bartender and the man in the conversation are employing expressions the viewer recognizes as formulas that are very common in social discourse. "What can I do for you?" is as common as "How can I help you?" when clerks or service employees are greeting customers. "Let's have lunch sometime" is as common as "Let's have coffee sometime" when people are quitting a conversation. The viewer knows this; Elwood P. Dowd doesn't recognize it. That dramatic irony yields humor to the scenes.

Throughout this text, the communication of ideas from one person to another has been described as one of the primary functions of language. Yet, when we greet people daily we often say things like "Hello", or "Pleased to meet you", or "Good morning, Mr. Green". These three expressions communicate absolutely no factual or substantive content; they are about as meaningful as that bit of social noise we saw earlier in "We should have lunch sometime". Despite the fact that "Hello", or "Pleased to meet you", or "Good morning, Mr. Green" may not communicate material or significant information, these three expressions actually communicate something else that is just as important. They are examples of the rules by which you and I govern the ways we interact with others. They represent **conventions**.

In chapter 2 we talked about the way we stand in elevator cars. Facing the sliding doors rather than the rear wall of the elevator car is a social convention. Holding your napkin in your lap during a meal is a social convention. Standing in line and waiting your turn ("first come, first served"), regardless of one's social or political status, is another social convention espoused in the United States.

SOME COMMON SOCIAL CONVENTIONS

Standing in line—called **queuing** in some parts of the English-speaking world—is a seemingly simple social convention, but this practice is grounded in more complex cultural values. Queuing began in Great Britain during World Wars I and II and was subsequently adopted as accepted and expected social practice in the United States, Canada, and a number of European countries.[1]

One theory suggests that countries valuing *time* stand in line for services; cultures not valuing time don't stand in line. One study found that Brazilians, known for not standing in line, own fewer clocks and watches per capita than similarly developed cultures.[2] This would support the theory.

A more important factor regarding queuing is the degree to which a culture values equality. In some Arab countries, for example, where women hold a social position inferior to men, it is common for men to cut in front of women at ticket windows and other places where queues form, a practice totally unthinkable in North America.[3]

A more complicated queuing convention is observed in Israel. Israelis are generally opposed to regimentation but hold dear to a commitment to fairness and equality. Consequently, people waiting for a bus in Israel resist forming lines. But, when a bus arrives, riders board the bus according to the first-come, first-served principle.[4]

These descriptions of standing-in-line customs illustrate how seemingly simple social conventions derive from basic values of the culture.

In the culture I know, we follow a number of social conventions: We routinely eat with a knife, fork, and spoon. Except for pizza, sandwiches, and other "finger foods," we don't eat with our fingers. Some cultures, on the other hand, use chopsticks instead of a knife, fork, and spoon. Some cultures eat with their fingers every day.

In the United States we drive on the right-hand side of the road; some cultures drive on the left. When a person of importance enters the room, we stand up; when we greet them, we shake hands. Some cultures don't follow these conventions.[5]

In the winter, I wear a hat. Without fail, I remove my hat when I enter my church. Protestants remove their hats as a sign of respect. A male Orthodox Jew, on the other hand, will always wear a head covering—a

---

[1]Malcom Gladwell, "Queue & A: The Long and Short of Standing in Line," *The Washington Post National Weekly*, December 21–27, 1992, 38.

[2]Ibid.

[3]Ibid.

[4]Ibid.

[5]Edward Anthony, "The Rhetoric of Behavior," *TESOL Matters*, October/November 1996, 1.

yarmulke—at synagogue and often in the home. This, too, is a sign of respect. The same basic value, respect, means wearing a hat in one culture, removing the hat in another.

At his second inauguration, President George W. Bush's University of Texas Longhorn salute was lost in translation in Scandinavia. Shocked Norwegians interpreted his hand gesture as recognition of another creature with horns, Satan. That's what it means in Norway when you lift your hand with the forefinger and the pinky fingers raised. For Texans, the gesture is a sign of affection for the University of Texas–Austin, and is usually accompanied with a shouted "Hook 'em Horns" at sporting events. In Norway, the gesture is a sign of tribute to Satan.[6] Two cultures attach different significance to the same sign.

FOR YOUR INQUIRY AND PRACTICE:

It is commonplace in the city where I live for men to wear baseball-style hats indoors; sometimes the hats are worn backward. Interview 8–10 people asking them how they feel about this practice? Is it a fashion statement? Are there age restrictions? Should male professors wear hats during class? Are the hats a sign of disrespect? A declaration of machismo? What's the convention?

We also observe conventions governing how close we stand to other people. In the United States, we tend to follow the "arm's length" principle, except with those with whom we are intimate. Other cultures— Latinos, Italians, French—are comfortable talking at a much closer distance. Neither convention is *correct* in an absolute sense; the different conventions merely reflect different cultural values.[7]

Restaurants conventionally have a host who will seat customers upon their arrival; short-order, fast-food eating establishments, even those with tables and chairs, allow the customers to seat themselves. This is not because of federal guidelines set for by the Food and Drug Administration in Washington, DC. The presence or absence of a host is a social convention.

Finally, despite what has been said about the liberating effects of language, there is an equally powerful *contradiction* because we are expected

---

[6]"Longhorn Salute Is Devilish in Norway," *Lincoln (NE) Journal Star,* January 22, 2005.

[7]Anthony, "The Rhetoric of Behavior", 23.

to follow several stringent language conventions. Those who violate these conventions of social discourse must be prepared to pay the social tax.

U.S. TELEPHONE CONVENTIONS

For example, we conventionally answer residential telephones in the United States with a simple "Hello." Sometimes we'll answer a residential telephone with "Hello, the Andersons" or "Anderson residence." I suspect the simple "Hello" is the most common. As relatively common as these methods of answering the telephone are in the United States, it's every bit as common in the United Kingdom for one to give the last four digits of the telephone number. My friend Graham Shaw (OBE) answers his London home telephone with "Hullo. Seven, eight, nine, four."

Not only are telephone conventions different in other parts of the English-speaking world, but they vary even more in other language groups. My daughter Sally has lived in Spain for 1 year and in Bolivia for 2 years. Here she shares her observations regarding home telephone conventions in Spanish-speaking homes.

SPANISH TELEPHONE CONVENTIONS
(BY SALLY ANDREWS)

A typical telephone call to a Spanish home will sound like this; notice that Miguel has placed the call to Carmen (the English translation is in parentheses):

Carmen:	Diga. ("Tell" or "say.") [This is a formal command.]
Miguel:	¿Está Javier? ("Is Javier there?")
Carmen:	Sí, ¿quién es? ("Yes, who is this?")
Miguel:	Soy Miguel. ("I am Miguel.")
Carmen:	Sí, un momento; ahora se pone ("Yes, just a minute; he's coming right now.")
Carmen [calling to Javier]:	Javier, ponte; es Miguel. ("Javier, come to the phone; it's Miguel.")

In Spain, the answerer begins the telephone conversation with a more formal statement than we conventionally use in the United States. The Spanish telephone answerer begins with *Diga* ("tell," "say") or with *Dígame* ("tell me"). This is generally although not universally true for both residential and business telephone answerers. Both *Diga* and *Digame* are commands to the caller to speak; the terms are not given as questions.

In other Spanish-speaking countries, however, these greetings will vary. In Mexico, for example, the answerer opens with *Bueno* ("well"); in parts of Latin America other common telephone greetings are *Hablame* ("talk to me") or *Aloh* (a variation of "Hello").

It is important to remember that telephones in most Spanish-speaking countries are extremely expensive, so costly in fact, that many homes do not have them. There is a toll charged for each local call, and the toll is calculated by the minute, similar to long-distance calls in the United States. Telephone conventions in Spain reflect this feature of the economic culture and, consequently, the telephone is used conservatively and sparingly. Speakers transact their business directly and quickly, with minimal "chatting," then they hang up the phone. Informal conversations are reserved for face-to-face meetings at cafes, parties, and other social events.

U.S. BUSINESS TELEPHONE CONVENTIONS

We follow a different set of conventions in the United States, however, when the telephone we're answering is a business telephone. The name of the business or organization is conventionally identified by the answerer, who will say something like "South High School," "First Presbyterian Church," "Moore's Market," or the excruciatingly long and synthetically chummy "Thank you for calling Waldo's, open 24 hours a day for your convenience, now at three locations. This is Jan. How may I help you?"

You can imagine the consternation you'd create if you answered your *home* telephone with "This is the Brown's: Bill, Betty, Bambi, and Bruce. How can we help you?" Or, if you called your bank you'd be surprised if you were greeted by the answerer with "Yeah? Who is this?"

Louis Whitmore, one of my night-class students who is a banker during the day, says that someone just *might* answer the telephone in this manner at his bank, but they would only do it *once*!

A relatively recent development with business telephones, especially at larger firms, is that the human operator at the central switchboard has been replaced by a computer-managed answering system. It has become somewhat common for a caller to a larger business to be greeted by: "Welcome to Acme Publishing Company. If you know the extension of the party you are calling, and if you are calling from a touch-tone phone, enter the extension number now. If you wish to place an order, press 1 now; if you have a question about the availability of a title, press 2 now; if you wish to speak to a sales representative, press 3 now; if you desire directory information, press 4 now. If you desire other information, press 5 now." This administrative practice is considered to be more efficient and economical. Though computer-managed answering and call-routing systems are no longer rarities, I don't believe they represent "discourse conventions," as we describe them in this text.

Some people believe the automated system is tedious. Others appreciate its efficiency. How do you feel about it? A "Ziggy" cartoon once presented Ziggy in the foreground of the cartoon panel, smoke billowing in the background. Ziggy is holding the handset and we read in the dialogue bubble: "This is your fire station. If you have a grease fire, push 1. If your basement is on fire, press 2. If a cat is up a tree, press 3. If you are on fire, press 4".[8]

DISCOURSE ROUTINES IN CONTEXT

In chapter 6 the diatypic features of field, tenor, and mode were described as environmental determinants of language. It is important to note that the setting, the environment, or the context of the language event shapes and determines the language used. The language choices we automatically make are influenced by the field, tenor, and mode. To believe, however, that a speaker says to him or herself "Let's see, now, I'm only going shopping for a loaf of bread and some milk, so I can leave my telephone voice at home," is to misinterpret how field, tenor, and mode exert their influences. It's not that overt.

Discourse and **discourse analysis** are areas of language study that have been the subject of a great deal of recent sociolinguistic research. For the purposes of a school program in LEA, however, our focus on discourse is limited to social and primarily oral exchanges and routines.

At the risk of my being what one of my daughters teasingly but knowingly calls "repetitively redundant," I want to help you recall that LEA stresses language as a *social* activity having to do with *people*. Language studied in LEA ought to be authentically human and ought to emerge from real human contexts.

In examining social discourse, it is important to add to this list some additional essentials. One of them is **connected language**. Many, but

---

[8.] "Ziggy," *The Lincoln (NE) Journal Star,* November 15, 1997, 15.

clearly not all, of the language events we experience daily are made up of two or more connected utterances. As we've observed in chapter 6, normal people simply don't wander around making one-sentence observations about the world.

An exchange of connected language might be as simple as one I encountered as I came to my office one morning:

Exchange 1:

(1) **Sharon:**   How's Larry this morning?
(2) **Larry:**   Fine, thanks. And you?
(3) **Sharon:**   I'm fine.

Or, an exchange might be more involved, like one I participated in on the telephone yesterday:

Exchange 2:

(1) **Larry:**   Hi. This is Larry Andrews. I'm calling about an over-
                 due book
(2)   notice I received in campus mail today.
(3) **Mary:**   Sure. What's your ID number?
(4) **Larry:**   628411
(5) **Mary:**   OK. Just a minute. (Enters number in library computer
                 and waits . . .)
(6) **Mary:**   OK. Here you are. Question?
(7) **Larry:**   I didn't check out the *Aging in America* book, yet the
                 notice says I have it and
(8)   that it's overdue.
(9) **Mary:**   OK. I'll mark it returned.
(10) **Larry:** Thank you. Is that all?
(11) **Mary:**   Yep.
(12) **Larry:** Fine. Bye.

These two examples of connected language are marked by the shared qualities of being astonishingly mundane and overwhelmingly ordinary. They are examples of direct speech, requiring very little interpretation. These two exchanges represent thousands of similar exchanges you and I participate in each week. Yet, you'll note that each of the two exchanges also follows certain conventions.

In Exchange 1, Sharon offers in (1) an **opening sequence**. As Finegan and Besnier point out, conversations are opened in socially accepted and recognized ways. A Greeting or an Opening Sequence is one method we have in society of saying "I recognize you" or "I want to recognize you."[9] It's a polite way to begin.

Because politeness is a trait valued by our society, it is conventionally required, albeit unspoken and unwritten, that the second speaker *acknowledge* the Opening Sequence-Greeting by being courteous and saying something mannerly in reply. Consequently, this tacit social requirement is satisfied by my utterance in (2).

The sentences in Exchange 1 are so formulaic that they actually convey little substantive content. They are important, however, for a different reason: *They provide some of the paste that helps to hold society together.*

Another Opening Sequence is shown in Exchange 2. In this case, I identify myself in (1) with a common beginning, Opening Sequence-Identification, which is used in hundreds of telephone conversations every day. The identification helps not only to identify the speaker, but also to solicit the answerer's attention, which is indicated in (3), (5), and (6).

Using the Opening Sequence-Identification convention on the telephone ("Hi. This is Larry Andrews.") is common in the Anglo-European culture in the United States, but is a convention infrequently used in the African-American culture as I know it. When an African American initiates an informal telephone call, he or she will most likely simply begin the conversation as soon as the answerer picks up the handset and says "Hello."

Why this difference? The Anglo-European culture values good manners; when an Anglo-European initiates a call to a friend, identifying yourself is the polite thing to do. The African-American culture also values good manners, but in addition it also places a very high value on *solidarity* and *community*; consequently, when an African American initiates a call to a friend, identifying yourself is unnecessary. When the caller starts talking the one called is simply *supposed to know* who is talking. It would be rude for the caller to identify him- or herself, questioning this *family* assumption.

Some Anglo-Europeans may not identify themselves when they call intimate friends and some African-American callers may sometimes identify themselves, but will likely do so indirectly. For example, a frequent caller to my home phone, a 30-year friend of my wife, will indirectly identify herself if I happen to answer the telephone with "My teacher!" because she took one of my courses at the university. Note that she doesn't say: "Hello, Larry. This is Marilyn. Is Ms. Ruth at home?"

---

[9]Edward Finegan and Niko Besnier, *Language: Its Structure and Use* (New York: Harcourt Brace Jovanovich Publishers, 1989), 344.

Another African-American caller to my home will identify himself indirectly if I answer the telephone and say, "My brother, how you doin'?" because he and I grew up together and played baseball together years ago in central Missouri; today, some 30 years later we are, quite coincidentally, living in the same city, attending the same church, and seeing each other frequently at the same social events. Note, however, that he *does not* say "Hello, Larry. This is David."

ADJACENCY AND UTTERANCE PAIRS

In a vein similar to Opening and Closing Sequences, Finegan and Besnier identify several **adjacency pairs**. Adjacency pairs are structural mechanisms society has found to be useful in organizing social conversations.[10] Questions, for example, are followed by Answers; an Invitation is followed by an Acceptance, and so on.

Question/Answer Utterance Pair

Speaker 1: Where's the morning paper?
Speaker 2: On the table.

Invitation/Acceptance Utterance Pair

Speaker 1: We're having some people for dinner Saturday and hope you can come.
Speaker 2: Thanks. We'd like that.

Assessment/Disagreement Utterance Pair

Speaker 1: Mr. Wilson is one of the great teachers around here!
Speaker 2: Oh? You obviously don't know him very well.

Apology/Acceptance Utterance Pair

Speaker 1: I'm sorry I called you so late last night.
Speaker 2: That's all right. No bother.

Summons/Acknowledgment Utterance Pair

Speaker 1: Say, Dave!
Speaker 2: Yes?

---

[10]Ibid., 341–344.

Adjacency pairs will follow a prescribed sequence, if they are to be successful and, given our definition of good English, comfortable to the participants. First, the pairs are *contiguous* and spoken by two speakers. When a speaker inserts an unrelated comment before giving an Answer to a Question, confusion and sometimes anger can result. For example:

Speaker 1:   Where's the morning paper?
Speaker 2:   They say it might snow tonight, and we're out of coffee. Have you seen my car keys? On the table.

On the other hand, a related response, not using a typical Question–Answer relationship, would be judged as acceptable:

Speaker 1:   Where's the morning paper?
Speaker 2:   It seems like the paper is getting later and later.

Second, the pairs are precisely *ordered*: Questions precede Answers, not vice versa (except on television's "Jeopardy"). Acceptances follow Invitations. Apologies can't be Accepted until they are offered.

Third, the pairs must be *matched*. It would be odd, for example, for the initial part of one adjacency pair to be followed by the second part of another.

Speaker 1:   We're having some people for dinner Saturday and hope you can come.
Speaker 2:   That's all right. No bother.

Elaine Chaika examines **utterance pairs**, which are similar to adjacency pairs. Utterance pairs are conversational sequences, too, in which the first utterance elicits a *prescribed* response. Common utterance pairs, according to Chaika, are:[11]

Greeting : Greeting
Question : Answer
Complaint : Excuse, Apology, or Denial
Request/Command : Acceptance/Rejection
Compliment : Acknowledgment
Farewell : Farewell

---

[11]Cited in Larry Andrews, *Language Exploration and Awareness: A Resource Book for Teachers*, 2nd ed. (Mahwah, NJ: Lawerence Erlbaum Associates. 1998), 169–170.

An opening sequence Greeting will elicit another Greeting in a prescribed reply. A Question prescribes an Answer. A Complaint calls for an Excuse, an Apology, or a Denial.

One of the profound features of oral language in its social uses is that we feel *compelled to reply* to those who initiate a conversation with us, as an examination of utterance pairs demonstrates. William Labov and David Fanshell describe **discourse preconditions**, unwritten and unspoken, that are at work: For example, when questions are asked, the questioner has a right or duty to ask a question; the one asked has a responsibility or obligation to give an answer.[12]

This Question: Answer precondition is implicitly understood by everyone in our society. It is the reason that when someone asks a question for which we have no answer we feel uncomfortable; we *must* reply we believe, and we must reply appropriately. An appropriate reply to a yes/no question is either "Yes" or "No" and we *must*, according to the precondition, use one of the appropriate replies. "Are you still beating your spouse?" is an old ploy based on this precondition. The precondition *compels* an answer, and it must be either "Yes" or "No."

Chaika extends the Labov-Fanshel precondition of Questions to cover *all* utterance pairs. Consequently, then, according to Chaika, not only does the Questioner have the right or duty to ask a question, but the Greeter has a right or duty to greet, the Complainer a right or duty to complain, and so on.[13]

We can summarize these amended discourse preconditions into the following:

DISCOURSE ROUTINE PRECONDITIONS

I. The first speaker has a right or duty to speak.
II. The second speaker has a responsibility or obligation to reply.

Closing sequences are as important as Opening Sequences. A Closing sequence cannot be used until at least one of the participants is ready for the conversation to end. Negotiating the timing of the Closing Sequence requires a keen notion of sensitivity, usually: The participants do not want to appear either curt or dawdling.

---

[12]Ibid., 170.

[13]Ibid.

We can't say, "I have no more to say on this matter." We can't say, "This conversation is finished." Rather than appear rude, we typically use socially acceptable *code words* to indicate that we're about to end a conversation: "Well . . . ," "So . . . " and "OK." being obvious and frequently used examples.

Speaker 1:   Well, it's been good seeing you.
Speaker 2:   Yeah! Take care.

Speaker A: So, do you think you can make it?
Speaker B: Sure! Thanks.

Speaker I: O.K., well, I think I'd better . . .
Speaker II: [Yeah, I need to get going, too.

Variations from the accepted conventions, just like other changes in the language, may be interpreted by some to represent social or linguistic decay. For example, here's a complaint recently sent to a newspaper advice columnist:

> Whatever happened to just plain "Goodbye?" [*sic*] It used to be a perfectly good word—a contraction of 'God be with ye'—but for reasons unknown, 'Goodbye' has fallen out of favor. In its place you get the pre-packaged exit line 'Have a nice day.' This hackneyed phrase is heard everywhere! Is there an appropriate response to this timeworn line?[14]

"Have a nice day" seems to be a rather harmless substitute for either "Goodbye," "Well, I'll be seeing you," or "So long." But, the letter demonstrates how riled some people can get when a language convention is tampered with.

On the other hand, some people like to toy with some of the conventions. It is fairly common, for instance, for some secretaries to conventionally ask those who have initiated a call to Mr. Executive, "May I tell him who's calling?"

A colleague of mine answers this question with a one-word reply: "Yes." That's all. He says no more.

Sometimes he varies the one-word answer with "Why? Who's he not talking to today?"

Another colleague uses a similar gambit when the telephone at home rings. If the caller asks, "Is Rolin [his son] there?" he'll frequently say, "Yes," then hang up the phone!

---

[14]"Have a Nice Day Raises Hackles," *Omaha (NE) World-Herald*, June 26, 1994.

I confess to having had a hand in convention baiting one evening. As my wife and I were driving to a restaurant with another couple, our conversation turned to the pseudofriendly practice of some waiters who introduce themselves to customers by announcing their first name. The four of us, thinking this convention was wearisome, plotted.

After having been seated, we were approached by our server who said, "Good evening. I'm Max. I'm really happy to be your server this evening." Acting out the plot we hatched, the four of us stood up, extended our hands as a sign of greeting and said, in turn: "Hi, I'm Jim." "Hello, I'm Mimi." "Hi, I'm Larry." "Hello, I'm Ruthie."

The waiter must have thought he had a quartet of loonies at Table 14!

TERMS OF ADDRESS CONVENTIONS

Whether to use a first name or a last name, and when either the first or last name is appropriate, or whether and when to use someone's title, and the like, is another sociocultural convention shaping our linguistic behavior. For example, in the culture in which I was reared, I learned early on to use the terms "Mom" and "Dad" with reference to my parents. This was the cultural norm, whether I was talking *about* my parents ("I can't go to the movie with you; Dad says I have to mow the lawn.") or *to* them ("Dad, can you please help me get the darned lawnmower started?").

You can imagine my astonishment when I was visiting a fifth-grade friend's house after school one day umpteen years ago and he said to his father, using the father's first name, "Les, can Larry and I have a coke?" Such brazen behavior! Was my friend completely devoid of manners?

Actually, my friend was following a usage pattern relatively, but clearly not solely, unique to his family. I believe the convention more often observed in the United States, but not universally, is for children to use a relationship name (Mother, Father, Mom, Dad, Mommy, Daddy, etc.) when they are talking to or talking about their parents.

Richard Hudson, an internationally recognized linguist at University College, the University of London, conducted an informal survey on family naming practices with members of the Language & Culture Discussion Group on the Internet. After analyzing the responses to his query, he speculated that addressing senior family members by their first names is still not the normal pattern and is likely, statistically, a minority practice.[15]

---

[15]Richard C. Hudson, "Naming Practices," posting to Language & Culture LISTSERV, July 11, 1995, language-culture@uchicago.edu.

I should add that the respondents to Prof. Hudson's admittedly unscientific survey were not only from the United Kingdom and the United States but from several countries.

I would speculate further that there are regions in the United States, however, particularly in the southern United States, where children will *never* address their parents by using the parents' first names; it simply isn't done. In other regions of the United States, the minority practice may be observed, however infrequently.

The conventions regarding naming practices can be studied more closely, by both you and your students, by completing the following chart, which was created by one of my students, Bill Collins. Naturally, the larger the number of participants completing the survey, the greater the likelihood that a clearer pattern of conventional naming practices will emerge. This activity could just as easily appear at the end of the chapter among the other Studend Explorations, but it seems especially relevant here.

TERMS OF ADDRESS

TERM	GIVE AN EXAMPLE	SITUATION (When and with whom is the term used?)
Nickname only		
First name only		
Mr. + last name		
Miss + last name		
Mrs. + last name		
Ms. + last name		
Ma'am		
Sir		
Title + last name		
Last name only		
Family relation + first name		
Family relation + last name		

CLASSROOM DISCOURSE

As you saw in chapter 3, Mary, Gary, and Mark had learned classroom discourse and were able to take on their appropriate roles with no adult direction or intervention. After having participated in any number of classroom discussions, they had implicitly learned how the teacher talks and how the students respond. For them, the roles followed a predictable formula.

I offer the following description of conventional classroom discourse because it is based on research and observations in a variety of classrooms. This is a description of what *is*, according to the research findings, not necessarily what *ought* to be:

1. Teachers do most of the talking in classrooms. Edwards and Mercer found that "across a wide range of teachers, classrooms and countries," teachers perform over 65% of the total talk.[16]

2. Teachers ask a lot of questions, and they already know most of the answers. Forestal found that 60% of the time teachers are talking, they are asking questions. The majority of these questions are "display" questions—questions for which the teacher is expecting one correct answer.[17] More often than not, "discussions like these are actually thinly disguised lectures.

3. Teachers do not wait for students to respond to questions. Forestal found that teachers usually give students 1 *second* to respond to a question.[18] What kind of an answer can you come up with if you have 1 second to think, to reflect? What kind of a question does a 1-second response elicit? Not an important one, I suggest.

The typical discussion in a classroom, based on these data, can be described by this simplistic formula: I-R-E.

I = the teacher Initiates a question.

R = a student Responds.

E = the teacher Evaluates the student's response.

Schematically, then, a discussion might look like this: I-R-E; I-R-E; I-R-E; I-R-E, and so on and so forth. I'll stop here, hoping that you'll be able to break the classroom discourse mold.

---

[16]David Edwards and Norman Mercer, *Common Knowledge: The Development of Understanding in the Classroom* (London: Heinemann, 1987), 20.

[17]Peter Forestal, "Talking: Toward Classroom Action. Perspectives on Small Group Learning," in Marvin Brubaker, et al. (eds.), *Perspectives on Small Group Learning: Theory and Practice* eds. Marvin Brubaker, Ryder Payne, and Kemp Rickett (Oakville, Ontario: Rubicon, 1990), 159.

[18]Ibid.

FOR YOUR INQUIRY AND PRACTICE:

Either audio- or videotape your classroom, or observe a classroom in which a discussion is planned. Focus your observation on the following:

1. Who's doing most of the talking?
2. How much "wait time" does the teacher allow for answers to questions?
3. Does the teacher evaluate, assess, or comment on every student response? Are students encouraged to elaborate?

Why is this focus on classroom discourse important?

THE COOPERATIVE PRINCIPLE

There's another way to describe and analyze conversations in an attempt to clarify how social talk succeeds or fails: the use of the **Cooperative Principle**. Describing how conversational speakers and partners cooperate with each other, illuminating the intricacies in oral communication, Paul Grice has defined the Cooperative Principle as:

> Make your conversational contribution such as is required, at the stage at which it occurs, by the accepted purpose or direction of the talk exchange in which you are engaged.[19]

The Cooperative Principle includes the following categories:

Category of Quantity. The Cooperative Principle's Quantity category is relatively simple: Speakers are expected (a) to provide as much information as is required (for the purposes of the current exchange), (b) but no more than is required.[20]

For example, if we ask Marilyn "Do you have any pets?," she will reply, "Yes, I have a cat." The category of Quantity allows us to assume, then, that she does not have other pets. She answered our question, we believe, by adhering to this category of the Cooperative Principle. Should we later discover that Marilyn also has a parakeet, a dog, and several

---

[19]Paul Grice, *Studies in the Way of Words* (Cambridge, MA: Harvard University Press, 1989), 26.

[20]Ibid.

hamsters, we would feel deceived. By violating the Quantity feature, Marilyn has violated the Cooperative Principle; she hasn't been a cooperative conversational partner.

The category of Quantity can be violated in an opposite manner, as well. Sometimes conversational partners will give more (oh, so agonizingly much, much more) information than was asked for. For example, we might casually ask Mary "Are you going shopping with us Sunday?" and receive the following tedious reply:

> Shopping? You must be joking. If you had any idea what my calendar looked like for the coming week, which starts with a meeting at 7:00 a.m. Monday, my mother's birthday by the way, and I forgot to call her last year because her birthday was on a Sunday and we were just swamped! I don't see how I can fit one more thing into my schedule and still have any time to sleep or eat.

About all that can be said about this tiresome and irksome reply is that if you ask certain kinds of people what kind of car they drive, they answer with a complete description of how the whole automobile was built! They tell us more than we really want or care to know. More generously, we can observe that this violation of Quantity makes the speaker an uncooperative— and tedious—conversational partner.

People who consistently violate Quantity by providing, on the one hand, too little information are known as secretive, sometimes as liars. Those who tell more than is necessary, on the other hand, are known as blabbermouths, boors, or even demagogues. Society will levy a heavy tax on them over time.

Grice adds an important note to the discussion of giving more information than is necessary. It might be claimed, for example, that doing so may not be a transgression but merely a waste of time. Grice contends, though, that overinformativeness may be confusing because it is apt to raise side issues and because it may also produce an indirect effect: Hearers may be misled, thinking there is some point to the excess information.[21]

Category of Relation.   This category assumes that what is said will be germane and relevant to the ongoing conversation.[22] An example of a relevant reply is illustrated in the Question/Answer utterance pair, described earlier. When following the Question "Where's the morning paper?," the

---

[21]Ibid., 26–27.

[22]Ibid., 27.

Answer "On the table" is a relevant comment. On the other hand, if we offer an invitation and say "We're having some people for dinner Saturday and hope you can come.", then "On the table." would not be relevant.

"Do you want to go to a movie next Friday?" is a Question/Invitation that calls for a predictable type of reply, one that will be relevant. "It's a stormy day and I have to call Uncle Freddy." is neither a cooperative nor a relevant response. It will be distracting, or it may create frustration or even anger.

Category of Manner. "Organization" could be a synonym to use in the discussion of this category, which assumes speakers will be both clear and orderly.[23] Dr. Allan Metcalf, Professor of English at MacMurray College and executive secretary of the American Dialect Society, calls President George W. Bush a language blunderer "of heroic stature," and points to this comment by President Bush, a classic violation of the category of Manner:

> And so, my state of the—my State of the Union—or state—my speech to the nation, whatever you want to call it, speech to the nation—I asked Americans to give 4,000 years—4,000 hours, over the next—the rest of your life—of service to America. That's what I asked—4,000 hours.[24]

Former President Bill Clinton has a reputation for being facile with the language, some believe too facile. Here is an example of one of Mr. Clinton's extemporaneous sentences, given as an answer to a reporter's question about the qualifications of a Secretary of State: "I want a Secretary of State who understands that we have obligations of continuity and obligations of change, and that basically the pillars of our national security and foreign policy ought to be a different but still very strong defense, a commitment to global growth and economic regeneration here, and the fulfilling of our responsibility as the world's sole superpower to try to promote democracy and freedom, and restrain the proliferation of weapons of mass destruction".[25]

What did he say? This stretch sentence proves that some politicians can answer questions in whole paragraphs. It also demonstrates that violations

---

[23]Ibid., 27.

[24]Allan Metcalf, *Presidential Voices* (Boston: Houghton Mifflin, 2004), 103–04.

[25]E. Leo McManus, "Presidential Rhetoric: Clinton Replaces Bush," *English Today*, October 1993, 14.

of manner—and in Clinton's case, violations of Quantity, as well—are bipartisan!

Category of Quality. We normally expect speakers and writers to say what they believe to be either true, or verifiable, or both.[26] Even when a conversation partner observes the categories of Quantity, Relevance, and Manner, a Quality violation makes the entire conversation (or writing) worthless, in the judgment of society. This category will not apply, of course, in joke-telling or humorous talk, but it certainly does apply to the vast majority of the social conversations we experience each day.

Speakers who violate this category of conversation will suffer the consequences. Sometimes they will be regarded as the constant group clown ("Can't you *ever* be serious?") and will not be taken seriously. Sometimes they will be recognized as individuals who are given to hyperbole ("Well, consider the source.") If their Quality violations are intentional and chronic, they will be avoided because everyone "knows" a liar when they see one!

The Cooperative Principle is routinely violated. Some of the violations come from those we may identify as wind-bags, unorganized, poor speakers, or liars. Other "violations" are not as serious or severe but simply are routine characteristics of oral discourse and conversations.

As chapters 1 and 7 illustrated, for example, structures that would ordinarily been classified as interrogatives really aren't interrogatives at all in some oral discourse, for example:

Speaker 1: Would you like to have this ticket to the concert?
Speaker 2: Is the Pope a Catholic?

Answering a Question with another Question technically violates the Cooperative Principle as it operates in adjacency pairs. In this example, however, Speaker 2's reply is not to be interpreted as a question.

Even when it appears that a respondent is being uncooperative, the conversational partners make adjustments and the Cooperative Principle is still at work. One of the reasons indirect speech acts "work" is the amount of personal and cultural knowledge and experiences shared by the participants. It's as if they are "talking between the lines."

Among the complicating features of indirect speech acts are the cultural values in the United States of a polite and an equal society. Although we may not want to be courteous or polite, and although we may privately

---

[26]Grice, *Studies in the Way,* 27.

believe that some people are more equal than others, we know that being courteous and behaving as if all were created equal are rotarian virtues good Americans are supposed to believe in.

Consequently, adjacency pairs are frequently altered so that they will adhere to cultural values. For example, in order to establish a more coequal atmosphere in my classrooms, I will often avoid initiating a Request/Command: Accept/Reject utterance routine and will substitute a Question/Answer pair by asking my students, "Will you please turn to page 99 in our text?"

I do this for a simple reason: in our culture it's bad to be dictatorial and give commands; it's good, on the other hand, to ask questions that sound like invitations, especially in classrooms! Actually, however, I'm telling and dictating to my students, "Turn now to page 99," but I'm *disguising* the Command.

Similarly, the question "Can you stop for a can of coffee on your way home?" is a Request/Command *disguised* as a question. Sometimes the disguise is intensified with the addition of "Can you stop for a can of coffee on your way home, *please*?" or the even sweeter, "Can you stop for a can of coffee on your way home, *please, honey*?"

You hear similarly disguised Request/Commands all the time. The following Request/Commands have been recently pawned off as Questions in my house:

> "Can you lower the volume on that Brubeck CD?"
>
> "Do you need to replace that old sweater?"
>
> "Is *that* what you're wearing to the party?"
>
> "Do you think you'll have time to take my things to the dry cleaner on your way to campus this morning?"

I'm certainly no genius, but I can tell you that I definitely know how to respond to these pseudo-Questions (actually Requests/Commands) asked to me by She Who Must Be Obeyed.

Sometimes we disguise Requests, primarily because we don't want to lose face. For example, instead of admitting that we're lost, forgetful, stupid, or all three, we'll ask for directions by saying: "Do you know the way to San Jose?" Or, "Excuse me, but do you have the time?" Others in our culture implicitly understand this feature of discourse, which is why they do not answer questions like the latter two with a simple "Yes" or "No. " However, there are those who love to toy with the conventions, which we've looked at earlier in this chapter.

Modesty is another public virtue, regardless of our private feelings about our accomplishments. As proud as we may be over a job promotion, a new article of clothing, a witty remark, and the like, we have been told over and over again: "Don't be a braggart!" Consequently, the Compliment: Acknowledgment utterance pair presents us with cultural etiquette problems.

Because of the societal virtue of Modesty, some people simply cannot accept and do not otherwise know how to Acknowledge a Compliment. They do not want to appear boastful. My friend Martha, for example, is a marvelous cook. (Actually, her name is Betty, but I have called her Martha for years, after the Martha in the Greek Scriptures who is always, seemingly, toiling in the kitchen.) At the conclusion of a meal she has prepared, people always compliment Martha because the food is always superbly, overwhelmingly, and totally magnificent; in acknowledging the Compliment, however, Martha always deflects Compliments by pointing out a weakness in the menu only she can know about ("I had to go next door to borrow an egg to fix this." Or, "I do wish our refrigerator made nicer ice cubes.").

Language users abide by a number of unwritten and unspoken contracts. The ability to use language with precision, elaboration, and spontaneity clearly has a liberating and enabling influence on us. Nevertheless, competent language users also intuitively know the rules of oral discourse routines, the social facts, and the principles of cooperative communication. If they decide to ignore the rules, it's certainly their choice to make, but they must be prepared for the social tax.

CMC AND "WRITTEN" CONVERSATION

CmC is the **acronym** (see chap. 5) used for *computer-mediated communication*. If you use e-mail, then you have used CmC. Computer-mediated communication is possibly the most widespread and most widely used technological development computer users around the world have experienced in the several years. Everybody, it seems, is using it.

E-mail has made a profound difference on the interactions I have with my students. At one time, I flatter myself to recall that students would stop by my office either to ask a question about an assignment or, simply, just to chat. Today, that seldom happens and I miss it. The reason for the change is e-mail. When a student has a question today, he or she will send me an e-mail message. On balance, I'm "talking" to more students than I used to, but e-mail has virtually replaced my office conversations with students.

E-mail has had much wider influences than those just described. Based on earlier estimates, it's safe to say that more than 829 million people in the world are using e-mail.[27] Some of those use e-mail from home computers for personal business; some are in an educational setting; others are in the corporate world. E-mail has become "a place for everything, from formal documents, to single-sentence greetings, and the functions of multi- recipiency and attachments make it a vehicle for newsletters, announcements, and reports."[28]

E-mail is so widespread throughout the business infrastructure that many organizations have had to establish policies governing the use of e-mail, primarily in an attempt to restrict its use to company business. "Some organizations totally ban the personal use of e-mail and IM [instant messaging] systems. Some allow limited use. If you're using it for personal reasons, and personal use is banned, that would be grounds for termination."[29]

Describing an earlier technological development, Postman points out that in creating the telegraph, Samuel F. B. Morse erased state boundaries, collapsed entire regions, and wrapped the North American continent in an information grid.[30] Similarly, I would expand, CmC has erased boundaries between whole *countries*, has collapsed entire *continents*, and has wrapped the *planet Earth* in an information grid!

Although CmC has become worldwide in a relatively brief period of time, its vehicles are being revised and updated, even as you read this sentence. Given this state of continuing change, what you're reading here about CmC may have already become either somewhat dated or even obsolete by the time you read this section of the text. Although the conventions governing CmC are in a state of flux, there are a number of observations we can make about the conventions appearing in this new form of conversation.

Please note that the last word in the preceding sentence is "conversation." This may seem odd, given the fact that when you read CmC messages on

---

[27]Li Lan, "E-mail: A Challenge to Standard English?", *English Today*, October 2000, 23.

[28]Ibid.

[29]"Watch What Is Written in E-Mails, Instant Messages," *Lincoln (NE) Journal Star,* July 26, 2004.

[30]Neal Postman, *Amusing Ourselves to Death* (New York: Viking Penguin, 1985), 65.

your computer screen, you are reading language in print. Nevertheless, one of the more remarkable features of CmC is its *speech like nature*. Although CmC is *written* language, it looks and behaves like *spoken language*.[31]

Consider this "conversation" between Brian and Les:

B1: you flying directly to DC on Monday night, right?
B2: you still flying to DC monday night?
L1: as it stands now, meeting on weds?
L2: instead of tues
B3: idiot Hess seemed to think you were there tues morning
B4: thot that mtg from 9 to 10 would solve
B5: if you not in ny I'm going to have mtg changed to wedne.[32]

This exchange disregards many of the conventions of printed language while it simultaneously appropriates several conventions typically associated with oral language. Some of the oral language conventions observed in this written language exchange between Brian and Les include:

- Using "right" as a tag question (see B1).
- Incomplete sentences (see L1)
- Interpersonal involvement, seen in the use of personal pronouns.
- Informal vocabulary ("idiot").
- Lack of need for conventional spellings ("ny," "mtg," "wedne").
- Strategies for brevity.[33]

The use of tag questions is customarily, not always, of course, but conventionally, used in oral discourse. We frequently say in a spoken discourse, a conversation, "I really like that new Dianna Krall CD, don't you?" In this instance, the tag question "don't you?" is a turn-taking marker; the first speaker is asking or inviting the conversational partner to speak.

Our oral conversations are characteristically marked by incomplete sentences, lacking the typical S-V-O pattern. In a typical *conversation*, we'll hear exchanges like:

---

[31]Denise Murray, "CmC," *English Today*, July 1990, 42.

[32]Ibid.

[33]Ibid.

Speaker 1: "Tired tonight?"
Speaker 2: "Umm. Busy day."

Conversations are also full of informal vocabulary. In written language, take this textbook as an example, we seldom use a term like "idiot" as a derogatory term (see B3). Back in chapters 1, 2, and 3, I might have taken exception to the language usage pronouncements of some prescriptivists, but I did not call them "idiots," "mental slugs," or "bald-headed Nazis." Terms like these might be used in the oral language of Howard Stern, Don Imus, Rush Limbaugh, or other radio or TV "shock-jocks," but most people would object to their appearing as expository prose in a university-level textbook.

In our uses of oral language, we'll frequently pay little attention to conventional spelling; "conventional written spelling" and "conversational uses of language" are dichotomies. We frequently, for example, speak words we can't spell, but we seldom write words we can't spell.

As the exchange between Brian and Les illustrates, brevity is valued. So it is with most of our conversations. As one observer has noted, e-mail, like conversation, favors the terse. Short lists, brief comments, and "one-liners" are often the units of thought in personal CmC.[34] For example, I recently sent an e-mail request to an adviser in my college's Student Services Center; I asked the adviser if she would please put a student-advising form in my mailbox. My request elicited the following "conversational" e-mail reply: "Larry. Will do. Laurie."

Further supporting the value of brevity, some e-mail authors will use abbreviations for common expressions, such as writing "Thx" for *Thanks* or *Thank you,* and "BTW" for *By the way.*

There are other novel uses of language in e-mail, also. Emphasis can be indicated by using either the italics or underscore function in an e-mail system (*italics,* *underscore*), but if the e-mail system doesn't have these functions, then all caps or asterisks will be used, as in "You MUST turn in your assignment on time," or "You * must * turn in your assignment on time."[35]

In oral language exchanges, we always clarify or intensify our intended meanings through the uses of a variety of nonverbal signals: a raised eye brow, a shrug of the shoulders, a wink, and the like. The subtle cues of

---

[34]John D. Cumming, "The Internet and the English Language," *English Today,* January 1995, 7.

[35]Gao Liwei, "Digital Age, Digital English," *English Today,* July 2001, 18.

voice inflection and body language are often lost on a computer screen, so e-mail correspondents will frequently make sure that intended jokes are identified by including a sideways grin, :-), or by the parenthetical addition of the printed word ("smile"). Displeasure can be accented by including a sideways frown, :-(.[36] One study found that some special CmC feature appeared at least once in every 32 words![37]

CmC, a relatively new form of discourse, is still developing its social, personal, and business routines. Its conventions are still in a state of flux, are not yet codified, and are taking shape on our computer screens as we speak, so to say.

FOR YOUR INQUIRY AND PRACTICE:

Summarize some discourse conventions (unspoken rules) observed by the participants in the following language events:

1. A telephone conversation between friends of the same age, same gender; between a 12-year-old and an aunt or uncle.
2. Meeting your major professor, principal, or superintendent in a supermarket checkout line.
3. A parent–teacher conference.
4. An interview with an excellent school system where you want to teach.

REVIEWING THE CHAPTER

Part One: *Place a (✓) beside each statement made in this chapter.*

___ 1. Social conventions are more universal than are rules and policies.

___ 2. Social conventions evolve from social values.

___ 3. Violators of discourse conventions are admired for their non conformity.

___ 4. True friends will not violate the cooperative principle.

___ 5. Language conventions are learned incidentally.

---

[36]Whitney Bolton, "CmC and E-Mail: Casting a Wider Net," *English Today*, October 1991, 35.

[37]Beverly A. Lewin and Yonatan Donner, "Communication in Internet Message Boards", *English Today*, July 2002, 34.

Part Two: *Place a (✓) beside each statement you think the text would agree with. Be prepared to explain* your answer.

___ 6. The environment affects language choices just like it affects clothing choices.

___ 7. The cooperative principle and the discourse preconditions are related.

___ 8. Cohesion matters more in oral rather than written language.

___ 9. "Spoken e-mail" is an acceptable oxymoron.

___ 10. Speakers of different ages follow the same discourse rules.

Part Three: *Place a (✓) beside each statement you agree with, based on what you know and what you've read in this chapter. Be prepared to explain your answer.*

___ 11. When in Rome, do as the Romans.

___ 12. Be neither the first nor the last to accommodate the new.

___ 13. Dress for success.

___ 14. Teamwork and individualism are not compatible.

___ 15. You can usually judge a book by its cover.

STUDENT EXPLORATIONS FOR DISCOURSE ROUTINES AND SOCIAL CONVENTIONS

EXPLORATION: X + Y = Z
DIRECTIONS: Make a list of some words you've used in your math classes that are seldom if ever used in informal conversations (like *sine, quotient, logarithm*).

1. Are there any words with special meanings in math that are also used in informal conversations?

2. Why are some words used exclusively in a particular content or subject matter area?

3. Would you agree that every content area in school is defined primarily by the language it uses? Why or why not?

***** ***** *****

EXPLORATION: It's Discourse, of Course
DIRECTIONS: To whom would you most likely say the following?

A. "Yo, dude. What's up? Wanna hang out later? By the way, cool shirt."
B. "Good morning. How are you today? Can we visit later today? Say, I really like your shirt."
C. "Good to see you. I'd like to talk with you sometime. Nice shirt!"

1. How do you decide how to talk to different people?
2. Does different language change the meanings in these examples?
3. Why do we use different language, depending on who our conversational partner might be?

***** ***** *****

EXPLORATION: Titles
DIRECTIONS: Watch the 10:00 o'clock or 11:00 o'clock news on the same television channel for 1 week, focusing your attention on one use of language: Under what circumstances and how do the broadcasters and reporters refer to people "in the news"? Do they always call the governor of the state "Governor"? Do they always refer to private citizens as "Mister," "Mrs.," or "Ms."? Do they sometimes use the first name of the individual being interviewed or talked about?

1. Are titles used for both men and women?
2. Are titles used for all people, regardless of gender or racial or religious background?
3. Who, and under what circumstances, is a person in the news referred to by his or her *first* name?
4. For which groups are titles most frequently used: elected officials (local, state, or national?), representatives of the military, members of the clergy?
5. What can you conclude from your observations about the station's terms-of-address policy? Does the policy treat all people equally?
6. Because thousands of viewers in your community watch this channel's newscasts nightly, weekly, and monthly, will the newscasters' and reporters' habits affect the *viewers' attitudes* toward those person interviewed or talked about or the *groups* they represent?

[Vary this Exploration by substituting a local or state radio or newspaper.]

***** ***** *****

EXPLORATION: Do You Hear What I Hear?
DIRECTIONS: Have you ever seen an adult walk into a room, maybe like yours at home, and ask, "You call this clean?" Or, did you ever watch a teacher enter unexpectedly a room full of talking classmates, and hear the teacher ask: "Do I hear noise in this room?" Questions like these really aren't *questions*. What are they?

1. Can you think of several examples similar to those just mentioned, which *say* one thing but *mean* another?
2. Why do we sometimes talk *indirectly*, saying one thing but actually meaning another?

***** ***** *****

EXPLORATION: Predicting Language
DIRECTIONS: Have you noticed that you can often predict how a speaker will end a sentence? Because you know the speaker well or because you know a lot about the topic (or both), you *know* how the sentence will end.

For each item in the following *series* of statements, identify (a) *who* the speaker is (generally, not a specific name), (b) *where* or *how* the statement was used, and (c) *who* is the intended receiver of the statement or message. Be prepared to defend your answers with specifics.
Here are the statements:

a. Ladies and gentlemen of the jury
b. Roger, Tango 778
c. This is to certify that
d. Dearly beloved
e. Soaring Temperatures to Continue
f. We'll be back right after this
g. Final Reduction
h. May I help you
i. Drive thru
j. Ladies
k. Beauty tips for cold weather
l. Off
m. Narrow ruled with margin
n. Shake before using
o. Stir until dissolved

***** ***** *****

EXPLORATION: Language Strategies

[Note to the teacher: You will need to bring to class a variety of magazines for this activity. The greater the variety, the better.]

DIRECTIONS: Select one of the magazines from the supply available. After you have had an opportunity to study the advertisements in one magazine, discuss the following questions:

1. Is the intended audience for the magazine primarily male or female? Is the language used in the ads more appealing to male or female readers? How do you know?

2. Share your observations about the ads in a small group. Do others in your group agree with your observations about the language patterns found in the ads? Is the agreement or disagreement related to male/female membership of your group?

3. Do magazines use a particular style of language intended to "speak to" the intended audience? Is this an appropriate or inappropriate use of language?

***** ***** *****

EXPLORATION: Telephone Discourse

[Note to the teacher: Task Cards will be needed for this activity. Sample tasks might include: (a) ordering pizza for a party; (b) getting a telephone number for L.A. Gear in Los Angeles; (c) Calling the state highway patrol for a report on interstate highway conditions; (d) Making a call on the 900 "Teen Line"; (e) calling your best friend to ask if he or she will call a special someone you like to see if that special someone likes you.]

DIRECTIONS: Using the two prop telephones in the class, role-play a telephone conversation in front of the class, using the Task Card you've drawn at random from the teacher. You will need one partner to complete this activity. After all of the conversations have been completed, let everyone answer the following questions:

1. How would you describe the differences in the language used in the different telephone conversations? Give specific examples to illustrate your answers.

2. What are the circumstances in the different conversations that affect how language will be used?

3. How is appropriate language use determined? What are some of the factors that determine how we will talk in different contexts?

***** ***** *****

EXPLORATION: Magazine Interviews
DIRECTIONS: In either the school library or media center, or at a news-stand or drugstore, locate a magazine containing an interview with a politi-cian, rock star, or film or athletic celebrity. Read the interview, then answer the following questions:

1. What is the purpose of the interview? Is the interviewer trying to reveal the "real" person behind the famous image? Is the purpose to bring forth an aspect of the subject's life that has heretofore not been widely known? Is there some other purpose?

2. What is the role of the interviewer? Does the interviewer use many or few questions? Does the interviewer become a part of the story, or is the interviewer part of the background?

3. What kinds of unstated "rules" seem to govern how interviews are conducted and then published in magazines?

***** ***** *****

EXPLORATION: Say Again . . .
DIRECTIONS: Watch an episode of "Barney", "MisterRogers Neighbor-hood", or "Reading Rainbow". Pay particular attention to the language used by Barney, Mr. Rogers, and the Rainbow host.

1. How would you describe the speech patterns used by these speak-ers? Considering their audience, do you think their speech patterns are or are not appropriate?

2. What would happen, do you think, if these speakers would use their television voices in the restaurant where they have lunch? In an automobile garage, explaining to a mechanic what's wrong with their car?

3. When is it either acceptable or unacceptable to change our speaking voices?

***** ***** *****

EXPLORATION: Find the Catch
DIRECTIONS: Some television ads seem too good to be true. Some ads want you to buy exercise equipment that will change your body structure and shape in 30 days, or even less! Other ads offer salves, ointments, and pills that will accomplish the same bodybuilding results ("Get rid of ugly cellulite!"). Too good to be true?

1. How would you describe the language in these ads? Is it scientific, medical, or technical, as we might expect?
2. Do you think ads like these tell the *whole* truth?
3. Do we expect advertisements to tell us the whole truth? The truth, *mostly*? The truth, *sometimes*? How much truth do we expect?

***** ***** *****

EXPLORATION: When Is Journalism Yellow?
DIRECTIONS: Collect and read two or three issues of tabloid newspapers that specialize in writing about fantastic events, secrets of famous people, and the like.

1. Do the articles cite sources for the information contained in the articles? Are the stories based on real evidence?
2. Are the articles telling the whole truth? The truth, mostly? Or the truth, hardly? How do you know?
3. Point out specific uses of language that would make the unsuspecting reader believe what's being reported is 100% true.

***** ***** *****

EXPLORATION: The Three Bears; or, the Trio of Stocky Mammals
DIRECTIONS: After listening to someone read aloud "Goldilocks and the Three Bears," ask for three groups of four people to reenact one of the scenes from the story. Which scene a group selects is left up to that group. The element of the story that will be changed, however, is the setting: the time and place. Have one group reenact Goldilocks in the original setting; one group's reenactment will be set in frontier Oklahoma in 1860; the third group's scene will take place in a posh condominium, today.

1. Discuss how the language used by the characters accurately reflected their age, locale, and relationships.
2. What seems to affect our language use the strongest: our age, where we are, or the people we're with?

***** ***** *****

EXPLORATION: It's Complimentary, Thank You
DIRECTIONS: Why do some people find it difficult to accept a compliment? When compliments are offered ("What a neat shirt!"), you sometimes don't hear a simple "Thank you," but what you hear is: "What? This old rag?"

For 1 day, focus your attention on the *complimenting language* you observe at school, on the bus, at the mall, and any other place you go. After collecting a day's worth of observed compliments, share your answers to the following questions with the class:

1. How many compliments did you observe? Is the number surprisingly large or surprisingly small?
2. Are compliments more common among men or women? Older or younger speakers?
3. How did those receiving the compliments respond? Were they pleased? Uneasy? What were some of their responses?
4. Why do so many people receiving a compliment avoid saying "Thank you"?

***** ***** *****

EXPLORATION: Literary License
DIRECTIONS: Select a well-known passage from literature, like Hamlet's soliloquy on death or Huck Finn's decision to save slave Jim. You and your teacher and classmates can identify several other passages. Rewrite your passage as it would appear in at least two of the following:

- an advice column
- a romance novel
- a textbook
- a TV soap opera
- a radio or TV advertisement
- a scene from an action-adventure movie
- a music video

1. What changes did you make, and why?
2. How did the changing audiences affect your choices of purpose, words, and tone?
3. How many different styles of writing are there, anyway? Why do different styles follow different rules?

***** ***** *****

EXPLORATION: Impersonating Language
DIRECTIONS: Pick out some public figures—politicians, athletes, entertainers—who are commonly impersonated on TV. ("Saturday Night

Live" continues to do this.). Make a list of the verbal and non verbal features the comedians are impersonating.

1. What are the verbal and nonverbal features you've identified?
2. If you were a public figure, what would a comedian do to impersonate you?
3. What sorts of "rules" or habits do the public figures seem to follow? What about you?

***** ***** *****

EXPLORATION: Say What, Say How?
DIRECTIONS: Select three to four television programs you enjoy and pay close attention to the characters' language. Make a note of recurring things they may say and how they say them.

1. Who is the targeted audience for each program, and how does the language used by the characters appeal to each audience?
2. In what ways do scripts and their language "fit" an audience?

***** ***** *****

EXPLORATION: I Wonder If Someone Could Help Me With This?
DIRECTIONS: With a partner, improvise one or two of the following situations, being faithful to the tone established:

- "Since you're going out to your car, do you think you could take the trash to the garage?"
- "I think the dog may want to go outside. Could you check on her?"
- "I'm so tired tonight, and the bathroom really needs to be cleaned."
- "Oh, there's the phone. I'm sure it's not for me."
- "Gosh, my back hurts today. Is that chair you're sitting in comfortable?"

1. Why don't we always say *exactly* what we mean?
2. Why do we sometimes avoid *telling*, *asking*, or *directing*?

***** ***** *****

EXPLORATION: O.J.T. = On-the-Job Talking
DIRECTIONS: Almost every place of employment or any other field of special interest (like a hobby) uses a special language.

1. Think about the place where you work, a hobby you enjoy, or an extracurricular activity you participate in. Make a list of words you especially use in this context and may not use in others.
2. How do these terms manage to be so important? Is learning them required or optional? Why?

***** ***** *****

EXPLORATION: How Do You Wink in Print?
DIRECTIONS: In oral language we can always shrug our shoulders, wink, smile, raise an eyebrow, or roll our eyes in order to emphasize the meaning of a spoken message. We can't do this with *written* language. How do we accomplish these emphases in written communication?

1. Make a list of ways writers emphasize parts of what they're trying to communicate. Sometimes they use words in capital letters, like "CAUTION" or "WARNING." Sometimes they use *italics* or **bold-face** print.
2. How are these conventions of written language helpful to readers?

***** ***** *****

EXPLORATION: The Context Made Me Do It
DIRECTIONS: Please read the following quotations:

- "They call me Mr. Tibbs!" (From *In the Heat of the Night)*
- "I wish you would stop bein' so good to me, Cap'n." (From *Cool Hand Luke*)
- "I'm sorry, Father. I didn't know."
  "Why are you sorry; because I'm a priest, or because you feel it's necessary to change your language to suit me? Well, don't. It only makes liars out of us both." (From *Going My Way*)
- "Yes, Daddy; No, Daddy; well, I don't care, Daddy."
  "Son, you can call me Father, you can call me Jake, you can even call me a son-of-a-bitch, but if you ever call me Daddy again, I'll knock you on your butt." (From *Big Jake*)
- "Yes, officer sir, we just sittin' here . . . restin' . . . me and Miss Daisy. We ain't doin' nothin' wrong."
  "Why, don't that beat all! A nigger and a old Jew lady travelin' together. My God." (From *Driving Miss Daisy*)

- "In this courtroom you will address me as 'Your Honor,' or you'll be thrown out and held in contempt of court!" (From an episode of *Perry Mason*)

1. Based on your reading of these quotations, and given what you may know about the films or television series each one comes from, how do people learn how to address those of higher authority? What happens if we us an improper term of address?

***** ***** *****

EXPLORATION: Yes, No, Well, Maybe So
DIRECTIONS: Think about these situations, all of which you want to say "No" to, then answer the questions that follow.

- Your mother tells you to take your younger brother or sister to the park.
- Your new boss asks you to work a double shift.
- Your teacher asks you to represent your class at a faculty meeting.
- Your neighbors want you to pick up their mail while they're out of town.
- Your grandmother tells you to bring your "significant other" to the Thanksgiving dinner at her house.

1. How would you say "No" in each of these situations?
2. Why is saying "No" easier in some contexts, and more difficult in other contexts?
3. Why does our language change from one context to another?

CHAPTER 8

Regional, Social, and Historical Variations

> *Language doesn't exist in a vacuum. It*
> *reflects all the life and variety and*
> *change and divisions which exist in society.*
> —David Crystal, *Who Cares About English Usage?*

Before you read this chapter, let's survey some of your linguistic attitudes. When you hear someone pronounce a word differently from the way you normally pronounce it, what's your reaction? How do you feel? What do you think about the person using the different pronunciation? Finally, where do your reactions come from?

WORDS, TOOLS, AND VARIATIONS

It's not unusual for teachers to compare *words* with *tools*.[1] In my garage I have four bookshelves, each one representing storage space for different kinds of tools. One bookshelf has a collection of tools used for interior and exterior house-painting jobs. Another bookshelf is where I keep my fishing paraphernalia. One bookshelf holds home-repair tools. The fourth bookshelf is my storage space for automobile-cleaning and maintenance tools.

Depending on the job at hand, whether I'm painting the trim around the garage doors or the walls in my study, I'll select the brushes or rollers most appropriate for the task. Whether I'm going fishing for bass in a local lake

---

[1]Larry Andrews, *Language Exploration and Awareness: A Resource Book for Teachers*, 2nd ed. (Mahwah, NJ: Lawrence Erlbaum Associates, 1998), 195.

or for crappie in a neighboring state, I'll select the most appropriate fishing rods and the tackle bag containing the lures most likely to attract the species I'm fishing for. Different automobile-cleaning tasks call for different tools, just like hanging a new print or changing a leaky faucet will require different tools. The intriguing fact remains, however, that my friends Larry Routh or Lee Naphew will use the same tools I might use for a home-repair task, but they will use the tools differently from ways I might use them, that is to say, with skill! Similarly, my father-in-law and I might select identical fishing rods and the same lures, but we'll use them differently.

The introductory analogy suggests to us that because people can use different tools for different purposes, they will use words differently, too. Consider how we produce a wide variety of linguistic creations, such as poems, shopping lists, laws for governments, letters to our friends, short stories, novels, reports, bills of sale, a last will and testament, a textbook, and so on, with word tools.

The ways a painter applies his or her vision through his brushes and paints will vary from studio to studio. His craft and technique enable him to create a portrait or a landscape that bears his artistic "signature." You can easily identify, for example, a work by Van Gogh, Gaugin, or Rembrandt.

The idea of characteristic *signatures* is familiar to those who enjoy music, too. A jazz enthusiast will be able to distinguish between the pianos of Dave Brubeck or Fats Waller in a moment; the same jazz fan will not likely confuse the singing of Johnny Adams or Joe Turner, or the big-band sounds of Duke Ellington, Stan Kenton, Count Basie, or Woody Herman. Country music fans would never confuse the voices of Trace Adkins or George Strait, or Reba Mackentire or Sara Evans.

To recall an idea from chapter 1, remember that people do not use language just like everybody else uses it. Like the painters or musicians, for instance, a writer will apply her vision through her talent at selecting and applying the tools of her trade—words—enabling her to create a work that bears her artistic *signature*. If you read a literary selection written by Emily Dickinson, then read one written by Toni Morrison, you'll recognize their differences right away. These two writers use language in different and unique ways, and each writer's use will bear her signature. Professional writers, however, are not the only ones who use language in characteristically personal ways.

It is well known that there are no two snowflakes just alike. Similarly, fingerprints are unique to each human. The same is true with the way each person uses language. This includes you, me, and every other person you know. The term **idiolect** is used to describe the uniquely individual ways each person uses written and spoken language. Individuals distinguish themselves from all other persons in a variety of ways, and their personal language use, their idiolect, is an important one.

The fact that each speaker or writer uses language in unique ways is illustrated by the omnipresent, almost off-hand comments we hear when a description of a recent conversation is recalled and one of the participants says, "You know, I can just hear Uncle Pete saying that!" or "Yes, that sounds exactly like something Mother would say!" We not only accept but we even enjoy and relish the distinctly individual uses of language we observe in the language of Uncle Pete, Mother, or any other person we like. Conversely, some people find the language differences exhibited by others to be unsettling, even intolerable, perhaps. Sometimes, on the other hand, individual speakers feel insecure when they are faced with a challenge of giving a report in class, at work, at church, or in some other public forum. (See chap. 3 and the discussion of the curriculum objective of **spontaneity**. They are afraid that the language pronunciations they use might cause them embarrassment. This is the downside of linguistic variation.

AMERICAN ENGLISH AND DIALECTS

The dominant language in the United States is **American English**, as you know. It is referred to by linguists as *American* English in order to distinguish it from *British* English, *Canadian* English, *Australian* English, and the like. Under the American English umbrella, there are numerous dialects.

Though some object to the use of the word *American* in the term American English because it subsumes, they believe, citizens of North America who don't live in the United States, I use American English because the overwhelming majority of linguists in the world use the term to describe the dominant language spoken in the United States.

Determining whether two varieties are either different languages or different dialects of the same language has been controversial, as almost all language topics are. Linguists usually use the criterion of **mutual intelligibility** as the litmus test. If two speech varieties are not mutually intelligible, that is, if speakers don't understand each other, then the varieties are usually considered separate languages. On the other hand, if the varieties are mutually intelligible, that is, if two speakers can still understand each other despite their different ways of pronouncing some words and despite their use of different words to name, identify, describe, or signify the same things, then they are using different dialects of the same language.

If you were to describe the *typical American* represented in the term **American English**, whom would you select? A department store clerk in Atlanta? A schoolteacher in Brooklyn? A carpenter in Minneapolis? A convenience store clerk in Dallas? A newspaper reporter in Des Moines? A realtor in Los Angeles? A police officer in Tucson? A beautician in Boston?

All of these people live in the United States. If we assume, moreover, that they are native American English speakers, it is very likely that the ways they use American English will differ to some degree. Their uses of American English will be mutually intelligible, but there will likely be a few ways their languages will differ. They might pronounce words like *bird*, *park*, or *either* differently. Their evening meal might be either *supper* or *dinner*. If they are having chicken for a meal, it might be prepared in either a *fry pan*, a *frying pan*, or a *skillet*. Their differing pronunciations and their using different words for the same event, object, or idea will not diminish their *typical American* status. These are exemplary Americans, and the differences observed in their language use represents the fact that they speak different dialects of the same language, American English.

Where is this discussion heading? Well, for the purposes of this text, we define American English as the dominant language in the United States, comprised of different dialects, which means that American English is not a unitary, single set of established linguistic behaviors. To the contrary, American English is a composite, the several dialects used by the typical Americans we described earlier.

VARIATIONS IN AMERICAN ENGLISH

Some people believe that *Standard English* is derived from some purer form of language, and even if there are different dialects in this country, one is "standard" and is preferred over all of the others. Some also believe that Standard English has direct ties to the British English that came to this country in the 17th century in the mouths of the colonists and, being the "founding language" of the United States, is the standard and is preferred. As we have observed before, however, the term Standard English is often difficult to define with precision.

Tom McArthur summarizes a common position among many linguists when he says that Standard English is a "widely used term that resists easy definition." More pointedly, he adds, "Some consider its meaning self-evident," whereas others see Standard English as "a convenient fiction, built on social elitism and educational privilege."[2] As people disagree on the definitions of Standard English, they also disagree on the definitions of American English.

Demo makes this issue clear when he says that "*Standard English* is a useful construct, especially for education, but it encompasses a range of dialects. A formal, standard variety of English, as reflected in dictionaries and grammars, is associated with written language, but it is unlikely that anyone speaks it. Speech communities use an informal standard that is a more flexible variety."[3]

The definition of American English, in my view, will vary just like the definition of *pizza*. What constitutes a pizza will depend on whether you're ordering your pizza in New York City, Chicago, San Francisco, St. Louis, or San Antonio. What constitutes *clothing fashion* for any age group will depend on whether one is buying clothes in Seattle, Los Angeles, Las Vegas, Houston, New Orleans, or Tallahassee. We could extend these examples of variability to almost any form of human behavior in U.S. cultures, but you already get the idea. If we can accept the fact that the ways food is prepared and the ways people dress will vary, can we also accept the fact that the ways they use American English will vary, too? The term *Standard American English* (SAE) is an idealized concept. SAE is a consolidation, a composite, of different dialects. Of course, the similarities among the dialects will outnumber the differences, but the differences, the variations are evident. The point is, SAE is not a unitary or a single or a fixed linguistic code.

FOR YOUR INQUIRY AND PRACTICE:

The traditional Thanksgiving Day dinner in the United States usually includes the basics of turkey, dressing, mashed potatoes, and gravy. In addition to these entrees, many families have an additional side dish that *must* be on the dinner table if the meal is to be an official Thanksgiving Day dinner. Does your family have a side-dish like this?

---

[2]Tom McArthur, ed., *The Oxford Companion to the English Language* (Oxford: Oxford University Press, 1992), 982.

[3]Douglas A. Demo, *Dialects in Education* (n.d.), http:www.cal.org/resources/RGOs/dialects.html.

Survey others to see whether they have an additional "must-have" side dish. How does this activity relate to our discussion of American English?

AFRICAN-AMERICAN VERNACULAR ENGLISH

An interesting and often overlooked contribution to American English was made by the slaves who were brought to this country by the early colonists. African Americans, the third largest minority group in the United States, have a unique cultural and linguistic history in this country. Their West African ancestors began arriving in what is now the United States about a decade after the British colonists. Whereas European immigrants came voluntarily, looking for new opportunities in America, West Africans came involuntarily—under compulsion and often in chains—and could look forward only to a life of slavery.[4]

Not only did the Anglo-European colonists dictated the arrival of the West Africans to the United States, but they also dictated where and how the West Africans would live. Consequently, the institution of slavery made it impossible for the slaves to be assimilated into the dominant culture, as the Anglo-European colonists could, or to maintain their culture under circumstances of their own choosing, as the Anglo-Europeans did. Therefore, because of these conditions, **African-American Vernacular English (AAVE)**, sometimes called **Black English Vernacular (BEV)** or **Ebonics,** developed differently from any other American language variety.[5]

One might assume, then, that AAVE has been influenced more by American English than vice-versa. However, a number of American English words are almost certain to have their etymological roots in West African terms, such as *jazz, tango, jumbo, impala, zombie, limber,* and *samba.*[6]

As you have read earlier (see chap. 5), American English contains many **borrowings** from other languages. Borrowing words from other languages is just one way the American English lexicon continues to reinvent itself. A small sampling of borrowed words, to supplement our chapter 5 discussion, include *kangaroo* (Aboriginal Australian); *commando* (Afrikaans);

---

[4]Nancy Faires Conklin and Margaret A. Lourie, *A Host of Tongues: Language Communities in the United States* (New York: The Free Press (Macmillan), 1983), 23.

[5]Ibid.

[6]Margaret Wade-Lewis, "The Status of Semantic Items From African Languages in American English," *The Black Scholar,* Summer 1993, 26.

moccasin, pecan, squash, and *igloo* (American Indian); *admiral* (Arabic); *Santa Claus* and *luck* (Dutch); *sauna* (Finnish); *coach* (Hungarian); *blarney* (Gaelic); *Sabbath, Satan,* and *hallelujah* (Hebrew).[7]

You can add to the list of borrowings additional borrowed words from the West African languages of the early slaves: *goober* (for peanut); *chigger, sweet talk,* and *banjo*.[8] Not only did the slaves learn American English, but they contributed to the American English language, as well.

THE DEVELOPMENT OF AAVE

AAVE continued its development long after the end of the Civil War. Although AAVE is not, in my view, a *dialect* of SAE, it represents another variation of the English heard in the United States. Some of the features that distinguish AAVE are:

- No final -*s* in the third-person singular tense (*he walk, she come*).
- No use of the verb "to be" in the present tense when it is used as a linking verb within a sentence (*They real fine, If you interested.*).
- The use of the verb *be* to mark habitual activity (*Sometime they be walkin round here.*).
- Use of *be done* in the sense of "will have" (*We be done washed those cars real soon.*).
- Use of *it* to express "existential meaning," heard in the SAE "there" (*It's a girl in my room called Kenetta.*).
- Use of double negatives involving the auxiliary verb at the beginning of a sentence (*Won't nobody do nothin bout that.*).[9]

These examples of AAVE *do not* represent a degenerate language. They represent a use of a variety of English that followed a different path to its own pattern of regularization.

It is important to point out that AAVE—which is an *idealized* concept, just like SAE—is certainly not spoken by all African Americans; similarly, someone born in Boston does not automatically speak Bostonian English.

---

[7]Robert Hendrickson, *American Talk: The Words and Ways of American Dialects* (New York: Penguin Books, 1986), 25–29.

[8]Ibid., 231–133.

[9]David Crystal, *The Cambridge Encyclopedia of Language*, 2nd ed. (Cambridge: Cambridge University Press, 1997), 35.

An individual born African-American is not predestined to speak AAVE. Whether an African-American person speaks AAVE or SAE is shaped by his or her environment, social status, occupational role and position, and the like.[10]

Furthermore, it's fairly common for a speaker of AAVE to switch registers, using SAE when the context demands it. For example, I have an African-American friend who is a physician. Another African-American friend is an attorney in my university's legal affairs office. Other African-American friends include several elementary, middle-level, and high school teachers with Masters Degrees, a middle-level principal, and a university representative engaged in student recruitment. I've observed all of them using AAVE in social settings with other speakers of AAVE. In their professional roles, they all routinely use SAE.

LINGUISTIC PREJUDICE

Some people continue to hold negative and prejudicial beliefs about less advantaged cultures in the United States, whether the minority cultures are African Americans, Hispanics, Vietnamese, hillbillies, or any other ethnic or geographic group. In these days of political correctness, they know that openly disparaging remarks aren't acceptable in society. For example, it is generally accepted in the United States, a country where all people are supposed to be created equally, that good citizens should behave in a democratic, egalitarian manner and they must avoid even the appearance of being prejudicial. Consequently, "certain speakers" can be criticized for using language that is "well, so different" that "effective communication is simply not possible."

As long as these prejudicial complaints are *disguised* in pseudo-linguistic terminology, they can sometimes successfully pass some public scrutiny. Actually, despite the region in which we live, we can almost always understand speakers from other areas of the country, even when their speech is seasoned with pronunciations and words unique to their local communities. Nevertheless, prejudiced statements can be made, some believe, provided that they are disguised as comments about "effective communication" or are disguised as pleas for the preservation of "Standard English" and "academic standards." Those who use these guises somehow feel justified and validated

---

[10]Monica Crabtree and Joyce Powers, *Language Files*, 5th ed. (Columbus: Ohio State University Press, 1991), 381.

because they have maintained, in their view, their own social, political, or economic superiority.

Others may be more open and direct. When I offer an alternate pronunciation of a word in my classes in order to illustrate a particular regional variation, I sometimes hear laughter, as if the alternate pronunciation is somehow "funny." Both on and off campus I hear some people say, "Hearing some people say *warsh* instead of *wash* just drives me crazy!" Would we offer the same judgments about the color of someone's skin or their religious beliefs?

EARLY LINGUISTIC INTOLERANCE

Negative attitudes toward language differences and variations are not a recent trend. People have always, it seems, been hypersensitive to linguistic differences. One of the earliest cases on record can be found in the Bible (RSV). In the Hebrew Scriptures in the Book of Judges (How appropriate!), for example, there is a description in chapter 12, verses 5–6, of the Ephraimites trying to cross the River Jordan so that they can flee from the Gileadites:

> And the Gileadites took the fords of the Jordan against the Ephraimites. And when any of the fugitives of Ephraim said "Let me go over," the men of Gilead said to him "Then say 'shibboleth'" and he said "sibboleth" because he could not pronounce it right. Then they seized him and slew him at the fords of the Jordan. And there fell at that time 42,000 of the Ephraimites.

The Ephraimites spoke a different dialect of Hebrew and could be recognized easily by their inability to pronounce the initial /sh-/sound in the word *shibboleth* (A *shibboleth* is an ear of grain). Consequently, instead of pronouncing the term in accord with the local dialect standard, *shibboleth*, the Ephraimites pronounced it *sibboleth*, using the /s/ sound instead of the initial /sh/ sound.

A similar observation is recorded in the Greek scriptures in the Book of Matthew (KJV) 26:70. Simon Peter is attempting to disassociate himself from Jesus and has denied that he even knows Jesus: "And after a while came unto him they that stood by, and said to Peter, 'Surely thou also art one of them for thy speech betrayeth thee." The *New Oxford Annotated Bible* renders Matthew 26: 72–73, Peter's denial, in language closer to what you are likely more accustomed to: "And again he denied it with an oath. After a little while the bystanders came up and said to

Peter, 'Certainly, you are also one of them for your accent betrays you." Indeed, dialects and language variations are not new. They are recorded in ancient Jewish and Christian texts.

The phonological differences in these illustrations are similar to the different pronunciations of the word signifying, for instance, the plant *sumac* in the United States, which I first encountered during my undergraduate days when I worked four summers at a summer camp in Vermont. "I imagine the *sumac* (which I pronounced "SUE-mack") is beautiful in October," I commented one day to my Vermont-native employer. "Yes," he answered, "the *sumac* (SHOE-mack, as he pronounced it) is colorful." I am grateful that he merely pronounced *sumac* as he customarily did and did not attempt to slay me on the banks of Vermont's Otter Creek because I used my Midland dialect pronunciation!

ALL LANGUAGES VARY

The fact that languages vary is not a new idea. As the quotations from the Bible illustrated earlier, dialects were a common feature in ancient Hebrew. Historical precedence, however, is not always appreciated by the young. In order to demonstrate the normality of language variation, here's an activity created by Kirk Hazen you can use with your students, assuming it will be age-appropriate for them.[11]

FOR YOUR INQUIRY AND PRACTICE:

The following words are all regular verbs. The past-tense marker <-ed> that is used with them comes in three different phonetic forms, /t/, /d/, and /ld/.

1. hop	2. knit	3. kick	4. score	5. stretch	6. bag
7. bat	8. explain	9. need	10. side	11. flex	12. burn

Pronounce each of these words aloud in the past tense. Note especially the *sound* of the <-ed> past-tense marker for each one. Sort the verbs into three columns according to which past-tense marker is used.

---

[11]Kirk Hazen, *Teaching About Dialects*, October, 2001. http://www.cal.org/resources/digest/o1o4dialects.html.

/t/	/d/	/Id/
_____	_____	_____
_____	_____	_____
_____	_____	_____
_____	_____	_____

This activity helps students understand that language variation is very normal; language variation is something every English speaker participates in. They see that there is more than one way to say <-ed>, and the choice follows a pattern. If the root word ends in /t/ or /d/, the <-ed> ending is pronounced /Id/. If the root word ends in a voiced sound other than /d/, the <-ed> ending is pronounced /d/. If the root word ends in a voiceless sound other than /t/, the ending is pronounced /t/. If you aren't familiar with the terms *voiced* or *voiceless*, see note 12.

This activity demonstrates that language variation is not haphazard; language variations follow patterns. Another example that may be familiar to you is the intrusive /r/ one hears in the speech of some when they say, "Well, the idear of it!" The intrusive /r/, attached to a word ending in /a/, is fairly common, although not universal, in the pronunciations of those speakers in Eastern New England and New York City, but only when the next word begins with a vowel. With this pattern, we would predict hearing either "Well, the idear of it!" or "Chinar is in Asia." We would *not* expect to hear the intrusive /r/ in the sentences "The idea can't work." or "China will sell thousands of cars this year." The intrusive /r/ follows a pattern, too.

Many people grow up with the ethnolinguistic attitude that *their* native language is the *best* language. Cruz humorously describes this attitude as laying claim to "the birthright of every native speaker of every language in the world—that of thinking that my language is better than anybody else's."[13] It is commonplace for people (not you, of course, nor I, but *they*)

---

[12] Crystal, *The Cambridge Encyclopaedia*, p. 289, demonstrates voicing this way: Place your thumb and forefinger on either side of your Adam's apple, then make the sounds [zzzz] and [ssss]. The [zzzz] sound is voiced, creating a vibration as sound is created in your vocal folds behind the Adam's apple; the [ssss] sound is voiceless. With your fingers still on either side of your Adam's apple, say the words *time* and *dime*. The /t/ at the beginning of *time* is voiceless; the /d/ at the beginning of *dime* is voiced. You'll get the same effect with *kong* and *gong*.

[13] Isagani R. Cruz, "A Nation Searching for a Language Finds a Language Searching for a Name," *English Today*, 7, no. 4 (1991) 17.

to hear other speakers use "strange" terms and pronounce some words in "weird" if not "wacky" ways. Cruz delightfully captures this attitude:

> Like everyone else, I do not think of myself as having an accent, although all my American friends think I speak English with a heavy Philippine accent and all my 'pure' Tagalog friends think I have a Manileno accent. Like American southerners who think that Jimmy Carter was the only recent president who did not have an accent, or like American fans of the Beatles who thought they had a funny accent when the Beatles themselves thought they were affecting an American accent, I am completely deaf to my own idiolectal idiosyncrasies.[14]

The distinguished historian Bernard Lewis, a prodigious scholar at the University of London and later at Princeton University, offers a similar comment, this one, mind you, from a native English speaker who is trying to balance emotion and reason: "I know in my heart that the English language is the finest instrument the human race has ever devised to express its thoughts and feelings, but I recognize in my mind that others may feel exactly the same about their languages."[15]

When we put our native language pride aside, we recognize and accept the fact that the Chinese speak Chinese, Germans speak German, the French speak French, and Spaniards speak Spanish. So it goes around the globe from one language family to another. The existence of language families demonstrates that people who speak *with* one another speak *like* one another.[16]

The opposite of this principle ought to be fairly obvious as well: People who *do not* regularly talk with one another *do not* talk like one another. Consequently, what one finds in the language world is similarities of usage among those who associate with each other and some differences in usage between those groups who have little or no association with each other.

As Finegan and Besnier further illustrate, even the most casual observers of language in the United States are aware of language variation in this country when they point out that someone speaks with a Boston accent,

---

[14]Ibid.

[15]Bernard Lewis, "I'm Right, You're Wrong, Go to Hell," *The Atlantic Monthly*, May 2003, 39.

[16]Edward Finegan and Niko Besnier, *Language: Its Structure and Use* (New York: Harcourt Brace Javonovich, Publishers, 1989), 383.

with a Southern drawl, or in Brooklynese. These comments denote a sensitivity to and an awareness of the fact that language—including the elusive Standard English—has *regional* variations; which are sometimes rather loosely called *accents* or *dialects*.[17]

PHONOLOGICAL, GRAMMATICAL, AND LEXICAL VARIATIONS

One of the universally accepted linguistic principles is that *everyone* speaks with an accent, and in a dialect that is a subset of their larger language. *Accent* and *dialect*, however, are not synonyms. An accent is just one feature found within the broader concept of dialect. **Accent** refers only to a distinctive pronunciation, whereas **dialect** includes not only differences in accent, but variations in vocabulary use and grammar as well.[18]

Dialects are characterized by variations observed in three basic linguistic features:

1. **Lexical** or **vocabulary** variations.
2. **Phonological** or **accent** variations.
3. **Grammatical** variations.

For any observable and identifiable language variety to gain the status as a full-fledged dialect, it must have unique grammatical features; **dialect;** then, refers to any language variety in which the speakers use (a) similar pronunciations, (b) similar word choices, and (c) their sentences are *grammatically* different from other regional or social groups of speakers.[19]

FOR YOUR INQUIRY AND PRACTICE:

Although you may not have a budget sufficiently large enough to send teams of dialectologists into the field in order to obtain data regarding varying pronunciations of words, you can use your dictionary to learn about dialects. You should be able to find at least two pronunciations for the following words in any collegiate desk dictionary:

---

[17]Ibid., 382.

[18]Crystal, *The Cambridge Encyclopaedia,* 24.

[19]Andrews, *Language Exploration,* 203.

1. tomato	2. diapers	3. aunt	4. often
5. garage	6. greasy	7. get	8. police
9. across	10. iron	11. pecan	12. acorn
13. roof	14. herbal	15. when	16. sure

Phonological differences are illustrated by the different pronunciations you've heard for words, such as *idear* or idea; *wash* or *warsh*; *dinner* or *dinna*; *humor* or *yumar*; *human* or *yuman*; *toosday* or *tyusday*; *white* or *wite*; or *duty* or *dyuty*. Linguistically speaking, each of these pronunciations is as "good" or "correct" as another. A *toosday* deadline is certainly as final as one on *tyusday*. Anyone who performs a *duty* is obviously as responsible as one who does a *dyuty*. At the level of meaning, the pronunciations are equals. Any judgments regarding phonological variations are not linguist evaluations, but are social evaluations.

Grammatical differences are evident, for example, in the use of the second-person pronoun. In the United States, it is a characteristic of the Southern dialect for a speaker to ask "Are *y'all* ready?" In the North Midland dialect area where I live, speakers are more likely to ask the same question but in a different form: "Are *you* ready?"

The only conclusion one can draw from these differences has already been suggested: People who speak *with* one another speak *like* one another. Speakers of *y'all* use that pronoun because other speakers in their network use it. Brits often omitted the definite pronoun because that's one of the linguistic facts learned from members of their speech network. One grammatical pattern is neither linguistically superior nor linguistically inferior to another. Some patterns may, it is clear, become socially stigmatized, but that is a social and not a linguistic judgment.

Vocabulary differences are another aspect of dialects. For example, a heavy pan used for frying chicken may be called either a *frying pan*, a *fry pan*, or a *skillet*. At the meaning level, the terms are equal; the chicken will taste just as good, regardless of the name used for the container it is fried in. Furthermore, whether you use an *earthworm*, an *angleworm*, or a *red worm*, or a *fishing* (or *fish*) *worm*, I suspect—based on my own extensive empirical research—your chances of catching a 5 pound bass are about the same.

REGIONAL AND SOCIAL DIALECTS

There are hundreds of additional examples of grammatical, phonological, and lexical variations such as these, which are illustrative of dialects.

In fact, the patterns of regional variation are so identifiable that they can be mapped. Examples of how linguistic variations become regional clusters and can be represented on language maps are numerous.[20]

It cannot be stressed enough: **Regional dialects** represent *legitimate* and *alternative* ways either to pronounce words, to put sentences together grammatically, or to name or identify ideas, objects, and things. As we noted earlier, however, there remains a degree of intolerance leveled against those persons who speak a different dialect. The logic of this negative attitude is ironic because *any* dialect can be regarded as *different*. Remove yourself to another part of the country, and *you* are the different dialect speaker!

Alternatively, you can observe this intolerance without actually leaving for another part of the country. Simply recall the last time you were in a group and one of its members pronounced a word somewhat differently from the group's standard pronunciation. That variant pronunciation most likely either caused some members of the group to give knowing smiles to others, or it may have caused an overt laugh. When my family was living in London, it was fairly routine to hear my daughter's schoolmates ask her, in good nature: "Sally, say something in Yank. It's so funny." Sometimes, on the other hand, as you know from your own experiences, the laughter is not good-natured.

Linguistically, any one of the regional choices is as useful as another. Nevertheless, some of the choices will be favored and others will be stigmatized. These value judgments are *social-class* comments, however, and are not, however cleverly disguised, *linguistic assessments*. We know that just as dialects vary from one region of the country to another, they also vary—in the form of **social dialects**—from one social class of society to another. This is true where I live and I am confident it holds true in your city.

---

[20] Hans Kurath, *A Word Geography of the Eastern United States* (Ann Arbor: University of Michigan Press, 1949); Hans Kurath, *Studies in Area Linguistics*, (Bloomington: Indiana University Press, 1972); Hans Kurath and Raven McDavid, *The Pronunciation of English in the Atlantic States* (Ann Arbor: University of Michigan Press, 1961); William Labov, *Language in the Inner City* (Philadelphia: University of Pennsylvania Press, 1972); Roger Shuy, *Discovering American Dialects* (Champaign-Urbana, IL: National Council of Teachers of English, 1967); Frederick G. Cassidy, ed., *Dictionary of American Regional English* (Cambridge, MA: Belknap Press of the Harvard University Press, 1985); and Craig M. Carver, *American Regional Dialects* (Ann Arbor: University of Michigan Press, 1987).

One of the earliest and now classic studies investigating language variation across **social classes** was completed by William Labov. Observing that some New Yorkers pronounce the /r/ at the ends of words like *car, far* and *jar* and observing also that some New Yorkers do not, Labov investigated the presence or absence of the postvocalic /r/ among a number of New York speakers. Collecting data in three department stores—an expensive upper-middle class store, a medium-priced, middle-class store, and a discount store utilized mostly by working-class shoppers—Labov discovered that the presence or absence of postvocalic /r/ was, in fact, remarkably related to the social standing of the shoppers at the three stores: The upper-middle class store employees were much more consistent in pronouncing the /r/. The employees at the lower-class store hardly ever pronounced it. The middle-class store employees were moderate, somewhere between the higher- and lower-class pronunciations of /r/.[21]

In the United States, postvocalic /r/-dropping has been associated with lower-class speakers for some time. People in the United States who enjoy higher social status, on the other hand, usually pronounce the /r/. Labov's data confirmed these social practices and attitudes.

Ironically, on the other hand, in the United Kingdom, the general social opinion is just the *opposite*. More "refined" people, those from the higher social classes, *do not* pronounce postvocalic /r/, whereas those considered crude, rude, or uneducated (euphemisms for lower social classes) do pronounce it. These reversals of the pronunciation of postvocalic /r/ across social class divisions are very dramatic.[22]

The presence or absence of postvocalic /r/ is just one example of how language varies according to social class (**sociolect**). The UK, data are illustrative; they are completely opposite! In one city, pronouncing the /r/ is indicative of *upper-class* status; in another city, pronouncing the /r/ is indicative of *lower-class* status. Go figure. There is an important generalization to be made here: When it comes to matters of language usage, do not look to what you and I might call "logic" or "common sense." Look to those who are using the language.

Based on your own observations, you know about the evaluations and judgments some individuals make about other people according to how they pronounce, for instance, the /th/ as in "this" or "dis" (*this* woman vs. *dis* woman) or how they pronounce /-ing/ in "*running*" or "*runnin.*"

---

[21] William Labov, *The Social Stratification of English in New York City,* (Washington, DC: The Center for Applied Linguistics, 1966).

[22] Andrews, *Language Exploration,* 206.

Arriving at opinions and decisions about how others use language is a widespread activity. In fact, a prominent sociolinguist has declared that evaluation is a major concern of most language users![23]

Social-class differences will emerge in other linguistic features, too, not just the phonological. For example, what are the differences in your community between the lexical choices of *lunch* or *dinner*, or of *supper* or *dinner*, or the pronunciations of the initial vowel in the word *either*: Is it EEE-ther or EYE-ther? Unless your community is different from other communities in the United States, different social classes will typically use one of these options but not the other.

The reason for this is simple: Some dialects have more prestige than others because the *speakers* of certain dialects have more prestige. That is to say, it's not really the dialect *itself* that holds higher or lower prestige; it's the *speakers* of the dialect who are held in higher or lower prestige and this prestige is generalized to their speech.

My observations of this phenomenon also suggest that speakers of a more prestigious dialect will sometimes claim that they have difficulty understanding the speech of those using a less-prestigious dialect. Conversely, speakers of less-prestigious dialects seldom claim that they can't understand the speech used by more prestigious speakers. Now, I ask you, is this a language issue or a social-class issue?

Broadly speaking, Americans in the Midwest assume that New Englanders in general, and Bostonians in particular, are better educated, are more urbane, and are more genteel and refined, so the Midwesterner invests more prestige in the New Englanders' speech. Some Midwesterners may even copy it by adopting a pronunciation they believe to be indicative of New Englanders' urbanity and refinement, such as NIGH-thur instead of the more locally common NEE-thur.

Furthermore, Americans in general assume that British English is somehow more proper because we think the British people are somehow more proper. A cosmopolitan character in a film or TV production takes on even greater prestige and glamour if he or she has a British English accent.

There are a number of ways British English differs from American English, in terms of phonology, vocabulary, spelling, and grammar. Some of the differences are entertaining. Table 8.1 contains just a few *vocabulary* differences:[24]

---

[23]Deborah Cameron, *Verbal Hygiene* (London and New York: Routledge, 1995).

[24]From my personal notes, augmented by http://www.krystal.com/ukandusa.html and Orin Hargraves, "Cucurbits," *English Today*, October 2004, 52.

TABLE 8.1
British and U.S. Vocabulary Difference

Definition	British Word	U.S. Word
The dot at the end of a sentence	Full stop	Period
Unit of paper currency	Note	Bill
Day when offices are closed	Bank holiday	Legal holiday
Sharp object for putting items on wall	Drawing pin	Thumb tack
Last letter of the alphabet	Zed	Zee
Soft shoe worn for sports	Trainers, plimsols	Sneakers
Clothing item worn in morning	Dressing gown	Bathrobe
What you put in baby's mouth	Dummy	Pacifier
Area next to street where people walk	Pavement	Sidewalk
Place to buy medicines	Chemist	Drugstore
Business part of the city	Town centre	Downtown
Rear compartment of car	Boot	Trunk
Multilane highway	Motorway	Freeway, interstate
What you eat with milk, tea, or coffee	Biscuit	Cookie
Crunchy, thin-sliced potatoes	Crisps	Chips
Ground beef	Mince	Hamburger
Battery-operated light	Torch	Flashlight
Place for watching films	Cinema	Movie theater
Portable telephone	Mobile	Cell phone
Long green vegetable, cucumber family	Corgette	Zucchini
Rounded purple vegetable	Aubergine	Eggplant

There are numerous spelling differences between British and American English, too. I had a student from Canada one semester who had grown up in the British English tradition. She thanked me at the end of the semester, telling me that I was one of the few professors she'd had who had not counted off for her British spellings (*theatre, centre*, etc.). My daughter Sally completed the equivalent of the 9th grade in a London comprehensive school during my appointment at the University of London. She came home in tears one afternoon; she had received a "D" on her Human Reproduction unit exam because she consistently used the American English spelling of *fetus* instead on the British English *foetus*! I trust you'll be more judicious with your students from other cultures.

To put it bluntly, some people in the United States are more highly regarded than others. Those who are economically, culturally, or politically more powerful benefit from higher social esteem. You may want to object to this fact, believing that it is neither just nor right, but, nevertheless, it is so. Given the sociolinguistic relationship between a person's social standing and a person's language, certain language usages are judged as either "good" or "bad," depending, on who is using them.[25]

As Walt Wolfram, a distinguished professor of sociolinguistics puts it, "It is often shocking to realize how extensively we may judge a person's background, character, and intentions based simply on the person's language, dialect, or, in some instances, even the choice of a single word."[26] For example, at an earlier time *ain't* was considered to be a perfectly acceptable contraction for *am not*. When *ain't* is used today as a normal part of one's speech pattern, however (I'm excluding here the use of *ain't* for special emphasis or for humor.), *it* has become so stigmatized that its use serves as a marker of nonstandard speech. As Conklin and Lourie describe the regular use of *ain't*, "An *ain't* user is judged [by society] not only to be speaking nonstandard English but to be ignorant, insensitive, dumb, even dirty—stereotypes of lower-class people."[27] On the other hand, if speakers use conventional pronunciations, speak quickly and fluently, and use few hesitations (like *ums* or *ers*), they are likely to be judged by society as more competent and more socially prominent.[28]

---

[25]Conklin and Lourie, *A Host of Tongues*, 115.

[26]Walt Wolfram, *Sociolinguistics*, Linguistic Society of America, http://www.lsadc.org/web2/socioling.html.

[27]Conklin and Lourie, *A Host of Tongues*, 115.

[28]Crystal, *The Cambridge Encyclopaedia*, 23.

DIALECT AFFILIATIONS

Our dialects are the products of several influences. Initially, we are born *into* a language network, the style of language used by our caregivers. The immediate speech network—a mother, a father, an older sibling, or other caregivers—provide our first language models. And, as has been said before, people who speak *with* one another talk *like* one another.

Very few people, though, spend their entire life with their social contacts limited to the close-knit home circle. As one's social environment expands, one's language networks increase in number. Our language is affected, subsequently, to the extent that we come into contact with a larger circle of friends and colleagues at school, at worship, at work, and at play. It is through these relationships that our social networks are created, which in turn cause our use of language to resemble the linguistic features—phonological, lexical, and syntactical—of the persons in each network.

A dialect, then, can also be viewed as any variety of a language spoken by a given network or community of people, or by a *regional, ethnic,* or *social* group. Whereas Robert Hendrickson describes only three main regional dialect areas in the United States, Kurath accounts for many more.[29] Hendrickson's book is written for a general audience of readers, whereas Kurath's reports, representing the results of extensive fieldwork, are of more interest to professional linguists in general, dialectologists in particular. The actual number of U.S. regional dialect areas, depends, of course, on how finely the definitions are drawn.

The fact is, at least for the more general language student, the total number of regional dialects is not all that important. The reason for this is relatively simple: As a matter of fact, *every* city, town, and village has its unique dialectical language forms. Growing up in Central Missouri, I had a high school friend who lived on Again Street (pronounced AA-gun). Thirty miles south from where I live today you'll find the town of Beatrice (pronounced Bee-AT-truss). Closer to home, in a number of elementary school classrooms I'm hearing younger language users pronounce the word put as "pert". Some New Yorkers do not tell a meddlesome soul "You're driving me crazy." Instead, they say "You're driving me to Poughkeepsie." That's where the mental hospital is.[30] With minimal fieldwork you can identify similar language uses unique to your locality.

Actually, one dialect is no better nor no worse than another. It is *people* who attach social prestige to some varieties and stigmatize others. These

---

[29]Hendrickson, *American Talks,* 17; and Kurath, *A Word Geography.*

[30]Hendrickson, *American Talk,* 194.

are social, however, not linguistic judgments. How and why these social judgments, which is another form of stereotyping, take place is an important area for discussion your classroom.

LANGUAGE AND CULTURE

Elsewhere in this book (see chap. 5) we talked about the inherent relationships between language and culture. Given the magnitude of that relationship, and given the fact that variations exist in language at the local, regional, and social-class levels, we need to address language and culture as an aspect of *cultural dialect.*

For an opener to this topic, let me take you with me to a Level V (Advanced) English as a Second Language (ESL) class I observed recently. The teacher and the students were engaged in an informal "state of the class" discussion, and they were talking about how much English the students had learned in a relatively brief period of time.

The teacher, Marilyn Deppe, said to her students, "Let's try to remember the first English words you learned." One of the students recalled the trips he had made with his mother to the grocery store. As a result of these trips, one of the first English phrases he learned was: "Paper or plastic?" In his home culture, that question would not be asked.

Cultural variations can be observed at an international level, beyond the confines of an ESL classroom. In May of 1995, then Secretary of State Warren Christopher responded to criticisms from the Republican Party that President Clinton's recent trip to Moscow had accomplished little. In Moscow, Christopher said: "In the business of diplomacy, you frequently score runs by hitting singles. And I think the President hit a series of good solid singles that'll add up to scoring a great many runs."[31] To most Americans, understanding the language used with baseball, Christopher's comments were clear enough. But, don't you suspect, that many in the Moscow audience, unfamiliar with the baseball metaphors, wondered just what Mr. Christopher had said?

Look at other cultural-specific metaphors:

- "It's your turn to step up to the plate and see if you can advance our proposal."

---

[31]Dilin Liu and Bryan Farha, "Three Strikes and You're Out," *English Today,* 12, no. 1 (1996): 36.

- "Three strikes and you're out" is a phrase borrowed by U.S. lawmakers for a crime bill that will imprison criminals who have three offenses.
- Some commentators refer to Japan as being a "major player" in the "big league" of the world economy.[32]

To many people in the world, these baseball metaphors—relatively common usages in the United States where baseball and its language are well-known—would have little meaning.

The earlier contrasts we made between a small number of British English and American English words reflect cultural differences, too. There are many other examples, too numerous to mention here, except for one. Accompanying one of my colleagues at the University of London for lunch at a corner pub one day, I ordered a half-pint of lager and a roast beef sandwich. The waitperson asked me, "Do you want salad with that?" Thinking a nice side salad would go well with the roast beef sandwich, I told her I'd like the salad. When my sandwich was delivered to our table, a piece of lettuce, a slice of onion, and a slice of tomato were on the plate. "Shall I put these [the "salad"] on your sandwich for you," the waitperson asked? *Salad* has a more limited definition in a London pub!

Closer to home, the language of the classroom culture is becoming a more fertile area for linguistic research. Earlier investigations 40 and 50 years ago examined classroom verbal interaction; that is, what kinds of student talk and what kinds of teacher talk take place? Questions? Answers? Student-initiated talk or responding talk only, and the like?

As the children of immigrants and refugees continue to increase in number in U.S. classrooms, and as No Child Left Behind legislation places more focus on individual student performance instead of group aggregated data, the differences between the language of the school culture and the language of the child's home culture become increasingly significant in the learning–teaching enterprise.

Speaking in general terms, Duranti has observed that, "So much of social hierarchy is both represented by and instantiated through speech that the study of any social system would not be possible without an understanding of the language that supports and represents such a system."[33]

---

[32] Ibid., 37.

[33] Cited in Betsy Rymes, "Eliciting Narratives: Drawing Attention to the Margins of Classroom Talk," *Research in the Teaching of English*, February 2003, 381.

In classrooms the social, the textual, and the cognitive are inextricably linked through talk every day. In schools, however, *one way* of speaking and one set of *approved* discourse routines is made primary. These routines are seldom, if ever, taught directly but are a part of the sociocultural knowledge that middle-class students raised within a particular literate tradition bring to school with them.[34] To use another sports metaphor, this creates a sloping playing field for some students. Although there has been some excellent scholarship in this area of inquiry, there hasn't been enough.

LANGUAGE VARIATION OVER TIME

Just as language varies from one city to another, one geographic region to another, one social class to another, and from one country to another, it also changes from one age to another.

How far back in history can we trace the roots of modern American English? You'd be surprised. Far, far, back in time, possibly 5,000 years or more. Current linguistic scholarship is more accurate, but not nearly as humorous, as the account of English language history provided by "Mr. Language Person," a created persona of the syndicated newspaper humorist Dave Barry: "The English language is a rich verbal tapestry woven together from the tongues of the Greeks, the Latins, the Angles, the Klaxtons, the Celtics, and many more other ancient people, all of whom had severe drinking problems."[35]

We'll not go back into history quite that far. Let's begin when English first immigrated to what we now call the United States. Language variation began in the United States shortly after the first colonists settled here. American colonists—remember that they were speaking the Early Modern English; language (EMnE) of Milton and Shakespeare—upon their arrival at the very beginning of the 17th century, added many new words to their vocabulary that were descriptive of their experiences in the New World. Many of these words were adapted from Native American words, words like *catalpa, hickory, pecan, squash, tamarack, hominy, succotash, chipmunk, muskrat, opossum, raccoon, skunk,* and *woodchuck.*[36]

Furthermore, the homeland language of immigrants is usually "frozen." That is to say, immigrants continue to use their homeland language in

---

[34]Ibid.

[35]Cited in Steven Pinker, *The Language Instinct* (New York: Morrow & Company, 1994), 246.

[36]Conklin and Lourie, *A Host of Tongues,* 75–76.

isolation from the changes that are taking place in the language of "home" from where they immigrated. Consequently, American colonists were too isolated from England to keep up with the changes that were taking place in British English.[37] For example, the colonists brought with them the word *druggist*, which came into use in British English in during the 17th century. In the middle of the 18th century, the British began to substitute *chemist* for *druggist*. The older form, *druggist*, from which we also derive the term *drugstore*, persists in the United States today.[38]

During the same time period the people "back home," the British, began to substitute the word *autumn* for the word *fall*. Unaware of this change, the colonists continued to use the word *fall*, a seasonal term most speakers of British English consider to be archaic.[39] Speakers in the United States continue to use *fall* today.

There were also pronunciation changes that took place during this time period. The colonists brought with them the vowel sounds in *derby*, *clerk*, and *Berkeley*, which are still predominant in American English today. Yet, in the mid-18th century, speakers of British English began to alter the vowel sounds in those words so that they were like the vowel used in *dark*. Today, speakers of British English pronounce the word *derby* so that it is rendered as "*darby*". The word *clerk* is rendered as "*clark*" and *Berkeley* is spoken as "*Barkley*".[40]

Regional variances are comparatively easy to detect; language changes taking place over the years are not as easily discernible. They are like the changes in a growing human: Only by stopping to examine a photograph, for example, or to measure a child with a yardstick do we notice that changes have occurred. Language change is inevitable, constant, inexorable, and slow; it moves just like the slow yet doggedly determined steadiness of an iceberg.

FOR YOUR INQUIRY AND PRACTICE:

The *etymological fallacy* is an erroneous notion that the earlier, older, meaning of a word is more accurate than a later meaning. The fact is, people will use words differently in successive generations,

---

[37]Ibid., 76.

[38]Ibid.

[39]Ibid.

[40]Ibid.

altering the older meanings. A collegiate desk dictionary can help you learn how these words have had different meanings given to them over time.

marshal	steward	hussy	minister	lord	nice
lewd	lust	stupid	bonfire	angel	nate

Even folder examples can come from English surnames. For example, some English surnames derive from colors: *Brown, White*, and *Green* are three very common examples. Yet, it's very unusual to see the surnames *Red* or *Yellow*. I have a colleague named Bob Brown. I've seen Betty White on TV. My wife's boss is named Gray Green. On the other hand, do you know anyone named Roger Red or Yvonne Yellow? Maybe Reed or Golden, but not Red or Yellow.

This naming custom began in medieval times when surnames were based on nicknames. (See Ken Follet's novel *Pillars of the Earth* for a fascinating account of how English surnames began.) Many nicknames were based on physical appearance, like the color of hair (brown, black). Other names were based on one's vocation (for example, surnames like *Arrowsmith, Barber, Carpenter, Cook, Cooper, Fletcher, Fowler, Forester,* or *Forrester, Mason, Merchant, Miller, Skinner, Smith, Tailor, or Taylor, Tanner, Wheeler, Warden*) or a family's geographical location; hence Green comes from "by the green."[41] Do you know of anyone named Underhill?

USING CHURCH TEXTS FOR TIME VARIATION STUDY

Earlier in this chapter I quoted three different translations of the Bible. I used these quotations to make an important point about dialects; you'll recall that I made no reference to my religious beliefs. When I quote the Bible, however, the reactions are often mixed.

The separation of church and state is a matter of constitutional law in the United States. Unfortunately, many teachers bend over backward to avoid any discussion of religious topics. Consequently, a treasure chest of language history goes unused. It is possible, nevertheless, to use different translations of the Bible to study historical changes in the English language. Moreover, Protestant hymnals contain excellent examples of how the English language has changed over the years. You can bring these

---

[41]"Q & A," *The Atlantic Monthly*, October 1992, 14.

examples into your classroom without attempting to intimidate or convert your students to accept a particular theology or denomination. You should, though, inform your building principal about your use of these texts in order to deflect potential parental complaints.

For example, thousands of churchgoers sing hymns each week with minimal attention to the historical uses or meanings of some of the words. Nevertheless, consider what students can learn about historical variations in English when they examine the texts of hymns like the following:

- Just as I am, without one plea,
  but that thou blood was shed for me,
  And that thou **bidst** me come to thee,
  O lamb of God . . . "
- "Happy the man whose hopes rely on Isreal's God
  he made the sky, And earth and seas with all their **train** . . . "
- "Beneath the cross of Jesus I **fain** would take my stand . . . "
- "For the Lord our God shall come,
  And shall take his harvest home;
  From his field shall in that day All offenses purge away,
  Give his angels charge at last In the fire the **tares** to cast,
  But the fruitful ears to store In his **garner** evermore."

In the hymn *Come Thou Fount of Every Blessing,* the second verse begins, "Here I raise mine **Ebenezer** . . . ." Thousands of churchgoers sing that hymn with great regularity—and they don't have the foggiest idea about who, what, or where an Ebenezer might be! We don't use Ebenezers anymore.

Any collegiate desk dictionary will enable students to learn about the earlier meanings of the words highlighted in **boldface** in the proceeding list.

WHO MAKES THESE CHANGES?

Changes occur in language because people create the changes. It is a linguist's axiom that whenever a new language form is needed, society will create it. Conversely, when a linguistic form is no longer needed, society will stop using it. For example, about 40 to 45 years ago, *victrolas* were replaced by *record players* in homes where there were those who enjoyed playing recordings of music. The record player was later replaced by a *hi-fi*, which in turn was replaced by a *stereo*, then it became a *boom box,* and finally a *CD player*. Within the same time-frame, the *icebox* was replaced by a *frigidaire*, which was subsequently replaced by a *refrigerator*. Similarly, words like *icon, mouse, pad,* and *drag* have been used by speakers and writers of English for hundreds of years. The advent of computers, however, created a new use for these existing words.

Speakers of Spanish have faced a recent challenge, created by scientific developments involved in the act of cloning one life form from the genetic material of another. The Spanish language already had a noun for the word clone (*un clon*), but had no verb form. As I write this chapter, the verb form in Spanish for "to clone" has been rendered both as *clonar* and as *clonear*. In time, one of these infinitives ("to clone") will emerge as the standard form.

Speakers of English face a similar challenge with telephones. The word *dial* can be used as either a noun or a verb. With the touch-tone telephone replacing the rotary telephone, people really don't *dial* (v.) telephone numbers anymore. The Supreme Court of language use—the people who use the language—hasn't yet settled on one word to replace the verb *dial*. I've heard *select, press, enter*, and *touch*, but consensus will likely take a while.

These are obvious examples of word changes that take place between and among generations. However, individual words aren't the only linguistic features subject to change. Another aspect of time change can be observed in *pronunciations*. I have a friend who goes cross-eyed and stiff-legged whenever he hears someone say "NUKE-kya-ler" for "NUKE-lee-ar." The former pronunciation can be heard with increasing regularity and *may* become the standard pronunciation. Another test item in this category is realtor. Are you hearing it pronounced in your community as a two- or a three-syllable word?

Not only do pronunciations change over time, but *spellings* change, as well, although they are the slowest uses of language to change. Greenbaum, for example, analyzes the increasing use of a newly spelled form: *could-be*, as in "Could-be, he'll be here Friday."[42] *Could-be* is a fairly common informal utterance and with increased use its spelling could become more widely accepted. This use of *could-be* seems to be a fore-runner to the fairly widespread *wanna-be*, which no longer causes heads to turn when it's used.

Similarly, I hear and read the word data used as a singular noun, even in the most prestigious journals I read, as in "The data *is* inconclusive." In

---

[42]Sidney Greenbaum, *Studies in English Adverbial Usage* (Coral Gables, FL: University of Miami Press, 1969), 109.

my graduate school days, it was always" the data *are* inconclusive." To speak or write otherwise was, back in those days, the kiss of death.

Sometimes society ascribes a new *meaning* for an existing word. If the new meaning catches on, then over a period of time we have yet another time variation. For example, in the preradio United States, the word *broadcast* was largely limited to agricultural uses, as in "broadcast the seeds over plowed land." Postradio, the existing word took on a newer meaning. *Crash* has a similar history revolving around the advent of computers.

Changes such as these are recorded in the *Oxford English Dictionary (OED)* the largest dictionary of the English language. The *OED* records, century by century, the histories of meanings that have evolved for English words. Etymologies in some desk dictionaries provide more limited word histories. These etymologies will reveal that many words have changed significantly over the years. As a matter of fact, some changes in meaning have been so widespread that they can be described in the following ways:

1. **Elevation**: The meaning has become more elevated, more prestigious. "Nice" once meant "ignorant" or "not knowing." An "economist" was a "housekeeper" or "house manager." Today, "nice" is a good word. An "economist" is a scientist.

2. **Degradation**: The meaning has degraded into a more pejorative, disparaging, or negative sense. "Smirk" once meant "smile;" a "gossip" was originally a "godparent," and anything "awful" once was "awe-inspiring."

3. **Generalization**: A specific meaning becomes more general. The word "butcher" once meant "slayer of goats." Today, a "butcher" prepares all kinds of meats. A "zone" is more than a "belt."

4. **Specialization**: A general word becomes more specific or specialized in meaning. The word "starve" originally meant "to die." An "angel" was simply a "messenger."[43]

Perhaps the most significant change in the English language took place at the Battle of Hastings in the year 1066. When William the Conqueror defeated the Anglo-Saxons, he established his own county and municipal system of government by naming fellow Norman-French to administrative positions. Similarly, the church, court system, and schools were administered by William's Norman-French appointees, most of whom spoke French as

---

[43] Monica Crabtree and Joyce Powers, *Language Files,* 5th ed. (Columbus: Ohio State University Press, 1991), 327.

their first language. French quickly became, therefore, the undeclared but nevertheless "official" language in England.

To make a long and very interesting story disappointingly short, 1066 is the reason English has such an astonishing array of Anglo Saxon, Germanic, French, Greek, and Latin language features today. English is built on a Germanic grammar system, on top of which we have a large number of Romance language words. The linguistic shotgun wedding brought about by William the Conqueror engendered the use of Romance Language counterparts for existing Anglo-Saxon words like loving (*amorous*), cow (*beef*), deep (*profound*), sharp (*poignant*) and hut (*cottage*).[44]

Inasmuch as the French language became the language of "official" England, it is no surprise that it also became the language of "social" England, especially higher society. This is why the preceding italicized terms in parentheses have higher prestige than their Anglo-Saxon synonyms: They were, and are still considered by many today, more "refined" words because they were used by the "better" folk. Even today, some 1,000 years or so after the Norman Conquest and the subsequent elevation of the French language to a position of social prestige, if a speaker wants to demonstrate that he or she possesses *savoir faire*, they will do so by inserting a French expression into their language.

REGISTER IN LANGUAGE

Throughout our lives, we learn many different varieties of language. A "speech variety" can also be a **register** of language. Registers are the varieties of language used by a particular group of people. Some registers are occupational registers because people in the same profession use similar language, that is, schoolteachers talk like schoolteachers, physicians talk like physicians, attorneys talk like attorneys, engineers talk like engineers, and so on.[45]

Some registers are based on special interests. When I'm fishing with my friend Norm Magruder, we use terms like *Rooster Tail, drag, shad,*

---

[44]See Albert C. Baugh and Thomas Cable, *A History of the English Language*, 3rd ed. (Englewood Cliffs, NJ: Prentice-Hall, 1978); and Robert McCrum, William Cran, and Robert MacNeil, *The Story of English* (New York: Elisabeth Softon Books-Viking, 1986). Of particular human interest is the story of the Norman Conquest, which is depicted in David Howarth, *1066: The Year of the Conquest* (New York: Dorset Press by arrangement with Viking-Penguin, 1978).

[45]Jack Richards, John Platt, and Heidi Weber, *Longman Dictionary of Applied Linguistics*, (London: Longman Group UK Limited, 1989), 242.

cast, and *jig*. These terms are commonly used in fishing, not in bridge, not in swimming, not in baseball or football. You have special interests and hobbies whose languages, varieties, or registers you know as well as I know those associated with fishing.

Some registers are social. Those in certain social roles are expected by the other members of their "group" to use linguistic behavior conventionally "appropriate" to that group. A financially successful individual who aspires to join a prestigious country club, but who continues to use language such as "ain't", "It don't matter to me", or "We was hoping to join this club," will not, in all likelihood, be admitted.

Not only do we learn many registers or **codes**, we also are skilled at switching from one code or register to another, depending on which one is contextually appropriate. No one needs to remind you, for example, that you speak to the superintendent of schools in your school district in one variety, yet use another variety when you speak to a loved one or to your pastor or to the person who carries your groceries to your car or puts them in the trunk of your car at the supermarket.

A excellent example of the rapidity of some code-switching took place in my family recently. My wife, suffering from a painful bone spur on her left heel, went to the podiatrist for relief. The podiatrist, like my wife, is an African-American female. Using her physician's SAE register (code), the podiatrist gave my wife a professional greeting, asked the appropriate professional questions about symptoms in a medically appropriate manner, inquired studiously about the onset of the pain, and the like, then toward the conclusion of the examination she asked my wife to walk to the end of the examining room and then return to her chair.

Observing my wife's manner of walking, the podiatrist switched to a more colloquial, informal register used conventionally among African-American women ("sister talk"), and she exclaimed, in AAVE, to my wife: "Girl, I can't tell which crazy way you walkin'."

For the duration of the session they talked about issues of mutual interest to African-American women who live in a predominantly Anglo-European community: where the other has her hair done, the best place to buy cosmetics, and so on. The context, and, thus, the language register had changed.

ATTITUDES TOWARD LANGUAGE VARIATION AND CHANGE

There are several myths about language use, some of them directly related to language diversity and variation. Some people, for example, are confident that the dominance of the English language in the Untied States is threatened, given the increases in immigrant and refugee children in our schools as well as the large Hispanic population in the Untied States. Some believe English literacy rates are low because language minority students don't want to learn English. Perhaps you've heard some of the other myths: The media are ruining English usage; women talk too much; children don't speak or write properly anymore; Black children are verbally deprived; and the meaning of words shouldn't be allowed to vary or to change.[46] The majority of contemporary linguists would disagree with all of the myths in the preceding sentence, but their views are seldom expressed in letters to the editor of the local newspaper, nor do they go to the local school district's board of education meetings to voice their current concerns. Consequently, the myths tend to survive, despite the fact that they aren't true.

Language change is inevitable and normal, and, for the most part, moves with the speed of a snail. Actually, only a very small part of the whole of language undergoes a perceptible change at any given moment, but the visible part that is undergoing change can create quite a stir. We may judge language change as *progress* if we approve of the change or have no strong feelings about it, or we may label it as *decay* if we don't like it.

People's responses to variations and changes in the language could probably be placed along a continuum, ranging from Positive on one end to Negative on the other (with Who Cares? in the middle). Aitchison deftly captures the essence of the two views in the title, as well as the content, of her book *Language Change: Progress or Decay?*[47]

The relatively recent spelling of *lite* for *light* may cause some to grumble. Similarly, there is a sharp generational division between younger language users, on the one hand, who effortlessly use the word *shit* and, on the other hand, older speakers who consider it a four-letter taboo word to be avoided by everyone except those who are morally bankrupt.

If a teacher had heard me utter the word *shit* in the school corridor, I would have been referred to the building principal, who would have suspended me from school for several days; today, *shit* is not an uncommon

---

[46]See Terrence C. Wiley, *Myths about Language Diversity and Literacy in the United States* (Washington DC: ERIC Clearing house, ED407881, 1997); and Laurie Bauer and Peter Trudgill, eds., *Language Myths* (New York and London: Penguin Books, 1998).

[47]Jean Aitchison, *Language Change: Progress or Decay?* (New York: Universe Books, 1985).

FIG. 8.1.　New spelling of light.

word overheard in the school hallway, the playground, or the parking lot. Times, people, and language change.

The public use of the word *condom* today is readily accepted by some, but is objectionable to others. Nevertheless, as several TV comedians have observed, "Do you need evidence that language changes? Remember the old days when you'd go into a drugstore and say, 'I want a pack of cigarettes, and [in a whispered voice] a pack of condoms.' Did you ever think you'd walk into the same drugstore and say, 'I want some condoms,' and then add in a whispered voice, 'And a pack of cigarettes'?" Social use has dramatically changed our responses to those two words.

We may call changes such as these changes in the language, but I suspect it's actually not the language, per se, which has changed. More accurately, *people* (communities, networks, or generations) have changed their uses of, responses to, and attitudes toward language.

LANGUAGE VARIATION IN LITERATURE

As the divisions among oral and written language learning continue to become more indistinct in school curricula, teachers and learners will see that literature texts can contribute much to the students' metalinguistic awareness. Teachers will be familiar with the attempts of Charles Dickens, Josh

Billings, and Mark Twain, to cite a few classic examples, to depict as accurately as possible the regional and social speech patterns of their characters. These speech patterns help to establish and maintain the readers' understandings of the characters' contexts, motivations, and abilities to resolve (successfully or unsuccessfully) whatever conflicts they may face.

A number of more contemporary writers accomplish some remarkable outcomes with their applications of aspects of linguistics. The books I'm about to discuss have remained favorite reads of students of variety of ages for years.

William Hogan's *The Quartzsite Trip* tells about P.J. Cooper, an English teacher, who selects a seeming unrelated collection of high school seniors to participate in an excursion into the wilderness each year during spring break (Easter vacation in the novel). Students' "good works" do not assure an invitation; the invitation is "given." The language of the novel supports these religious themes through repetition of place names and the characters' names, dates, and the like. Similarly, the novel assumes verselike structure in its paragraphing, producing, in conjunction with the language elements already mentioned, a biblical tone. The religious themes are artfully developed through Hogan's writing.[48]

A similar comment can be made about Margaret Atwood's *The Handmaid's Tale*. This speculative fiction is set in the future and is narrated by a female character Offred, a handmaid whose "job" is to bear children for the Republic of Gilead. Women in Gilead no longer use their birthnames but are defeminized and rechristened: Offred, Ofwarren, Ofglen, and the like. Service women who cook and clean the dormitories are referred to only as "the Marthas" (see the New Testament). Public discourse among the handmaids is liturgical:

> "The war is going well, I hear," she says.
>
> "Praise be," I reply.
>
> "We've been sent good weather."
>
> "Which I receive with joy."
>
> "They've defeated more of the rebels since yesterday."
>
> "Praise be," I say.[49]

Blitzcat, by Robert Westall, offers readers both n heroic story of a cat attempting to find her way home during World War II as well as an opportunity to

---

[48]William Hogan, *The Quartzsite Trip* (New York: Avon Books, 1980).

[49]Margaret Atwood, *The Handmaid's Tale* (New York: Ballentine Books, 1985), 26.

observe a number of language usages that show how British English varies from American English. Westall is a Brit and spells accordingly, using the standard British English spellings of *defenceless, learnt, favour, pyjamas,* and *paralysed,* to name a few. Lexical variations are also apparent: *windscreen, fortnight, potty* (crazy, dotty, daft), and *sods* (as in "poor sods").[50] Other British English usages are throughout the book, enabling to reader to make linguistic observations by completing linguistic "fieldwork" without leaving the reading table or desk.

A Day No Pigs Would Die, by Robert Newton Peck, continues to be read and loved by each generation who "discovers" the novel. The novel enables readers to observe several aspects of language, especially how the language of younger speakers differs from older ones. Rob, the narrator and son of Haven Peck, uses language and slang (*heck, damn, darn*) far removed from the more traditional language of his conservative Quaker father.[51]

This discussion could extend indefinitely, but available space allows me to mention only one more writer. Consequently, I'll invite you to read and share one of my favorite writers: Molly Ivins. In her collection of newspaper and magazine articles, *Molly Ivins Can't Say That, Can She?*, Ivins' wit and perspicacity are made sharper as she describes the goings-on of state and national politicians by adopting the dialect of a Texan. She renders the Texas dialect through respellings like: *Meskin* (Mexican), *bidness* (business), *lookahere* (look here), *bob war* (barbed wire), *gennlemen* (gentlemen), *wimmin* (women), *how yew?* (how are you?), and *hail fahr* (hell fire!)[52]

These books are good reads. They also provide us and our students with opportunities to see perfectly normal language variations at work in literature.

REVIEWING THE CHAPTER:

1. How are *accent* and *dialect* different?
2. What variables contribute to the shaping of one's *idiolect*?
3. Does isolation tend to challenge or to preserve the status quo?
4. Should mastery of SAE remain a primary objective of the language arts curriculum?

---

[50]Robert Westall, *Blitzcat* (New York: Scholastic Inc., 1989).

[51]Robert Newton Peck, *A Day No Pigs Would Die* (New York: Dell Publishing Company, 1972).

[52]Molly Ivins, *Molly Ivins Can't Say That, Can She?* (New York: Random House Inc., 1991).

5. Which three linguistic variations constitute a dialect?
6. Do social and regional variations ever occur simultaneously?
7. How are *language* and *culture* related?
8. Is the older definition of a word more accurate or less accurate?
9. What changes faster, changes in pronunciation or changes in spelling?
10. How are necessity and invention related?

STUDENT EXPLORATIONS FOR
REGIONAL, SOCIAL, AND HISTORICAL VARIATIONS

EXPLORATION: Language Changes
DIRECTIONS: Some people believe changes in our language mean that it is falling apart and going to the dogs. The fact is, language *does* change. If we like the change, we call it *progress*. If we don't like it, we call it *decay*.

1. Talk with your grandparents, or someone their age. What differences have they seen in how the English language has changed during their lifetime. Do they approve or disapprove of the changes?
2. Talk with your parents, or someone their age. What differences have they seen in how the English language has changed during their lifetime. Do they approve or disapprove of the changes?
3. Why, do you think, people from different generations regard language changes differently?

***** ***** *****

EXPLORATION: Wicked, Groovy, Rad
DIRECTIONS: Make a list of some slang terms you once used but no longer use. Can you identify some slang terms your parents and grandparents once used? (Ask them.)

1. How did you, your parents, and your grandparents learn these slang words?
2. What made you stop using some slang words?
3. How do you decide which slang words are "in" and which ones are "out?"
4. Who determines which language is more or less appropriate?

***** ***** *****

EXPLORATION: What's for Dinner, or Supper?
DIRECTIONS: Think of all the words you know that are used to describe eating practices: *dinner, supper, lunch, snack, tea, brunch,* etc.

1. Organize your lists according to the time of day you'd eat them.
2. Can some words signify more than one mealtime?
3. Are there some mealtimes that have only one name?
4. Do some of the names of meals suggest formal or informal dining?
5. Who makes the decisions regarding the names of mealtimes?

***** ***** *****

EXPLORATION: Hymn Language
DIRECTIONS: Look up the meanings for the italicized words in the following lines, taken from well-known hymns.

A. "Amazing grace, how sweet the sound, that saved a *wretch* like me . . . "
B. "Rock of ages, *cleft* for me . . . "
C. "Before Jehovah's *aweful* throne . . . "
D. "Now let the *vault* of heaven resound . . . "

1. Do you use any of these words today?
2. How do these words and their definitions illustrate how language changes over time?

***** ***** *****

EXPLORATION: Nursery Rhyme Time
DIRECTIONS: Here are some lines from well-known nursery rhymes with one word in italics. Look up the italicized words in your dictionary.

A. "Ring around the *rosie* . . . "
B. "Sing a song of *sixpence* . . . "
C. "A *diller* a dollar, a ten o'clock scholar . . . "
D. "*Pease* porridge hot . . . "
E. "Ride a *cockhorse* to Banbury Cross . . . "

1. Do any of the definitions you found surprise you?
2. Do the definitions help you to understand the nursery rhymes better?
3. Why do you suppose these words are no longer in common use today?

***** ***** *****

EXPLORATION: The Math Code
DIRECTIONS: Here is a list of words you use in ordinary conversations. They are also used in the study of mathematics. What can each word mean in both circumstances?

a. *square*   b. *cube*   c. *root*   d. *table*   e. *base*
f. *power*   g. *real*   h. *domain*   i. *rational*   k. *property*

1. What are the differences between the different uses of these words?
2. Can you think of other words that are used in special ways in other school subjects?
3. How does this activity help you to clarify what is meant when people talk about "the meaning" of a word?

***** ***** *****

EXPLORATION: What's in a Name?
DIRECTIONS: A dictionary can reveal interesting facts about languages. Using cither the dictionary you normally use or one you might borrow from the media center or a foreign language teacher, what do you think some of these family names meant originally?

Armstrong, Abbot, Aguilar, Armour, Arrowsmith
Baker, Brewer, Brewster, Barber
Chen, Cooper, Carter, Cutler, Carpenter, Chandler, Cook
Dale, de Leon
Elder
Flores, Fischer, Fuller, For(r)ester, Fletcher, Fowler
Goldschmidt, Garland, Granger
Hidalgo, Hunter, Huerta
Issacson

Jardine

Kaplan, Kaiser, Knox, Knight, Kaufmann

Lansberg, Laine, Li

Miller, Merchant, Mason, Masterson

Nelson

O'Donald

Palmer, Pei

Quentin

Rodriguez, Radcliffe, Roth, Rosenberg

Schneider, Silverberg, Schwarz, Skinner, Smith, Santos

Tanner, Tailor (Taylor)

Underhill

Vintner

Wheeler, Wu, Wright, Warden

Xavier

Yates, Yin, Young (Younger)

Zimmer

What is the story of *your* family name?

***** ***** *****

EXPLORATION: The Water River
DIRECTIONS: The word avon is a Celtic word meaning "water." William Shakespeare was born in Stratford, England, which is located on the Avon River (or, "the River Avon" as speakers in England would say it). Does this mean that the Celts called this river "the Water River"? Examine a highway map for your state, looking especially at the names of the towns and cities. You'll probably find several place names with similar endings, like -polis, -ton, -ham, -ley, field, -worth, and -ing, to name a few.

1. What are the most often used place names in your county or state?
2. According to your dictionary and your own speculation, what did (do) these names mean?
3. Were these towns and cities named after people, places, or events?
4. Are there any remaining ethnic relationships between the names of these towns and their current residents?

5. Given your research findings, what can you conclude about the place names you've studied and the people who originally settled these areas in your state?

***** ***** *****

EXPLORATION: TV Homework

DIRECTIONS: For a period of 1 week, try to watch as many episodes as you can of one type of television program: mysteries, medical programs, programs about attorneys, families, fishing programs, sit-coms, and so on. Regardless of which type of program you select, you'll find they all contain similar characters: the stern judge, the hostile witness, the gruff doctor, the kindly nurse (or vice versa), the heroic or the humorous detective. These characters frequently share several language characteristics, regardless of the particular program.

1. What are some of those characteristics?
2. Why do "all" characters of a certain type use these language features?
3. What is the effect of these repeating language features on the other characters? On the viewer?
4. What does this Exploration lead you to believe about language stereotypes? Or, language groups or communities?

***** ***** *****

EXPLORATION: Pen Pals #1

DIRECTIONS: With the help of your teacher, principal, or school superintendent, locate pen pals in another state (as far away as possible) who are in the same grade in school as you are. Send them your list of slang terms with your definitions.

1. Which terms or phrases on your list do they recognize? How many do they actually use?
2. Ask them to send you also their own list of slang with definitions, then you can analyze their list. How many of their words do you recognize? How many do you actually use?
3. Why, do you think, are the lists different?

***** ***** *****

EXPLORATION: Pen Pals #2
DIRECTIONS: Select three or four poems your class has read, then send copies of the poems and an audiotape to your pen pals. Ask them to tape-record themselves as they read your poems. (You might send them a tape-recording of people in your class reading the poems, too.)

1. When you listen to them reading the poems, do you hear any differences in the ways they read the poem? Do they stress different words?
2. Do they use different intonations at the end of a line or sentence?
3. Do they pronounce individual words differently?
4. Do the varying pronunciations mean that they're wrong and you're right in the way the words are pronounced, or that they're right and you're wrong? Or, do the variations signify something else?

***** ***** *****

EXPLORATION: Pen Pals #3
DIRECTIONS: Send your pen pal class another audiotape and ask them to talk informally as they answer several questions you send them on a brief questionnaire. For example, you might write questions that would ask them to describe their school, favorite teachers, favorite songs and rock groups, best movies, and so on. When the tape is returned, analyze their speech as you did in the proceeding Exploration, Pen Pals 20.

1. Do they stress different words?
2. Do they use different intonations at the end of a line or sentence?
3. Do they pronounce individual words differently? Why?
4. Do the varying pronunciations mean that they're wrong and you're right in the way the words are pronounced, or that they're right and you're wrong? Or, do the variations signify something else?

***** ***** *****

EXPLORATION: Variant Pronunciations
DIRECTIONS: Your dictionary includes a lot of information about words: different meanings people use for a word, the different pronunciations a word may have, and from which language the word came from

originally. What pronunciations does your dictionary include for these words?

again

garage

orange

roof

strength

tower

wash

1. Which dictionary pronunciation is closest to how you normally pronounce each word?
2. Why does the dictionary include more than one pronunciation for these words?
3. How would you respond to the statement, "The first pronunciation is the preferred pronunciation"?

***** ***** *****

EXPLORATION: New Ways for Old Words
DIRECTIONS: Sometimes people will give a familiar word a new spelling, a new pronunciation, or even a new meaning. For one day try to keep a record of the new ways people are using old words (using the word *lite* instead of *light*, for example) by using the New Language Log on the next page. When your day of language observation is finished, bring your completed log to class and answer the following questions:

1. What was the most frequent *type* (spelling, pronunciation, or meaning) of new language you observed?
2. Why do you suppose there were more examples of this type than the others?
3. What would happen if you used any of the new language uses in your written work at school? Would it matter? Would your grade be lowered?
4. Based on your observations of new language uses and your discussions of them with your friends, how would you describe the

reactions of people to changes in the language? Who are the ones who seem to care most about the changes? Or, who seems to care the least?

NEW LANGUAGE LOG

Date of observations: _____

Example   Where observed   Used by whom?   Why was it used?

***** ***** *****

EXPLORATION: ". . . them that speak leasing . . . "
DIRECTIONS: Changes in language are not limited just to slang, or to our general vocabulary. The Bible demonstrates language change, too. Here are five sentences taken from the King James Version of the Bible; note especially the *italicized* words.

> A. I would not have you ignorant, brethren, that oftentimes I purposed to come unto you, (but was *let* thereto), that I might have some fruit among you also, even as among other Gentiles. (Romans 1:13)
>
> B. Let them wander up and down for meat, and *grudge* if they be not satisfied. (Psalms 59:15)
>
> C. And he will appoint him captains over thousands, and captains over fifties; and he will set them to *ear* his ground, and to reap his harvest, and to make his instruments of war, and his instruments of his chariots. (1 Samuel 8:12)
>
> D. Thou shalt destroy them that speak *leasing*: the Lord will abhor the bloody and deceitful man. (Psalms 5:6)
>
> E. But their eyes were *holden* that they should not know him. (Luke 24:16)

1. What do you think the italicized word means in the context of each one of these sentences?
2. Locate each one of these passages in another Bible translation (New English, Jerusalem, Revised Standard Version, Philips, etc.) and see if the alternate version helps your understanding of the italicized words.
3. Finally, consult your dictionary. Look up the italicized words and see if you can determine how the italicized words have changed in

meaning over the years and have taken on the meanings you are more familiar with today.

***** ***** *****

EXPLORATION: Invited Variation
DIRECTIONS: Invite to your class someone who originally comes from a different part of the country. Explain to your guest that the class is studying normal language variations. You can decide how best to elicit oral language from your guest: Ask your guest to describe his or her extended family, a special hobby, or his or her job.

1. In what *specific* ways are the guest's pronunciations or word choices different from yours? Similar to yours?
2. Ask the guest which local pronunciations, word choices, or other expressions used commonly in your community seem "odd" or "different"?
3. What does this exchange lead you to believe about "standard" or "expected" ways of talking in a particular community?

***** ***** *****

EXPLORATION: Linguistic Fingerprints
DIRECTIONS: Without explaining that you are doing so (observing normal and natural language is essential in this, observe one person you know well throughout 1 school day. Record in a language log what your person says to whom. Pay particular attention to recurring words, expressions, or pronunciations your person uses consistently throughout the day.

1. Share the final notes in your log with your friend. The contents of the log will help to describe your friend's *ideolect*, the unique ways each individual speaks.
2. Discuss the log with your friend. Can your friend explain any influences (other friends, a parent, a relative, a teacher) on his or her ideolect?
3. How do our very personal ways of using language develop? In what ways is our language like the language of all people, like the language of some people, and like the language of no other people?

***** ***** *****

EXPLORATION: You Say Goodbye, and I Say Hello
DIRECTIONS: While expressing similar and related sentiments, our different ways of greeting people can produce a special effect or flavor. Think of the different ways we say "Hello" and "Goodbye." For a day, maybe 2, observe the different ways people greet you and the ways people indicate that they are leaving.

1. How often do you hear any of the following expressions:

EXPRESSIONS OF "HELLO"	EXPRESSIONS OF "GOODBYE"
Hi	Bye
Howdy	Bye-bye
How do	See ya
Greetings	Ciao
Hullo	So long
How are you?	Farewell
What's going on?	Adieu
Hey	Toodle-oo
Hola	Cheerio
How's it going?	See you later
What's happening?	Fare you well
What's up?	Good night/evening
Good morning/afternoon	Be seeing you
Hey, dude	Adios

Which hello/goodbye expressions can you add to this list?

2. How many of these expressions have you actually used? Where have you heard any of these expressions? Which expressions are used by older speakers? Younger speakers?
3. Which expressions are formal? Informal?
4. Some of these terms have been borrowed from other languages. Can you identify the original language?
5. Why is it helpful to have so many options available for saying hello and goodbye?

***** ***** *****

EXPLORATION: The Right or Write Word
DIRECTIONS: Examine this list of words, doing the following:

a. Circle a word if you usually use it.
b. Put a star (*) beside a word you would think strange for an older person to use.
c. Put an "X" beside those you never use.

truant	ditch	hooky	mongo
smidgen	grass widow	humongous	corn
micro	poke	pone	sack
cornbread	snob	bread	squash
hare	uppity	lightbread	jack rabbit
Johnnycake	hollow	feud	booze
divorcee	skunk	reckon	cave
play-pretty	moonshine	redneck	heck
gleek	polecat	guess	rumble
toys	whiskey	figger	bag
cushaw	kinfolk	bunny	fight
conceited			

1. Compare your answers with others in your class. Are there any interesting or surprising differences or similarities in your marked words?
2. Using words from this list, the school principal might report that a student was truant, a parent might say the student played hooky, but the student might say she ditched school. Can you find similar teams of words? Who might use one of the words in the teams you've identified?
3. Why do different speakers select different terms in order to communicate similar ideas?

***** ***** *****

EXPLORATION: Some Dialect Fieldwork
DIRECTIONS: Read the following, then select the answer that reflects what you usually and most often say.

Where do you get water from?
  a. tap   b. faucet   c. spigot

What do you fry eggs in?
a. fry pan pan   b. skillet   c. frying pan

What do you eat at an athletic contest?
a. frank   b. wiener   c. hot dog

What might you eat for breakfast?
a. hotcakes   b. flapjacks   c. pancakes

What is a *tavern*?
a. bar   b. sandwich c. inn

What is a *whip*?
a. licorice   b. strap   c. path

When do people eat *lunch*?
a. noon   b. morning   c. afternoon

1. Contrast your answers with others in your class. Discuss why some people might use different terms for the same idea or object.

2. Have you heard other members of your family use any of these words? Who? How old are they? Where do they live?

4. Can you add to the preceding sentences, giving different terms for the same idea or object?

5. How do we decide which word we will use in the sample sentences seen here? How is the decision made?

***** ***** *****

EXPLORATION: Leave It to Beaver and Bart
DIRECTIONS: Watching television carefully can help us learn a great deal about language. Watch one episode of "Leave It to Beaver" and one episode of "The Simpsons." How many specific differences in language use can you observe? For example, how does Beaver greet his father; how does Bart greet Homer?

1. What slang terms did you see in the episodes?

2. How do Beaver's conversations with his friends differ from that ways Bart talks to his friends?

3. How do the conversations between Beaver and Wally differ from those between Bart and Lisa?

4. How do the parents on the two programs talk to their children?

5. What are some of the reasons for the language differences you've observed in these programs?

***** ***** *****

EXPLORATION: Good, Bad, or Ugly?
DIRECTIONS: Visit with a grandparent or a person old enough to be a grandparent about changes they've observed in the way language is being used today. Do they think the changes are examples of progress? Of decay? You might talk about the following:

1. What about "taboo" words? They seem to be used more casually today, in conversation, on TV. Is this acceptable?

2. What about the emphasis on gender-neutral words, like *fireperson* instead of *fireman*?

3. "Private products," for both men and women, and advertised openly. Is this a good idea?

4. What do the responses you receive tell you about language change?

***** ***** *****

EXPLORATION: What's in a Name? (An illustrative language exploration activity using literature, based on *Great Expectations*)
DIRECTIONS: Charles Dickens enjoyed using language for a variety of purposes. In *Great Expectations*, Mrs. Joe uses a stick she calls the "tickler" to beat Pip and Joe with. Miss Havisham's name includes the word *sham*; a "sham" is a trick, an attempt to delude another. Now, let's consider some more words from *Great Expectations*.

1. Who and what is Estella? Look up the word *stellar* in your dictionary?

2. What is "Satis House"? Look up the word *status* or the word *satisfy* in your dictionary.

3. Consider Joe Gargery for a moment. Look up the word *gargantuan* in your dictionary.

4. Do the names of people, places, and things matter in literature? Why, or why not?

***** ***** *****

EXPLORATION: Social Climbing Up, Up, and Away
DIRECTIONS: Read the following groups of words, and or each group, decide who is more likely to use them:

davenport	sofa	Couch
bubbler	drinking fountain	water fountain
soda	coke	pop
restroom	bathroom	john
brunch	lunch	dinner

1. How many of these words do you use? Which ones would you *never* use?

2. Why are different words used to express the same idea?

3. How do you decide which words are more or less appropriate to use?

CHAPTER **9**

Meanings and General Semantics

*The concepts people live by are derived only from
perceptions and from language, and since the perceptions
are received and interpreted only in the light of earlier
concepts, man comes pretty close to living in a house that
language built, located by maps that language drew.*
—Russell F. W. Smith, *Linguistics in Theory and Practice*

Before you read this chapter, think about what makes "dirty"
words *dirty*? What should be done, if anything, to people who burn
flags; why? Would you rather buy an article of clothing from a *sales-
clerk* or from an *apparel broker*; why? Finally, the Latinate words
for "going to the bathroom" are more acceptable than are their
Anglo-Saxon counterparts; why?

WHAT'S IN A NAME? WORD MAGIC!

Starbuck is a character in Herman Melville's 1851 novel *Moby Dick*.
Starbuck serves as the first mate on the *Pequod*, the whaling ship under
the command of the mad Captain Ahab. Melville's Starbuck is strong,
steady, and loyal, and goes down with the ship and Captain Ahab. Starbuck
is a character in the play, *The Rainmaker*, and also appears in a television
science-fiction series, *Battlestar Galactica*.[1] Starbuck has more recently
become immortalized since a national coffee franchise has assumed
his name.

---

[1]http://www.who2.com/starbuck.html.

The chain of coffee shops offers three cup sizes, but they aren't the more traditional *small, medium,* and *large.* The sizes they use are *tall* (small), *grande* (medium), and *grande supremo* (large). What has actually been changed here? Does coffee served in a *tall-, grande-,* or *grande supremo*-sized cup taste better? Probably not. Is tall bigger than small? Doubtful. This terminology is an example of **word magic**.

Mr. Language Person, humorist Dave Barry's alter-ego, says, "Unfortunately, we consumers, like moron sheep, started actually using those names [for cup sizes]. Why? If Starbucks decided to call its toilets 'AquaSwooshies,' would we go along with that? Yes! Baaaa!"[2]

Words and names are important, as we've observed numerous times. Sports teams are known in the United States by a variety of names: *Tigers, Lions, Bears, Cubs, Orioles, Cardinals,* and *Giants,* to name a few. As the professional leagues continue to approve franchises in new cities, however, I'll bet you the cost of this book that no new team will be named the *Rats, Hippos, Sloths,* or *Tapirs.* The reason is simple: word magic.

The magical influence of language can be observed in languages all around the world. The belief that words can control objects, events, and people is evident in the uses of magical formulae, litanies of names, and many other rites in black and white magic and in organized religion.[3]

For example, when someone sneezes we automatically say *Bless you* or *Gesundheit* ("health"), following a custom of warding off disease by using the right words. In religious ceremonies clergy will say words like *I baptize you . . .* or "*I now pronounce you husband and wife*". The saying of the words becomes *the act* of baptism or *the act* of marriage. At sports events cheerleaders lead the spectators in chanting special incantations, like *DEE-fense, DEE-fense,* in hopes that the chanting will magically inspire or enable the team to greater levels of performance.

The mystique of words can affect the choices of names for things. In 1868, the name of the Japanese city called *Edo* was changed to *Tokyo* ("eastern residence"), symbolizing a new period in Japanese history.[4] In Russia, historical events caused the city of *St. Petersburg* to become *Petrograd,* and later it was changed again to *Leningrad.*

---

[2]Dave Barry, "Mr. Language Person Returns in a Grande Way," *Lincoln (NE) Journal Star,* October 10, 2004, sec. K.

[3]David Crystal, *The Cambridge Encyclopedia of Language* (Cambridge: Cambridge University Press, 1991), 8.

[4]Ibid., 9.

In politics, names matter. Who, for instance, could have opposed the Republican Party's *American Dream Restoration Act*? Similarly, who would speak in opposition to the Democrats' *Middle Class Bill of Rights*? *Because* voters sometimes have difficulty dealing with the details of proposed legislation, the *name* given to a proposed bill becomes part of the substance of the proposal.[5]

You'll hear politicians use the following words with predictable and monotonous regularity: *flag, prosperity, common sense, family values, corruption, liberal, left-wing, right-wing,* and *decay.* Why? Because these words have a magical effect on people. The saying of the words triggers immediate, and often unthinking, positive or negative responses.

Automobile names are revealing, too. Manufacturers use names like *Blazer, Explorer, Saturn,* and *Lexus,* but not names like *Tank* or *Tug.* And, you'll not likely ever, ever see another boat named *Titanic.* Why? Word magic.

Here are some successes and failures in the naming of products. To what extent did the name changes matter to the buying public?

- *Orange Roughy*, a sweet-tasting, mild-flavored fish, was once called *slimehead*.
- *Canola oil*, a substitute for cholesterol-rich cooking oils, was once called *rapeseed oil.*
- *Fair Lady*, the name of Nissan sports cars that had been sold in Japan with considerable success, was introduced to the U.S. market under a new, more masculine name: the Z-series, *240Z, 300Z.*
- *Pschitt,* a popular soft drink in France, failed miserably when it was introduced in the United States. (Enough said!)
- *Slime eel*, found in the New England fishing waters, was changed to *hag fish.* (Why bother?)
- *Gruntfish*, sometimes called *hogfish*, from the Carolinas, was changed to *pigfish.* (Again, why bother?)[6]

From recent wars a number of words and terms have been produced, each one an attempt to conjure a meaning separate from reality. *Hot contact point*, for example, is a place where soldiers get shot at. *Collateral damage* refers to the accidental killing of noncombatant civilians. *Mouseholing* is not something done in an animated cartoon broadcast on Saturday morning

---

[5]"What's in a Name? Success," *Lincoln (NE) Journal Star,* June 18, 1996, sec. A.

[6]Ibid.

television; it refers to blowing a hole in a side wall of a house in order to avoid using the front door, which might be booby-trapped.

Finding the right term for the enemy in Iraq has been a struggle. What, or who, are they: *thugs, assassins, rebels, guerillas, insurgents, resistance,* or *fedayeen*? *Resistance* evokes World War II heroics á la the movie *Casablanca*. *Rebel* calls to mind the good guys in *The Empire Strikes Back* and possibly *Lawrence of Arabia*.[7]

FOR YOUR INQUIRY AND PRACTICE:

Collect a number of display advertisements, those with pictures, from magazines directed to special audiences (publications like, but not limited to, *Jet, Ebony, Tennis, Runner's World, Successful Farming, Family Circle, Cosmopolitan, Esquire*, etc.). How does the language used in the advertisements "speak" to the intended audience? Is there any "word magic" at work?

More often than not, it's not *what* is said, but *how* it is said that matters. For example, what do you think of when you hear or read the word *welfare*? To some people, the word *welfare* conjures up images of cheating low-lifes who are buying expensive automobiles with welfare checks. *Welfare* can also describe programs whose primary aim is to provide shelter, food, and health care for poor children or *welfare* can describe the costs for daycare for those who are trying to work their way off welfare roles.

In order to clarify how people felt about welfare, the *New York Times* conducted a survey, which is of significant semantic interest. Notice especially the language used in each question and the corresponding answers:[8]

Do You Think Government Spending on Programs for Poor Children Should be Increased, Decreased or Kept About the Same?

Increased	47%
Decreased	9%

---

[7]Geoffrey Nunberg, *Going Nucular: Language, Politics, and Culture in Confrontational Times* (New York: Perseus Book Group, 2004), 92.

[8]"How You Say It Matters," *Lincoln (NE) Journal Star*, March 9, 1995.

Same	39%
Don't know	6%

On the other hand, consider these results, when the *same question*, essentially, was worded differently:

Do You Think Government Spending on Welfare Should Be Increased, Decreased, or Kept About The Same?

Increased	13%
Decreased	48%
Same	36%
Don't know	3%

By carefully revising the language used in the two questions, which were asking people how they felt about the *same issue*, the *New York Times* reporter received diametrically opposite responses. Words, in this example, and the meanings the respondents attached to the words used in the questions, performed their magic.

You might remember these data, by the way, the next time you read or hear about the results of a "scientific poll." A pollster with good verbal skills can ask questions that will insure the preferred results!

Words and symbols, as well as the meanings invested in those words and symbols, are important to many people. Places of worship are full of symbols important to the denomination: Stained-glass windows, paintings, sculpture, and wall hangings depict lambs, doves, arks, stars, boats, angels, candles, crosses, rainbows, flags, banners, and the like. Homes are decorated with green plants, memorabilia from vacation trips, religious icons, and photographs of significant family members and events.

Here is a statement from a writer of a letter to the editor who feels deeply about a particular symbol: the U.S. flag:

Two weeks ago my mother, daughter and I were in Lincoln for some meetings and were fortunate enough to take in several Star City holiday festival activities, including the December 5 parade. While the parade was enjoyable for all three generations, I remain disturbed by one thing. As the color guard rounded the corner, only a handful of people stood for the passing of the flag. Among those already standing, only a few paused to salute. As my mother and I rose and I placed my two-year-old's hand over her heart, I inquired of those around me, 'Isn't anyone going to stand a salute the flag?' The puzzled looks from parents and children alike were shocking. I felt sorry for the veterans [bearing the flag] passing by. Since I am not from Lincoln, I am curious. Do the elementary school children receive any lessons in flag etiquette? Do the parents share in the processes if there are? Standing to salute is such a simple thing and it has a tremendous heritage behind it. No wonder our society is in such turmoil if even the simplest acts of civility are starting to fall by the wayside.[9]

I'm including this letter to the editor for a simple reason: to demonstrate how deeply one person feels about one symbolic act. Whether you or I might agree or disagree with the writer of the letter is another matter. The fact remains, different people will ascribe significantly different meanings to symbols.

The author of this letter isn't alone in her regard for the flag. Recently, a city councilman in a nearby city introduced a proposal with the hope that it would be endorsed by the city council and then be forwarded to the state legislature for statewide enactment. The proposal would require all public school students to begin each school day by saluting the U.S. flag and singing the national anthem.[10] These symbolic acts, the councilman said, would discourage crime and gang activity.

On my campus there was a recent controversy created when an undergraduate student, Anglo-European, from North Carolina put a Confederate flag in the window of his room in the dormitory. According to newspaper accounts, his friends and roommates describe the young man as shy, nice, and "not a racist." For him, the stars and bars symbolized home and his Southern heritage. Another student, African-American, attached a different set of meanings to the flag in the window. To her, the flag symbolized oppression and slavery and she complained about it to the campus student affairs office.[11] The issue was resolved with no further publicity, and I include it here simply to illustrate how people can have divergent views regarding the same symbol.

In another well-publicized circumstance, a 64-year-old Vietnam veteran flew his U.S. flag upside down on his backyard flag pole as a protest against the war in Iraq. "This doesn't mean anything against the boys and girls in the war right now," he said, "they're doing their job. I just wanted to express myself on my own land."[12]

---

[9]Letter to the editor, *Lincoln (NE) Journal Star*, December 18, 1992.

[10]"Make Students Salute Flag, Councilman Urges," *Omaha (NE) World-Herald*, November 17, 1996, sec. B.

[11]"Confederate Flag Causes Flap," *Lincoln (NE) Journal Star*, September 14, 2004, sec. A.

[12]"Flag Desecration Charges Against Vietnam Veteran Are Dismissed, *Lincoln (NE) Journal Star*, November 12, 2004, sec. B.

As symbols go, the U.S. flag is powerful.

Foods can assume symbolic significance, too. A browned and glistening turkey in a roasting pan is a symbol of Thanksgiving. Watermelon can be either a symbol for the hazy, lazy days of summer, or a trite and banal symbol denigrating African Americans.

Following the lead of Stolichnaya, vodka had replaced gin, scotch, and bourbon as the top-selling spirits in the United States by 1976, a position it has continued to hold for almost three decades. After the Soviet downing of Flight 007 in 1982, however, sales of Russian products like Stolichnaya vodka tumbled, leaving a ready market for the Swedish vodka, Absolut.[13] Boycotting Stolichnaya was a symbolic act by U.S. vodka drinkers.

During World War I, in an attempt to fight Germany on the home front, many in the United States refused to use the Germanic *sauerkraut* and renamed it *liberty cabbage. Dachsunds* became known as *liberty dogs.* When France refused to become a part of the coalition President George W. Bush attempted to create for hostilities against Iraq, many diners stopped listing *French fries* on their menus, replacing them with *freedom fries*.[14] The dog breed itself wasn't changed; neither were the foods. The names, however, the *symbols* for the foods and the dog breed, were changed.

Individuals in a certain line of work can change their names, symbolizing a profession with, ostensibly, more professionalism and more prestige. This is how *undertakers* became *morticians* and *janitors* became *sanitary engineers*. Not all members of an identifiable group will agree with the semantic changes, as this writer demonstrates:

> As someone who respects words, I am bothered when people try to gain more respect by changing what they call themselves. The progression is almost always from clarity to vagueness; we know what janitors do, but are less sure what custodians and sanitary engineers are responsible for. My own profession in now in a wholesale flight from the words *library* and *librarian* with a similar loss of meaning; we know what libraries and librarians are, but not what learning resource centers and information specialists will do for us.[15]

This writer goes on to lament the change in the professional titles of those educators formerly known as librarians. Clearly, she resists what these changes symbolize.

---

[13]Corby Kummer, "Flavorless No More," *The Atlantic Monthly*, December 2004, 189.

[14]Nunberg, *Going Nucular*, 79.

[15]Marylaine Block, "Change a Word, Change a World," *My Word's Worth*, March 27, 2000, http://www.marylaine.com/myword/wordmean.html.

All of the preceding examples illustrate, I hope, the significance people invest in symbols and how these symbols represent significant meanings for them. In our everyday lives ceremonial singing, chanting, and speaking are routine events in our culture. Civic organizations typically open their meetings with a group recitation of the Pledge of Allegiance to the U.S. flag, or by singing the national anthem, or with a prayer, or with all three. At major sporting events at the intercollegiate and professional levels, the spectators sing the national anthem. At worship, congregations read in unison various collects, scriptures, prayers, and responsive readings. At mealtime, a prayer is spoken. All of these are examples of word magic.

In my macrofamily, word magic was used in relation to the before-eating blessing: Anything you sneak from the table *before* the prayer automatically turns into fat! So warned, we learned to mind our manners!

IT'S "ONLY SEMANTICS"

Some of the terminology associated with the study of language is frequently misused. For example, the differences between *grammar* and *usage* are blurred when a charge is made that someone "doesn't know his grammar." More often than not, those who say this are actually describing their personal preference for a particular style or *usage*, such as the distinctions in the uses of *lie/lay, fewer/lesser, and between/among*; avoiding prepositions in sentence-final positions; or trying to assiduously avoid split infinitives. These represent *usage* variations, not errors in *grammar*. **Usage** denotes the ways people actually perform oral and written language within the wide range of available options. **Grammar**, on the other hand, usually refers to a description of how words and phrases normally relate to each other in oral or written sentences in a language, their morphology and their meanings.

Similarly, the terms *rhetoric* and *semantics* are sometimes misused, often in an unfavorable sense as if the terms themselves were negative labels for bad language usages or habits. Some people will comment, for instance, that "If you can cut through his campaign rhetoric, Mr. Smith might be a good candidate for mayor."

Likewise, you have heard, I imagine, any number of heated discussions brought to an abrupt end by the charge: "Well, that's just a matter of semantics!" This judgment has stopped many conversations.

A statement such as the last one is either an overt or an uninformed attempt to disregard and then to dismiss differences of opinion, belief, and perception as being insignificant or petty annoyances created by the different meanings the conversational participants have constructed. How *meaning* can be downgraded in this manner is nothing short of pathetic.

Usually the person who alleges that a difference of opinion is "only semantics" is attempting to minimize the different meanings the discussants have ascribed to the words and terms being used to define and describe one's *beliefs*.

The meanings and beliefs we hold in our minds are not, in my view, objects of minimal importance. Quite to the contrary, they collectively represent one's sense and apprehension of the universe.

The word *semantics* is derived from the Greek *semantikos*; *significant"* comes from *semainein*, "to signify," "to mean."[16] As practiced by General Semanticists, semantics is the study of signification, the study of the relationship(s) between and among symbols, names, and meanings.

As I said in chapter 1, to most people, *meaning* is the most interesting aspect of language. In this chapter let me elaborate by adding that most people find meaning to be not only the most interesting but also the most *consequential*!

SEMANTICS AND LINGUISTICS

The field of General Semantics was introduced to U.S. language scholars by Alfred Korzybski, through his book *Science and Sanity: An Introduction to Non-Aristotelian Systems and General Semantics. Science and Sanity* created quite a stir after its publication, and the general semantics movement flourished in the United States in the 1940s and 1950s.[17]

As Hasselriis points out,[18] among the reasons for this burst of interest was the publication of S. I. Hayakawa's *Language in Action*.[19] Still reeling from the successes of Hitler, Mussolini, and others who had perfected the use of "the big lie" and other deliberate misuses of language, the

---

[16]Alfred Korzybski, *Science and Sanity: An Introduction to Non-Aristotelian Systems and General Semantics,* 4th ed. (Lakeville, CT: International Non-Aristotelian Publishing Company, 1958), 19.

[17]Ross Evans Paulson, *Language, Science and Action: Korzybski's General Semantics: A Study in Comparative Intellectual History* (Westport, CT: Greenwood Press, 1983), 87–88.

[18]Peter Hasselriis, "From Pearl Harbor to Watergate to Kuwait: Language in Thought and Action," *English Journal,* 80, no. 2 (1991): 28.

[19]S. I. Hayakawa, *Language in Action* (New York: Harcourt, Brace and Company, 1941).

reading public was ready to learn about how *meaning* is perceived, made, received, and filtered, and how to detect intentional distortions in language. Hayakawaya's book, as well as the teachings and writings of Stuart Chase, Wendell Johnson, and Irving Lee, helped readers examine language use through what many considered to be completely new lenses. Interest in General Semantics was keen. In fact, in December 1941 *Language in Action* was the Book-of-the-Month Club selection, a truly auspicious achievement for a book about the study of language!

Shortly thereafter, however, academic linguistics experienced a fundamental paradigm shift. In 1957 Noam Chomsky published *Syntactic Structures*, the first articulation of transformational-generative grammar, which de-emphasized semantics.[20] Chomsky's ideas have been the central, defining force among U.S. linguists in particular, and to some extent among linguists in the larger, global linguistics community, since 1957. Sooner or later in most language discussions, linguists describe or define their beliefs in relation to their agreement or disagreement with Chomsky.

Since the late 1950s, the field of linguistics in the United States has experienced unprecedented oscillations in the amount of attention paid to meaning, and the status of semantics in the discipline in general. University students entering courses and programs of language study in the past 20 to 25 years have little understanding or appreciation of the bias against semantics that held sway in the 1960s and early 1970s.[21]

ALFRED KORZYBSKI AND GENERAL SEMANTICS

Alfred Korzybski, philosopher, mathematician, amateur linguist, and professional engineer, is generally regarded as the "father" of the field of general semantics. Korzybski's book *Science & Sanity: An Introduction to Non-Aristotelian Systems and General Semantics* was first published in 1933, and it established the science of General Semantics. Some of Korzybski's observations and principles of General Semantics are as follows:

Meaning Is Not in Words, But in People. Meaning is not something to be received, extracted, caught, or got from a symbol, a word, or a page;

---

[20]Paulson, Language, Science, 87.

[21]William Labov, preface *On Semantics*, by Uriel Weinrich (Philadelphia: University of Pennsylvania Press, 1980), vii.

rather, meaning is what people assign or attach to the symbol or the word. In other words, we don't *get* but we *give* meanings to symbols and words.[22]

For example, people are not likely to connect or associate a meaning to a word beyond their experience. Unless you are familiar with the languages cited here, the Spanish word *taza* or the Tongan word *ili* will remain only splotches of ink on paper for you. These words do not *tell* you anything. It follows that the same would be true for any word from any language we don't know.

That meaning is not in things but in people is not only evident when considering verbal symbols, but is also true for nonverbal, or graphic, symbols. An example of this can be found in the search by traffic engineers for a sign to post at the side of a street or road in order to alert motorists that they are nearing a school and should, therefore, drive with caution. The sign that was first designed used the lamp of knowledge as a symbolic, nonverbal warning that "there's a school ahead and children may be in the street" statement. However, many people did not recognize the lamp of knowledge and did not, obviously, ascribe any meaning to it at all. Only later was the primitive outline of a school building used, and because people could create successful meaning from this shape, it replaced the earlier sign.

Because meaning resides within the experiences or schemata of people, language is open to multiple interpretations. As a high school junior observed in a Spanish IV class recently, "Language means different things to different people. I guess that's why we have lawyers." Out of the mouths of babes . . .!

Words Are Not What They Refer To.   An object or a feeling, Korzybski pointed out, is *unspeakable*. A toothache or a chair, for example, may be *named* or *described* by words, but the naming or the describing are *not* the same thing(s) as the *condition*. **The condition itself is fundamentally unspeakable and it simply exists.**[23] A word can be a symbol for or a name for a definition. Whether the word is a symbol or a name, however, it is an *abstraction*, removed from the level of absolute objectivity, which is always *unspeakable*.[24]

A more familiar paraphrase for this Korzybskian understanding (that words are not what they refer to) is "the word is not the thing." From the writings of Piaget, for example, we know that children equate names and

---

[22]Korzybski, *Science and Sanity,* 21–22.

[23]Ibid., 34.

[24]Ibid., 92.

things. Perhaps you are familiar with the apocryphal comment made by a child: "'Pig' is a good name for that animal because it's so dirty!" Of course, a statement like this ignores both the symbolic and the arbitrary nature of language. First of all, when we say the word *pig* we've only said a word; we haven't uttered the actual condition or thing. Articulating the word *pig* is to say the name of a definition. Second, if *pig* were the perfect name for the animal in question, then every language used on Earth would use the word *pig* when referring to the animal in this illustration. This is clearly not the case, however, because we know that the animal we are discussing may be known by the name of *cerdo* to some people, as *schwein* to some, or as *cochon* to others, to cite but three examples.

Not only does this understanding from Korzybski help to remind us of the arbitrary feature of language, but it also means that even if we are in a community of same-language speakers, saying a word is not the same as "saying" the thing the word refers to, the *referent*. Though a word is only a symbol referring to a referent (thing), it can be, nevertheless, a symbol to which people ascribe a great deal of emotion.

Confusing a word with the word's unspeakable referent results, for example, in cautions to children that they must avoid saying "dirty" words. It is implicitly assumed that having the word in one's mouth is the same thing as having the actual referent or "thing" in one's mouth: That's why one legendary punishment for using "dirty" language is to wash the culprit's mouth out with soap!

One of the reasons people employ **euphemisms** is to avoid the semantic dilemma of having a dirty, unmentionable or indelicate word or thing in their mouth. This is one reason why we use terms like *bathroom*, *restroom*, and *powder room* when, in fact, we go to this room with no intention of taking a bath, resting, or powdering.

I confess that I intentionally exploited this confusion once. Back in my junior high school teaching days, I happened one afternoon after school to come upon some of my students who were hanging out in the school parking lot. They were using language of the "blue" variety. In fact, their language was bluer . . . no, it was the *bluest* I had ever heard. My uninvited and unexpected presence startled them; they waited for a dressing-down. Instead of giving them a "You-should-be-ashamed-what-would-your-parents-think?" speech, or a more academic "Only-those-with-limited-language-or-imagination-use-language-like-that" lecture, all I said was: *"Do you eat with those mouths?"*

They stared back at me in stunned silence, not fully realizing but dimly suspecting what I had accomplished with my brief question. Although they lacked the words to articulate the concept, they realized I was playing some form of word magic. I had turned a taboo event into a "thing" and it was lodged in their mouths.

Every society has taboo words. The taboo words, however, are only arbitrary and symbolic referents to other objects or conditions. Remember that a map is only a map, a representation; it is not the actual, objective, and ultimately unspeakable territory. I did not explain this to my students, but I think they were fussing with the general notion.

There is more to be said about euphemisms than has been described here. Euphemisms, which are used for several purposes beyond these illustrations, are described in more detail later in this chapter.

Language Operates on Varying Levels of Abstraction. This is another Korzybskian notion. Some language, for example, operates at a higher or a lower level of abstraction, or concreteness, depending on how "close" the language is to its otherwise unspeakable but verifiable referents.[25] The following sentences progressively move from the more abstract and general to the more concrete and specific:

> I'm shopping for clothes.
>
> I'm looking for a new shirt.
>
> I need a new tennis shirt.
>
> I want a white, ribbed-collar knit shirt.
>
> I want a white, ribbed-collar knit shirt with an alligator on the leftbreast.

It is clearly useful to know whether one is hearing or reading language that is more or less abstract or concrete. Better comprehension and understanding result when we can detect highly abstract claims made about a product being advertised, a candidate running for office, or a vague question asked by a student. In the two former examples, we can decide whether we'll purchase the product or vote for the candidate. For example, the word *value* is very popular in advertising and in politics. How many products claim to be "the best value for your money"? All political candidates run for office promising to uphold "family values."

In the case of the student's question, we'll know whether to ask her to repeat the question, ". . . and please be more specific." When we ask for "more specific" restatements in this manner, I suspect we are usually asking

---

[25]Ibid., 389.

the questioner to be less abstract and try to use more specific, more concrete language.

Meaning Has "Direction." If you are familiar with the terms *connotation* and *denotation*, then you already understand a great deal concerning this observation from Korzybski. He used the terms **intensional** (connotation) and **extensional** (denotation) to describe the two directions meaning can take.

The clearest distinctions between intensional and extensional meanings have been provided by one of Korzybski's former students, and one of his clearer translators, S. I. Hayakawa. Hayakawa points out that the extensional meaning of an utterance is that which it refers to in the extensional, physical, verifiable, but unspeakable state of being. An extensional meaning cannot be expressed in words because it is, fundamentally and essentially, the actual (and unspeakable) territory. We can refer to and illustrate an extensional meaning we may have in mind by putting our hands over our mouths and pointing at an extensional meaning, whether it's a tree, a dog, a pencil, a radio, or any other object.[26]

Obviously, however, we can't always point at an object, feeling, or a condition. In the real world of authentic language use, we seldom cover our mouths in an attempt to communicate unspeakable actualities. This is why understanding and using the more familiar term *denotation* is helpful.

We can use the concept of denotation to refer to that which is being talked about. When I mentioned my Maltese dog in chapter 4, I could not explain what I meant to explain to you by pointing to him, thus communicating to you the extensional meaning, *my dog*. Nevertheless, in the language you and I read, the word *dog* denotes a class of animals in the world, and you easily understood that this word included the pet I was referring to.[27]

On the other hand, the *intensional meaning* of an expression, sentence, phrase, or word is that which is suggested (connoted) inside one's head. Certain words conjure up positive or negative feelings, good or bad connotations that we ascribe to them.[28]

The languages we speak, write, hear, read, and encounter every day will usually have both extensional (denotation) and intensional (connotation)

---

[26]S. I. Hawakaya and Alan R. Hawakaya, *Language in Thought and Action,* 5th ed. (New York: Harcourt Brace Jovanovich, 1990), 36.

[27]Ibid., 36–37.

[28]Ibid., 37.

meaning, and at other times one type of meaning will be much more predominant. For example, if a report you're reading uses the symbol /Σ/ then you may have an understanding of its extensional (denotation) meaning, one that will likely be free from intensional meanings, or connotations. On the other hand, an advertising slogan inviting everyone to "Come see the softer side of Sears" or another that claims that Panasonic is "just slightly ahead of our time" are statements having no extensional meanings. They are, however, loaded with a variety of intensional meanings and connotations.

Identification.   According to Korzybski, **identification** is a "semantic disturbance" consisting of errors in meanings.[29] What I take Korzybski's discussion to mean is that some people cannot or do not distinguish a factual report from an inference, one teenager from another, or one Democrat or Republican from another. In the Korzybskian sense, as I understand this concept, identification means something more like *identicalification* because a person who suffers from this "disturbance" identifies similar conditions, events, people, and things as *identical*.

In practice, identification is at work in someone's language/thinking when you hear that someone say "Look at that crazy woman driver! Why can't women learn to drive?" The person who might say this is treating *all* women drivers as *one identical* motorist.

Similarly, we can hear or read related comments about how it comes to be that *all* New Yorkers are pushy and rude, *all* Blacks are natural athletes and have innate rhythm, *all* Jews are wealthy because they are shrewd and marginally ethical negotiators, and *all* mothers-in-law are nosy and overbearing. Additional examples abound *identifying*, in the special Korzybskian use of the term: bankers, school administrators, politicians, clergy persons, football players, English teachers, and any other identifiable group you care to name.

Identification can certainly simplify the world we live in, but it's a disturbing, inaccurate behavior that results in a faulty map of reality. The fact is, there are no two instances, Blacks, Jews, mothers-in-law, football players, or other conditions or circumstances that are identical.

Korzybski's solution to this circumstance was to suggest the use of index numbers, thereby affixing a superscript (**indexing**) so that, for example, when we say the word dog, we will remind ourselves that we are meaning dog[1] (my particular pet, a Maltese dog, named Christopher Robin), not

---

[29]Korzybski, *Science and Sanity,* 452.

Dog$_1$

FIG. 9.1.   Korzybski's solution to identification.

dog^2 (Rex and Ardis Bevins' Maltese pet dog, named Scruffy), or dog^3 (Jim and Caryl Bryan's pet dog, named Spencer), or dog^4 (the ugly, loud dog next door, named Dammit Shut Up) . . . and so on, through dog^z.

Obviously, Korzybski's solution of indexing is impractical, although I suspect, given the imperious tone of his writing, he intended for everyone in the world to use indexing. My suggestion is to take Korzybski at his best, not his worst: *Think* indexing, and you'll accomplish the same thing.

As an attempt to deflect semantic disturbance, or *meaning disturbance*, indexing reminds us that as we participate in language events concerning people, objects, conditions, and propositions, we are considering only *one* case or instance from a larger universe of events and objects. Indexing also helps us keep in order the houses our language is building and our maps to those houses more accurate.

EUPHEMISMS AND JARGON

Language critics frequently cite the use of euphemisms and jargon as the chief roadblocks to clear meanings, using them as examples of what Korzybski would call "semantic disturbance." Euphemisms and jargon, they will maintain, are attempts to hide true meaning because the uninitiated listener or reader will be misled. Calling a 5-year-old automobile with 74,000 miles on the odometer, for example, a *pre-owned* or an *experienced* instead of a *used* car would seem to be an illustration of this type of misleading language.

The use of the term *experienced automobile* is an attempt to enhance the value of a used car. "Sure," the used-car salesman might say, "this car is 10 years old, but it's *experienced*." Well, I think to myself, I want a dentist who is experienced; I want a physician who is experienced; I know that Steve Anderson, the man who figures my income taxes each year, is experienced. Experience, I conclude, is good. "So," I ask the used-car salesman, "are those brand-new, *inexperienced* cars in the showroom cheaper?"

Postman defines a euphemism as "an auspicious or exalted term (like 'sanitation engineer') that is used in place of a more down-to-earth term (like 'garbage man')." Euphemizing is, he suggests, an attempt to give a prettier name to an uglier reality.[30] This definition would seem to fit the preceding illustration concerning the *preowned* and *experienced*, but nevertheless, *used* car.

It should be pointed out, however, that applying prettier names to uglier realities is not always a deceitful practice. Sometimes we use euphemisms out of our desire to be sensitive to others. For example, Postman calls "Operation Sunshine," the name for a series of hydrogen bomb experiments conducted by the U.S. government in the South Pacific, one of the more detestable euphemisms used in recent years. It is deceitful.[31] The purpose of Operation Sunshine was to develop a thermonuclear bomb for killing. More recently, Iraqi civilians who were killed during Operation Desert Storm were referred to by Pentagon sources not as "nonmilitary Iraqi citizens who have been accidentally killed" but as "collateral damage."

On the other hand, we may euphemize and substitute *passed* or *passed away* for *died*. We do this not because we are attempting to be deceitful or to hide the truth, but because we are sensitive to the emotional state and needs of those who have experienced a recent death in their family.[32]

There is nothing *inherently* wrong with the use of euphemisms. Euphemisms, like all other aspects of language and any other tools, are neither intrinsically moral nor intrinsically immoral in and of themselves. A hammer is an amoral object that can be used either in the construction of a new home or in the smashing of automobile headlights. Our judgment should not be focused on the tool, but on the user, the intent, and the outcome. So it is with euphemisms. Do they hide the truth or are they attempts to be considerate? What is the user's intent, and what is the outcome?

---

[30]Neil Postman, *Crazy Talk, Stupid Talk* (New York: Delacorte Press, 1976), 208.

[31]Ibid.

[32]Ibid., 212.

FOR YOUR INQUIRY AND PRACTICE:

How many euphemisms can you think of for the following terms? Why are they used?

bathroom, corpse, crippled, drunk, fat, pimples, Jesus! (profanity), **God!** (profanity), **retarded, death**

Some examples you can examine for your own practice in the consideration of intent and outcome are the following: Internal Revenue Service (tax collector); nervous wetness (sweat); facial blemishes (pimples); convenient terms (20% annual interest); full-figured or queen-size (fat, large); shortfall (mistake); daytime drama (soap opera); cleaning up the historical record (shredding or falsifying official documents); terminate with extreme prejudice (assassinate an enemy agent without a trial).[33]

One way to test language use in order to determine whether it is or isn't euphemistic doublespeak involves an analysis proposed by Hugh Rank.[34] To analyze the full context in which language, intent, and outcomes occur, Rank asks these questions:

1. Who is saying what to whom?
2. Under what conditions?
3. Under what circumstances?
4. With what intent?
5. With what results?

FOR YOUR INQUIRY AND PRACTICE:

Observe either an interview, a press conference, or a public meeting that is televised on the national networks or on one of your local cable channels, or read an account of one of these types of meetings

---

[33]William Lutz, "Notes Toward a Definition of Doublespeak," in *Beyond 1984: Doublespeak in a Post-Orwelian Age*, ed. William Lutz (Champaign-Urbana, IL: National Council of Teachers of English, 1989), 7.

[34]Ibid., 4.

in your local newspaper. Analyze the questions, answers, and other comments using Rank's Doublespeak Analysis. What are your conclusions about the presence or absence of doublespeak in the meeting? Is truth valued?

Studying semantics, euphemism, or doublespeak in classrooms is not something we do because we hope to educate our students so that they will graduate as full-fledged cynics. We can return to Korzybski for better reasons to study semantics.

As early as 1933, Korzybski understood the power and control language can exercise over people when he observed that:

The affairs of man are conducted by our own man-made rules and according to man-made theories. Man's achievements rest upon the use of symbols. For this reason, we must consider ourselves as a symbolic, semantic class of life, and those who rule the symbols, rule us.[35] (emphasis added)

More recently, Charles Weingartner suggests that the study of semantics "can do more to help students become more perceptive and sophisticated users of language than can any other form of language study" in the school.[36] You may or may not agree with Weingartner's assertion concerning the centrality of semantics in a language curriculum, but there's little doubt about its importance.

The study of meaning and meaning making is a matter of human interest and consequence. As Elaine Caccia suggests, our students' becoming effective citizens in the world is based on their effectiveness with language. "In saying this," Caccia continues, "I'm not referring to matters of effective usage and style. Competence in these areas may contribute to effective use of language, but dwelling there will never reveal the heart of the matter."[37] Putting semantics to work in the classroom will.

---

[35]Korzybski, Science and Sanity, 76.

[36]Charles Weingartner, "Semantics: What and Why," *English Journal,* vol. 58, no. 8 (1969): 1214.

[37]Elaine Caccia, "Getting Grounded: Putting Semantics to Work in the Classroom," *English Journal,* 80, no. 2 (1991): 55.

REVIEWING THE CHAPTER:

Part One: *Place a (✔) beside each statement found in the chapter.*

___ 1. Some words trigger automatic responses.
___ 2. Noam Chomsky is considered to be the "father" of general semantics.
___ 3. Euphemisms obscure clear communication.
___ 4. The word is not the thing.
___ 5. Those who rule the symbols rule.

Part Two: *Place a (✔) beside each statement you believe the author would support. Be prepared to defend your answer.*

___ 6. Grammar, syntax, and usage are, generally, synonyms.
___ 7. Symbols are recognized universally.
___ 8. Taboo words tend to be more concrete than abstract.
___ 9. Words are either intensional or extensional, but seldom both.
___ 10. Semantics relies heavily on one's emotions.

Part Three: *Based on your understanding of this chapter, and considering what you know as an educator, place a check beside each statement you can support. As usual, be prepared to defend your answer.*

___ 11. The architect's blue-print is not the building.
___ 12. Knowledge and belief are not the same.
___ 13. If it looks like a duck, walks like a duck, and quacks like a duck, it must be a duck.
___ 14. Some people just don't "get it."
___ 15. Good teaching revolves around showing, not telling.

STUDENT EXPLORATIONS FOR MEANING AND GENERAL SEMANTICS

EXPLORATION: Patriotic Language
DIRECTIONS: Language can cause us to do many things if it's powerful enough. Here is some language taken from magazine advertisements during different wars.

A. In times of war, in times of peace, use Parshall's Universal Flour. (WWI)
B. You've done your best, now do your bit. (WWII, war bonds)
C. Admiral Halsey is counting on you. (WWII, war bonds)
D. Keep America moving. (Iraq war, General Motors)
E. Add your voice to the push for peace. (Iraq war, antiwar rally)

1. What are the emotional effects of these slogans?
2. What audience is the slogan addressing? How do you know?
3. What does this activity help you understand about language and the setting in which it occurs?

***** ***** *****

EXPLORATION: You're So Vain
DIRECTIONS: Read *Oedipus the King (of the Road),* at http://www. chaos.umd.edu/misc/story.html.

1. How is the language on automobile vanity plates different from standard written language?
2. How is the language on automobile vanity plates similar to e-mail?
3. What is e-mail, another form of written language or a different type of language altogether?

***** ***** *****

EXPLORATION: Frindle
DIRECTIONS: In Andrew Clements' novel *Frindle,* Nick starts calling his writing pen a *frindle.* This change has a big influence on his family, friends, and teachers.

1. Select a common item—a notebook, your shoes, your belt, or the like—and give it a new name. Use this new name for at least a week, but don't tell anyone why you are using the new name.
2. How do people react to your new name for the item?
3. What does this activity tell you about how people form a general consensus about the meanings of words?

***** ***** *****

EXPLORATION: Meanings in Flux
DIRECTIONS: Here is a list of items advertised in newspapers and magazines. Examine the ads in newspapers and magazines selling these products. What pictorial associations are made in the advertisements with the item: happy families, tired workers, sexy men and women, and so on?

a. wrist watches   b. shoes   c. automobiles   d. alcohol
e. telephones   f. cigarettes   g. clothes   h. luggage

1. What is the advertisement *really* selling?
2. Is the association between the item and the picture or illustration reasonable, in your view? Is it far-fetched?
3. Where does *meaning* reside? In the advertisement or in the reader?

***** ***** *****

EXPLORATION: Which Word Is Better?
DIRRECTIONS: How many different synonyms can you think of for the following words?

A. dumb   B. cool   C. midget   D. happy
E. fat   F. bathroom   G. disabled   H. neighborhood

1. For each of the alternate meanings you were able to think of, when would you use them? With whom?
2. Why do we use different words meaning essentially the same thing in different circumstances?

***** ***** *****

EXPLORATION: Where Do You Want to Live?
DIRECTIONS: People live in places like Paradise, California; Comfort, Texas; Boring, Oregon; Friend, Nebraska; and Peculiar, Missouri. A visit with a U.S. atlas will help you discover a number of additional unusual place names. Make a list of at least 10 cities or towns with unusual names.

1. Go to the Internet and see iof you can discover how each town or your list acquired its name.
2. Is there any "magic" involved in selecting the name for a town or city? What were the town founders trying to communicate when the town was named?

***** ***** *****

EXPLORATION: Pleasant Words for Unpleasant Realities
DIRECTIONS: Examine the following lists then circle the word with the strongest negative association. Try to do this in a group.

A. big-boned, fat, overweight
B. die, pass away, pass on
C. elderly, aged, old
D. stupid, dumb, half-witted
E. restroom, bathroom, powder room
F. operation, war, conflict
G. poor, lower class, hard up
H. off, murder, slay
I. corpse, body, cadaver
J. crazy, mad, insane

1. Did you and your friends agree on which word was the most negative?
2. Do the words in each group mean exactly the same thing?
3. Why do we use alternative words for each of the events illustrated in these groups?

***** ***** *****

EXPLORATION: Words We Know
DIRECTIONS: Think about a vocation you're interested in, one of your hobbies, or your favorite school subject. Brainstorm by yourself, creating a list of terms used in the vocation, hobby, or subject. Read your list to a partner.

1. How many terms on your partner's list were unknown to you? How many of your terms were unknown to your partner?
2. If a term or word is unknown to you, is the word less real? Where do you locate these terms and words in your sense of reality? Are these words more or less alien to you than words from another language?
3. Where do our words and the concepts they represent come from, especially those used in the special interests we have?

***** ***** *****

EXPLORATION: The Meaning Is in Here, Somewhere
DIRECTIONS: Almost every word that we use can evoke sharp and well-defined images. Here is a short list of common, everyday words. For each word make a list of words and terms you associate with that word.

music	**dog**
cat	**mother**
car	**holiday**

1. Compare your lists with those lists created by others in your small group.
2. How can you explain the range of associations attached to each of these rather simple words?
3. Based on the discussions in your group, what can you conclude about *meanings* and where they come from?

***** ***** *****

EXPLORATION: Synonyms
DIRECTIONS: For each key word shown in **boldface** type, write several words that are used as synonyms for the key word.

Example: **policeman**: officer, buttons, cop, flatfoot

woman:

man:

teacher:

doctor:

actor:

politician:

1. Do all of the synonyms evoke the same meaning as the key word? What additional meanings do each of the synonyms bring?
2. In what contexts might you use one of the synonyms for the key word?
3. Do you find that some of the synonyms are more powerful than the others in evoking more positive or more negative images of each key word?

***** ***** *****

EXPLORATION: Jargon
DIRECTIONS: Technical magazines abound at newsstands; many are in a library or school media center. Locate three technical magazines—such as *Personal Computing*, *Modern Aviation*, or *American Cinematographer*—and make a list from each magazine of 10 words you may recognize but do not ordinarily use.

1. Examine the sentence from which you took the word and try to explain to a partner what you think each term means.
2. Do you know anyone who uses or might use these terms more often than you do? How did they learn these terms?
3. Are these special-use terms "jargon"? What purpose is served by using special-use words such as these?

***** ***** *****

EXPLORATION: Are These Shoes Experienced, Preowned, or Used?
DIRECTIONS: After examining a pair of old shoes located in some central spot in the room, brainstorm with a partner as many words you can think of to describe the shoes.

1. Put your list of words into categories, like *size*, *color*, or *material*.
2. Using the descriptive words, write a limerick or short poem about the shoes using as many words as you can from each category.
3. Now, examine your poem and substitute for each descriptive word you've used the category name.
4. What has happened to your poem? What is lost in the poem when you use the names of the categories instead of the descriptive words?

***** ***** *****

EXPLORATION: Word Rainbows
DIRECTIONS: Using advertisements printed in color from catalogs, the Sunday newspaper, or circulars received in the mail, identify the *names* of as many different colors as you can that are used either in an illustration or in the description of an item.

1. Place the individual names of colors with others of its "family" of colors, using the chart on the following page. (For example, "teal" and "eggshell blue" will go with "blue.")

2. How many of the more specific color names come from foods, like "apricot," "olive," "tangerine," or "apple red"? How many of the names come from nature, like "sky" or "dusk"?

3. Will the choice of color names enhance the product's image for the prospective buyer or shopper, in your judgment?

4. Is there a *logical* connection between the names selected and they objects they refer to?

WORD RAINBOWS
Using the advertisements available, categorize the color names you've identified with the color groups shown here.

Black: _____

_____

White: _____

_____

Blue: _____

_____

Red: _____

_____

Yellow: _____

_____

***** ***** *****

EXPLORATION: Nonesuches
DIRECTIONS: In a small group, read Lewis Carroll's "Jabberwocky," Dr. Suess' *How the Grinch Stole Christmas*, Dr. Seuss' *The Lorax,* or any other selection of literature that uses a relative large number of nonsense words.

1. Write down at least five of the nonsense words and try to give them definitions, according to how and where they are used in the sentence in which they appear.

2. Discuss your definitions with the meanings created by other members of your group. As you compare the several meanings suggested, can your group agree to advocate *one* of the definitions as the best?

3. Reread orally some of the sentences, substituting the created meanings for the original nonsense words. Do the nonsense words or the created definitions add more to or subtract more from the enjoyment of the selection?

***** ***** *****

EXPLORATION: Buffalo Breath

DIRECTIONS: It's very unlikely that you'll ever see an advertisement on television or in your local newspaper for a new cologne called "Buffalo Breath." The names of colognes—for either men or women—more often than not want to connote a different kind of image for the user than "Buffalo Breath" might create. Who wants to smell like "Buffalo Breath"? Don't you prefer "Obsession"?

Divide the class into several groups of three or four, then have the group select one family of products: toothpastes, colognes, underarm deodorant, hair lotions and treatments, perfumes, aftershave lotions, skin creams and ointments, and the like.

Each group should collect as many different ads as possible for its "family" of products from newspapers and magazines; listen for your products being advertised on the radio; they are probably advertised on television, too.

1. What are the various *names* used for these products?
2. What features do the names used have in common?
3. Why are the names selected by the companies creating these products?
4. Are the names selected because the company intends to create an image for its *product* or for the *person* who uses the product?
5. What is the producer of this product really trying to sell? The product only?
6. Most of these ads will include people using the product. How are they presented in the ad? How do their physical appearance and their actions support the intended image?
7. Based on your observations, what can you conclude about the process involved in naming a product?

(You might repeat this activity, examining the names of breakfast cereals, cars [family sedans, mid size, or compact—be specific], floor waxes and polishes, liquid household cleaners, or any other product line.)

***** ***** *****

EXPLORATION: Tears in My Ears

DIRECTIONS: Many years ago there was a popular song that included the line: "I've got tears in my ears from lying on my back in the bed while I cry over you." Many disc jockeys used the entire line as the song's title, which meant that it took almost as long to announce the song as it did to play it on the air! Where do song titles come from?

Divide the class into teams of two, then assign each team a year, beginning with the current year and counting back at 10-year intervals. (One group will have 1995, another 1985, another 1975, and so on.) Either use back copies (from your local library) of *Billboard* magazine or *Radio and Records* magazine, or interview a DJ at your favorite radio station and find out the titles of the most popular song for each month of your assigned year.

1. Are the titles serious or humorous?
2. Are the titles representative of a male or a female orientation?
3. What are the basic topics of the most popular songs during your year?
4. If any of the titles seem weird to you, what makes them that way?
5. Based on what you know about history—or, you might do a little library research—do the song titles reflect what was going on in the world during your year?
6. Based on your research, what can you conclude about the relationship between popular music and what's going on in the news? Do some songs (as seen in their titles) reflect what listeners are interested in and care about? Or, do the songs shape or determine what people are interested in and care about?

***** ***** *****

EXPLORATION: Similar, but Different

DIRECTIONS: *Synonyms* are usually thought of as words having the same, or nearly the same meaning. It may be more useful for you to emphasize the *nearly* in this definition because people tend to make very fine distinctions in how they use words. Here is a grid giving you the opportunity to grade some common words. For Set #1, put an "X" in the column that best describes each word in relation to the other four. Then, do the same for Set #2.

Set #1	*Solemn*	*Earnest*	*Sober*	*Serious*	*Intense*
love					
affection					
adoration					
devotion					
passion					

Set #2	*Solemn*	*Earnest*	*Sober*	*Serious*	*Intense*
sorrow					
anguish					
grief					
sadness					
woe					

1. Compare your rankings of the words in the two sets with members of your group. Try to determine on what grounds your rankings are alike or different.
2. Based on your rankings and the subsequent discussions, why do you think people give different shades of meanings to the same words?

***** ***** *****

EXPLORATION: " 'The Time Has Come,' the Walrus Said . . ."
DIRECTIONS: You may recall the title of this activity from *Alice in Wonderland*. Walruses are important animals to many Eskimo tribes, just as chickens, steers, fish, and pigs are to other peoples. Eskimos have several names for the walrus:

nutara	baby walrus
ipiksalik	2-year-old walrus
tugar	walrus with tusks
timartik	big male walrus

aiverk   lone walrus
naktivilik   mature walrus

1. Can you think of reasons why Eskimos have more names for the walrus than we have in our language?
2. Is there an animal name in your language that has several versions?
3. Predict the number of names an Eskimo might have for "horse."
4. How can you account for the differences in the number of terms your language might have for *dog* or *horse* and compared to Eskimo? And, why does an Eskimo have more terms for *walrus*? What does this contrast tell you about how a language portrays the world around us?

***** ***** *****

EXPLORATION: Tintinnabulatory Effects
DIRECTIONS: Dogs and cats make the same actual sounds all around the world. The various world languages, however, represent these sounds in different ways. Each language represents the sound of a thunderclap, a gunshot, and a sneeze differently, although the actual noises made are probably identical anywhere on Earth.

Try to match the following English terms with their French counterparts.

English Terms	**French Terms**
boom	achoum
splash	glouglou
glug-glug	badaboum
pooey (stinky)	plouf
achoo	pouah
bang-bang (gun)	miam miam
knock-knock	boum
yum-yum	pan pan
smack	clac
tickle-tickle	youopi
hurray, goody	oh la la la
Oh dear	hic
hiccup	guili guili
ouch	toc-toc
bang (door)	aie, ouille

(Answers: achoo/achoum; glug-glug/glouglou; boom/badaboum; splash/ plouf; pooey (stinky)/pouah; yum-yum/miam miam; knock-knock/toc toc; ouch/aie, ouille; bang (door)/boum; bang-bang (gun)/pan pan; smack/clac; hurray, goody/youpi; Oh dear/oh la la la; hiccup/hic; tickle tickle/guili guili)

1. Given these different spellings for the same sounds, do readers of French and readers of English "hear" the same things?
2. Which spellings of these sounds come closer to representing the *real* sound?
3. Do the different spellings of the similar sounds illustrated in this activity carry different meanings in either language?

***** ***** *****

EXPLORATION: Animal Images
DIRECTIONS: When you hear someone claim that "It's raining cats and dogs" you are hearing animal imagery. Can you imagine how difficult it would be to explain this image to one who speaks Spanish, German, or any other language? Here are some common animal images from English with their French counterparts.

English	**French**
to play leapfrog	jouer a saute-mouton (to play leap sheep)
a scardey-cat	une poule mouillee (a wet hen)
to have goose pimples	avoir la chair de poule (to have hen flesh)
clever as a fox	malin comme un singe (clever as a monkey)
You can't teach an old dog new tricks.	On n'apprend pas a an singe comment la grimace (you can't teach a monkey how to make faces)
to open a can of worms	un vrai panier de crabes (a real basket of crabs)
to be hungry as a horse	avoir une faim de loup (to be hungry as a wolf)
to have bats in the belfry	avoir une araignee au plafond (to have a spider on the ceiling)

1. Can you speculate why each language uses the animals found in their respective expressions?

2. Do the uses of different animals change the basic meanings of the expressions?

3. Explain why you agree or disagree with the statement: "A language is not right or wrong; it's just different."

***** ***** *****

EXPLORATION: Birds of a Feather . . .
DIRECTIONS: Proverbs are universal; all peoples of the world have have them in their languages. Here are some proverbs you have probably heard before, with their French counterparts.

English	**French**
When in Rome, do as the Romans (do).	Il faut hurler avec les loups. (You must howl with the wolves.)
Actions speak louder than words.	Faire et dire sont deux. (To say and to do are two.)
Live and let live.	Il faut que tout le monde vive. (All the world must live.)
I'm at my wit's end.	Je suis au bout de mon latin. (I'm at the end of my Latin.)
Out of sight, out of mind.	Loin des yeux, loin du coeur. (Far from the eyes, far from the heart.)
The more, the merrier.	Plus on est de fous, plus on rit. (The more fools there are, the more they laugh.)
Birds of a feather flock together.	Qui se ressemble, s'assemble. (Those who resemble, assemble.)
Put your money where your mouth is.	Selon ta bourse gouverne ta bouche. (According to your purse, govern your mouth.)
Calling a spade a spade.	J'appelle un chat un chat. (I am calling a cat a cat.)
Where there's a will there's a way.	Vouloir, c'est pouvoir. (To want is to be able.)
Nothing ventured, nothing gained.	Qui ne risque rien, n'a rien. (He who risks nothing, has nothing.)

1. Which of these proverbs are most alike? Which are most different?

2. What are the purposes of proverbs? Why do people use them? Do proverbs reveal anything about those who use them?

3. Do you think language shapes the thoughts in proverbs, or do the thoughts shape the language. Or, to ask this question in a more proverbial way, what came first: the chicken (language) or the egg (idea)?

***** ***** *****

EXPLORATION: Be a Good Sport

DIRECTIONS: Scan the sports section of your local newspaper, read an interview in a sports magazine, or watch a television sportscast and identify three examples of euphemisms. Examples might be calling a bad decision made by a game official or a stupid play by a player a "mental error" or a "judgment call." Or, an athlete who has been arrested for drunken driving, drug use, or some other illegal behavior is described as "having off-the-field difficulties."

1. Who used the euphemisms you've identified? The sportswriter? The interviewer? The athlete?

2. In your judgment, what was the user of the euphemism trying to say or *not* say?

3. Why were the euphemism used? Was effective communication achieved?

***** ***** *****

EXPLORATION: Are You Sick, or What?

DIRECTIONS: In groups of four to five, brainstorm as many terms or phrases you can think of that are used in society to describe physical or health-related conditions. Some examples are:

Flu or cold   "under the weather"
                         "have the sniffles"
Pregnancy   "expecting"
                         "blessed event"

Using the list of euphemisms your group has listed, answer the following questions:

1. How do you think these euphemisms originated? Are the euphemisms harmful to anyone?
2. Compare the terms on your list. Is society more comfortable using euphemisms for certain physical circumstances or conditions?

***** ***** *****

EXPLORATION: Gobbledygook
DIRECTIONS: "Gobbledygook" is bloated, inflated language that tries to overwhelm the reader or listener with words, the bigger the better! Select a brief article from a newspaper or magazine and rewrite it using as much gobbledygook as you can. Your dictionary or thesaurus will be helpful.

1. Who normally uses gobbledygook, bloated, inflated language?
2. Check the etymologies (word histories) of your bigger words. Which languages did they come from? What does this reveal about the history of English?

***** ***** *****

EXPLORATION: Pearl Jam on Toast
DIRECTIONS: Make a list of five of your favorite music groups' names and then look up each word in the name in your dictionary. Compare your list with others'.

1. Do any of the names have anything to do with music?
2. Do the words in a group's name relate?
3. What seems to be the purpose in selecting the name for a group?

***** ***** *****

EXPLORATION: Is It Scarlet or Red O'Hara?
DIRECTIONS: Bring to class four magazine ads for lipstick, blush, or eye shadow. For each color named in the ad ("Desert Dream"), supply the name of an actual color ("peach"). Compare your lists with others', giving them only the advertiser's name, not the actual color; can they guess the color?

1. Are there any patterns in the names of cosmetics?
2. Does the advertiser's name influence your opinion of the product?

3. What seems to be the primary purpose in selecting names for cosmetics?

***** ***** *****

EXPLORATION: Beauty Is in the Beholder's Eye
DIRECTIONS: In a group, brainstorm and make a list of some names used in your school to depict certain groups. "Athletes" are sometimes called "jocks"; "studious students" are sometimes called "nerds"; "hackers" may be "computer violators," and the like.

1. Show your list to some parents, teachers, and other "older" persons. Can they guess what your names depict? Does age make a difference?
2. Are some terms more positive or more negative?
3. Are terms like these unique to a particular group of language users? Why are these names used?

***** ***** *****

EXPLORATION: To Buy or Not to Buy
DIRECTIONS: Advertisements in magazines use both words and pictures to describe the products they are selling. Collect (a) one new-car advertisement, (b) one cigarette ad, (c) one soft-drink ad, and (d) one hair-care product ad. Be prepared to answer the following questions for your collection of advertisements:

1. What are the key words used in each advertisement?
2. Do the advertisements use any stereotypes? Why or why not?
3. What meaning(s) do these words communicate to you? Are the words direct, concrete, and factual, or do they suggest additional meaning(s)? How do you know?

***** ***** *****

EXPLORATION: With Deepest Sympathy
DIRECTIONS: Whenever a friend has experienced a death in his or her family, we send our friend a greeting card expressing our sympathy. In groups of three or four, brainstorm as many words you can think of that are used as euphemisms for *death*.

1. Why do some people use euphemisms when writing or talking about death?

2. Might some people be offended by some of the euphimistic words on your list?

3. Why do some people use euphemisms? Are euphemisms good or bad, in your judgment?

CHAPTER **10**

The Languages of Intolerance and Discrimination

Sticks and stones may break my bones,
but words will never hurt me.
—American folk proverb

Before you read this chapter, consider your role as a teacher of the English language arts to young people who are in the process of becoming adults. What should you do when you hear them using intolerant, stereotyped, racist, sexist, or any other type of hurtful language?

- Ignore the situation(s), believing that in time the students will stop using these words?
- Punish the guilty in some manner in accord with the policies of your school building and district?
- Calmly, clearly, but cogently explain to the student(s) that "that kind" of language is simply not allowed in your classroom?
- Do something else?

In *A First Look at Communication Theory*, Em Griffin points out that Alfred Korzybski, founder of General Semantics, believed that the essence of being human was the ability to communicate. Vegetation transforms energy from the sun into organic nutrients. Animals aren't planted, so they improve their lot in life by moving about. Only humans have the capacity to use communicative symbols in order to share the accumulated experience of the past, to frame the questions leading to a more promising future, and to share practical information as we tell our children how to grow food, which snakes are poisonous, and how to find a job.[1]

Communication is a special, distinctive trait, but we don't always do it successfully. That's why we encounter ambiguous sentences like "The shooting of the hunters was awful" or "The chicken was too hot to eat."

Several newspaper accounts provide similar ambiguities. Here's a true headline, from a local newspaper: "Volunteers Needed to Help Torture Survivors". In a Florida newspaper, we read "Homeless Man Improves After Car Runs Into Him". In another Florida newspaper, a headline announces, "Midwest Storm Blamed for Wisconsin". An obituary in a New York newspaper acknowledges, "To Everyone and Anyone who was in any way involved in my husband's passing, a Heart Felt Thank You."[2]

When communication isn't successful because of humorous syntactic ambiguities, we laugh. There are other communication circumstances, however, that aren't funny. For example, when two California high school teams were playing a baseball game, several fans from Castro Valley, whose team members were mostly White, taunted and yelled racial slurs at two African-American players on the team from Ashland. When the game ended, as the two teams were passing each other observing the politically correct end-of-game handshaking, the shoving and punching began. A player from one team swung a baseball bat at a member of the opposing team; the intended victim ducked, however, and a spectator who was looking the other way was struck in the back of the head. He later died from the injury.[3]

Professional athletes head-butting referees, spitting on umpires, throwing towels in coaches' faces, physically and verbally attacking both opposing players and fans in the stands, and using the widely publicized "trash talk" all contribute, the umpire at the baseball game said, to younger players believing such behavior is acceptable. "The whole thing happened over words," the umpire commented.[4]

Words, in and of themselves, may not, in fact, *directly* inflict injury, but in this case, words helped to create an environment—a *context*, to use a term commonly used in this text—in which injury and death resulted.

---

[1] http://www.afirstlook.com/archive/gensem.cfm?source=archther.

[2] Dave Barry, "Mister Language Person Returns in a Grande Way," *Lincoln (NE) Journal Star*, October 10, 2004, sec. K.

[3] "Youth Baseball Brawl Deadly," *Lincoln (NE) Journal Star*, May 20, 1993.

[4] Ibid.

Hurtful words, however, are not always used in overt ways; sometimes they are covert and they slip into conversations when a speaker believes, unthinkingly, that he or she is being especially clever or funny. For example, several years ago I conducted an all-day workshop for a K–12 school faculty during the week prior to the opening of classes in the fall. A month later I returned to the school in order to visit with the faculty about their successes or to address any questions they might have had about the learning strategies I had presented a month earlier in the all-day workshop.

At the end of the follow-up visitation day, a teacher approached me and apologized for having missed the back-to-school workshop because she was in the hospital, having just given birth to her first child. "How nice," I said, "what kind did you have?" A nearby teacher interjected: "White!" Then he laughed. I did not. The "joke" wasn't funny.

Maybe my "what kind" question was poorly framed. I think, however, that given the context the teacher understood what I was asking. I was asking her, as I'm confident she understood, whether her newborn was either male or female, but I was more than astonished by the nearby teacher's interjected "humor."

At a time when major U.S. corporations pay millions of dollars in damages to African Americans who have been discriminated against or harassed in the workplace, when African-American automobile drivers are racially profiled and stopped by law enforcement officers for no apparent reason, how, I asked myself, how could anyone—especially a teacher!—offer such a blatantly racist remark in the guise of a "joke"? If I were an African American, I doubt that he would have made the remark, which makes his "humor" all the more pernicious.

OVERT INTOLERANCE

Sometimes, it's not a person, per se, who is damaged by language. Sometimes a *process* is harmed. One would like to think that in the halls of Congress in Washington, DC, where issues of supreme importance to the citizens of the United States are resolved, the political discourse would reflect a solemn obligation to high-mindedness and statesmanship. As you may have heard, this isn't always the case.

Recently the vice president of the United States and a senior member of the U.S. Senate exchanged sharp words concerning the vice president's ties to an international energy services corporation that had received sole-source contracts (No bids required.) in Iraq. These contracts were worth millions of dollars to the company. The vice president ended the argument with an unstatesman-like "Go fuck yourself."[5] There goes the solemn obligation to serious political discourse!

Four-letter taboo words aren't the only culprits in the process of fogging-up our thinking. After France refused to join the United States' coalition to invade Iraq, the media had a field-day with the term *Gallic*. *Gallic* isn't a familiar term to many people, being a fancy adjective like *Hibernian* for the Irish, *Caledonian* for the Scots, and *Teutonic* for the Germans, words journalists keep handy to evoke national stereotypes. Given the recent relationships between the United States and France, the term *Gallic* has come to suggest stereotypically "those stupid French are at it again!"[6]

STICKS, STONES, AND WORDS

You probably have heard the proverb quoted in the headnote to this chapter. It has been in use for well over a century in the United States. Parents and other adult caregivers have taught this adage to children whose feelings have been bruised by others with some well-aimed and generally demeaning or hurtful words.

Typically, proverbs like "Sticks and stones . . ." are usually reserved for resolving conflicts or disputes with or among children. "Haste makes waste" and "First come, first served" are classic examples.[7]

For those with interests in language history, the "sticks and stones" proverb can be traced back to the beginning of the 19th century. Hugh Henry Brackenridge, an early explorer of the Missouri River Valley, wrote in his *Gazette* in 1801: "Hard words, and language break nae bane." In 1814 Gouverner Morris, a Philadelphian active in the American Revolutionary War, wrote a strikingly similar idea in his *Dairy and Letters*: "These are mere words—hard words if you please, but they break no bones."[8]

---

[5] Helen Dewar and Dana Milbank, "Cheney Dismisses Critic With Obscentity," *The Washington Post*, June 25, 2004, sec. A.

[6] Geoffrey Nunberg, *Going Nucular: Language, Politics, and Culture in Confrontational Times* (New York: Perseus Books Group, 2004), 84–85.

[7] Neil Postman, *Amusing Ourselves to Death* (New York: Viking Penguin, 1986), 19.

[8] Jere Whiting Bartlett, *Early American Proverbs and Proverbial Phrases* (Cambridge, MA: Harvard University Press, 1977), 496.

These first written uses of this familiar proverb are included here for two reasons: First, the history of language is always interesting. Second, I suspect that from the times of Brackenridge and Morris, to the first time you heard the proverb, and up to and including yesterday no doubt, when someone somewhere told a tearful child: "Well, you just remember, dear, sticks and stones . . . ," the proverbial poultice did not, in fact, actually resolve a dispute or conflict, nor did it make the hurt go away.

I further suspect that the proverb has probably never provided either short- or long-term relief. Unquestionably, its use enables a parent or some other caregiver to express nurturing love for the affected child, a linguistic event that needs to occur frequently, and its importance in this respect must not be diminished, but the pain that words can inflict remains. (Can't you recall a time *you* were the subject of name-calling?) Sticks and stones hurt, as the proverb acknowledges; but, despite the proverb's denial, words hurt, too. And the hurt is frequently more acute and longer lasting than the proverb pronouncers might imagine or prefer.

WHY SOME PEOPLE HAVE MANY NAMES

Peggy Sullivan's novel *Many Names for Eileen* tells the story of a young girl, Eileen, who enjoys a busy Saturday with her mother and father. Throughout the day Eileen meets a variety of people, each of whom calls her by a different name: "Missy," "Curlytop," "Princess," "Little Ella," "Tiger," and "Sport." At the end of her busy day, Eileen asks her mother why all the people she's met have called her by all of these different names instead of by her real name. Her mother replies that there may be several reasons for all of the names, but probably the most special reason is that the child who is *loved* has many names.[9]

It is a different matter, on the other hand, for those children who grow up in a more hostile culture, one that attaches to them stereotyped labels, words containing built-in judgments about them or other assumptions about their worth as human beings: words like *Jewboy, Fag Girl, Crip, Boy, Bitch, Nigger, Dago, Queer*, or *Spic*. Children who have been called by names like these—usually over a period of years—clearly do not believe that they have many names because they are loved!

Most speakers in the United States, however, have learned over the past 15 to 20 years that *overt* use of most of these labels is a cultural taboo in

---

[9]Peggy Sullivan, *Many Names for Eileen* (Chicago and New York: Follett Publishing Company, 1969).

polite society and they should not be used in public. Their overt use violates the Rotarian virtues associated with the tenets of a democratic and multi cultural society where all people are supposed to have been equally created and enjoy impartial and unrestrained opportunities.

As an example of *some* progress in the declining use of hate speech, ask almost any group of persons under the age of 21 to fill in the blank in the sentence, "Eeny, meeny, meinie mo, catch a _____ by the toe," and they'll likely use either the word *tiger* or perhaps *spider*.

My generation and culture used a different word.

Despite such recent changes, however, there remains in our contemporary society other uses of demeaning language and nonverbal behavior. For example, there have been recent reports of a fraternity hosting a Fiji Islander party, featuring a Harlem Room in which black-faced partygoers ate fried chicken and drank watermelon punch. At another university, two Whites posted a Sambo-like defacement of a picture of Beethoven in the Black studies dorm.[10]

At Columbia University, an African-American columnist in *The Columbia Daily Spectator* denounced Jewish criticisms of The Million Man March by saying: "Lift up the yarmulke and what you will find is the blood of millions of Africans weighing on their heads." After the first O. J. Simpson trial, a flyer was circulated at the University of Southern California campus warning that "I need to alert all the whites that the niggers [will] take up arms and defend themselves." At Emory University in Atlanta, two black students found a note under their door that read: "You niggers [better] never sleep."[11]

A LARGER SOCIAL ISSUE

Do these reports only substantiate the claims of some people who believe that in any collection of humanity as large and as diverse as a university student body there are bound to be some feather-brained zanies who will say and do anything? Well, maybe. But racist terms like these aren't confined either primarily or only to university campuses. It's an issue the larger society can share.

---

[10]"Hate Speech on the College Campus," *Lex Colligi* (Nashville, TN: College Legal Information, Inc., vol. 14, no. 3, 1991), 1.

[11]"Many Campuses Seethe With Racism," *Lincoln (NE) Journal Star*, October 25, 1995, sec. C.

To validate this statement you can examine your own experience. For example, you likely know that public schools, business firms of all sizes, and governmental and public service agencies either employ or are seeking to employ specialists charged with the responsibilities of improving ethnic and multicultural tolerance, sensitivity, and understanding among their students, faculty, and workforce.

As far away as Jinan, China, for example, employees have received guidance about how they must improve their linguistic etiquette. The city's bank, in an attempt to be more customer-friendly, has directed the tellers that they must never use 90 "uncivilized" sentences and phrases, including "That's not my responsibility," "What's the rush?," "Wait over there," "Go complain if you want" and "Can't you see I'm busy?"[12]

The borough council in Raritan, New Jersey, passed unanimously a ban on public cursing. "Cursing in public should be banned," said one of the council members, "but since people can't seem to do it voluntarily, it's up to [us] lawmakers."[13]

A large, metropolitan newspaper recently established a policy on the use of vulgarity and "bad taste" in language. The editor of the newspaper explained that syndicated columns, wire service stories, and locally produced reports have been edited, and words deleted have included, for example, "butt" and "wee wee." Furthermore, a syndicated column using the word "ballknockers" was not even published by the newspaper. A comic strip exploiting the rhyme between "Uranus" and "your anus," and another comic making a reference to "big hooters" were both withheld from publication.[14]

Whether you agree with the various steps reported here, all of this activity indicates that there must be a sufficient amount of intolerant and demeaning language and behavior in the larger society that is causing schools, agencies, and businesses to try to do something about it.

I recently read in my local newspaper about the director of a state agency who has placed a voluptuous light switch cover in his office that depicts a woman with bare breasts. Each morning as he flips up the switch and he "turns on" the lights, a woman is reduced to one feature: her anatomy. Walter Gottlieb claims that movies not only reflect our collective

[12]"Chinese Bank Bans Tellers From Using 90 Rude Phrases," *Lincoln (NE) Journal Star*, April 25, 1995.

[13]"N.J. Town Votes Cursing Ban," *Lincoln (NE) Journal Star*, October 13, 1994.

[14]"Readers Praise Our Anti-Crudities Stand," *Omaha (NE) World-Herald*, October 16, 1994, sec. A.

bigotry and hatred, but also reinforce them. He says this after reviewing a series of Hollywood films that for the past several years have exploited Jewish stereotypes.[15]

I do not pretend to understand all of the reasons for the overt or covert uses of intolerant, prejudicial, and demeaning language. Nor am I posturing, claiming that English language teachers (we precious few) are the sole bastions of sanity in a world gone linguistically loony. On the other hand, I am fairly well convinced that the relationships between thought and language require that you and I attend to language that diminishes and hurts others.

I am suggesting that we cannot ignore this language, and that we *judiciously* bring it into the classroom so that students have the opportunity to examine and to explore racist or sexist language and behavior following the approach that is advocated in this book for the study of other aspects of language.

To put this idea in a clearer context, and as a brief review, we can recall that prescriptive "Do say" and "Don't say" exhortations are seldom, if ever, successful. Simply *telling* or *commanding* students "Do not use that term [*homo, coon*, etc.] in this room!" will be, in the long run, about as successful as our trying to dictate to them that "The past tense of *dive* is *dived*, not *dove*! Do not use the term *dove* in this room!"

Simply banning or prohibiting certain words and phrases is nothing less than substituting one form of dogmatism for another. Our job, as I see it, is *education*, not *training*. As we discussed in earlier chapters, a prescriptive approach seldom motivates students to examine their linguistic behavior in a meaningful or permanent manner. We may temporarily suppress a language usage on the surface, but down in the deeper structures the student's attitudes, values, and thought structures, the components of *self*, will either remain unchanged or may even become more steadfast.

Similarly, some students are not aware that sentence-initial adverbs, agentless or passive sentences, or any other isolated aspect of language might somehow be offensive to others. Likewise, among some of those same students, there are those who are either unaware or are only dimly aware why *girl, cameraman, crip, fag,* or *fox* may be offensive to others or why these words are insulting. Without a fuller awareness, they see little need to modify their language. So, they don't.

I have some crude data on my desk, collected at random from some high school students, that suggest that demeaning and derogatory terms are

---

[15]Walter J. Gottlieb, "Next Comes a Thick Yiddish Accent," *The Washington Post National Weekly*, September 9–15, 1991, 25.

sometimes used without regard to what the terms might actually mean, but are used as ritual insults almost generally, ambiguously, and indiscriminately. For example, one student defined *fag* as "a term you use for anyone you don't like."

Consequently, this chapter suggests an approach to the examination of demeaning language that is consistent with the approach previously advocated for other aspects of language. If learners are going to gain an understanding of and greater control over their language, they need to explore language in its actual social contexts, its real-time uses and both its intended and, possibly, unintended outcomes. Subsequently, our students' more intentional and more informed choices will follow, given time. Remember, they are linguistic *apprentices*.

This chapter examines racist, sexist, and other examples of language of intolerance and discrimination. It is important to stress once more, however, the inseparability of language and context, which includes participants, their relationships, and their communicative intent (See the tenor, field, and mode discussion in chap. 6.). Though we may agree that *girl* may be considered sexist language in one context, remember that it may not be in another.

For example, a graduate student complained to me once about one of her professor's habits of constantly referring to the class as "men and girls." He routinely and customarily used this expression, according to the student, in a consistent manner throughout the course as a habitual expression. She was offended.

On the other hand, African-American women of almost all ages use the word *girl* as a term of *cohesiveness* and *endearment*. It is an expression of *sisterhood*. They will routinely use "Say, girl . . ." in their conversations with each other and no one is offended. I've heard several Anglo-European women trying to adopt the use of *girl*, and my best estimation is that they understand the words, but not the music.

The professor's reported use of *girl* is an example of unexamined, probably unintentional but, nevertheless, sexist language; the latter, in my experience, is not. There are other examples of language use that is demeaning in one context ("You worthless son-of-a-bitch!"), but is not in another. ("Hey, you old son-of-a-bitch! Gosh, it's good to see you!")

One reason people use hurtful language is because they acquire this language and the semantic houses, fields, and maps it represents just like they acquire all of the other parts of their language of nature and of nurture. It was acquired indirectly and implicitly from their culture. Like their patterns of pronunciation and grammar, these vocabulary words are a part of the surrounding linguistic atmosphere they breathe.

In order to validate this statement you can conduct some armchair research.

FOR YOUR INQUIRY AND PRACTICE:

Watch television for several hours or for 1 hour several times. Or, alternatively, thumb through several national magazines for general audiences. Make a simple tally sheet. Then count the number of products that are advertised through a stereotyped association with female posteriors or cleavage; or, with associations between male decisiveness and dominance, sometimes linked to corresponding female indecision or submission. What are the results of your research?

Must women always be portrayed as being sexy and alluring, even when cleaning toilet bowls, scouring dirty pots and pans in the kitchen sink, or shopping for breakfast cereal? These images are not ones I advocate, but they permeate the media.

Must men always be strong, John-Wayne-Hair-on-the-Chest-Get-Out-of-My-Way-Pilgrim types who are the center of attention because they make rational and rapid decisions? Many advertising campaigns seem to suggest as much.

Where do these stereotypes come from? Do the advertisements, especially the more ubiquitous ones on television, merely reflect commonly held cultural stereotypes or do they create them? Postman maintains that this question has receded into the background of intellectual thought in the United States because television and its messages have permeated our society to such an extent that "television has gradually *become* our culture."[16] Quentin J. Schultze et al. are in general agreement with this view and suggest in their book *Dancing in the Dark: Youth, Popular Culture and the Electronic Media* that popular culture must be taken very seriously inasmuch as it is not only the *vehicle* but the *creator* of social attitudes and values.[17]

---

[16]Postman, *Amusing Ourselves*, 79.

[17]Quentin J. Schultze, Roy M. Anker, James D. Bratt, William D. Romanowski, John W. Worst, and Lambert Zuidervaart, *Dancing in the Dark: Youth, Popular Culture and the Electronic Media* (Grand Rapids, MI: Eerdmans, 1991). For related analyses, see also John P. Ferre, ed., *Channels of Belief: Religion and American Television* (Ames: Iowa State University Press, 1991); and Gregor T. Goethals, *The Electronic Golden Calf: Images, Religion and the Making of Meaning* (Cambridge, MA: Cowley, 1991).

A tentative answer, then, to the question posed earlier asking whether advertisements either reflect or create cultural stereotypes is, in both instances: "Yes." Advertisements, I believe, both reflect and create stereotypes. Advertisements are seldom too far ahead of cultural values and are probably never lagging too far behind what society might consider true or important. Consequently, we can speculate that an advertising agency's images of men, women, and ethnic groups spin in a circular fashion reflecting, maintaining, reinforcing, creating, hence reflecting, maintaining, reinforcing, and so on, society's collective views. If the images violated the public's expectations, they would most likely disappear. So far, they haven't.

It's tempting at this point to cite any number of television (or magazine or newspaper) advertisements and commercials that exploit male, female, and ethnic stereotypes, none of them flattering. But such a citation would become obsolete as soon as it's printed; the ads change so quickly. The stereotypes don't, however, as the armchair research you completed earlier demonstrates.

Advertisements on television can't stand, however, as the sole perpetrators of stereotypes. In addition to television advertisements, examine also display advertisements in popular magazines, tabloids, and some newspapers. You'll discover recurring ethnic and sexual themes.

The messages are clear. It's an *either–or* world: You can be either beautiful or ugly (and lonely), sexy or dowdy (and lonely), manly or wimpy (again, lonely). The choices are clearly in the hands of the consumer: Buy this hair-care product, drink this liquor, purchase Product X, and sex appeal is yours. You might conclude that Love Potion No. 9 is the primary advertising account supporting the media.

A CONFESSION

I have a friend who once had a severe drinking problem. He always needed a drink to "get going." Before going to a party, he'd always have three or four drinks at home in order to "get ready" for the party. At the party, then, he'd have more drinks. Then he'd go home, he's told me, and have several more drinks so that he could "relax" and "unwind." About 15 years ago—weary from a perpetual hangover and strained friendships—he sought professional help and he hasn't had a drink since. I'm proud of his success, but he's not. "Larry," he's said to me several times, "I'm still a drunk. I'm just a *recovering* alcoholic. I don't drink right now."

In the same sense of my friend's usage, I confess to you that I'm a recovering racist and sexist language user. The fact that I'm writing this chapter doesn't get me off the hook.

It's always dangerous when you and I believe we've achieved a Utopian state of linguistic perfection, an achievement others (The Unclean) should strive to attain. A case in point: During a summer session class I was explaining a significant sociolinguistic fact. "A colleague of mine," I told the class, "is a Nigerian national who came to the United States to go to a university. While in school, he met a woman from Mississippi; they fell in love and were married. Whenever his family members from Nigeria come for a visit, they are shocked at his behavior. In Nigeria, sex roles are rigidly observed—there's woman's work and there's man's work. The distinctions are very clear. His relatives cannot understand how he can lower himself to help her with her household chores."

Well, I thought with consummate pride, I had, once again, made a significant sociolinguistic point! The perspicacious professor strikes again!

Valorie Foy, one of the students I've enjoyed having in class for reasons you'll immediately recognize, asked me after class: "Larry, why were the tasks *her* household chores? Why didn't you refer to them as *the* household chores?"

My keen insight turned into embarrassment. Val's comment reminded me that whenever I do something stupid, I mean *really* stupid, I usually do it with my lips, larynx, teeth, and tongue: the articulators of speech. Inadvertently, I demonstrated that I am a recovering sexist.

SEXIST LANGUAGE

Owing to the efforts of activists in the United States, considerable attention has been given to the relationships between language and gender in recent years, mainly as a consequence of concern over male and female equality. A number of criticisms have been offered, many of them linguistic, emphasizing how language constitutes a male-oriented view of the world. This view, it is argued, leads to a denigration of the role of women in society.[18]

The issue that has generated considerable attention is the grammatical lack of a gender-neutral, third-person-singular pronoun in English, especially

---

[18]David Crystal, *The Cambridge Encyclopedia of Language* (Cambridge: Cambridge University Press, 1991), 46.

in its use following indefinite pronouns, as in *If anyone wants a copy, he can have one.* What if the "anyone" is a *she*?[19]

In terms of vocabulary, there are other examples. For instance, consider the use of "male" items in contexts having little to do with gender as in *the man in the street, one man one vote, Stone Age man,* and the like. There are also women in the general public and women who vote, and there were women in the prehistoric times, facts the unexamined usages gloss over.

In English there are few grammatical forms, vocabulary items, or patterns of pronunciation that are used exclusively by either men or women, but there are differences in *frequency* of use. For example, women frequently utilize **tag-questions** at the end of a sentence (e.g., I really liked that movie, *didn't you*?) more than men do. Similarly, women frequently use more emotive adjectives (*super, lovely*), exclamations such as *Goodness me* or *Oh dear*, and intensifiers, like *so* and *such* (e.g., It was *such* a busy week!).[20]

Men and women frequently adopt different discourse strategies when they are engaged in mixed-gender conversations. Women, on the one hand, will typically ask more questions and utilize more **backchannels**, which are expressions of conversational encouragement, like *Hmmmm, Yes, Uh huh,* and *Oh, I see.* On the other hand, men are more likely to interrupt (up to three times as much it has been reported), to dispute what has been said, to ignore a woman's comment, to introduce more new topics, and to make more declarations of fact or opinion.[21]

One writer has made a clear distinction between the cross-purposes men and women have in mixed-gender conversations: the women are using *rapport-talk* and the men are using *report-talk*.[22] For men, according to these distinctions, talk is for information; it is transactional language. For women, talk is interactional language, showing involvement, caring, and interest.

In one analysis of school textbooks, male pronouns were four times as common as were female pronouns. In another study, 220 terms in English were identified for sexually promiscuous women, but only 22 for

---

[19]Ibid.

[20]Ibid., 21

[21]Ibid.

[22]Deborah Tannen, *You Just Don't Understand: Women and Men in Conversation* (New York: Ballantine Books, 1990), 77–79.

sexually promiscuous men.[23] The linguistic bias against women becomes obvious.

In order to stress this point, I've used a compliment barrage activity in my classes. I ask the class to identify a student we all know well. With the student's permission, he or she sits in the middle of a circle while the rest of us call out attributes of the student we all admire. After about 2 minutes I call the activity to a halt. I ask the student in the center, "How did you feel?" "Embarrassed," is the typical reply, "embarrassed, but good." Then I conclude by asking the entire class, "How would you feel if people said *negative* things about you, not for 2 minutes, but for 2 months, 2 years . . . or all your life?" The point is made.

Space limitations preclude an exhaustive analysis of male–female speech differences here. And certainly, not all women and men utilize the strategies I've described. If you're interested in pursuing this topic further, I invite you to read both the popular and scholarly writings of sociolinguists like Deb Cameron, Jennifer Coates, and Deborah Tannen. Their writings are clear and they help to dispel a number of myths about the speech strategies of the sexes. The world of language use is complex and can seldom be explained away by blithely saying, "Well, that's just the way women (or men) are."

THE TWO-VALUE ORIENTATION

Korzybski dealt with this simplistic, *either–or* view of the universe in his descriptions of the multiordinality of language. He believed that words have indefinite meanings, depending on the contexts in which they are applied. He was concerned that people tend to think with language that is limited and constrained to *either–or*, or to *biordinal* choices.[24]

Korzybski suggested that people tend to think in bi-polar opposites, leaving little or no room for gradualized positions or ideas in between. Examples of this idea are fairly common. For instance, some people find it astonishingly easy to sum up otherwise very complex philosophical, political, or religious ideas on the bumper stickers they place on their cars. "America: Love it or Leave It" was popular for a while. More recently I've seen "I've found it!" Another bumper sticker depicts the image of the

---

[23]Crystal, *The Cambridge Encyclopedia*, 46.

[24]Alfred Korzybski, *Science and Sanity: An Introduction to Non-Aristotelian Systems and General Semantics* (Lakeville, CT: The International Non-Aristotelian Library Publishing Company, 1958), 14.

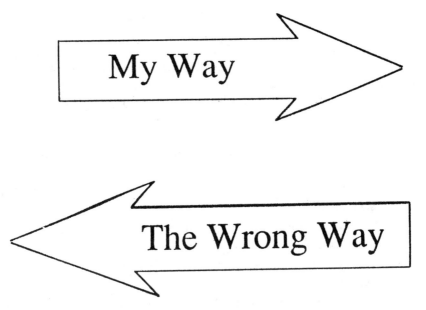

FIG. 10.1.   Example of two-value orientation.

Statue of Liberty printed on one side with the two-value choice "Speak English or Get the Fuck Out!" printed on the other. This is similar to one I saw just last week: "One nation, one flag, one language."

There are more proverbs expressing two-value orientations. For example, you've probably heard a few like the following:

1. There are two sides to every question.
2. You're either a part of the problem or a part of the solution.
3. You're either a Democrat or a Republican.
4. You're either right, or you're wrong.
5. Either you support the president, or you're opposed to him.
6. Do it my way or the wrong way.
7. Are you a man or a mouse?
8. Good Catholics [Baptists, Lutherans, Jews, etc.] don't do that.
9. Are you with me or against me?
10. Isn't that just like a woman?

Ignoring any middle ground or middle position in circumstances like these is illustrative of what Korzybski described as a **two-value orientation,** an orientation toward people, events, and circumstances that leads to only two possible choices.

As you reflect on two-value orientations, on the other hand, you may come to the conclusion that there will be times when they are inappropriate; there are, on the other hand, times when they are acceptable and appropriate. For example, you might look at the following and ask yourself whether a two-value orientation is or is not appropriate:

1. Should the ordination of gay and lesbian clergy be allowed in your church? Any church?

2. Should public tax dollars be used to support minority-student scholarships?

3. Should you force a 2-year-old to hold your hand while crossing the street?

4. Is it fair or just to require a 16-year-old to observe an 11:00 p.m. curfew?

5. Do you support the establishment of dress codes in schools, especially codes banning gang colors?

6. Should your local, state, or the federal government have any authority regarding membership criteria and quotas at private clubs?

7. Should all employees be required to participate in United Way or Community Chest pledge campaigns?

9. Should the U.S. Constitution be amended in order to make English the official language of the United States?

10. Should prayers be allowed, or mandated, in public school classrooms?

11. Should women of child-bearing age who are convicted for drug use be forced to have court-ordered contraceptives implanted surgically? Should they be sterilized?

12. Should university athletes with scholarships providing full payment of tuition, room, board, and books also receive free private tutoring to help them pass their courses?

13. Should fathers of newborn babies be allowed maternity or family leave from their places of employment?

14. Should you adhere to the posted speed limit on the interstate highway at 2:00 a.m.?

15. Should you park in a "Handicapped Only" parking space when you'll be in a supermarket only long enough to pick up a loaf of bread?
16. Should persons of the same gender be allowed to marry?

Not all of the preceding examples are of equal social, personal, or moral import. Nevertheless, I'm sure you get the idea. Although each of us will eventually arrive at a decision in cases such as these illustrations, the decisions are seldom simple yes–no propositions, a fact that will be clearer if you discuss the statements in a group of three or four people.

We can take the analyses you completed as you considered the a forementioned statements and transpose them into the realm of language marked by racism, sexism, prejudice, and bigotry. If these and other issues are multiordinal, can't we accept the multiordinality of people, too?

THE LANGUAGE OF PREJUDICE

Allport suggests that *language* plays a major role in both the development of and maintenance of prejudice, given the interdependent and intimate links among perception, thought, and language. He points out that some of the labels we apply to people are stronger in their emotional connotations than are others. He calls the more powerful ones **labels of primary potency**.[25]

For example, we may say a woman is an expert speaker, a thorough student, and a faithful employee. When we add that she is also a *blind* person, then the feature of *blindness* outweighs all of the other features. Among labels used to describe someone, Gordon Allport says, *blind* is more potent. Many physical and ethnic labels (crippled, disabled; Asian, African American, Native American) are examples of labels of primary potency.

What is at issue here, of course, is the fact that labels of primary potency blind us to most of the other attributes and characteristics an individual might possess. Labels of primary potency stop thought; they are examples of language "doing" our thinking for us. Labels of Primary Potency prevent alternative or additional perceptions and descriptions. They refer to only one aspect of a human being, but not any others.

---

[25]Gordon Allport, "The Language of Prejudice," in *Language Awareness* Paul Escholz, Alfred Rosa, and Virginia Clark, eds. (New York, St. Martin's Press, 1986), 261–70.

Left-handed people, for example, can also be considered as hard workers and thrifty shoppers. People with black hair can also be good mothers, excellent tennis players, and rapid readers. These illustrative descriptors appear to be relatively equal in emotional connotation and one feature does not overshadow or diminish another one. Add the term *gay* or *lesbian* to any of these attributes, and the less potent traits all but disappear.

Labels of primary potency, according to Allport, conjure up in the minds of some people connotations that are much stronger, almost always negative and hostile, and overshadow other attributes. Consequently, in such cases, Blacks are *only* Blacks, with no other recognizable or significant features. Jews are *only* Jews and nothing else really matters. Hispanics are *only* Hispanics, and nothing else is important. *Women* are only *Women*. A *crip* is a *crip*. *Wops* are *wops*. *Gays* are, well . . . you know.

The use of these labels reduces persons to *one* dimension: a stereotype. End of thinking. End of discussion. These labels prevent our seeing the fuller person, as the writer of the following letter to the editor attempts to illustrate:

> Our [gay and lesbian] children have partners celebrating their fifth, 10th and 15th anniversaries. They own homes and mortgages, have car payments, gardens, lawns, neighbors, dogs and cats and they hold jobs. They pay taxes. They also have brothers and sisters, grand-parents, related kinfolks and friends.[26]

If you are one who cannot or has not been described by one of the labels of Primary Potency, then you may be less likely to be disturbed by their use in society. Obviously, on the other hand, if you or someone you love has been called *timber-nigger* (a crude form of double jeopardy aimed at Native Americans) or *porch monkey*, or if you or a friend have been the target of another bumper sticker I saw recently that read "Save a fish, spear an Indian," then you understand how mean and demeaning they are.

Haven't you wondered where these bumper stickers come from?

I am not trying to convert either teachers or their students into feminists, or any other kind of *-ists*. I am suggesting, however, that racist, sexist, or demeaning language ought to be understood and avoided, and I am using our earlier definition of "good english" (see chap. 6) as the rationale:

Good English is marked by success in making language
choices so that the fewest number of persons
will be distracted by the choices.[27]

---

[26]Letter to the editor, *Lincoln (NE) Journal Star*, September 7, 1991.

[27]Robert C. Pooley, *The Teaching of English Usage* (Champaign-Urbana, IL: National Council of Teachers of English, 1974), 5.

Knowing that some will be distracted and offended by the use of *Boy,* *Fox, Coon,* or any other label of primary and negative potency is reason enough not to use it. We can try to get our own linguistic houses in order in our efforts to help students become more spontaneous, precise, and elaborative with language. "Good English" is the more traditional educational aim, and we have defined it in such a way that its social uses are clearly important.

Regardless of how you may feel personally about the use of *mailman* versus *mail carrier*, or using *man* as a generic, neutral noun encompassing both male and female, let's review some ideas from chapter 6. Part of our definition of "good English" says that the language used will be comfortable to *both* speaker and listener. Think of it this way. If you are hosting a dinner party this weekend and plan to burn incense in an attempt to create the atmosphere desired, will you insist on burning the incense if you know one of your guests is allergic to it? Similarly, should we continue to use words and expressions when we know others are distracted by their use?

This determination of "good English" requires us to recenter the focus of conversation. We *refocus* our talk from "I" to "we," or from "me" to "us." This requires, for many of us, a totally different way of looking at the universe!

I understand and appreciate the fact that the forces of "political correctness" force some people to avoid topics of genuine interest. Do all gay men lisp? Are African Americans better kissers because they have bigger lips? These and other questions are seldom asked because if they were, the question asker might be labeled as *homophobic* or *racist*. Well, knowing that a legitimate question left unsaid maintains a status quo of ignorance, Phillip Milano started www.yforum.com several years ago. At this site, people can ask any questions that help to demystify real or perceived human differences.[28]

When conversations, news stories, editorials, television programs, classroom instructional materials, political campaigns, and advertising campaigns utilize or exploit labels of primary potency, making some people appear to be unidimensional, it is another way of making the targeted group less than human. It makes them subhuman. "Anyone who believes that certain people *are* subhuman will find it easy to treat them *as* subhuman. The end result can be mountains of baby shoes in storehouses, lamp shades made from human skin, and soap made from human fat."[29]

---

[28] Leonard Pitts, Jr., "Go Ahead—You Can Ask the Unaskable," *Lincoln (NE) Journal Star*, September 13, 2004, sec. B.

[29] Morris Engel, *The Language Trap* (Englewood Cliffs, NJ: Prentice-Hall, 1984), 106.

Given our earlier description of English teacher as language cop, not much is likely to be gained, in my view, by dogmatically banning or prohibiting demeaning language, although its use can't be condoned. Attempts to modify or to control language through prescriptive legislation inevitably fail.

The student explorations at the end of this chapter are examples of classroom activities through which students can become more aware of and sensitive to language and images of intolerance and discrimination. Personal explorations like these are more likely to be effective than will be teacher- or adult-centered exhortations.

The topic of demeaning language must be approached with a fine, sensitive hand in classrooms. It is not to be studied because we want either Anglo-European students or young men to feel more guilty about racist or sexist language in society. Nor is it to be examined so that beleaguered non-White minorities or young women might gain a small measure of smug victory and relief in our classrooms.

It is studied, as Engel reminds us, because we have it in our power either to degrade or to enhance and beautify ourselves and our world by the way we use language.[30]

I understand and fully appreciate the fact that some may believe this comment is hopelessly idealistic, but I leave you with this question and challenge: If you, a professional language teacher, do not enable your students to use language in ways that will enhance and beautify themselves and their worlds, who will?

REVIEWING THE CHAPTER:

Part One: *Please place a (✓) by the statement if it represents what the author **says** in chapter 10. Be prepared to defend your answers with references to the text.*

    ____ 1. Many children do not believe they have many names because they are loved.

    ____ 2. Intolerant stereotypes are primarily limited to university campuses.

    ____ 3. Banning the use of intolerant language is not likely to be successful.

---

[30]Ibid.

___ 4. Language may be intolerant in one context but not in another.

___ 5. Attempts to control language through prescription inevitably fail.

Part Two: *Place a (✔) beside each statement you believe represents what the author **means** in chapter 10. Be prepared to support your answers with references to the text.*

___ 6. Two-value orientations enhance our perceptions of the world.

___ 7. Two-value orientations are usually wrong.

___ 8. People may unknowingly use demeaning language.

___ 9. Teachers may affect surface structures in their students' language use.

___ 10. People learn hurtful language just like they learn other aspects of language.

Part Three: *Based on your reading of chapter 10 as well as other readings and your experiences as an educator, place a (✔) beside any statement below you connect with the chapter and can support.*

___ 11. Birds of a feather flock together.

___ 12. A weed is any plant out of place.

___ 13. Beauty is in the eye of the beholder.

___ 14. Guns don't kill; people kill.

___ 15. An ounce of prevention is worth a pound of cure.

STUDENT EXPLORATIONS
FOR LANGUAGES OF INTOLERANCE
AND DISCRIMINATION

EXPLORATION: What Is Funny?
DIRECTIONS: Revisit your childhood and watch several TV cartoons.

1. Do the characters in the different cartoons use different language or do they all use the same language?

2. Do any of the cartoon characters portray stereotyped roles? How can language reinforce a stereotype?

3. Interview a parent; what was his or her favorite cartoon as a child? Was language an important part of the cartoon's humor?

4. Do the cartoons you've seen reflect societal beliefs, stereotypes, and the like?

***** ***** *****

EXPLORATION: It's a Man's World
DIRECTIONS: How might you rewrite the following lines from popular culture so that they aren't referring only to one gender?

a. Where's my dinner, woman?
b. White men can't jump.
c. There's no crying in baseball.
d. You may kiss the bride.
e. Men are from Mars, Women are from Venus.
f. She thinks my tractor's sexy.

1. How often do stereotyped labels come into the language of popular culture?
2. Do people use these labels intentionally or unintentionally?
3. Does this language reflect society's values, do you think?

***** ***** *****

EXPLORATION: Degenderizing Designations
DIRECTIONS: Some occupations have gender-neutral titles, such as *teacher, librarian,* and *lawyer.* Can you retitle the following, making each one more gender-neutral?

a. fireman
b. stewardess
c. salesman
d. garbage man
e. craftsman
f. chairman
g. fisherman
h. lineman
i. paperboy

1. Are some titles more easily made gender-neutral than others? Why?
2. Why do you think some gender-specific job titles remain in use?
3. What does the general society prefer, do you think, gender-neutral or gender-specific job titles?

***** ***** *****

EXPLORATION: Advertising Inserts
DIRECTIONS: Examine the advertising inserts that come with the Sunday edition of any newspaper. Try to separate the merchandise being advertised in these inserts into categories: computers and other technological items; home maintenance; sportswear and gear; furniture; home appliances; and the like.

1. As you examine these advertisements, do some try to appeal more to men? To women?
2. Are some stores advertised in the inserts *women's* stores or *men's* stores? How do you know?
3. Can gender assignment be avoided in advertising?

***** ***** *****

EXPLORATION: "'Mawnin!',' says Brer Rabbit."
DIRECTIONS: Stereotypes are standardized, uncritical, and unthinking images or prejudgments some people use in their views of other people and the world. Stereotypes can be found in literature, advertising, television programs, political advertisements, music, and mealtime conversations. Humorous literature frequently uses stereotypes as it pokes fun at people and their behavior. The *Uncle Remus* stories by Joel Chandler Harris, for example, employ heavy use of stereotyped language. Harris' stories depict the way Southern White Anglo-Saxons perceived African Americans in the 1800s in the United States. Focusing on the characters of Brer Fox and Brer Rabbit, the language and action of the stories represent stereotypical Black English Vernacular. Read the first 20 paragraphs of "The Wonderful Tar-Baby Story," then answer the following questions:

1. List the words in the passage that are used to form the reader's opinion or interpretation of the characters.
2. Explain how these words create stereotypes, and whether they help or harm our interpretations.

3. How do these words and the sentences they're taken from affect the way the reader perceives people living in the South in the 1800s?

4. Based on your understanding of this passage, the words you have been examining, and your general knowledge, do writers continue to use these stereotypes today?

***** ***** *****

EXPLORATION: Driving With Latka

DIRECTIONS: "I could drive this taxi with both eyes tied behind my back!" This sentence is just on example of many stereotyped uses of language by a non-native speaker seen on the syndicated channel television program "Taxi." Latka Gravas is depicted as never getting English quite right, presumably as many non-native speakers of English do not.

Watch an episode of "Taxi." Notice in particular the common stereotypes the program's writers use in Latka's speech. Then, be prepared to discuss the following:

1. List some of the language stereotypes used to portray Latka's character.

2. What are some of the words or phrases Latka uses that demonstrate his misunderstanding of English?

3. Do you find Latka's English usage humorous or distracting?

4. Do you believe Latka's English is an accurate representation of how non-native speakers use English?

5. Based on this discussion of one episode of "Taxi," as well as other television programs you've seen, what can you determine about television's use of language stereotypes? Are they always funny? Can they be harmful?

***** ***** *****

EXPLORATION: Are You What You Drive?

DIRECTIONS: "What's a 'rent [parent] doing in a load [great car] like that?" is an example of a sentence you might hear someone say when their stereotyped ideas about the type of automobile a parent *ought* to drive are proved false. Why do so many people associate the type of car a person owns to be a reflection of that person's personality or social status? Or, why do some believe owning a particular type of car will automatically bestow on them either new personality or a different position in society?

Using automobile ads clipped from newspapers and magazines, create a collage demonstrating the various ways advertisers use stereotyped language in order to entice potential buyers.

1. Make a list of the various names of cars appearing in your collage. Can you group these names into categories (for example, under Cats you could include cougar, lynx, bobcat).

2. What types of stereotypes do these names and/or categories conjure? What personality stereotypes do they suggest?

3. How are these examples of stereotyped language used to the advantage of the advertiser? The automobile company? The potential purchaser?

4. Based on your analyses of stereotyped language used in automobile advertising, do you believe society is affected one way or another by this language?

***** ***** *****

EXPLORATION: Every Light in the House Is On
DIRECTIONS: The titles of popular country songs sometimes appeal to stereotyped ideas about men and women and their relationships. Listen to a local country radio station and examine the titles of popular songs and the corresponding themes developed through the verses. Are there stereotyped themes, characters, or other patterns you can identify?

1. What are some titles of currently popular country songs? Do the songs used stereotyped language in depicting men, women, or themes?

2. Are these uses of language intentional or unintentional, in your view?

3. Based on these analyses, what do the titles suggest about people who listen to country music? Is there a stereotyped view of them? Do you agree or disagree with this view?

***** ***** *****

EXPLORATION: Here Come Angel and Stud-Boy
DIRECTIONS: Terms of endearment are frequently used in spoken exchanges between members of the opposite gender. Some of the terms are positive, but some have negative connotations. Brainstorm with others

in your class, listing as many terms of endearment you can remember hearing people use during the past week.

1. Distinguish between the terms used for men and women. Do the terms group themselves into categories (physical Characteristics, special talents, ethnicity, etc.)?

2. What do these categories and terms suggest about possible stereo-typed views of men and women? When do we begin to learn these terms?

3. Based on these discussions, do you think terms of endearment affect people's view of themselves?

***** ***** *****

EXPLORATION: Cheers
DIRECTIONS: Which character in the cast of the syndicated television program "Cheers" is more likely to ask: "Yeah, and how would you like a hook in your mouth?" The characters in the program are defined for the viewer largely through the language they use. Watch an episode or two of "Cheers."

1. Explain how language is used in stereotypical ways by the writers of "Cheers" in order to characterize Frazier, and his level of edu-cation and training; Carla, and her working-class social status; or Woody, and his Midwest origins and values.

2. How would you describe the *tone* of the conversations taking place in the Cheers bar? How does this conversational tone provide a set-ting for the language stereotypes identified in Question 1?

3. Do you believe the stereotyped language used by the characters depicted in "Cheers" reflects society in general?

***** ***** *****

EXPLORATION: Caveat Emptor
DIRECTIONS: Used-car advertisements use language in several uncon-ventional ways. Sometime "used" cars are called "program cars," "expe-rienced cars," or "preowned cars." In order to lure buyers to the sales lot, sales agents will describe "easy terms," "instant credit," and the like. Easy for whom? Is it really *instant*? Examine several advertisements for used cars, either on television or in newspapers, then prepare a parody of a

used-car commercial in which you use the stereotyped language you've observed in order to sell a car. (Select any car you think is a real dog.)

1. What are some of the more frequent terms commercials use to describe used cars? Are these terms accurate or misleading, in your judgment?
2. How do these terms put the prospective buyer at a disadvantage?
3. What is the general effect of language that distorts? Consider the point of view of *both* the seller and the buyer.

***** ***** *****

EXPLORATION: Love Is a Simply Splendored Thing
DIRECTIONS: "Will Zack ever return the searing love Kimberly so desires? Will Kimberly ever find the cache of words in her heart's vocabulary in order to explain to Zack how she yearns for him?" This sentence could have come from one of any number of grocery store romance novels. The language used in these novels is very dramatic, formulaic, and stereotyped as it describes the soft-spoken woman who falls hopelessly in love with an athletic-looking man who inevitably is a member of a different social class. It's the basic Romeo and Juliet story told over and over again, moving around the country from St. Louis, to Miami, to Southern California to Anywhere, U.S.A. Only the geography is different. Locate a grocery store romance novel, then select and read a 100-word passage at the beginning, middle, and the end of the book.

1. What phrases and language clichés are used in the passages to describe the characters? How does this language use affect your view of the characters?
2. Why do these novels rely so heavily on stereotyped language? Is this language use harmful to anyone?

***** ***** *****

EXPLORATION: The Sexy Toilet Bowl Cleaner
DIRECTIONS: An implicit message in several TV commercials seem to suggest that there is one acceptable image of the Ideal woman and any woman can attain that ideal if . . . she uses this shampoo or that toilet bowl cleaner, or washes her family's clothes with a particular detergent. Bring to class several color display advertisements from a variety of popular magazines.

1. What stereotypes of men or women are used in your ads?
2. Are there recurring words or phrases used in the ads, regardless of the product being advertised?
3. What are some results of the stereotyped views of men and women as they are depicted in advertisements?

***** ***** *****

EXPLORATION: You're Such a @&*$%!
DIRECTIONS: Look at the following list of words. They are frequently used as derogetory terms. What characteristics make them so negative?

a. snake
b. dog
c. cow
d. pig
e. rat
f. bug

1. Why do some people use these names applied to other people? What is the intended result?

***** ***** *****

EXPLORATION: Have You Come a Long Way, Baby?
DIRECTIONS: Here are a number of phrases commonly used today. How might you change them?

a. The girls at the office . . .
b. It's a man's job . . .
c. I now pronounce you man and wife . . .
d. The fabric is man-made . . .
e. Women are not good at math . . .
f. All men are created equal . . .
g. A woman's place is in the home . . .
h. Man's best friend is his dog . . .
i. Real men don't cry . . .

***** ***** *****

EXPLORATION: She's Always a Woman . . .
DIRECTIONS: Try to obtain either audio copies or printed lyrics of songs popular in the 1950s, 1960s, 1970s, 1980s, and 1990s. Listen to the audio copy or read the printed version.

1. How are men and women portrayed in these songs?
2. How would you describe the relationships between men and women as they are portrayed in these songs?
3. As you examine male–female relationships as portrayed in popular music over the years, how are the relationships similar? How are they different?
4. Do you think language affects our views of other people? Why or why not?

CHAPTER **11**

When Some of Them Don't Speak English

*"Well, then, why ain't it natural and right for
a Frenchman to talk different from us?
You answer me that."*
—Mark Twain, *Adventures of Huckleberry Finn*

Before you read the following chapter, consider the following telephone conversation:

"Dr. Andrews, this is Jane Doe, the high school counselor at Midway High School. We have three new students from (name any country) who came to my office just two days ago to begin school here and their English language proficiency is, well, very limited. Their teachers aren't sure how to help them in their classes. Can you give us some, like, really quick advice?"

I've had several conversations like this one. In this example, I've changed only the names of the counselor and the school.

What advice would you give to the counselor and to the teachers?

The numbers of children for whom English is a new language continue to increase in our schools. These are children from immigrant and refugee families, and some of them were born in the United States to parents who cannot speak English.

According the U.S. Office of Education's Office of English Language Acquisition, Language Enhancement, and Academic Achievement for Limited English Proficient Students, the percentage of limited English proficient students enrolled in kindergarten through 12th grade nationwide from the 1991–1992 through the 2001–2002 school years increased 95%, from 2,430,712 to 4,747,763 students. During that same decade, the overall school-age population increased by 12%.[1]

Although the presence of language-minority students—students whose primary language is a language other than English—has been a factor in U.S. schools since the school doors first opened in the 18th century in this country, identifying and agreeing on the best ways to teach these students continues to challenge schools, policymakers, and communities.[2]

El Cenizo, Texas, created a solution in 1999. El Cenizo is 15 miles south of Laredo and is, literally, a border town. The population of El Cenizo is 7,800, and 98.9% of its citizens are Hispanic, many of whom speak no English. In an attempt to make the town's official business meetings more understandable to its citizens, the town council declared that Spanish would be El Cenizo's "official" language![3] When the news filtered northward it set off a firestorm. English First, the organization dedicated to the proposition that English should be the dominant and official language of the United States, fearing a domino-like effect across the country, likened El Cenizo to "the Quebec of the U.S."[4]

I offer El Cenizo's "solution" to the challenge of teaching English as a new language with tongue in cheek. The town council was simply trying to get its Spanish-speaking citizens involved in local government issues. They had no idea, apparently, that their decision would be in the national news. But, language issues can easily become emotional issues, as the Ebonics debates, the Whole Language debates, and the El Cenizo controversy all attest.

Because of the enormity of the United States, many of us spend our lifetimes immersed in a monolingual, English-speaking environment.[5] For example, I can get in my car and drive for 5 hours in *any* direction, get out of my car, and the language I'll hear spoken on the local main street, radio, or television, or read in the local newspaper will be the same language I routinely speak and read at home. I'm not unique. Many people in the United States, perhaps you, too, can make the same comment.

---

[1]Jill Davidson, "English Language Learners in Essential Schools," *Horace*, Winter 2003, http://www.essentialschools.org/cs/resources/view/ces_res.286.

[2]Ibid.

[3]Linda Gorow, "Texas Town Makes Spanish Official, Stirs War of Words," *The Boston Globe*, August 28, 1999, sec. E.

[4]Ibid.

[5]Donna M. Brown, "One Person's Opinion," *English Journal*, December 1996, 13.

With only one or two exceptions, however, few people in the rest of the world can make this generalization. In that regard, then, several of us in the United States *are* unique.

People in other parts of the world can drive for 5 hours—or sometimes much less—in any direction and encounter *several* language groups. What this illustrates is that many of us in the United States are linguistically land-locked. Except for those of you living near ethnic enclaves in major metropolitan centers or those of you living in a border state, we in the United States are largely, but not totally, of course, surrounded by linguistic sameness: the English language.

I do not mean to suggest that the dominance of the English language is a negative factor, or that we are inherently stupid or lazy people because of our lack of experience with other languages and cultures. It is unfortunate, though, that this lack of experience with other language groups causes some to view other languages and other cultures as being of little or no value or importance, and causes some either to ignore or to avoid those who do not speak fluent English.[6]

In some cases, according to Betancourt, there are openly antagonistic attitudes toward persons who speak other languages. She suggests that especially in those states that have enacted English as their "official language," the discussions have encouraged hostile feelings toward non-English-speaking citizens.[7]

A national White supremacist group has circulated leaflets in those cities in my state where there are substantial numbers of Hispanics employed in the beef-processing industry. At the top of the page, the leaflet proclaims *Not immigration but INVASION!* and warns that the English language and U.S. culture are under attack. This same group recently leafleted a neighborhood not too far from my home, warning about the dangers of Black-on-White crimes.[8]

In the largest city in my state, the same group leafleted several neighborhoods on Martin Luther King, Jr., Day. These leaflets decried interracial marriage, immigration of non-White persons to the United States, and multiculturalism.[9]

---

[6]Ibid., 14.

[7]Ingrid Betancourt, *Wilson Library Bulletin*, February 1992, 38.

[8]Butch Mabin, "South Lincoln Target of Fliers," *Lincoln (NE) Journal Star*, December 22, 2004, sec. B.

[9]"Supremacists Leave Leaflets in Omaha," *Lincoln (NE) Journal Star*, January 18, 2005, sec. B.

These antagonistic events have been isolated events, but they illustrate Bettencourt's point.

THE GROWING NUMBERS OF ENGLISH-LANGUAGE LEARNERS

Earlier in this chapter you read the data describing the remarkable growth of the English Language Learner (ELL) population. Some have estimated that as many as one third of all of the students attending urban schools in the United States use English as their *second* language.[10]

Even in the relatively sparsely populated state in which I live, both the larger and the smaller school districts are facing a common challenge: meeting the learning needs of a growing number of children whose first language is not English.

I know of two smaller school districts serving towns with populations in the 5,000 to 6,000 range. If anyone had suggested to school personnel in these districts a decade ago that among their greatest challenges in the beginning of the 21st century would be trying to meet the needs of English Language Learners, they would have laughed at the suggestion. They certainly aren't laughing today, however, as the telephone conversation reported at the headnote to this chapter illustrates.

What all of the aforementioned tells me is, I believe, fairly clear. Unless or until there is a dramatic reduction in immigration quotas that might be established by the U.S. government, I can guarantee you that sooner or later—and it's likely to be sooner—you will have a student, perhaps several students, for whom English is their second (or third, or fourth) language, and, furthermore, their English language proficiency will not be the same as that of your native English-speaking students! What do you do, then, when not all of your students speak English?

I cannot deliver in this single chapter a complete K–12 teacher-education program that will certify you as an ELL teacher. If you are interested in such a program, your state colleges or universities may offer one. Because one chapter in one book can't tell you everything you need to know about second language acquisition and pedagogy, I'm going to

---

[9]"Supremacists Leave Leaflets in Omaha," *Lincoln (NE) Journal Star*, January 18, 2005, sec. B.

[10]"One Nation, One Language," *U.S. News & World Report*, September 25, 1995.

inject a subtitle for this chapter: *A Practical and Introductory Guide for the Classroom Teacher*.

WHO ARE THESE STUDENTS?

Theodore Sizer opened the 2002 Fall Forum of the Coalition of Essential Schools with these words:

> We recognize the fact that no two of our students are exactly the same, and that each changes over time. All this bubbling variety is inconvenient. It would be handy if each thirteen year old was a standardized being, pumping no more or fewer hormones than any other thirteen year old and speaking no language other than formal English. Life as a teacher would be easier if each of our charges was so predictable.[11]

What Sizer is emphasizing in his remarks is that our ELL students are remarkably different, few if any speak formal English, and some speak no English at all. Teaching certainly is inconvenient!

Who are these children and young adults who look to you to help them learn in school? They are the sons and daughters of immigrants or refugees from Bosnia, Russia, Ukraine, Sudan, Croatia, Mexico, Vietnam Haiti, and a host of other nations. They may have come to the United States with the assistance of family members who immigrated earlier, years ago. Or, they may have come with the assistance of a local social service agency or church. Or, they may have immigrated to the United States completely on their own.

Furthermore, remember that each family has a *story*. Some of the stories are narratives of dogged determination and achievement. Some of their stories are nothing less than horrific! As John Skretta, a local high school principal and a former graduate student of mine who taught me a lot, wrote in his ELL Internship journal several years ago: "That human beings could endure, or should have to endure and overcome, the physical, emotional and psychological threats some of my ELL students have faced, is testimony to the incredible resiliency of the human spirit."

Finally, but by no means conclusively, some of these learners, a number of whom have never before attended school, are in your community and school because they *want* to be there and are happy to be there. They have come to the United States and have, consequently, avoided the

---

[11]Davidson, "English Language Learners."

life-or-death threat of ethnic or political "cleansing," or, they have rejoined their family, or they have newfound opportunities for education and for employment.

On the other hand, some are here *against* their will; their parents made the decision to immigrate to the United States and the son or daughter had, absolutely, no vote in the matter. They were finessed. When they came to the United States, they left behind their best friends, their own culture and customs, and their own language. In the words of a well-known science fiction writer, Robert Heinlein, they are strangers in strange land . . . and they may not like this strange land!

SOME NOTIONS ABOUT TEACHING ELL LEARNERS

As we begin our *Practical and Introductory Guide for the Classroom Teacher*, there are a few notions worth remembering about the ELL learners in your classroom.

ELL Learners Are, First of All, Human Beings; They Are People.[12] This may seem obvious, but, sometimes, it is either forgotten or ignored. For example, I have seen a 15-year-old immigrant student placed in a fifth-grade classroom. His English language proficiency wasn't the same as the native English speakers of the same age. He was, clearly, the oldest and the largest learner in the room, much too large for the flip-top desk he tried to cram his body into. Furthermore, he had the interests of a 15-year-old person, not a 10-year-old. He had no friends in this room. He was clearly embarrassed and anxious. For him, school was not a "safe place."

I have seen a 12-year-old student from Bosnia placed in a classroom dedicated to the needs of "retarded" learners. Because of her limited English proficiency, she was classified by the school as a "retarded" learner. This young woman knew what was happening to her, and she resented the treatment she was receiving.

Both of these learners, however, are *people*, just like their American age-mates. Their only "problem" was that they didn't speak fluent English. The schools forgot they these students were human beings with the same needs and interests of their native English-speaking peers.

In addition to these violations of human relationships, there is a significant linguistic fault: The two young people I've described needed to be

---

[12]Pat Rigg and Virginia G. Allen, eds., "Introduction," in *When They Don't All Speak English* (Champaign-Urbana, IL: National Council of Teachers of English, 1989), viii.

placed with first language students; the ELL students will learn a lot of English from them.

ELL Students Learn English in Order to Accomplish What They Need and Want to Accomplish With Those Who Speak English.[13] ELL learners need to learn English that will help them *now*, not someday in the future.

To illustrate: One of my students shared with the class one night the first sentence he learned in a foreign language course, which was (translated into English), "I have a green pencil box." Twenty years later, he said, he's still *waiting* for an opportunity to use that sentence! As you might imagine, he may need to wait a few more years.

ELL learners need to do *immediate* things with English: how to ask for help or for directions, how to ask a question in class, how to go through the lunch line and ask for a preferred entrée, how to ask for a bus transfer-slip, how to give an answer to a question in class, and the like.

The ELL Student's Growth in English Proficiency Develops Globally, Not Linearly.[14] ELL learners don't acquire English in a linear sequence by learning nouns first, verbs second, adverbs third, then pronouns, and so on. They learn "chunks" of language in meaningful contexts. Please, do not waste their time by assigning drills and worksheets that focus on isolated fragments of language; rather, keep them engaged in talking and writing activities with their English-speaking peers in which they must use English in order to satisfy age-appropriate, meaningful classroom learning assignments.

Won't these activities present a variety of challenges to the ELL learners and to their English-speaking peers? Of course; next question?

In time the ELL learners will learn both English and content, more rapidly than you might assume. Plus, peers are effective—and relatively more patient—mentors than you or I might be.

Language Develops in a Variety of Contexts.[15] When you were acquiring language, you did so by playing different types of games with your family; by listening to read-aloud poems and stories and by talking about them; by looking at pictures in a variety of books; by going to the mall and talking about what you saw; by going to the grocery store; by riding in the family car or in a bus; by talking about what you were seeing.

---

[13]Ibid., ix.

[14]Ibid., xi.

[15]Ibid., xii.

I have a friend who teaches ELL science. The curriculum called for a unit titled "The Rain Forest"; her students from Iraq and Jordan recognized the separate words *rain* and *forest*, but had little understanding of the larger, compound concept, "rain forest." She took the students to a nearby zoo that has a reconstructed rain forest. The students enjoyed the trip, had a meaningful experience, and the unit meant something to them.

All of the field trips you can arrange—or piggy-back with another teacher in your building—will be useful, but the field trips don't need to be "fancy." A walk around the block, or a trip to a local grocery store, fire station, hospital, drugstore, or even your own home will provide your ELL learners with language-rich experiences.

Additionally, keep a supply of word games available; take your old magazines to school. Bring the local newspaper and telephone book to class; they employ many uses of language you cannot assume your ELL learners are familiar with.

Focus Your Attention on General Literacy, Not Isolated Skills. Once again, review your own experiences, or, if you are a parent, those of your children. When language learners acquire language, their family members don't devote Mondays to reading, Tuesdays to talking, Wednesdays to writing, and the like.

In an English-speaking home with a younger language learner, literacy events take place in an integrated manner: A parent reads a letter from a relative, talks about the letter and the relative with the learner, then the child "writes" a letter, real or imaginary, using some conventional spellings, some not, maybe some invented spellings, or perhaps only what adults might call "scribbling."

In English-speaking homes adults read to children, make shopping lists, and talk about what's for lunch. The children talk with the adults about the letters, the lists, and the menu; they'll frequently create their own stories, lists, and menus, in both written and oral forms.

I am not suggesting that you duplicate these illustrations in your classroom. If you think they'll work, try them. I am, however, suggesting that reading-writing-listening-speaking events are normally and naturally *intertwined*. Read aloud to your students, then talk about what you've read. Use wordless picture books and invite the class to create the narration and dialogue. Have the students draw or write their own stories or poems. Discuss the stories. The students will learn language and conversational conventions, story structures, the differences between expository and narrative prose, the importance of sequence, and the like.

Include Your ELL Learners in All Classroom Activities. The vast majority of classroom teachers I know are humane, caring people who are dedicated to helping others to learn. They know that classrooms should be "safe" environments in which predicting, speculating, and exploring are to be encouraged, without the students fearing failure.

Furthermore, they know that no learner should suffer embarrassment; learning is, among other things, emotional. When people are threatened, they learn little; when they feel safe, they learn more.

Consequently, some well-intentioned teachers will not call on ELL learners in class discussions. Fearful that the ELL learner might not know an answer (as if all of the English-speaking students will!) or might mispronounce the language, the well-intentioned teacher doesn't call on the ELL learner as often. *Let's avoid embarrassment* seems to be the ruling assumption. On the one hand, this is understandable.

In the long run, however, strategies such as this, no matter how altruistic they may be, *do not help* the ELL learner. It pushes him or her to the social and educational periphery of the class. These "humanistic" attempts, in fact, remove the ELL learner from meaningful content-related discussions and from the culture of the classroom. You must include your ELL learners in all of the activities in your classes; the alternative is to harm them with misguided kindness, however well-intentioned, which makes them marginalized citizens in the classroom.

WHO OWNS ENGLISH?

Before we examine the structure of meaningful learning activities for ELL students in the next section of this chapter, I believe it's important for you too look in a mirror and ask yourself some hard questions about your general attitudes toward the English language, like who "owns" it, what are reasonable expectations for ELL learners, how you'll respond to student miscues, and the like.

I suspect the majority of English language scholars would agree today with the position advanced by McArthur in his preface to the *Oxford Companion to the English Language:* "English is the possession of every individual and every community that in any way uses it, regardless of what any other individual or community may think about it."[16]

---

[16]Cited in Jiang Yajun, "Metaphors the English Language Lives By", *English Today*, July 2002, 62.

Not everyone, however, agrees with McArthur. Standing in stark contrast to McArthur's position is this from Enoch Powell, a British politician: "Others may speak and read English—more or less—but it is our language, not theirs. It was made in England by the English and it remains our distinctive property, however widely it is used and learned."[17] In addition to either ignoring or simply not knowing about the foundations of the English language laid by non-English speakers like the Angles, Saxons, Jutes, Norse, and Norman French, Powell's proprietary attitude toward English is not a warm but is a constrained invitation to those who would learn English: You can learn English, he seems to be saying, but remember your proper place.

Robert Burchfield, editor of the *Oxford English Dictionary*, sums it up, in my view, with this statement:

> English has also become a lingua franca to the point that any literate educated person is in a very real sense deprived if he does not know English. Poverty, famine, and disease are instantly recognized as the cruelest and least excusable forms of deprivation. Linguistic deprivation is a less easily noticed condition, but one nevertheless of great significance.[18]

The teacher's view of language defines as well as limits the ways he or she will *perceive* the uses of English. If there are "abuses" of English, it's the "enemy" who is doing the abusing and the teacher, then, becomes the "protector." With this metaphorical view, it's only a small step for a teacher to see him or herself as noble and courageous, involved in a battle against bad people who seek to degenerate "our" language.[19] I trust you will avoid this view.

DESIGNING ELL CLASSROOM STRATEGIES

First of all, let me clear the chalkboard: Some teachers believe that fully certified ELL teachers possess a mysterious repertoire of *magical* strategies enabling them to help immigrant/refugee children learn English. This is, however, not the way it is.

Certified ELL teachers are not wizards of the arcane; they do not employ academic alchemy. They modify successful, proven practices in order to meet the needs of their students. All good teachers do the same thing.

---

[17]Ibid.

[18]Ibid., 60.

[19]Ibid., 57.

As a transition, revisit with me an early Indiana Jones movie, *Raiders of the Lost Ark*. In the first scenes we see Indy and his guide attempting to take a bag of jewels from a protected dais. Indy takes the bag, he and the guide race out of the cave—chased by a large, rolling boulder—only to be met by a dastardly villain. Indy heroically flees and runs as fast as he can to his airplane, parked on a conveniently nearby lake, and he escapes! Whew!

In the next scene we see *Dr*. Indiana Jones, an Ivy League professor of archaeology, all tweedy and frumpy, leather patches at the elbows, delivering a lecture to his students. As Indy's lecture approaches a dramatic denouement, a rude school bell rings, interrupting and signifying the end of class. The students gather up their notebooks, stuff them into their book bags, and start filing out of the room. As the students exit, Indy shouts after them, "Remember, read chapter 6 for the next class!"

That's how Professor Jones gives assignments to his students. It's a *counterexample* of effective practice, described here as a model to *avoid*. With all students in general, and with ELL learners in particular, the assignment phase of a reading assignment in any classroom is crucial. A more effective assignment will include the following:

- **The assignment will build upon the learners' prior knowledge of the topic.** The teacher will describe in very direct language how the next assignment is related to the topic covered yesterday, last week, or in the last unit of study. Or, the teacher may ask the class to brainstorm about the topic of the next assignment, listing their comments on the chalkboard, then organizing these comments into related clusters. If the class lacks sufficient prior knowledge, provide direct experience that will give them the knowledge (the trip to the zoo's rain forest, described earlier, is an excellent example).

- **The assignment will introduce important new vocabulary words.** Presented in the actual context in which they appear in the text, the new words are introduced. Perhaps the students can figure out the meaning of the word by seeing how it is used in the sentence. If not, the teacher can provide the meaning. Be selective in choosing words, however. You can't teach your students all the words they might not know. Consequently, introduce vocabulary that name *key concepts* in the assignment and that are likely to be *encountered again* in the study of the subject at hand.

- **The assignment will provide clear direction, purpose, and meaning.** Through the use of graphic organizers, Venn diagrams, structured overviews, and the like, the teacher can help the readers to focus their attention. For example, some reading materials compare and contrast two characters, two countries, or two forms of government; some texts provide a description of causes and effects of events in history or in proper versus improper nutrition. Some texts are organized by providing a list or a sequence, as in the ordering of the planets in our universe or in naming the characteristics of the more successful first colonies. When readers know beforehand that they are reading an assignment in order to determine one of these relationships as they read, their reading will have greater purpose and meaning, the underpinnings of successful comprehension.

- **The assignment will provide opportunities for the learners to integrate language activities.** After reading the text, the class may be asked to write a more complete description of how, for example, Jim and Huck Finn are similar and dissimilar characters (compare–contrast), or why the Battle of Bull Run took place and why it was significant (cause–effect). Some of these writings can be read aloud for further class discussion.[20]

FOR YOUR INQUIRY AND PRACTICE:

Review both the section "Some Notions About Teaching ELL Learners" and the characteristics of effective assignments. In how many ways are the notions and the characteristics interrelated?

WHAT ABOUT GRAMMAR AND CORRECTNESS?

Second language learners (L2 learners) aren't likely to be as proficient in their oral and written uses of English as their native English-speaking

---

[20]For a more complete discussion of effective assignments and follow-up activities, see Suzanne F. Peregoy and Owen F. Boyle, *Reading, Writing and Learning in ELL: A Resource Book for K–12 Teachers,* 2nd ed. (White Plains, NY: Longman, 1997), 281–84.

peers; they may never achieve that standard. What should we do, then, when L2 students make usage errors?

As one teacher describes it, "I was pleasantly surprised to learn there has recently been a shift away from preoccupation with surface errors in the teaching of L2 writers."[21]

Surface errors in usage should not be viewed as an L2 learner's failure, but as a natural part of the language-learning process. In fact, errors that do not get in the way of the L2 student's reading or writing comprehension are often overlooked.[22]

Many L2 learners are eager to achieve grammatical accuracy; they want the teacher to correct all of their unconventional usages, spellings, pronunciations, and the like. This is, however, a daunting task. Consequently, Leki makes two useful suggestions: First, focus your corrections on those errors that have the greatest social stigma; and, second, watch for patterns of errors L2 students may be making in your class. If patterns become obvious to you, then you can help your L2 learner(s) through a 15- to 20-minute mini lesson addressing the matter.[23]

AND NOW, IN CONCLUSION . . .

The chapter has tried to provide some basic suggestions to teachers who have the responsibility for helping immigrant children whose first language is not English to achieve in school. For additional help, you should talk with an ELL teacher in your building or district. He or she can provide both collegial support and suggestions for teaching L2 learners. Also, don't forget the foreign language teacher. She or he is familiar with approaches to teaching in a second language acquisition context; they'll likely be happy to help you.

Although L2 learners may, at first, seem to present a challenge you'll never be able to meet, in time and with patience and practice, both you and they will learn. They will be learning a lot about a new culture, the English language, and the content of your course. The beauty of your relationship with these students is, so will you.

---

[21]Pamela Sissy Carroll, Frances Blake, and Rose Aan Camalo, "When Acceptance Isn't Enough: Helping ELL Students Become Successful Writers," *English Journal*, December 1996, 28.

[22]Ibid.

[23]Ibid.

REVIEWING THE CHAPTER

1. Approximately how many people in the United States speak a language other than English in the home?
2. Is teaching ELL learners an experience relatively few teachers will have?
3. Do you believe ELL learners ought to be placed in special classes?
4. Should ELL learners be allowed to use their native language in school?
5. Will a fish out of water learn to swim better?
6. What should an ELL student learn first: accurate pronunciation or accurate spelling?
7. What's more important for the ELL student, to learn English for social purposes or for classroom purposes?
8. If you could select one major goal for an ELL learner, would it be improved speaking or improved writing abilities?
9. Should an ELL learner consult a dictionary every time an unfamiliar word is encountered?
10. Does practice always make perfect?

***** ***** *****

If you have a younger ELL learner in your classroom, say from ages 7 to 11 or 12, you can use some of these suggestions, offered by one of my ELL teacher friends, Rita Smith. *If you believe that some of these ideas are not age-appropriate for your students, adapt them and make them more appropriate.* Rita is one of the best teachers on the planet and is worthy of emulation!

PREPARING YOUR CLASSROOM FOR ELL LEARNERS

by Rita Smith Lyon, ELL Teacher
Meadowlane School
Lincoln, Nebraska

Before Your Students Arrive:

1. Prepare a list to hang by the door that includes the students' names and bus number. Keep this list updated throughout the year!

2. Provide picture cues that include the daily schedule and other daily activities such as choices for Learning Centers.

3. Translate for parents notes that contain important school information. One way to do this is to assemble a bag that includes school forms and a translated description on a cassette tape of how to fill out the forms. A tape recorder should also be included.

4. If you are unfamiliar with the customs, eating habits, greetings, and so on, of your new ELL students, read an appropriate *Culturegram*. *Culturegrams* are or should be available in your school media center or from your ELL teachers.

5. Ask ELL teachers, former students, or translators in your district how to say "hello" in your new students' first language.

6. Celebrate diversity! Show diversity in your classroom in the literature you choose, the pictures you hang, and in the activities you plan.

7. Label and picture objects and areas in your classroom.

On Your Students' First Day:

1. When the buses arrive, attach a name tag for each student in the bus windows. The name tag should include the student's name and bus stop address.

2. Give each student a button name tag that includes the student's name and the teacher's name or classroom number.

3. If your students eat lunch at school, prepare a lunch chart that provides pictures of the choices on the school menu.

4. Prepare a Good Manners Chart with your students that has the classroom rules written and pictured. Role-play the rules with the students.

5. Role-play other classroom and schoolwide activities, such as Friday Folders, Popcorn Friday, lunchroom routines, lining up, taking turns, and so on.

6. Assign a buddy to each new ELL student. Buddies can help new students learn the routines of the classroom.

7. Establish a consistent routine in the classroom. Students will learn from "Saying, Watching, and Doing."

Other Ideas:

1. Use pattern books! Students enjoy and learn from books they can read again and again. *Brown Bear, Brown Bear, What Do You See?* is a good example of a pattern book. It is also fun to let the children make book rewrites with these books.

2. Use photos of all your students in books and room displays. An *Alphabet Name Book* is fun to make and students will read it over and over again!

3. Provide many hands-on activities and modify activities to meet ELL students' needs. For example, in a Food Unit students could (a) walk to the nearest grocery store, (b) bake and eat different foods, (c) set up a "Classroom Cafe" to practice ordering food off a menu, and (d) sort food in different ways, by color, size, food groups, and so on.

4. Read books such as *We Are All Alike, We Are All Different*. Have the children make paper-doll people that show the different-colored skin tones and different dress of students in the room.

5. Provide modeling in all activities. Use "Read and Do" charts with your activities that show the directions in written and picture form.

6. Make picture/word charts for each unit and/or new vocabulary words in books you're using.

7. When printing material that students will see, make sure your printing is very clear and that each letter is separate, not connected as in cursive writing.

8. Use sign language when introducing new vocabulary words or new concepts. Students will enjoy learning the signs and the visual cues are helpful reminders.

9. Incorporate music whenever possible into your units of study. Students enjoy singing. The actions and repetition of words will be helpful to English Language Learners.

STUDENT EXPLORATIONS FOR WHEN ALL OF THEM DON'T SPEAK ENGLISH

EXPLORATION: Catching Some Z's
DIRRECTIONS: "Catching some z's" is one way people in the United States describe *sleeping*. Have you heard any other ways to describe *sleeping* in the United States? If you need some help, ask a teacher or an English-speaking classmate. Try to make a list of *sleeping* terms.

1. How many terms did you have on your list?
2. How any ways do you describe sleeping in your home language?
3. Why do we use different ways of naming the same activity?

***** ***** *****

EXPLORATION: Saying What's On Your Mind
DIRECTIONS: Here is a list of expressions commonly used in the United States. What do you think they really mean?

  a. He is acting funny.
  b. It beats me.
  c. It costs an arm and a leg.
  d. Don't count your chickens before they hatch.
  e. Go with the flow.
  f. Time to hit the sack.
  g. Don't pull my leg.
  h. Try not to jump the gun.

  1. Do expressions like these make English easier or harder to understand?
  2. Why don't people just say exactly what they mean?
  3. Why do you think expressions like these are used so widely?

***** ***** *****

EXPLORATION: Tune In Next Week
DIRECTIONS: The teacher needs to bring to class a videotaped episode of a currently popular soap opera. Show some of the episode first with no volume and ask the class if it can interpret what the characters' moods and attitudes are based on their nonverbal behaviors, facial expressions, and the like. After this discussion, replay the videotape with the audio on.

  1. How do the characters' body language support the spoken language used?
  2. What are some relationships among body language, intonation, and communication?

***** ***** *****

EXPLORATION: Pause, and Take Five
DIRECTIONS: Select a paragraph from a book being used in class. Read the paragraph aloud with the students, clearing up any unfamiliar words or pronunciations. When the students are comfortable with the paragraph, copy it onto a transparency, breaking the sentences according to the natural pauses, not necessarily the punctuation marks, used in the oral reading.

> If your oral reading is typical
> you'll probably find
> that the sentences will assume
> a vertical form
> something like this.

1. Which words in the text's paragraph are emphasized when it is read silently? Why?
2. Are the same words emphasized when the paragraph is read aloud? How do we decide when to pause when reading aloud?
3. What are some of the differences between reading aloud and reading silently? Do these differences affect our understanding of what we read?

Bibliography

Aitchison, Jean. *The Articulate Mammal*. London: Unwin Hyman, 1989, 5.

———. *Language Change: Progress or Decay?*, New York: Universe Books, 1985.

———. *Words in the Mind*. Oxford: Basil Blackwell, 1987.

Akmajian, Adrian, et al., *Linguistics: An Introduction to Language and Communication*. 3rd ed. Cambridge, MA: MIT Press, 1990.

Allington, Richard. "What I've Learned About Effective Reading Instruction." *Phi Delta Kappan*, June 2002, 744–45.

Allport, Gordon. "The Language of Prejudice." In Edited by Paul Escholz, Alfred Rosa, and Virginia Clark. *Language Awareness*, New York: St. Martin's Press, 1986.

Andrews, Larry. *Language Exploration and Awareness: A Resource Book for Teachers*. 2nd ed. Mahwah, NJ: Lawrence Erlbaum Associates, 1998.

———. *Linguistics for L2 Teachers*. Mahwah, NJ: Lawrence Erlbaum Associates, 2001.

Annie's Mailbox. *Lincoln (NE) Journal Star*, November 21, 2004.

Anthony, Edward. "The Rhetoric of Behavior." *TESOL Matters*, October/November 1996, 1, 23.

Appplebee, Arthur N. *Contexts for Learning to Write: Studies in Secondary School Instruction*. Norwood, NJ: Ablex Publishing Corporation, 1984.

———. *The Teaching of Literature in Programs With Reputations for Excellence in English*. Albany: University of New York-Albany Center for the Learning and Teaching of Literature, Report 1.1, 1989.

———. *Tradition and Reform in the Teaching of English: A History*. Urbana, IL: National Council of Teachers of English, 1974.

Associated Press. "Have a Nice Day Raises Hackles." *Omaha (NE) World-Herald*, June 26, 1994.

———. "Longhorn Salute Is Devilish in Norway." *Lincoln (NE) Journal Star*, January 22, 2005.

———. "Watch What Is Written in E-Mails, Instant Messages." *Lincoln (NE) Journal Star*, July 26, 2004.

———. "Wrong Turn on Foul Word Spells Loss." *The Lincoln (NE) Star*, September 24, 1991.

Astor, Gerald. *The Baseball Hall of Fame 50th Anniversary Book*. New York: Prentice Hall, 1988.

Atwood, Margaret. *The Handmaid's Tale*. New York: Ballentine Books, 1985.

Auel, Jean. *The Valley of Horses*. New York: Bantam Books, 1982.

Aulbach, Carol. "The Committee of Ten: Ghosts Who Still Haunt Us." *English Journal*, March 1994, 16.

Baron, Dennis. *Guide to Home English Repair*. Champaign-Urbana, IL: National Council of Teachers of English, 1994.

Barry, Dave. "Mister Language Person Returns in a Grande Way." *Lincoln (NE) Journal Star*, October 10, 2004.

Bartlett, Jere Whiting. *Early American Proverbs and Proverbial Phrases*. Cambridge, MA: Harvard University Press, 1977.

Bauer, Laurie, and Peter Trudgill, eds. *Language Myths*. New York and London: Penguin Books, 1998.

Baugh, Albert C., and Thomas Cable. *A History of the English Language*. 3rd ed. Englewood Cliffs, NJ: Prentice-Hall, 1978.

Berlitz, Charles. *Native Tongues*. New York: Grosset & Dunlap, 1982.

Betancourt, Ingrid. *Wilson Library Bulletin*, February 1992, 38.

Block, Marylaine. "Change a Word, Change a World." *My Word's Worth*. March 27, 2000. http://www.marylaine.com/myword/wordmean.html.

Bolton, Whitney. "CmC and E-Mail: Casting a Wider Net." *English Today*, October 1991, 35.

Boyer, Ernest L. "Literacy and Learning." In Edited by Michael F. Graves, Paul Van Den Broek, and Barbara, M. Taylor. *The First R: Every Child's Right to Read*. New York: Teachers College Press, and Newark, DE: The International Reading Association, 1996.

Braddock, Richard C., Richard Lloyd-Jones, and Lowell Schoer. *Research in Written Composition*. Champaign-Urbana, IL: National Council of Teachers of English, 1963.

Brown, B. Bradford, and Wendy Theobald. "Learning Contexts Beyond the Classroom: Extracurricular Activities, Community Organizations, and Peer Groups." In *The Adolescent Years: Social Influences and Educational Challenges*, Ninety-Seventh Yearbook of the National Society for the Study of Education. Edited by Kathryn Borman and Barbara Schneider. Chicago: University of Chicago Press, 1998.

Brown, Donna. "One Person's Opinion." *English Journal*, December 1996, 13, 14.

Bruner, Jerome S. *Child's Talk*. New York: W. W. Norton, 1981.

Bryson, Bill. *Mother Tongue*. London: Penguin Books, 1991.

Burchfield, Robert. "The Oxford English Dictionary," In *Lexicography: An Emerging International Profession*. Edited by Robert Ilson. Manchester, England: Manchester University Press, 1986.

Caccia, Paul. "Getting Grounded: Putting Semantics to Work in the Classroom." *English Journal* 80, no. 2 (1991): 55.

Cameron, Deborah. *Verbal Hygiene*. London and New York: Routledge, 1995.

Carlson, Robert G. *The Americanization Syndrome: A Quest for Conformity*. New York: St. Martin's Press, 1987.

Carroll, Pamela Sissy, Frances Blake, and Rose Ann Camalo. "When Acceptance Isn't Enough: Helping ELL Students Become Successful Writers." *English Journal*, December 1996, 28.

Carver, Craig M. *American Regional Dialects*. Ann Arbor: University of Michigan Press, 1987.

Cassidy, Frederick G., ed. *Dictionary of American Regional English*. Cambridge, MA: Belknap Press of the Harvard University Press, 1985.

Chapman, Raymond. "A Versatile Suffix." *English Today* 7, no. 4 (1991): 39, 41.

Chinese Bank Bans Tellers From Using 90 Rude Phrases. *Lincoln (NE) Journal Star*, April 25, 1995.

Chomsky, Noam. *Syntactic Structures*. The Hague: Mouton, 1957.

Clarke, Mark A. "The Dysfunctions of the Theory/Practice Discourse." *TESOL Quarterly*, Spring 1994, 15.

"Confederate Flag Causes Flap." *Lincoln (NE) Journal Star*, September 14, 2004.

Conklin, Nancy Faires, and Margaret A. Lourie. *A Host of Tongues: Language Communities in the United States.* New York: The Free Press (Macmillan), 1983.

Connors, Robert J., and Andrea A. Lunsford. "Frequency of Formal Error Patterns." *College Composition and Communication* 39 (1988): 395–409.

Crabtree, Monica, and Joyce Powers. *Language Files*, 5th ed. Columbus: Ohio State University Press, 1991.

Cruz, Isagani R. "A Nation Searching for a Language Finds a Language Searching for a Name." *English Today* 7, no. 4 (1991): 17.

Crystal, David, ed. *The Cambridge Encyclopedia of Language.* 2nd ed. Cambridge: Cambridge University Press, 1997.

———. *Who Cares About English Usage?* London: Penguin Books, 1984.

Culotta, Elizabeth, and Brooks Hanson. "First Words." *Science*, February 2004, 1315.

Cumming, John D. "The Internet and the English Language." *English Today*, January 1995, 7.

Cummins, Jim. "Language and the Human Spirit." *TESOL Matters* 23, no. 1 (2003): 1.

Davidson, Jill. "English Language Learners in Essential Schools." *Horace*, Winter 2003. Available at http://www.essentialschools.org/cs/resources/view/ces_res.286

Dear Abby. *The Lincoln (NE) Journal Star*, August 4, 1992.

———. *The Lincoln (NE) Star*, August 12, 1992.

———. *The Lincoln (NE) Star*, August 4, 1993.

Demo, Douglas A. *Dialects in Education.* http://www.cal.org/resources/RGOs/dialects.html.

Dewar, Helen, and Dana Milbank. "Cheney Dismisses Critic with Obscentity." *Washington Post*, June 25, 2004.

Edwards, David, and Norman Mercer. *Common Knowledge: The Development of Understanding in the Classroom.* London: Heinemann, 1987.

Elbow, Peter. *What Is English?* New York: The Modern Language Association, and Champaign-Urbana, IL: The National Council of Teachers of English, 1990.

Engel, Morris. *The Language Trap.* Englewood Cliffs, NJ: Prentice-Hall, 1984.

Erman, Brit. *Pragmatic Expressions in English: A Study of "You Know," "You See," and "I Mean" in Face-to-Face Conversation.* Stockholm: University of Stockholm, Stockholm Studies in English, 1987.

Fairman, Tony. "Mainstream English." *English Today*, January 2002, 58.

Ferre, John P., ed. *Channels of Belief: Religion and American Television.* Ames: Iowa State University Press, 1991.

Fillmore, Lily Wong, and Catherine Snow. *What Teachers Need to Know About Language.* 2000. http://www.cal.org.ericcll/teachers.pdf.

Finders, Margaret, and Susan Hynds. *Literacy Lessons.* Columbus, OH: Merrill Prentice Hall, 2003.

Finegan, Edward, and Niko Besnier. *Language: Its Structure and Use.* New York: Harcourt Brace Jovanovich Publishers, 1989.

Finegan, Edward, *What Is "Correct" Language?* Linguistic Society of America. htp://www.lsadc.org/fields/index.htm.

Fitzgerald, F. Scott. *The Great Gatsby.* New York: Collier Books, 1980.

"Flag Desecration Charges Against Vietnam Veteran Are Dismissed." *Lincoln (NE) Journal Star*, November 12, 2004.

Flaherty, Frances. "Lexicography Odds and Ends." *The Atlantic Monthly* 271, no. 1 (1993): 40.

Flexner, Stuart Berg. " 'Preface' to the *Dictionary of American Slang*." In *Language Awareness.* 4th ed. Edited by Paul Escholz, Alfred Rosa, and Virginia Clark. New York: St. Martin's Press, 1986.

Forestal, Peter. "Talking: Toward Classroom Action. Perspectives on Small Group Learning." In *Perspectives on Small Group Learning: Theory and Practice*. Edited by Mark Brubadier, Ryder Payne, and Kemp Rickett. Oakville: Ontario: Rubicon, 1990.

Freire, Paulo. "The Adult Literacy Process as Cultural Action for Freedom." *Harvard Educational Review* 40 (1970): 205–221.

Gee, James Paul. "Literacy, Discourse, and Linguistics." *Boston University Journal of Education* 171, no. 1 (1989): 5–25.

Giles, Howard, and Peter Robinson. *Handbook of Language and Social Psychology*. New York: John Wiley & Sons, 1990.

Gladwell, Malcom. "Queue & A: The Long and Short of Standing in Line." *Washington Post National Weekly*, December 21–27, 1992.

Goethals, Gregor T. *The Electronic Golden Calf: Images, Religion and the Making of Meaning*. Cambridge, MA: Cowley, 1991.

Goodlad, John. *A Place Called School*. New York: McGraw-Hill, 1984.

Gorow, Linda. "Texas Town Makes Spanish Official, Stirs War of Words." *Boston Globe*, August 28, 1999.

Gottlieb, Walter J. "Next Comes a Thick Yiddish Accent." *Washington Post National Weekly*. September 9–15, 1991.

Greenbaum, Sidney. *Studies in English Adverbial Usage*. Coral Gables, FL: University of Miami Press, 1969.

Greenspan, Stanley I., and Stuart G. Shanker. *The First Idea: How Symbols, Language, and Intelligence Evolved From Our Primate Ancestors to Modern Humans*. New York: De Capo Press, 2004.

Grice, Paul. *Studies in the Way of Words*. Cambridge, MA: Harvard University Press, 1989.

Halliday, M. A. K. *Learning How to Mean: Explorations in the Development of Language*. London: Edward Arnold, 1975.

———. "Linguistics in Teacher Education." In *Linguistics and the Teacher*. Edited by Ronald Carter. London: Routledge & Kegan Paul, 1982.

Halliday, M. A. K., Augus McIntosh, and Peter Strevens. *The Linguistic Sciences and Language Teaching*. Bloomington: Indiana University Press, 1964.

Harder, Kelsie B. *Illustrated Dictionary of Placenames, United States and Canada*. New York: Van Nostrand Reinhold Company, 1976.

Hargraves, Orin. "Cucurbits." *English Today*, October 2004, 52.

Harris, Raymond. *The Language Myth*. London: Duckworth & Company, Ltd., 1981.

Hartwell, Patrick. "Grammar, Grammar, and the Teaching of Grammar." *College English* 47 (1985): 105–27.

Hasselriis, Peter. "From Pearl Harbor to Watergate to Kuwait: Language in Thought and Action." *English Journal* 80, no. 2 (1991): 28.

"Hate Speech on the College Campus." *Lex Colligi* 14, no. 3 (1991): 1.

Hayakawa, S. I. *Language in Action*. New York: Harcourt, Brace and Company, 1941.

Hayakawa, S. I. and Alan R. Hayakawa. *Language in Thought and Action*. 5th ed. New York: Harcourt Brace Jovanovich, 1990.

Hazen, Kirk. *Teaching About Dialects*. October 2001. http://www.cal.org/resources/digest/o1o4dialects.html.

Hendrickson, Robert. *American Talk: The Words and Ways of American Dialects*. New York: Penguin Books, 1986.

Hillocks, George. *Research on Written Composition*. Urbana, IL: National Council of Teachers of English, 1986.

Hockett, Charles F. "Logical Considerations in the Study of Animal Communication." In Charles F. Hockett. Edited by *The View From Language*. Athens: University of Georgia Press, 1977.

Hogan, William. *The Quartzsite Trip*. New York, Avon Books, 1980.

Holden, Constance. "The Origin of Speech." *Science*, February 2004, 1316.

The Holy Qur'an, S.xxx.22.

"How You Say It Matters." *Lincoln (NE) Journal Star*, March 9, 1995.

Howarth, David. *1066: The Year of the Conquest*. New York: Dorset Press by arrangement with Viking-Penguin, 1978.

Hudson, Richard C. "Naming Practices." Language & Culture LISTSERV. July 11, 1995. language-culture@uchicago.edu.

Ivins, Molly. *Molly Ivins Can't Say That, Can She?* New York: Random House, 1991.

Kaplan, Jeffrey. *English Grammar: Principles and Facts*. Englewood Cliffs, NJ: Prentice-Hall, 1989.

Korzybski, Alfred. *Science and Sanity: An Introduction to Non-Aristotelian Systems and General Semantics*. 4th ed. Lakeville, CT: International Non-Aristotelian Publishing Company, 1958.

Kummer, Corby. "Flavorless No More." *The Atlantic Monthly*, December 2004, 189.

Kurath, Hans. *Studies in Area Linguistics*. Bloomington: Indiana University Press, 1972.

————. *A Word Geography of the Eastern United States*. Ann Arbor: University of Michigan Press, 1949.

Kurath, Hans, and Raven McDavid. *The Pronunciation of English in the Atlantic States*. Ann Arbor: University of Michigan Press, 1961.

————. 'Preface' to *On Semantics*. Edited by Uriel Weinrich. Philadelphia: University of Pennsylvania Press, 1980.

Labov, William. *Language in the Inner City*. Philadelphia: University of Pennsylvania Press, 1972.

————. *The Social Stratification of English in New York City*. Washington, DC: The Center for Applied Linguistics, 1966.

Lakoff, George, and Mark Johnson. *Metaphors We Live By*. Chicago: University of Chicago Press, 1980.

Lan, Li. "E-mail: A Challenge to Standard English?" *English Today*, October 2000, 23.

Lee, Laurie. *The Edge of Day: A Boyhood in the West of England*. New York: William Morrow and Company, 1960.

Letter to the editor. *Lincoln (NE) Journal Star*, September 7, 1991.

Letter to the editor. *Lincoln (NE) Journal Star*, December 18, 1992.

Lewin, Beverly A., and Yonatan Donner. "Communication in Internet Message Boards," *English Today*, July 2002, 34.

Lewis, Bernard. "I'm Right, You're Wrong, Go to Hell." *The Atlantic Monthly*, May 2003, 39.

Lipton, James. *An Exaltation of Larks*. New York: Viking Penguin, 1991.

Liu, Dilin, and Bryan Farha. "Three Strikes and You're Out." *English Today* 12, no. 1 (1996): 36–40.

Liwei, Gao. "Digital Age, Digital English." *English Today*, July 2001, 18.

Long, C. C. *New Language Exercises for Elementary Schools*. Cincinnati and New York: Van Antwerp Bragg and Company, 1889.

Lutz, William. "Notes Toward a Definition of Doublespeak," In *Beyond 1984: Doublespeak in a Post-Orwelian Age*. Edited by William Lutz. Champaign-Urbana, IL: National Council of Teachers of English, 1989.

Mabin, Butch. "South Lincoln Target of Fliers." *Lincoln (NE) Journal Star*, December 22, 2004.

"Make Students Salute Flag, Councilman Urges." *Omaha (NE) World-Herald*, November 17, 1996.

Mandelbaum, David. *The Selected Writings of Edward Sapir*. Berkeley: University of California Press, 1949.

"Many Campuses Seethe With Racism." *Lincoln (NE) Journal Star*, October 25, 1995.

Marshakj, David. "No Child Left Behind: A Foolish Race Into the Past." *Phi Delta Kappan*, November 2003, 229–31.

McArthur, Tom, ed. *The Oxford Companion to the English Language*. Oxford: Oxford University Press, 1992.

McCrum, Robert, William Cran, and Robert MacNeil. *The Story of English*, New York: Elisabeth Softon Books-Viking, 1986.

McManus, E. Leo. "Presidential Rhetoric: Clinton Replaces Bush." *English Today*, October 1993, 14.

Metcalf, Allan. *Presidential Voices*. Boston: Houghton Mifflin, 2004.

Milroy, James, and Leslie Milroy. *Authority in Language*. London: Routledge & Kegan Paul, 1985.

Murray, Denise. "CmC." *English Today*, July 1990, 42.

"N.J. Town Votes Cursing Ban." *Lincoln (NE) Journal Star*, October 13, 1994, 5.

Nebraska Reading/Writing Standards, Grades K–12. February 6, 1998. Lincoln: Nebraska State Board of Education.

No Child Left Behind. http://www.nochildleftbehind.gov.

Noguchi, Rei R. *Grammar and the Teaching of Writing: Limits and Possibilities*, Champaign-Urbana, IL: National Council of Teachers of English, 1991.

Nunberg, Geoffrey. *Going Nucular: Language, Politics, and Culture in Confrontational Times*. New York: Public Affairs Perseus Books Group, 2004.

"One Nation, One Language." *U.S. News & World Report*, September 25, 1995, 38–40.

Ornstein, Allan, and Daniel U. Levine. *Foundations of Education*. Boston: Houghton Miffllin, 1993.

Paulson, Ross Evans. *Language, Science and Action: Korzybski's General Semantics: A Study in Comparative Intellectual History*. Westport, CT: Greenwood Press, 1983.

Peck, Robert Newton. *A Day No Pigs Would Die*. New York: Dell Publishing Company, 1972.

Peregoy, Suzanne F., and Owen F. Boyle. *Reading, Writing and Learning in ELL: A Resource Book for K–12 Teachers*. 2nd ed. White Plains, NY: Longman, 1997.

Perera, Katherine. "The Language Demands of Schooling." In *Linguistics and the Teacher*. Edited by Ronald Carter. London: Routledge & Kegan Paul, 1982.

Piaget, Jean. *The Language and Thought of the Child*. London: Routlege and Kegan, 1965.

Pinker, Steven. *The Language Instinct*. New York: Penguin, 1990.

———. *Learnability and Cognition: The Acquisition of Argument Structure*. Cambridge, MA: MIT Press, 1991.

———. *Words and Rules: The Ingredients of Language*. New York: HarperCollins Publishers, 2000.

Pitts, Leonard, Jr. "Go Ahead—You Can Ask the Unaskable." *Lincoln (NE) Journal Star*, September 13, 2004.

Pooley, Robert C. *The Teaching of English Usage*. Champaign-Urbana, IL: National Council of Teachers of English, 1974.

Postman, Neal. *Amusing Ourselves to Death*. New York: Viking Penguin, 1985.

———. *Crazy Talk, Stupid Talk*. New York: Delacorte Press, 1976.

"Q & A." *The Atlantic Monthly*, October 1992, 14.

Readance, John E., R. Scott Baldwin, and Thomas W. Bean. *Teaching Content Literacy: An Integrated Approach*. 8th ed. Dubuque, IA: Kendall/Hunt Publishing Company, 2004.

"Readers Praise Our Anti-Crudities Stand." *Omaha (NE) World-Herald*, October 16, 1994.

Richards, Jack C. *The Language Teaching Matrix*. Cambridge: Cambridge University Press, 1997.

Richards, Jack, John Platt, and Heidi Weber. *Longman Dictionary of Applied Linguistics*. London: Longman Group UK Limited, 1989.

Rigg, Pat, and Virginia G. Allen. Introduction to *When They Don't All Speak English*. Champaign-Urbana, IL: National Council of Teachers of English, 1989.

Roller, Cathy M. *Variability, Not Disability*. Newark, DE: International Reading Association, 1996.

Romaine, Suzanne. *The Language of Children and Adolescents*. Oxford, Basil Blackwell, 1984.

Rosenthal, Jack. "9/11." September 1, 2002. http://nytimes.com/2002/01/magazine/01 ONLANGUAGE.html.

Rymes, Betsy. "Eliciting Narratives: Drawing Attention to the Margins of Classroom Talk." *Research in the Teaching of English*, February 2003, 381.

Sampson, Geoffrey. *Schools of Linguistics*. London: Century Hutchinson, 1987.

Schultze, Quentin J., et al. *Dancing in the Dark*: *Youth, Popular Culture and the Electronic Media*. Grand Rapids, MI: Eerdmans, 1991.

Shafer, Gregory. "Reforming Writing and Rethinking Correctness." *English Journal*, September 2004, 66.

Sheidlower, Jesse. "Elegant Variation and All That." *The Atlantic Monthly*, December 1996, 112.

Sherwin, Stephen. *Four Problems in Teaching English: A Critique of Research*. Scranton, PA: International Textbook Company for the National Council of Teachers of English, 1966.

Shetier, Emily. "Dictionary Man." *VIP*. 2004. http://www.journalism.nyu/pubzone/vip.

Shuy, Roger. *Discovering American Dialects*. Champaign-Urbana, IL: National Council of Teachers of English, 1967.

Smagorinsky, Peter. "'Growth through English' Revisited." *English Journal*, July 2002, 27.

Smith, Lana J., and Dennie L. Smith. "The Discussion Process: A Simulation." *Journal of Reading*, April 1994, 583.

Snodgrass, Mary Ellen. *The Great American English Handbook*. Jacksonville, IL: Perma-Bound, 1987.

Squire, James R., and Roger K. Applebee. *High School English Instruction Today*, New York: Appleton–Century–Crofts, 1968.

Stewart, George R. *American Place Names*. New York: Oxford University Press, 1970.

———. *Discourse Analysis*. Oxford: Basil Blackwell, 1983.

———. *Educational Linguistics*. Oxford: Basil Blackwell, 1986.

Stubbs, Michael, "The Sociolinguistics of Writing: Or, Why Children Aren't Adults." In *Readings on Language, Schools, and Classrooms*. Edited by Michael Stubbs and Hillary Hiller. London and New York: Methuen & Company, 1983.

Sullivan, Peggy. *Many Names for Eileen*. Chicago and New York: Follett Publishing Company, 1969.

"Supremacists Leave Leaflets in Omaha." *Lincoln (NE) Journal Star*, January 18, 2005, 3.

Tajun, Jiang. "Metaphors the English Language Lives By." *English Today*, July 2002, 59.

Tannen, Deborah. *You Just Don't Understand: Women and Men in Conversation*. New York: Ballantine Books, 1990.

Trudgill, Peter. "Standard English: What it Isn't." In *Standard English: The Widening Debate*. Edited by Tony Bex and Richard J. Watts. London: Routledge, 1999.

Truly, Pat. "Self-Censorship Growing Tedious." *Lincoln (NE) Star*, October 27, 1994.

The United States Dictionary of Places. New York: Somerset Publishers, 1988.

VanDeWeghe, Richard. "Spelling and Grammar Logs." In *Non-Native and Nonstandard Dialect Students*. Edited by Candy Carter Champaign-Urbana, IL: National Council of Teachers of English, 1982.

Vygotsky, Lev. *Thought and Language*. Cambridge, MA: MIT Press, 1962.

Wade-Lewis, Margaret. "The Status of Semantic Items From African Languages in American English." *The Black Scholar*, Summer 1993, 26.

Wallraf, Barbara, ed. "Word Fugitives." *The Atlantic Monthly*, December 2004, 196.

Weingartner, Charles. "Semantics: What and Why." *English Journal* 58, no. 8 (1969): 1214.

Wells, Gordon. *The Meaning Makers: Children Learning Language and Using Language to Learn.* London: Heinemann, 1986.

West, Fred. *The Way of Language.* New York: Harcourt Brace Javonovich, 1975.

Westall, Robert. *Blitzcat.* New York: Scholastic Inc., 1989.

"What's in a Name? Success." *Lincoln (NE) Journal Star*, June 18, 1996.

Whorf, Benjamin. "A Linguistic Consideration of Thinking in Primitive Communities." In *Language, Thought, and Reality.* Edited by John Carroll. Cambridge, MA: MIT Press, 1956.

Wiley, Terrence C. *Myths About Language Diversity and Literacy in the United States.* ERIC: ED407881, 1997.

Will, George. "ESPN Pervades the Cultural World." *Lincoln (NE) Journal-Star*, November 7, 2004.

Wilson, Kenneth G. *Van Winkle's Return: Change in American English 1966–1986.* Hanover, NH: University Press of New England, 1987.

Winchester, Simon. *The Meaning of Everything.* Oxford: Oxford University Press, 2003.

———. *The Professor and the Madman.* New York: HarperCollins Publishers, 1998.

Wolfram, Walt. *Sociolinguistics.* Linguistic Society of America. http://www.lsadc.org/web2/sociling.html.

Wolk, Allan. *The Naming of America.* Nashville, TN: Nelson Publishing, 1977.

Word Court. *The Atlantic Monthly.* July 1996, 112.

Yajun, Jiang. "Metaphors the English Language Lives By." *English Today*, July 2002, 57, 59, 60, 62.

"Youth Baseball Brawl Deadly." *Lincoln (NE) Journal Star*, May 20, 1993.

Yule, George. *The Study of Language.* Cambridge: Cambridge University Press, 1985.

Ziggy. *The Lincoln (NE) Journal Star*, November 15, 1997.

Index